M

ENDURING VIETNAM

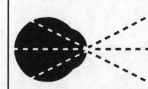

This Large Print Book carries the Seal of Approval of N.A.V.H.

ENDURING VIETNAM

AN AMERICAN GENERATION AND ITS WAR

JAMES WRIGHT

THORNDIKE PRESS
A part of Gale, a Cengage Company

Farmington Hills, Mich • San Francisco • New York • Waterville, Maine
Meriden, Conn • Mason, Ohio • Chicago

LIBRARY OF CONGRESS CATALOGING-IN-PUBLICATION DATA

Names: Wright, James Edward, 1939– author.
Title: Enduring Vietnam : an American generation and its war / by James Wright.
Description: Large print edition. | Waterville, Maine : Thorndike Press, a part of Gale, a Cengage Company, [2017] | Series: Thorndike Press large print popular and narrative nonfiction | Includes bibliographical references.
Identifiers: LCCN 2017015638| ISBN 9781432840402 (large print : hardcover) | ISBN 1432840401 (large print : hardcover)
Subjects: LCSH: Vietnam War, 1961–1975—United States. | Vietnam War, 1961–1975—Influence. | Large type books.
Classification: LCC DS558 .W76 2017b | DDC 959.704/3373—dc23
LC record available at https://lccn.loc.gov/2017015638

Published in 2017 by arrangement with Macmillan Publishing Group, LLC/St. Martin's Press, an imprint of Penguin Publishing Group, a division of Penguin Random House, LLC

This book is dedicated to that American generation who honorably served in the Vietnam War. And this book salutes those who sacrificed. Their stories deserve to be known and their lives remembered.

The difficulty of this American generation's war and the controversies it engendered made their willingness to serve, and the sacrifices that they made, the greater and not the lesser.

CONTENTS

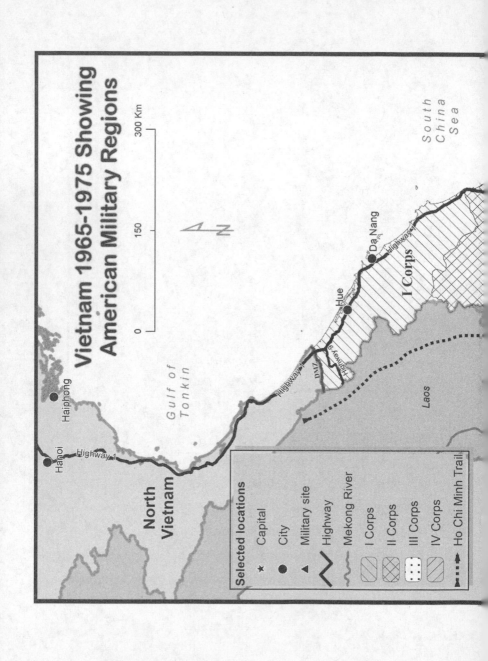

Vietnam 1965-1975 Showing American Military Regions

North Vietnam

Hanoi

Highway 1

Haiphong

Gulf of Tonkin

0   150   300 Km

Da Nang

Highway 1

Hue

I Corps

Highway 9

DMZ

Highway 1

Laos

South China Sea

Ho Chi Minh Trail

Selected locations

★ Capital
● City
◄ Military site
⌇ Highway
〰 Mekong River
▨ I Corps
▧ II Corps
⬚ III Corps
▨ IV Corps
▪▪▪ Ho Chi Minh Trail

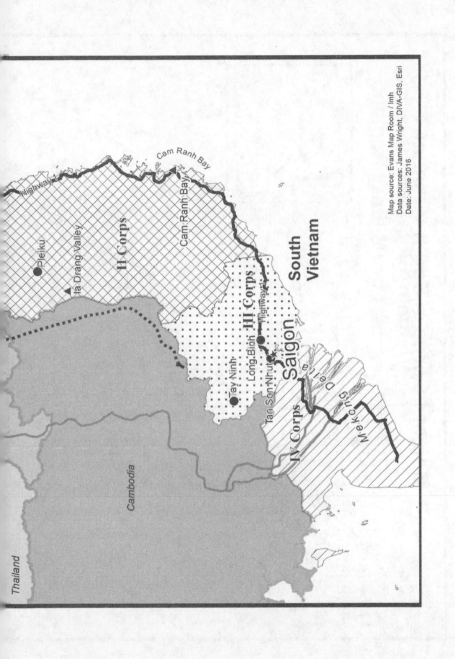

Map sources: Evans Map Room / lmh
Data sources: James Wright, DIVA-GIS, Esri
Date: June 2016

Map of I Corps in South Vietnam

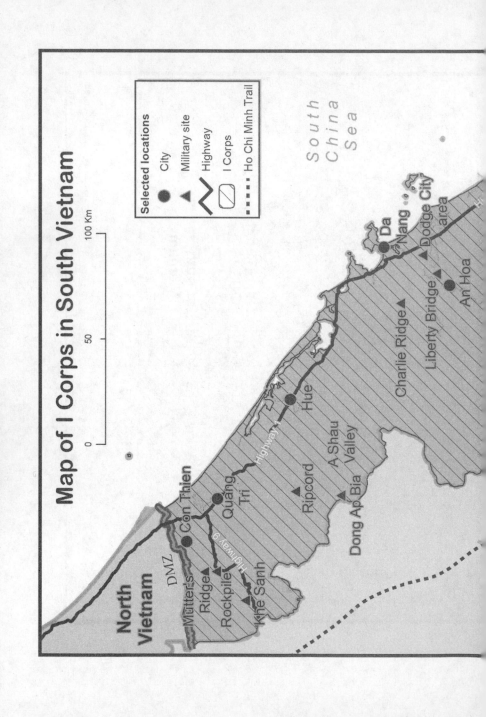

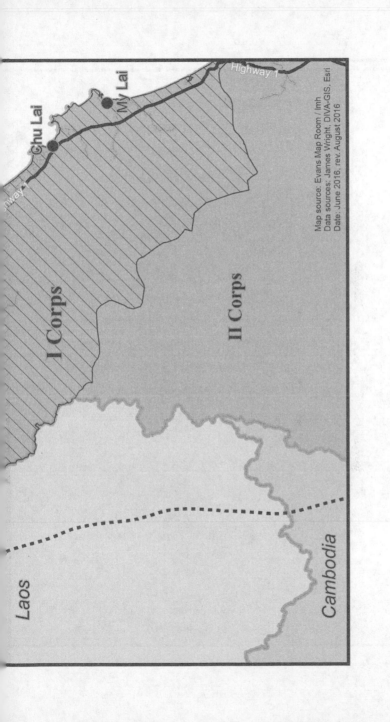

Chu Lai

My Lai

Highway 1

I Corps

II Corps

Laos

Cambodia

Map source: Evans Map Room / lmh
Data sources: James Wright, DIVA-GIS, Esri
Date: June 2016, rev. August 2016

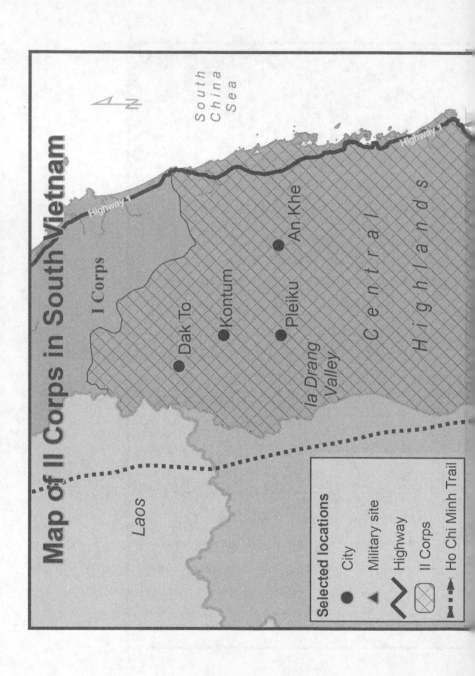

Map of II Corps in South Vietnam

South China Sea

Laos

I Corps

Central Highlands

Dak To

Kontum

Pleiku

An Khe

Ia Drang Valley

Highway 1

Highway 1

N

Selected locations

- ● City
- ▲ Military site
- 〰 Highway
- ▨ II Corps
- ▪▪▪ Ho Chi Minh Trail

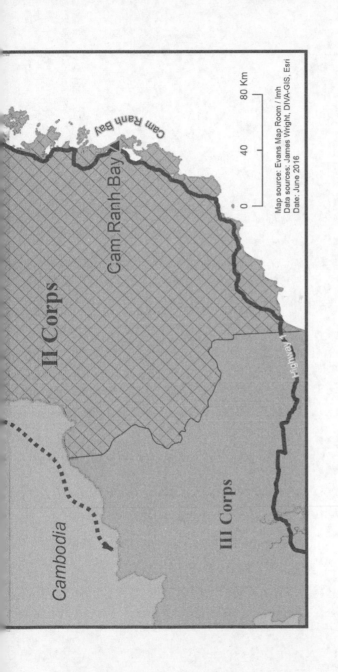

II Corps

Cam Ranh Bay

Cam Ranh Bay

Highway 1

III Corps

Cambodia

Map source: Evans Map Room / lmh
Data sources: James Wright, DIVA-GIS, Esri
Date: June 2016

0   40   80 Km

PREFACE:
VISITING VIETNAM

In early September 2014, I stood at the top of Dong Ap Bia in Vietnam's A Shau Valley. Bordering Laos in the northwestern part of the old South Vietnam, this steep and imposing mountain was Hill 937 on U.S. military maps from the Vietnam War period. Local Montagnard tribesmen called it "the Crouching Beast." The American soldiers who fought there knew it as "Hamburger Hill."

For eleven days in May 1969, units of the 101st Airborne Division had fought North Vietnamese regulars, largely from the 29th Regiment but also the 6th and 9th Regiments, for control of this hill. Today there is a memorial at the top placed there in 2009 by the Socialist Republic of Vietnam celebrating "a victorious place." Yet in fact it wasn't their victory, at least not then, not in that battle. The Americans prevailed, but the North Vietnamese returned. Six years later they would occupy Saigon and win the war.

I was on the hill forty-five years later

because I was writing this book on the Vietnam War. I was part of a very small group that included two North Vietnamese Army (NVA) veterans of this 1969 battle. I had met them that morning in the nearby village of A Luoi, and they quickly accepted my invitation to join me in a climb of Dong Ap Bia. Our group also included an American army veteran who had served there at this time but not in this battle, as well as two young Vietnamese men. One was the son of a southern Vietnamese man who fought with the National Liberation Front (NLF), known as the Viet Cong, and the other the son of a soldier with the South Vietnamese Army, the Army of the Republic of Vietnam.[1] The latter had spent some time in a reeducation camp after the war ended. I had been traveling through Vietnam battle sites because I wanted to see the places where Americans fought, especially in May and June 1969.

The contrasts between that distant war and modern Vietnam are everywhere. At Cu Chi, the extensive old tunnels are preserved as a tourist attraction, and there is a gruesome display of punji stick traps and other devices used against the Americans. The old airstrip at Dak To in the Highlands, where the 299th Engineers had fought against North Vietnamese forces based in Cambodia, is still desolate, barren, and deteriorating. The bunker where 9 American soldiers died had

18

been filled and leveled, with manioc growing nearby and local farmers drying it on the old runway. Mutter's Ridge up above Highway 9 continues to be a forbidding-looking place, in the midst of equally forbidding places, known by Americans who fought there as Razorback and the Rockpile.

Outside Hanoi, on the street adjacent to the lake where jagged fragments of a B-52 remain jutting from the water, is a restaurant called Cafe B52. In English, the sign promised that inside, in addition to coffee, Wi-Fi was available. And south of Da Nang, a cemetery is at the spot on the road where an army chaplain and 5 others died when their vehicle struck a mine in June 1969. This cemetery contains and celebrates the remains of National Liberation Front and North Vietnamese Army soldiers who died in the "American War."

Southwest of Da Nang we spent some time in and near the area the marines called "Dodge City." It indeed was a place filled with gunfights. South of Hill 55, I wanted to visit a rice paddy where Billy Smoyer was one of 19 marines in Kilo Company of the 3rd Battalion of the 7th Marines who died in an ambush on July 28, 1968. Billy was a star hockey and soccer player at Dartmouth who had joined the marines upon graduation. He came from a comfortable New Jersey family and probably could have deferred or even

19

found an exemption from service. Instead, he said that the war shouldn't be fought only by the sons of miners and factory workers. I buried a Dartmouth hockey puck in the rice paddy where Second Lieutenant Smoyer died less than four weeks after arriving in Vietnam.

In a tragic coincidence, a Dartmouth classmate and friend of Billy Smoyers's, Duncan Sleigh, died in another ambush less than five months later just two miles away. Duncan was in Mike Company of the 3rd Battalion of the 7th Marines. They lost 14 men in that ambush and Second Lieutenant Sleigh was awarded the Navy Cross posthumously for his effort to shield a wounded marine from another grenade. The marine survived but Sleigh did not. I buried a small New Hampshire memento in that rice paddy.

North of the pilings from the old Liberty Bridge, four of us were looking across a field at the slope where several U.S. marines died on May 29, 1969, on the last day of Operation Oklahoma Hills. A smiling teenage Vietnamese boy stepped out of a house and waved to us. Then his grandfather came out and greeted us and invited us in for tea. He had lived in that house for his entire eighty-five years. He served during the war with a local NLF unit. He told us that in the 1960s, during the day he farmed and at night he fought. Looking out from this home, looming above this peaceful place, remained the heavy and dark green hills that Americans called Charlie Ridge. The U.S. troops seldom went there and never stayed long. As we walked along the pathway from the home of this veteran, we passed a group of young children playing. They smiled and shouted proudly in English, "Hello!" And one flashed the common V fingers greeting, ironically evoking the American antiwar peace sign.

But Dong Ap Bia has remained Hamburger Hill — very steep, more than three thousand feet high, red clay and rocks, slippery after a summer shower that began our trek. Jungle heat and humidity slowed our pace. Modern Vietnam has hardly touched this place. After the 1969 battle, soldiers described the hill as looking like a moonscape — artillery and bombs and herbicides having torn and burned trees and undergrowth. The land, at least superficially, had now recovered. Double- and triple-canopy growth had returned, with incredibly dense foliage and shrubs, much of which would have been familiar to those men of the 187th of the 101st Airborne who hurried from their helicopters there on May 10. Now the Crouching Beast was silent, or at least the chaotic sounds of war had been replaced by a cacophony from unfamiliar birds and animals and insects.

Hidden in the brush were signs of an old

battle: bomb craters holding pools of stagnant water; charred wood in the underbrush; occasionally the rotted hulk of a once large tree still stood defiantly, marked by apparent bullet holes. And hidden in the foliage near the peak we occasionally saw dark tunnel entrances, small squared holes just large enough for a man to slip in or out from the underground complex that once ran through the hill. My companions who had been there with the North Vietnamese Army quietly pointed them out.

Before our small group began our descent from the top of Dong Ap Bia, I told them that I wanted to leave behind something I had brought with me. I had grown up in Galena, Illinois, an old mining town. I worked for a time there in the mines, and my boss was a World War II veteran with a Purple Heart. He was a good man and a good boss. I came to know his son as an English student at the local high school when I taught there in a student teaching program. This young man, Michael Lyden, had died in May 1969 with the 187th on Hamburger Hill when a rocket-propelled grenade fired by a North Vietnamese soldier struck him and killed him instantly. So I dug a small hole and left behind a piece of lead sulfide called galena. I had been keeping this on my desk since I had picked it up in the Graham Mine fifty years earlier. Now a small piece of his hometown could remain in Vietnam, on top of the hill that my young friend never reached.

This book is about his war. About his generation's war. About America's War.

"One morning in Saigon she'd asked what it was all about. 'This whole war,' she said, 'why was everybody so mad at everybody else?'

I shook my head. 'They weren't mad, exactly. Some people wanted one thing, other people wanted another thing.'

'What did you want?'

'Nothing,' I said. 'To stay alive.'

'That's all?'

'Yes.' "

— FROM TIM O'BRIEN,
THE THINGS THEY CARRIED

INTRODUCTION:
A GENERATION GOES TO WAR

Enduring Vietnam is about the generation that grew up in post–World War II America and about their war. During the 1960s, and likely even more so as the years have passed, many of them would reject the ownership implicit in calling the American War in Vietnam "their war." But it was that generation's war. As youngsters, most joined older generations in supporting it at the outset and, still essentially as youngsters, many finally served in it. If not always eagerly or even willingly, they served. They may legitimately deny responsibility for starting the war — their parents' and grand-parents' generations did that for them — but they cannot deny that this war marked them profoundly. And they marked the war. It was *Their* War. This generation is often called the baby boomers, a description that I use de-scriptively but somewhat reluctantly when considering this subject, since there is some-thing light and flippant about the title and there was nothing light and flippant about their war.

My primary focus is on those members of the generation who served in Vietnam. Describing their experience requires an overview of the American war, a framing of that engagement. Within this framework I provide a more detailed focus on the spring of 1969. I tell the story of some of the men — and women — who died there in that spring during the intense combat that preceded an explicit shift in the war's assumptions, objectives, and rhetoric. These personal stories illustrate my strong belief that accounts of war need to be more than critical analyses of national presumptions and strategic goals, and more than studies of the tactics, objectives, and results of the conduct of the military operations on the ground. These are all essential parts of the story of war. But they often neglect the human experience — and the human cost. While some Americans were intensely debating the Vietnam War, other Americans were fighting it — and dying in it.

I have sought primarily to understand and to tell the story of those Americans who were the war fighters, perhaps a half million or six hundred thousand men over eight years of regular ground war, approximately 25 or 30 percent of the more than two and one half million U.S. troops who served in Vietnam. As the war went on, increasingly they were baby boomers. These men — and the women who served with them in medical or other combat support specialties — were fully and not peripherally a part of their generation. And they were on the ground for their generation's war.

In addition to these combat troops, there were roughly two million Americans who served in noncombat missions, and their contributions and service were substantial. They worked to sustain and protect the fighting force and to advance the overall mission of support for the South Vietnamese government and people. And many of them served in vulnerable posts or took on exposed assignments that could at any time have subjected them to an attack by the enemy.

Over ten million baby boomers served in the armed forces in the 1960s and early 1970s. Nearly 27 million young American men reached eighteen, draft age, between August 1964 and March 1973. More than 2.2 million of them were drafted and 8.7 million enlisted in military services. Nearly 10 percent of the men in that generation went to Vietnam.[1] As the war went on in the 1960s, draftees as a proportion of those serving in the military increased. But the majority of those who served enlisted, willingly as volunteers or less willingly in response to or in anticipation of a draft call. Most were not deployed to Vietnam but were posted elsewhere at U.S. bases or at sea. They too served when called, were always on standby for Vietnam deployment, and their service is a part of their generation's account.

The images of the 1960s that resonate today are of Woodstock, youthful rebellion, of a generation leading protests against the war, against authority, and against convention, embracing new musical sounds considered revolutionary, of a time remembered romantically as the decade of "Peace and Love," of the Beatles and of the Age of Aquarius, and, indeed, of times that truly were a-changin'. But it is necessary also to remember that for many of that era there is also a powerful memory of the *thump-thump-thump* of helicopters flying over the hills and treetops of Vietnam and the smell and feel of rice paddies or of humid jungle.

More young Americans in the '60s died in Vietnam, over 58,000, than went to jail for refusing to serve in the military or moved to Canada to avoid serving. This book is about the experience of those who served — not to impugn those who protested what they believed was an unnecessary or unjust war, one that was sometimes immorally cruel in its execution. After all, it turned out that they were largely correct. But there is more to their generation's story — and their generation's war — than that. For the baby boomer generation not only challenged the war, they also experienced it. And that experience, on the ground in Vietnam, was far more complex and more nuanced than persistent stereotypes of atrocities committed, of mutiny and fragging and antiwar activities in a haze of drugs. Each of these images came to have some basis, especially in the last years of the war, but by no means can they stand as fair generalizations of the conduct of most of those who served.

The American War in Vietnam was a powerful force in American life. But for most Americans it was more metaphor than experience. "Vietnam" was a word used to describe a policy, an engagement, to refer to a distant, mysterious place. Vietnam represented an unpleasant activity occurring on behalf of the United States. It represented something increasingly considered negative in the decade of the 1960s.

A friend recently returned to Vietnam to see again the places where he fought in late 1968 and early 1969. He particularly wanted to visit the rice paddy where a close college friend and hockey teammate, Billy Smoyer, died. He shared with me his reflections on this as well as an exchange he had with a high school classmate, whom I then contacted. The veteran observed that "my story is one small paragraph in that much larger history of our generation at war that was, for many only part of our '60s upheaval." His high school friend wrote him:

Your time in 'Nam resonates with me, quite deeply. Like many of our generation, Vietnam was at the center. From 1965 to 1975, Vietnam seemed (to me) the black hole around which that decade floated. The music, the protests, the drugs, the clothing, the long hair, the changes in academic curricula, the attitudes towards the "Establishment," Chicago in 1968, Watergate, Nixon, Nixon's resignation, LBJ not running for reelection, McGovern, free speech, Woodstock, Altamont, rights for Blacks and women, environmental concerns, open sexual mores . . . . seemed to float around the darkness that was Vietnam. Like many, I spent a number of years making sure I did not go to 'Nam.

Educational and then a medical deferment enabled this man to avoid serving in the military. He continued his education and then began a lifelong career as a high school English teacher. But "then, in the late '70s, the dark hole that was Vietnam began to almost haunt me. In trying to understand who I was, and what those ten years meant and how they formed and informed me." He devoted himself to learning more about Vietnam — but always with the recognition that like the blind men trying to define an el-

32

ephant by touch, it is hard to ever truly know this "black hole" that touched and haunted all of his generation.[2]

Certainly all Americans knew about the war in Vietnam at the time, but only a small percentage truly *knew* it. Politically, culturally, morally, the war — and its images — overwhelmed the period. And it assuredly was a war on which all Americans came to have an opinion. They based their views on their understanding and assessment of the wisdom and, for some, their judgments about the morality, of this major war. These opinions seldom were informed by the experience of the generation that was engaging in this war. And in truth, most who experienced Vietnam and have since spent a lifetime reflecting on it would acknowledge that they did not truly "know" their war with all of its sectors and layers and varieties and "need to know" compartments.

By focusing on the American on-ground experience, it is not my intention to obscure or challenge the sharp criticism of the assumptions, judgments, and, yes, the deceit that led the United States into that war. The war was conducted with ambivalence and uncertainty, conditions exacerbated by very general and shifting objectives, and by restraints and conflicting instructions from Washington based upon political rather than military calculations. Senior policy makers never provided an honest public assessment of the war's progress and its costs. In the field, the war officially entered into on behalf of the Vietnamese was carried out too often with indifference toward the residents of the country or even with willful cruelty in which the noncombatant Vietnamese civilians were innocent casualties. It would be shameful to minimize these things, just as it would be slanderous to many good men to suggest that all American troops behaved as indifferent or willful thugs.

As a number of critics then and scholars later have agreed, among the baby boomer generation, the burden of American military service and even more specifically of combat service was not equitably shared. The sons of blue-collar families, African American, Hispanic, and Native American young men were disproportionately out in the jungles of Vietnam. And while many, increasingly more as the war went on, were not eager to serve, it was also the case that not all were there as reluctant draftees. These young men were often serving because of their sense of patriotism and obligation, of what many considered their responsibility; some served because they hoped that military service could expand their future opportunities. Despite the inequities, a large part of an iconic American generation served there — *and served well.* If it was largely a blue-collar war, it surely was not uniformly one. College students and college graduates were also on the front lines. And by no means only as officers.

Enduring Vietnam is not a war story, but it is a story of war experiences focusing on the American ground war in Vietnam that took place from 1965 to 1973 — the period in which U.S. troops were in the country engaging in combat with Communist forces. The war in Vietnam unambiguously became an American War by the summer of 1965. If there was a history that explained the steps that led to this engagement, this was not a history that made it inevitable. The World War II generation that was assuming positions of leadership in American public life came into these roles seared by their war and committed to avoiding any repetition of what they considered the mistakes that led to it. Unfortunately, their steps to avoid a repeat of World War II moved the nation to another war, and one that was very different from their own experience.

The American War in Vietnam was never only, or even primarily, about Vietnam. The rhetoric in the 1950s and '60s described the American commitment there as a recognition of responsibility to protect democracy and to save an imperiled nation. Nonetheless, the conflict essentially was about international tensions that appeared to be playing out in Vietnam. The cold war, with the United

States and its allies competing with the Soviets and the Chinese, shaped much of the American strategy in Vietnam. Combat operations on the ground were aimed more at drawing lines and making statements, about perceptions and consequences in a larger global context, about establishing negotiating markers and bargaining chips, than they were military operations with an immediate — or even a clearly defined — military goal.

Domestic politics also influenced the rhetoric and the promises that framed this war. Presidents from Harry Truman to Richard Nixon, including Dwight Eisenhower, John Kennedy, and Lyndon Johnson, based their decisions partly on domestic political considerations. At their best, actions taken as a result of sensitivity to the political interests and wishes of constituents can be examples of democracy at work. At their worst, they can be illustrations of cynicism and manipulation. Unfortunately, in the case of this war, many steps showed leaders at their worst. Finally, too often the decision to fight in Vietnam was personalized, was reduced to a flexing of personal muscle, of individual machismo and national strength. Lyndon Johnson's insecurities, his insistence on showing his toughness, his manhood, surely played out here, as did John Kennedy's resolve to demonstrate that he had the maturity and strength to face down Communist leaders.

The diplomatic and the political developments, the broader global context, and the public perceptions of the war are critical elements in understanding it. They all revolved around "Why are we in Vietnam?" which politicians and their constituents increasingly asked after 1965. While there had been opposition to the war from the outset, within a few years the war became increasingly a focus of public concern and public dissent, and of growing cynicism about the purported purpose of the war and skepticism about the official narrative of its rationale, its conduct, and its costs. Of course, many still question why the United States went to war in Vietnam. And "no more Vietnams" is an assertion made without any sense of a need to explain what it means. Ongoing debates focusing on the Vietnam experience pretty consistently describe it as a mistake — a mistake in commitment or a mistake in execution. Or both.

As important as these analyses of the war were and are, they and the debates around them can be reductive. They focus on diplomacy and politics, on interpretations of meaning and consequences, and they wrestle with conduct and morality, with assessments of the judgment of leaders. At this macro level, the accounts too readily generalize the actual experience of war. The war on the ground becomes background rather than foreground. Wars are easier to start — if not to end — if they are considered abstract dramas about slights or presumed threats or strategic goals built upon principles projected to distant places. Then those engaged in them can be reduced to general descriptive categories and faceless units and numbers ("A marine company today engaged . . ." "Twenty-five soldiers were killed when . . .").

After all of the conversations about origins and strategies and political consequences, wars are about combat, what in recent times is sometimes glibly called "boots on the ground." Most of the decision makers and debaters can at best only imagine that experience. And typically they describe it with numbers or anecdotes, selective numbers and anecdotes that best support their intellectual or political position.

While some scholars have focused on the Vietnamese history of this era, a critical and often missing dimension of Western narratives about the American War in Vietnam has to do with the Vietnamese experience. If the war was fought basically as a result of a cold war competition that transcended Vietnam, it was nonetheless fought on Vietnamese ground. It was not another "world war." In fact, the major East-West competitors in the cold war strived to contain it. But fundamentally it was a war in which Vietnam was the local arena for a worldwide contest. Yet a critical part of the war's rationale had to do with the imputed aspirations and motives of the Vietnamese, North and South.

Explanations about the American War in Vietnam typically have focused on the Vietnamese as cruel ideological aggressors, ambitious and manipulative political leaders, or innocent victims, but seldom treat them as active participants shaping their own drama. The critics of the war especially came to consider the South Vietnamese as victims and their leaders either as American puppets or profiteers and narcissists victimizing their own people — corrupt, incompetent, and undemocratic. In fact, they also were driven by their own political and personal goals. The South Vietnamese vision was not simply one choreographed in Washington.

And the North Vietnamese leaders, in the popular narratives, were seldom understood as engaged participants, strategic and manipulative with their own agenda. Instead, they were bloodthirsty instigators who were the tools of Chinese and Soviet masters of a Communist threat. Or else they came to be seen as little more than hapless victims of American airpower who were only seeking to have their own nation. Of course, the North Vietnamese were far more than merely passive victims. They too fought a cruel war, and their leaders were actively involved in framing their own objectives and strategies. They too had an agenda, and they did more than react to American initiatives. They too could be hypocritical and cynical. And they were determined.

The Vietnamese civilians, North as well as South, truly were caught up in an extended global struggle that often dominated, but never negated, their own conflicts with historical, cultural, and religious roots. The civil war in Vietnam was not a singular fight about ideology, even if cold war cheering sections deemed it a surrogate for that. Many conflicting tensions and aspirations, rooted in religion, ethnicity, geography, history, and personal ambition, played out as well.

Those living in South Vietnam, the main combat arena, found themselves caught between contending forces that often were at best indifferent to the suffering of the non-combatants. This plight was destructive and senseless, from South Vietnamese and U.S. "resettlement" programs that removed entire villages from their historic homes, to American and South Vietnamese military or their agents executing suspected enemy supporters, destroying villages or, in extreme cases, massacring people such as at My Lai. There was no respite, no safe ground, in the South Vietnamese countryside, as revealed by accounts of North Vietnamese Army and National Liberation Front (Viet Cong) forces executing civilians they suspected of engaging with the "enemy" in places ranging from isolated villages to the city of Hué during the 1968 Tet Offensive. This ancient city became a massive killing ground for government officials and presumed Saigon sympathizers. And North Vietnamese treatment of South Vietnamese military and civilian officials, or those alleged to be supporters of them, following the fall of Saigon in 1975, is a gruesome story.

The Vietnamese were more than background, more than a tragic Greek chorus, hovering over the Americans fighting in their country. After all of the arguments seeking to support political and moral positions, after all of the sweeping generalizations and exaggerations, the American War in Vietnam was marked by high numbers of innocent victims. Of course, that is true of any war, but the best calculations are that a million or more Vietnamese civilians died between 1965 and 1975 as a result of the war. Some have tripled that figure.[3]

The American War largely was a war without front lines. It was built around small-unit actions intended to surprise the enemy or lure them into attacking. And battles were not so much won as they were concluded. Temporarily concluded. The objective was to kill enough opponents to dissuade the enemy from continuing the war. These kinds of activities do not lend themselves readily to

41

standard war story narratives, to tally sheets listing battles won. In the accounts of great battles in American military history, there are no examples from Vietnam.

Absent tangible military goals, it was hard to produce tangible military results. So the great debates during the war — and since then — about its conduct have often focused on the metrics that the military and their civilian leadership developed to measure "progress." Winning hearts and minds is not a measurable result, at least not one that generates periodic scores and tallies. The U.S. military was more sophisticated than the stereotyped image of an obsession with "body counts" suggests, but it surely used these as it struggled to find the real light at the end of the long tunnel. Vietnam had no benchmarks remotely comparable to those of the army sweeping from Normandy and on to Paris in the summer of 1944. There were no headlines shouting of territories won, of happy villagers cheering their liberation. There was no iconic flag raising such as at Iwo Jima in 1945.

In the late 1960s, the growing dissent against the American War in Vietnam focused on costs and consequences. Critics increasingly pressed the case for recognizing moral costs and moral consequences. As the scale of U.S. involvement grew, and the nature of the fighting intensified, as the war in Vietnam became the American War in Vietnam, so did the volume of reports and accounts from that country. These led to increasingly negative public attitudes toward the war and, for some, perceptions of the men fighting it.

The popular depictions of the soldiers and marines on the ground changed from 1965 to 1970, from original views of heroes in the jungle fighting to protect democracy. Certainly from 1965 onward, this narrative shifted as more Americans came to be critical of or at least uncertain about the wisdom of the U.S. buildup and expansion of combat operations. In order to mobilize the forces for this expanded engagement, the Pentagon needed to increase significantly the number of men drafted. This meant that draftees constituted a growing part of the U.S. forces just as American casualties increased markedly. As there were more draftees among the killed and wounded, some common perceptions of the troops deployed to Vietnam moved from heroic freedom fighters to innocent young men dispatched to fight a mistaken war, a cruel and tragic war.

Finally, by late 1969, especially following the public disclosures of the My Lai massacre of several hundred Vietnamese civilians in March 1968, some accounts depicted the Americans no longer as victims but as eager perpetrators of the war, perpetrators often high on drugs. Although neither innocent victim nor cruel participant was a majority

43

public view, these nonetheless often were dominating ones. Each was a condescending and grossly distorted generalization.

Among the more than 2.5 million American servicemen and -women in Vietnam, some may have fit easily into one or another of the stereotypes, but surely most did not. Many of those who served may have been unwilling, but they did not consider themselves hapless victims nor were they racist psychopaths. They came home quietly and stepped aside quickly, except perhaps for those who joined in antiwar activities. Most did not join in the protests, even those who shared some of the views of the group. Even though the American War in Vietnam likely had proportionately as many individual acts of courage and bravery and sacrifice as any other war, there was relatively little enthusiasm for publicizing these accounts — or, revealingly, perhaps even less interest in hearing them. The result was a hard and impersonal war narrative with few publicly celebrated military heroes, and an often difficult and lonely homecoming. U.S. Army lieutenant William Calley, convicted of leading the massacre at My Lai, is the most recognized name of those who served in the field in Vietnam. Most Americans would be hard-pressed to name even one person who quietly and honorably served. This compounds the tragedy.

For those who served there, Vietnam was a

pretty basic world in which they focused on survival as a daily goal. Participants in all wars do that, of course, but in Vietnam it became harder to project this personal goal, to imagine the daily experience, within a broader and grander set of military objectives serving critical national needs. Except for a brief period at the beginning, the American War in Vietnam lacked a nationally endorsed feel-good, big-story narrative in which the personal accounts could fit and be warmly embraced by a grateful nation.

Today, there is a substantial library of solid scholarly studies that enrich our knowledge of this war and its consequences. My understanding has been significantly enhanced by this literature. But I have turned often to the fictional accounts of the war — the informed fiction written by men who themselves fought in it. Vietnam veterans such as Karl Marlantes, Tim O'Brien, and Jim Webb are significant contributors. Webb's Robert E. Lee Hodges, Will Goodrich, and the indomitable "Snake"; Marlantes's Waino Mellas and the trials of Bravo Company; O'Brien's Norman Bowker and Kiowa and Paul Berlin — all of these characters helped me to understand better what it was like on the ground in Vietnam. These men, along with my many interviewees, encouraged me to describe the human face, the remarkable human adaptability, the tragedy, and even the humor that generation managed to find in a very cruel experience.

Enduring Vietnam is about the American War as a generation of Americans experienced it, with a close-up focus on the transitional spring of 1969. The four years following the introduction of combat troops in March 1965 marked a period of expanding troop levels and increasing combat operations. These years were marked by an attitude of resolution and a sense of purpose. They began with certainty and optimism, then witnessed the decline of these sustaining attitudes. Here, "enduring" describes an experience encountered. In the next four years, the United States steadily drew back from Vietnam. Those on the ground endured in a war that for most Americans quickly was sapped of confidence and optimism, of energy and purpose.

Beginning with the enemy's Tet Offensive in January and February 1968, Americans at home and in Vietnam were surprised when the North Vietnamese regulars and the National Liberation Front irregulars mounted a massive attack on American installations. The fact that Americans and their allies turned back these attacks, defeating the Communist forces, never quite compensated for the surprise. And for the remainder of that presidential election year, the drama of Vietnam was upstaged by, and perceptions about the war were fully incorporated into, the drama of politics. All of the candidates talked about Vietnam. And if their policy remedies were seldom clear, it seemed evident that voters expected the United States to change the objectives or the conduct of the war. The next year, the newly inaugurated President Nixon did — though his goals were as ambiguous, his unspoken objectives as cynical, as those of his predecessors.

By the spring of 1969, for those on the ground, the terms, the equivocal goals, and the common understanding of the war clearly had changed. This had been more of an evolutionary process than an abrupt shift. But the markers of the shift were clear. When President Nixon announced in mid-May 1969 that the United States was not seeking a military victory in Vietnam, this was not really a change in objectives; it was a public acknowledgment of military limits. This restraint was only implicit earlier, and it had gone largely unnoticed in the face of a fair amount of confident saber rattling. These more limited ambitions would be underlined when the Pentagon told the American military command in Vietnam to avoid any sustained battles such as the just completed fight for Hamburger Hill.

These developments, combined with the June 1969 decision and public announcement to shift more of the ground combat to the South Vietnamese Army, described as "Vietnamization," and the concurrent initiation of a drawing down of American forces in the country, portended the end of the American War. So the last four years, from 1969 to 1973, saw a different perception of the war. The troops in those years found it even harder to understand their mission and nearly impossible to ennoble it. At some level, a sense of national need and noble purpose may be necessary conditions for anyone to volunteer or to accede to go to war. By 1969, the national narrative seemed to lose all pretense of grandeur.

Chapters 1 and 2 describe the time of transition in the spring of 1969 in the United States and in Vietnam. Americans at home celebrated Memorial Day without quite knowing how to incorporate a controversial war into the national commemoration. As they wrestled with the meaning of the war, for many it was at most a distraction. On the ground in Vietnam, the battle for Dong Ap Bia, known by the American soldiers who fought there as Hamburger Hill, a place that was grinding them up, became a part of the debate over the war and added little to a national sense of optimism. That battle encapsulated within an eleven-day window many of the elements of the American War:

elusive tactical goals, unexpected sustained resistance from disciplined and tough enemy forces who seldom followed the American expectations, American troops who despite those surprises fought with courage, and a growing controversy in the United States about the need for the battle. All of these factors filtered into a broader debate back home.

Following this introduction to the changing ground of 1969, I describe how the United States and the postwar generation of young Americans found themselves fighting this war. The cynicism of the late 1960s and early 1970s and the growing American hostility toward the war had been preceded by — perhaps exacerbated or even caused by — the world-views that dominated the twenty years from 1945 to 1965. This had been a time of a growing and genuine fear of the threats posed by the cold war. And it was a time that America viewed itself as a strong, resolute, optimistic, generous, and self-sacrificing leader in a threatening world.

Chapter 3 describes the political, cultural, and diplomatic assumptions that marked American life in those years. None of these made involvement in Vietnam inevitable even if the dominant leadership of the country defined their initiatives as clear lessons of history, of necessary assumptions of commitments, and of resolute responses to challenges faced.

The context is important, for it framed the world in which this generation grew up, one of presumed threats and assumed responsibility. Chapter 4 describes this understanding of the world. The baby boomers did not suddenly drop into Vietnam. They grew up in a nation in which the draft had always loomed and leaders and teachers warned them of their need to be prepared to defend their country. Many members of this generation took this responsibility seriously. As criticism of the war increased and as many young people protested it, it is remarkable that even as enthusiasm for the assignment waned, many still stood up to serve.

Chapter 5 describes what it was like to serve in Vietnam in those early years of the war. The development of a major American military presence with the infrastructure to support it is a dramatic story — and one that underlines that this now was the American War. Those men and women deployed there seldom found Vietnam evoking memories of the World War II narratives with which they had grown up. The nature of this war and the environment the men and women faced had little relationship to their expectations. They did assume their assigned roles — even as they held on to many aspects of the society they had left behind temporarily. You could take them out of American culture, but all of the military training could not take their culture from them. This was the generation of the '60s.

By the election of 1968, Americans had wearied of the costly struggle in Vietnam. The Tet Offensive the previous winter seemed to underline that the war would not have a quick and successful resolution. A brief transitional section describes the political shake-up that resulted in the election of Richard Nixon and the steps he took to defuse the war politically. It would prove to be a time of transition that would eventually mark the end of the American War.

Chapters 6 and 7 provide a detailed look at the time that was the hinge for this changeover. In the thirty days before President Nixon's June 8, 1969, announcement of Vietnamization and drawdown, the American War in Vietnam stayed on its aggressive course before abruptly shifting to adapt to the changing ground of political realities and the adjustments in war aims and strategies in Washington. Chapter 6 tells the stories of some of those who served during this transition. It is enriched by their own accounts, which recall the experience of a war that was different from their parents' war. And different from the war they had expected. The details of their daily lives and their struggles and sacrifices and frustrations defined their war.

Chapter 7 describes the process of homecoming. Serving in Vietnam involved a regular term of deployment and of rotation home. This chapter focuses on the human cost of the war for those Americans who served and for those who waited for them. Not all who came home did so whole of body. And some came home in aluminum military coffins. Some, still missing in action, never came home at all.

Chapter 8 describes the second half of the eight-year American ground involvement in Vietnam. These were the Nixon years, years in which politics, international and domestic, shaped tactical operations. In a complex global contest, the military role was more to threaten or to punish and less to gain and to secure. The war began with military activities accelerating even as their strategic purposes were often non-military. The war ended with a deceleration of military activity and with most operations serving as feints to secure nonmilitary goals. Or as muscle flexing or punishment aimed at achieving political resolutions. In its final years, the American War became even harder to explain and a much harder war to serve in. Nonetheless, and despite a real deterioration in traditional military discipline, the troops continued to serve well and to die in a war whose purpose on the ground was reduced to survival.

Chapter 9 summarizes the enduring experience of Vietnam for the generation that served there — and their country's enduring negative image and embarrassed memory of it. The persisting images and stereotypes have tangible sustained consequences for the veterans. Both in the haunted national consciousness and in the troubled memories of those who served, "Vietnam" is a story that has no end. And in this phase, "enduring" shifts from a verb to an adjective. Americans were never as hostile to the veterans of the Vietnam War as the legends suggest. And they have never become as warm toward them, or as comfortable with them, as the narrative promises. The reconciliation has been — and remains — complicated. Support for veterans of this war evolved from perfunctory to platitudinous.

Serving in Vietnam was of course a burden. Despite popular tales of romance and heroic and often bloodless drama, serving in any war is a burden. But perhaps unlike any other American war, *having served* in this war also became a burden. It is hard ever to feel pride for serving in your nation's war if it is always described as a negative example, as a war that should not have been fought — or, if fought, should not have been fought the way that it was. Or should not have had the embarrassed conclusion that it did. It is hard to express pride to those who were not there if the most commonly remembered event of the war was the massacre of civilians at My Lai. So the veterans of Vietnam tried to fade quietly back into American society.

While I have learned a great deal from studies and from published accounts of the Vietnam War, much of my discussion of the combat experience is based upon published and unpublished reflections and on interviews with men and women who were part of that experience, with a primary focus on those who served in Vietnam in the spring of 1969. I am grateful to the more than 160 individuals who agreed to be interviewed. For some it was the first time they had talked about their role in their war.

They often did so because they shared my interest in telling the story of those who were there and who never returned except in a military coffin. Of course, the narrators' own stories themselves became a critical part of this account. The interviewees are not a random cross section of those who served in Vietnam. Because I was seeking to talk to those who had served with men who had died, I have a highly disproportionate number of combat veterans, army and marine ground troops, infantrymen, the "grunts." Sometimes described as the tip of the spear, their experiences relate most directly to the realities of war. I have used their personal reflections and accounts as essential components of a larger story.

■ ■ ■ ■

It might be appropriate to offer a brief personal note regarding my own experience and my purpose here. I served in the Marine Corps for three years, enlisting at age seventeen in 1957. I didn't serve in Vietnam and never engaged in any combat activity. As a graduate student at the University of Wisconsin in the 1960s, and as a new faculty member at Dartmouth College beginning in 1969, I came to have an increasingly critical view of the war, its shifting and unclear objectives and the costly engagement. My criticism was directed at policy makers and not at the troops on the ground. Since 2005, I have been involved in activities supporting veterans of the wars in Iraq and Afghanistan. And since 2009, my work as a historian has focused on understanding better the experience of veterans of American wars.

My 2012 book *Those Who Have Borne the Battle: A History of America's Wars and Those Who Fought Them* represents this focus. While writing that book, I was struck again and again by the positive views Americans had of veterans of the Iraq and Afghanistan wars compared to those who had served in Vietnam. This book is a follow-up effort to better understand — and to introduce — the Vietnam veterans and their war.

Enduring Vietnam is at one level a history of the Vietnam War. As a professional historian depending largely on scholarly studies, memoirs, accounts, and contemporary media, I have taken care to try to tell this story accurately and well. But on another level, this book offers an opportunity for those who served there, and some of their families, to tell their story. This is history at a personal level. Of course, there is nothing more personal than war and its costs. My goal is to fit these elements into the broader history of that war while also using them to illustrate and to make personal that history. And finally this book represents some of my own reflections, informed by my career and work as an academic historian, a scholar, and influenced by my own experiences as a veteran and as an activist on behalf of veterans. Vietnam Veteran Bernie Edelman wrote, "Perhaps because we have been so long caught up in arguing the wisdom of the war, as a nation we have only belatedly come to recognize the sacrifices of those who were sent to fight."

On Veterans Day in 2009, I was honored to be invited to speak at the Vietnam Veterans Memorial in Washington. It was a cool, rainy morning, and the audience included a number of veterans of the war and the families of those who died there, including a group of Gold Star Mothers sitting in the front row. I

56

could not presume to speak for them, but I could attempt to speak to them. I talked about some people whose names were on the Wall, telling the stories of Michael Lyden and Billy Smoyer. I recalled that just a few months earlier my wife, Susan, and I had visited the American Cemetery at Colleville-sur-Mer at Normandy, where "we walked among the graves for some time, reading the names . . . We thought of lives cut short and of dreams unrealized and wanted to know more about them."

I concluded my remarks, standing in front of the Wall that then had names of more than 58,000 American servicemen and -women who had died in Vietnam:

> Casualties of war cry out to be known — as persons, not as abstractions called casualties nor as numbers entered into the books, and not only as names chiseled into marble or granite.
> . . . We need to ensure that here, in this place of memory, lives as well as names are recorded. Lives with smiling human faces, remarkable accomplishments, engaging personalities, and with dreams to pursue. We do this for them, for history, and for those in the future who will send the young to war.

This book is not a compendium of memories; it is a work of history that seeks to understand why America in the 1960s sent its young to war, to remember who the Vietnam generation was and how they had grown up, to reflect on why this generation served and sacrificed in a war that drifted in purpose and declined in public support. Finally, I focus on the human face, the human cost, of war. It is a cost that by no means is paid in full when the shooting stops. *Enduring Vietnam* is a study of a generation and of those who served and sacrificed.

1
MEMORIAL DAYS

On Friday, May 30, 1969, there was a late spring heat wave in the northeastern United States. The Connecticut Valley area of Massachusetts had a terrific storm the night before, but most of the country experienced pleasant if warm weather. It was auspicious for the day that customarily symbolized the beginning of summer — Memorial Day. Except, as with so many things in American life that year, it was a time of transition and confusion. The holiday was actually observed on different days in 1969, with a number of states having celebrated it on the previous Monday, May 26. But there was more dividing the nation than just a date on the calendar.

Memorial Day had begun following the Civil War. As early as 1865, a group of free African Americans took the day to recognize the Union veterans buried in temporary graves at a racetrack in Charleston, South Carolina. Over the next few years, more and more communities gathered to remember those lost in the war. In 1868, General John A. Logan, president of the Grand Army of the Republic, an organization of veterans of the Union Army, distributed a letter calling on Northerners to remember the war dead by visiting and placing flowers on their graves.

Often called Decoration Day, this spring date for reflection within a few years would become a holiday in all states except for those formerly in the Confederacy. It wasn't until the twentieth century that it became celebrated nationally. After incorporating the old Confederacy, it evolved into Memorial Day, a day to acknowledge the dead of all American wars. This fit into a national narrative, patriotic and grateful, and served as a reminder of sacrifice and as a touchstone of unity. On Memorial Day 1969, in many communities speakers read from General Logan's letter urging this annual day of reflection.[1]

Memorial Day by then was about more than decorating graves and remembering the dead. Economically and culturally, it heralded summer. Most people enjoyed a day free from work. Family outings, picnics, the beach, baseball games, and special retail sales marked the day. Implicitly affirming these wide-ranging and "secular" activities, in 1968 Congress agreed to move the holiday from its traditional May 30 date to the last Monday of May, creating a three-day weekend. Many states followed. Some of the changes took effect immediately, while the federal holiday was not adjusted until 1971. So in 1969 there were two different memorial days. But on May 30, all federal offices were closed while the baseball games and the picnics and the Indianapolis 500 went on.

Americans were going to the movies in droves that weekend. The number-one box office movie was *Midnight Cowboy*. The pop music charts recorded that Americans were listening to the 5th Dimension's "Let the Sunshine In" from the musical *Hair* along with the Beatles' "Get Back," and Creedence Clearwater Revival's "Bad Moon Rising." The country charts reported that the top songs were Glenn Campbell's "Galveston" and Roy Clark's "Yesterday, When I Was Young." Beach books that weekend included bestsellers Philip Roth's *Portnoy's Complaint,* Mario Puzo's *The Godfather,* and Kurt Vonnegut's *Slaughterhouse Five.*

Chino, California, had a Fair and a Dairy Festival. In Del Rio, Texas, the Drifting Playboys were performing at a dance at the Hide-A-Way on Highway 90. *The New York Times* described New York on that day as a "ghost town in many neighborhoods . . . as people headed for the parks, mountains, lakes and the seashore." In Chicago, officials estimated that 175,000 people were on the city's beaches. An estimated 125,000 watched 64 units of servicemen, veterans, and Scouts in the annual parade from South Water Street to Van Buren Street. Washingtonians heading for the shore jammed the Chesapeake Bay Bridge for about five hours, beginning at 6:30 in the morning. Six were killed in a car-truck collision on Interstate 95 in Virginia.[2]

Workers at the National Space Center in Houston did not have a holiday; they were preparing for the Apollo 11 moon mission scheduled for late July. In small towns across the country, high school bands marched, speakers praised patriotic sacrifice, and picnickers filled parks. As one woman wrote to the *Chicago Tribune,* "There is a lingering softness about Memorial Day in a small rural community; a sort of gentle, mistlike earthiness in the air."[3]

In cities large and small, along with the outings, the picnics, and the gatherings, it remained as well a day for many to pause and remember. In Winona, Minnesota, the Garden Memorial Committee organized a tribute for the 5 members of that community who had died in Vietnam. The State Committee reminded citizens that 732 Minnesotans had died in that ongoing war. At Zuni Pueblo in New Mexico, 18 Gold Star Mothers, who had lost sons at war, attended the celebration of the members of that community who had died in the country's wars.

Shortsville, New York, had a parade and a buffet lunch at the American Legion post. The *Lowell Sun* published pictures of some of that city's war memorials and noted, "So long as granite and bronze shall last, so also will the City of Lowell and its residents be reminded of the supreme sacrifices made by its men who have given their lives in every war engaged in by the nation." In Columbus, Nebraska, there was a reading of Lincoln's Gettysburg Address and John McCrae's "In Flanders Fields."[4]

The nation's memory of wartime sacrifice had been expanded over the past several years. Beginning in 1965, combat dead from Vietnam had been coming home for burial following the 416 advisers and others who had died through 1964. By April 30, 1969, 33,641 Americans had been killed in Vietnam — but of course not all of their bodies had been recovered for burial.

The American experience in Vietnam and accounts of those who died there were not easily assimilated into the Memorial Day commemorations. Perhaps it is always hard for a current war to fit readily into the outline of memory. But this war seemed especially difficult for many to embrace. In the parades around the country, there were still a few Spanish-American War veterans and a number of World War I veterans who were the center of attention. They evoked a sense of history, a history remembered proudly. Korean War veterans were less visible and engaged. But the largest numbers of veterans in 1969 were of course from World War II. Still fairly young, most now only in their forties, they represented what the nation celebrated as the American way of war: clear objectives, citizen-soldiers responding to recognized threats, and unencumbered military action leading to unambiguous victory. Those who died in that war were warmly remembered. The parents of Ira Hayes came from the Gila River Reservation in Arizona to visit his grave at Arlington Cemetery. Hayes was the young Pima Indian marine who had helped to raise the flag on Iwo Jima in 1945. He died in 1965.[5]

On Memorial Day 1969, Americans were preparing to note the twenty-fifth anniversary of the D-day landing at Normandy, occurring on Friday, June 6. This dramatic story had no equivalent in Vietnam, or in Korea, for that matter: The Normandy landing led to heroic victory in a war framed by moral clarity. President Richard Nixon, himself a World War II veteran, proclaimed that D-day marked "a historical landmark in the history of freedom." He reminded the nation that the troops on the Normandy beaches left a legacy of "acts of valor which have been the inspiration and often the salvation of Western civilization."[6]

Around the country, while orators did not quite ignore the current war in Vietnam, the embrace was strained, and in some cases their comments were outright critical. The supportive remarks seemed often to be more inspirational reminders than tales of heroic deeds. The critical comments focused on the war rather than on those Americans fighting it. It was becoming harder to separate them. Speakers did call on Americans to applaud the service and to remember the sacrifices of Americans in Vietnam. President Nixon observed that "these young men and women are responding just as bravely today as their forefathers did on previous occasions when the call to duty came." He insisted, "Their sense of purpose, their personal courage, their professionalism and their loyalty are an inspiration to all."[7]

Vice President Spiro Agnew placed a wreath of red, white, and blue carnations at the Tomb of the Unknowns at Arlington National Cemetery. He noted that along with the thousands of graves of those remembered as heroes, "some died without special recognition." But all "were willing to die for freedom. We can do no less." He stressed that Americans were sacrificing in Vietnam because "if we allow the small and the weak to be devoured, the larger and stronger will infallibly become the prey."[8]

Vietnam had not yet entered into the

65

national narrative of war. The war was too current — and too controversial — for its tales to readily nestle among accounts of Gettysburg or Pointe du Hoc or Okinawa. One complication was that the current war was marked by small-scale company — and often only platoon-level — engagements. These involved troops defending against an ambush, walking into minefields, securing a trail or a slope. There were few sweeping, blockbuster engagements. In this war, out in the bush, "securing" meant only for the time being. There were no flags planted and no dramatic victories. This was by its nature a different type of war, which did not lend itself to heroic headlines. And the controversy over the war did not enhance the accounts of it.

Nonetheless, some people tried. In Manchester, Connecticut, a member of a local veterans' group reminded listeners of their debt to those who served, heroes who "shared in the preservation of this nation and her principles from the dark days of the Revolutionary War to the troubled days of the Vietnam War." In Sawtelle, California, a navy rear admiral urged the "adults" in his audience to remind the young that "freedom is not freedom from responsibility" and that sacrifices are necessary to keep "our freedom from being taken away." The adjutant general of New Mexico told a gathering that "we are all certainly proud of each and every one of our boys. They are doing their duty and accepting their responsibility."[9]

Patriotism alone could not minimize reminders of the cost paid for those who performed that duty. In Boston, the city dedicated an intersection as Robert G. Harris Square, honoring a Vietnam casualty. Harris, a Roxbury native who had been drafted in the fall of 1967, had been killed in April 1968 by a mortar round while serving with the Americal Division near Tien Phuoc. He died just ten days short of his twenty-first birthday. Lane Tech High School in Chicago had a special Memorial Day celebration, honoring the 24 graduates of that school who had died in Vietnam.[10]

In Madison, Wisconsin, a group estimated at five thousand followed the city's traditional Memorial Day parade with a march protesting the war in Vietnam. In Torrington, Connecticut, William Styron and Arthur Miller read the names of all of the Vietnam War dead during a twenty-four-hour vigil. Other peace groups read the names of the dead at gatherings in Rochester, Philadelphia, and Cincinnati. Mayor Philip Jones of San Fernando, California, had lost an eye fighting with the marines on Guam in World War II. He spent more than fifteen hours reading the names of Vietnam dead, asking, "How many more of our youth must be uselessly sacrificed before the killing is ended?"[11]

■ ■ ■ ■

Over the preceding two or three years, there had been a growing public concern about the war. For many Americans, particularly the young, these reservations had moved from unease to protest. Beginning with marches and rallies as early as 1965, galvanized by the Lincoln Memorial protests in October 1967, continuing on campuses and at the Democratic National Convention in Chicago in August 1968, the young marched and demonstrated. And although many in their parents' generation disapproved of these protests, it was clear that even among them support for the war had been declining markedly. A January 1965 Gallup poll reported that 28 percent of Americans thought it would be a mistake to send troops to Vietnam. By January 1969, that figure was 52 percent.[12]

The Tet Offensive in January 1968 in which NLF and North Vietnamese forces assaulted major American and South Vietnamese enclaves, including the American embassy in Saigon, proved to be a turning point — a psychological one, not a military one. Ironically, the Americans and their allies won these battles, including a major fight over the city of Hué. But the fact that they had been fought when most officials had insisted that the war was nearly over caused an erosion of public support. In November 1968, Richard Nixon won the presidential election in a contest against Lyndon Johnson's vice president, Hubert Humphrey. Although a strong supporter of the Vietnam engagement, Nixon was critical of its conduct and insisted that he had a plan to end the war. The protests did not abate.

During the spring of 1969, college campuses had experienced unprecedented protests, many of which resulted in injuries and/or arrests. Students occupied the president's office at the University of Iowa and at Dartmouth College. Protesters started fires at City College of New York, the University of Illinois, and Lincoln University in Jefferson City, Missouri. Someone shot at firemen at the University of Illinois and at policemen who came to Seattle (Washington) Community College.[13]

At Notre Dame, the senior class chose the antiwar presidential candidate in 1968, Senator Eugene McCarthy, as their "Fellow." Two years earlier, the graduates had selected General William Westmoreland, the commander of the Military Assistance Command, Vietnam, as "Patriot of the Year." The Harvard faculty voted just before Memorial Day to discontinue the university's ROTC programs. And at Berkeley there was a great battle over the student effort to claim a

"People's Park." Governor Ronald Reagan sent in the National Guard. Guardsmen also moved into the North Carolina Agricultural and Technical State University in Greensboro. Ten Quakers from Philadelphia were arrested on the steps of the U.S. Capitol when they began reading the names of those who died in Vietnam. Military recruiters began to be far more selective in determining which campuses to visit.[14]

Passions were almost equally high on the other side of the issue. There was a major pushback against the demonstrations. At the University of Wisconsin at Madison, scene of several major protests over the previous two years, the executive director of the Alumni Association reported that membership had declined: "Alumni quit because they feel this is a way they can strike back at the University for tolerating protests and unseemly behavior."[15]

Attorney General John Mitchell spoke of a "conspiracy" involving "professional militants." The columnist Mary McGrory reminded the administration that the dissent was far more universally supported than they believed.[16] The historian Henry Steele Commager warned students at Stanford that they needed to be careful in focusing their anger on universities, "the most unique and least corrupt institution in society." He said that even if universities acceded to all of the students' demands, "The war in Vietnam would go on, the draft would go on and all of today's problems would be the same as they were before."[17]

In fact, student protest was not so sharply focused. A Gallup poll in May 1969 that surveyed college students reported that the students' greatest concern was "Not enough say in running of college." Forty-two percent agreed with this. Only 11 percent said that the Vietnam War was their major "gripe." The "current inadequacies of society" and "adult and governmental authority" were both significantly greater concerns than the war, according to these respondents.[18] Nonetheless, war protest became the defining symbol of campus protesters in the national consciousness.

Every part of American society seemed to be sorting itself into sides. The July 11 issue of *Life* magazine had a cover story contrasting Dustin Hoffman and John Wayne, "A Choice of Heroes." It showed Wayne, the "Duke," in scenes from the new movie *True Grit* and Hoffman in scenes from his hit movie *Midnight Cowboy.* The differences were sharp. In regard to protests, Hoffman said, "The youth outburst in this country is a good thing. The kids are angry because the American leaders have made mistakes and refused to admit it." John Wayne in his comment, according to the reporter, "growls" that "the disorders in the schools are caused by immature professors who have encouraged activists."

By this Memorial Day, Americans were clearly divided over the war in Vietnam. And this marker day forced many to try to reconcile — or to confront — the proud national narrative of American wars with their current perception of this war. The New York Times editors published an editorial, "These Honored Dead." The newspaper described "a miasma of national regret, recrimination and disillusionment." The editors rejected turning to Abraham Lincoln's "classic" response to the question: To what end did they die? In this war, they insisted, it would not suffice to insist that we have an obligation to "resolve that these dead shall not have died in vain." The Times concluded:

The cause for which men have fought and died in Vietnam is peace — that is, a better understanding of how men can live together despite ideological antagonisms and conflicting interests. From their sacrifices, Americans have gained new wisdom and insight about the limits of their power, about the nature of Communist revolutions and guerrilla warfare, and about the character of their adversaries and of themselves. Comfortable illusions have been dispelled and disastrous temptations rebuked.

Brave men have paid with their lives for the hard-won wisdom. The responsibility of the living is to act upon that wisdom. If they do, if they have advanced in their understanding of that complex process called peace, then the men who have fallen in Vietnam have won a victory far more profound than the conventional triumph celebrated with bands and parades.

So in this view, the educational process and the intellectual lessons of this war may justify its costs. The problem was that dying for an enhanced national wisdom was not likely to be celebrated comfortably in the traditional Memorial Day celebrations and parades.[19]

The Washington Post was of a somewhat different mind on Memorial Day 1969. Their editors suggested, "The men who are doing the dirty work of the state in South Vietnam must feel like the Roman legions, cut off and at war amid a hostile enemy and none too certain of the support of their own countrymen." The *Post* insisted that:

those who fight this war are very properly heroes — because they fight to no applause, because the cause is not supported, because all of it is so unequal. It is as if all the injustices of life have been concentrated in one unlucky place, where the burden is borne by a brave few whose stake in its

73

outcome is very small. A man's death is no less because it occurs at Danang rather than Remagen, and an exploit like Hamburger Hill is no less gallant than Iwo Jima. But it is not common now to speak of gallantry, any more than it is to speak of heroes.[20]

These strained explanations of the nation's war and its costs were necessary. It was no longer possible to ignore the war; it had become the major focus of American discussion and debate. Since late 1967, Gallup had discovered that it was the number-one answer when pollsters asked citizens to identify the leading issue or problem facing the country. On Friday, May 30, the three national television networks, ABC, CBS, and NBC, presented nineteen Vietnam-related stories on their evening news telecasts. Eric Sevareid had a closing commentary on the *CBS Evening News.* Following Walter Cronkite's reminder that this was Memorial Day, Sevareid concluded that this holiday was aimed at remembering those Americans killed in the country's wars:

It is difficult to think of soldier heroes when so many are soldiers again in a war without glory, where the bravest are heroes only to their immediate comrades, unacknowledged by their country at large. This is fairly surely the most disliked, unbelieved-in war Americans have ever fought so its deaths are doubly bitter. . . .

There is something in us that insists our wars be moral crusades, and when the morality of the fighting is not clear and obvious, rebellious protest spreads across the land.

So anyone who visits the combat soldiers in Vietnam confronts a humbling mystery: young Americans fighting, not for glory, not for booty, not because their own land is directly threatened, not out of passion, living the worst life they have ever lived, while most of their countrymen, including most of their youthful peers, live the best life they have ever lived. But they do not quit; they climb the deadly hill again. This spectacle does not yield to logic or reason or even common sense, but somehow it evokes in all who see it a profound respect.

Holiday oratory, punditry, and commentary are artifacts of the mood, the understanding, of the moment. Clearly the Memorial Day events of 1969 were marked by divisions and emotion, by pleas for understanding and reminders of sacrifice. Vietnam figured in the center of all of this — but more abstractly than concretely, more metaphorically than literally, more politically than analytically. Except it was tangible and real for those serving in Vietnam and their families, for those back home worrying about the draft, and of course for the nearly 35,000 families of those who had already died in the war.

For the vast majority, however, lives went on. Americans were captivated by the preparations for the July launch from the Kennedy Space Center that would send Neil Armstrong, Buzz Aldrin, and Michael Collins to the moon on Apollo 11. Armstrong and Aldrin were scheduled to go to the surface and step out on the moon.

In New York, a group was proceeding with plans for a major outdoor music festival in August upstate in Wallkill. Local opposition would finally force a late summer movement of the program to Max Yasgur's farm at White Lake, not far from Woodstock. It was billed as "An Aquarian Exposition: 3 Days of Peace & Music." By early June, with Jimi Hendrix on board, joining Country Joe McDonald, Janis Joplin, the Grateful Dead, Creedence Clearwater, Joan Baez, and Crosby, Stills, Nash & Young, this was going to be a major event. It was a music festival rather than an antiwar gathering, but obviously it represented a substantial part of American culture that was increasingly hostile to the war in Vietnam.[21]

This was expressed in some novel ways. John Lennon and Yoko Ono, recently married, held a "Bed-In for Peace" at the Queen

Elizabeth Hotel in Montreal. It was a major event, covered widely by the media. It had been scheduled to be held in New York, but Lennon was not allowed to come into the United States because of his recent conviction for marijuana possession. He and Yoko Ono positioned themselves in a white double bed, wearing white, and over several days met with hundreds of visitors, including Allen Ginsberg, Timothy Leary, a Hare Krishna group, the jazz critic Nat Hentoff, disc jockey Murray the K, and Dick Gregory. Tommy Smothers joined them, and the conservative *L'il Abner* cartoonist Al Capp came to confront them. Lennon composed lyrics during that time, and on June 1, he and Ono and Tommy Smothers recorded "Give Peace a Chance," which quickly became the anthem for the antiwar movement. With its raplike chants touching on major themes and individuals of the culture of the 1960s, it was memorable for the plea of its chorus: "All we are saying is give peace a chance."[22]

At the Wellesley College commencement on May 31, the differences were sharpened by an exchange between the commencement speaker, Massachusetts senator Edward W. Brooke, and graduating senior Hillary Rodham from Park Ridge, Illinois. Rodham was the first Wellesley graduate to speak at her school's commencement. Protesting students had demanded a student speaker. Senator

Brooke was critical of radical protest. Rodham rejected the idea of politics as the art of the possible. She said that the challenge facing Brooke "and us — now — is to practice politics as the art of making possible what appears to be impossible." Rodham received an extended standing ovation from the four hundred graduates.[23]

In New York on May 29, a federal grand jury indicted eighteen young men for draft evasion — they had burned their draft cards at a protest rally. Two of the defendants had moved to London and six of them were in Toronto.[24]

Many of the wars in the nation's history had seen protesters and dissension, but there was a new element in the unpopularity of the current war. The original sense of shared moral purpose was eroding. By 1969, despite the persistent rationale that the Vietnam War was about halting the spread of communism, probably few would have disputed Sevareid's implicit reminder that this war was not a moral crusade. Most would have accepted his point that it was hard to find in Vietnam any "glory" — and they would not have disagreed with the *Post* editors that it was a war that seemed to lack stories of gallantry or heroes. Perhaps a majority would have even agreed with the *Times*'s conclusion that the best result of the Vietnam War was that it was providing a lesson on the errors of the war: "Comfortable illusions have been dispelled and disastrous temptations rebuked."

In speeches and articles, in demonstrations for and against the war, the Americans serving in Vietnam that Memorial Day weekend seemed to have become distant pieces and caricatures of a broad conflict that was generational and cultural, sectional and political. Protesters for the last two or more years had chanted, "Hey, hey, LBJ. How many kids did you kill today?" Still, very few of the protesters and critics were directly implicating the servicemen and -women in Vietnam. The story of the My Lai massacre in March 1968 would not become public until later that year. The Winter Soldier Investigation, where antiwar veterans would describe their own and others' crimes in Vietnam, was nearly two years away.

That Memorial Day weekend, when many Americans were arguing about the fighting in Vietnam, a small fraction of the nation's citizens were actually experiencing the war. And that experience was far from abstract. On April 30, the number of American troops serving in Vietnam peaked at more than 543,000. This represented about a quarter of 1 percent of the U.S. population and was approximately 7 percent of the eligible male population under age twenty-five. If most Americans did not know them personally, they nonetheless discussed them. American

79

troops serving at bases around the world did have a holiday for Memorial Day, but not those serving in Vietnam. War zones do not pause for holiday weekends.

It turned out there was a stand-down of sorts in Vietnam on May 30. The National Liberation Front had declared a forty-eight-hour cease-fire in honor of Buddha's Birthday. The South Vietnamese government and the U.S. Command countered with a twenty-four-hour cease-fire, beginning at 6:00 A.M. on Friday, May 30. There were accounts of a number of violations that the United States insisted had been initiated by the Communists. But there were few major fights during that period.[25]

On May 30, a group from the 1st Marine Division went to a church service at Yen Ne, near Da Nang. The *Chicago Tribune* reported that they considered the Buddha's Birthday truce "rhetorical jargon. It did little to insure survival." But they took the break and caught their breath in the summer heat. "The marines received the sacrament, then wandered off silently in small groups with rifles slung over their shoulders. The truce was nearly over. They would be moving out soon."[26]

Twenty-four American servicemen died during the cease-fire. Coming into the traditional Memorial Day of that year, 1,411 Americans had already died in Vietnam in May. And over the three-day weekend, 110 more would die.

The median age of the Americans who died in those three days was twenty-one. Eighteen were teenagers. Twenty-seven were married. Ninety-four were white, and 16 were African American. Thirty-eight were draftees, 9 were officers. Eighty-five served in the army, 21 were marines, 3 were in the navy, and 1 was serving in the air force. Fourteen were from California, 7 were Texans, 9 came from Illinois, 6 were from Georgia, and 6 were from Michigan. Forty were from the South. Buddha's Birthday or not, the war in Vietnam was not on holiday.

Jerome Collins turned twenty-one on Mother's Day just a few weeks before his death. His family lived on the river in Magnolia Springs, Alabama. They were Creole, proud descendants of a settlement on Mobile Bay that dated from the eighteenth century when French and Spanish explorers and adventurers came there. Some remained, living with local Indians and then with escaped slaves, forming their own isolated settlement and culture. This group had been described by a sociologist during the Great Depression as an independent enclave that resented its white neighbors for identifying them as part of the black subculture of Alabama. They insisted that they were not black.[27] But in the segregated Alabama of the 1960s, Jerome Collins and his siblings and neighbors were

81

not allowed to enroll in the white schools. Most of them attended St. John's parochial school. Ten Collins children went there.

Jerome's family farmed and fished and hunted and gathered oysters. His friend Helen Trammel remembered him as a gentle spirit, very artistic and musical. He was a crack shot and taught Helen and her sister Faith how to shoot and skin rabbits. He spent as much time as he could on the river and was a good athlete who ran everywhere he went. Jerome, "Romey," as he was called by friends and family, liked to play the guitar and sing Hank Williams classics — especially "Your Cheatin' Heart" — but his favorite song was "Green, Green Grass of Home." He was a quiet but sometimes exuberant young man, and when he got excited or something delighted him, he would jump up and say, "Shakespeare!"

Jerome enlisted in the army in the spring of 1968, soon after graduating from high school. He was facing the draft and decided to join. His younger brother Allen, fourteen years old at the time, recalls that he saw Romey only once after enlistment. He was home on leave before he went to Vietnam. That was the last time. Allen said that Jerome served his country knowing that he might not come back and he seemed okay with that. His younger sister Lucy recalls that as he was leaving, he gave his sisters some ice cream, and hugged and kissed them. It was the first time he had ever done that. And he told her that he probably would not see them again.[28]

Jerome arrived in Vietnam on January 31, 1969. After processing, he was assigned to the 173rd Airborne Brigade and sent up to the Central Highlands. Here they were trying to halt the North Vietnamese Army effort to move troops from Laos to the coastal plains in support of the NLF forces. An infantryman, he joined a Scout platoon that engaged in patrols and helped to secure the highway between Mang Yang Pass and An Khe. On a mission the night before the Buddha's Birthday cease-fire, Collins's group secured a village and then pursued NLF soldiers into tall grass, where they were ambushed. When the enemy detonated a Claymore mine, 7 members of the Scout patrol were hit. They were medevaced out. Virgil Hamilton died immediately and Collins apparently survived only briefly; Steven Owen of Long Beach, California, was badly wounded and died on May 31. The other 4 wounded members of the patrol survived.[29]

Back in Magnolia Springs, Jerome Collins's family had no telephone and little communication with the broader world. When they first learned from the army that their son had been killed, they were not sure whether it was Jerome's older brother Dawn, who was also in the army, or Jerome. Lucy

83

said that when Jerome's body was returned almost two weeks later and the family was permitted a viewing, he looked to her like he wanted to get out of the casket. His favorite flower, the bird-of-paradise, was placed near his casket for his funeral at St. John's Church.

On May 30, Gwen Miller was at her home in Ottumwa, Iowa, with her infant son. Iowa was one of the states that had already moved the holiday to a Monday that would anchor a three-day weekend. So Memorial Day of 1969 in the Hawkeye state had been on May 26. Gwen was an Ottumwa native and she had married her college sweetheart, Terry Vernon Miller, in 1967. Now they had a three-month-old son, Christian.

Gwen Cheatum's and Terry Miller's fathers and others in their families worked at the local John Deere factory. Yet even though they had gone to the same high school, the two of them didn't really meet until they were students at Northeast Missouri State Teachers College. Both were art majors and had been involved in some of the antiwar discussions at the school. It was unusual for the draft board to select someone like Terry Miller, who was married and still had a semester of teacher training to finish his art degree. But in the summer of 1968, he was drafted. The fact that his wife was pregnant was not a basis to change his draft status.

Gwen urged Terry to go to Canada, where they could start a new life. He said that even though he opposed the war, he accepted his obligation to serve. But he assured his family and friends that he would never shoot anyone. Following basic training, Terry Miller actually volunteered to go to Vietnam. He did this because he knew that the policy was to provide soldiers with a leave to go home before deployment. This would enable him to be with Gwen when their baby was born. Terry Miller met and held Christian in February 1969, and a few days later his family saw him off at the Ottumwa airport. He told Gwen that he did not want her to say "Good-bye." She kissed him and told him that she loved him.[30]

In March, Terry Miller joined the 4th Battalion of the 21st Infantry, part of the Americal Division. They were north of their base camp at Dak To, out on Firebase Amy, near the borders of Vietnam, Laos, and Cambodia. They were lifted out for patrols or ambushes, and most of their contact was with soldiers from the North Vietnamese Army. On the night of May 29, their company was positioned on a hill while some of the group went out on ambush. Terry Miller remained on the defensive perimeter of the night position. They were assaulted that night, and Terry Miller was killed, along with Louie Leija, who was in the same foxhole. Because the hill was very rocky, it had not been possible to dig deep foxholes, and so the two soldiers were killed by small-arms fire. When the ambush team came back in the morning, the men remaining on the defensive perimeter had wrapped their comrades' bodies in their ponchos and were waiting for a helicopter to take them out.[31]

Terry Miller had instructed the army to notify his parents rather than his wife if he was killed or injured. He did not want Gwen to confront any difficult news alone. So when her father-in-law came to her house with two soldiers on the afternoon of May 30, Gwen knew immediately what had happened.

It took ten days for Terry Miller's body to be returned. As was customary, the family was permitted to view the body in private. Gwen recalled that his face was bloated and his chest was "sunken," probably as a result of gunshot wounds. Contrary to custom, she asked that the casket remain open for the wake. She wanted friends to see him and to know this was real. She sat in the funeral home alone overnight with her husband's body.

Forty-five years later, she recalled that night, sitting off to one side, when a woman came in and approached the casket and stood there looking at Terry's body. Gwen recognized her as the woman who also had given birth in the hospital when Christian was born. The other woman had several children already and her husband didn't come by to see her. When Terry came in with flowers for Gwen and learned that the other woman had no visitors, he went out and bought flowers for her. Some one hundred days later, this woman came at night to the funeral home, when she thought no one else would be there, to visit Terry.

Terry's funeral was on June 9, and he was buried in the Ottumwa Cemetery. The City Council ordered flags to be flown at half-staff in his honor. But at Gwen's request, the U.S. Army Honor Guard did not fire their rifles in the customary burial salute at the cemetery. She did not want gunfire at Terry's grave. She told the army representatives that there had been enough gunfire around her husband. Nor did she allow the local television station news crew to film the ceremony.[32]

On May 30, the Quincy, Massachusetts, newspaper published a brief obituary for James Hickey, a nineteen-year-old marine who had been killed in a mortar attack three days earlier. His family, their very close Irish American community, and the citizens of Quincy were all devastated. Quincy would lose 27 men in Vietnam.

Jimmy Hickey grew up in a culture where military service was part of life, part of the rite of passage for many in his blue-collar community. And in this milieu, joining the marines was the preferred choice. Jimmy Hickey had been prepared to drop out of high school and join the marines with some friends in 1967, but he changed his mind because he didn't want to leave his girlfriend. His friend David Pitts did join with this group. In February 1968, David Pitts was killed, along with several marines in a mortar attack on their position in Hué during the Tet Offensive.

Jimmy Hickey and five friends dropped out of school a month before graduation and joined the marines following David Pitts's death. As one of his friends said, Pitts's death "devastated us . . . Something just reached inside of you and said, 'This is reality. This is real.' " By this time Hickey and his girlfriend had broken up. Jimmy was part of a very tight-knit community, one that valued loyalty, and now he was prepared to go to Vietnam. He was there within several months. He wrote to "My Darling little sister" Carol and told her that he missed everyone. "I hate being here because I have no idea what's going on back home."[33]

Hickey wrote to his friend Jack Croall, one of the group that had joined in 1967 and was now home in Quincy recovering from wounds suffered in Vietnam. He admitted that he missed his friends and would like to have a chance to be with them, and that he still felt the same about his former girlfriend — "Something like that takes a lot longer to get over than I thought." He also was bored at his artillery post and was ready for some action.[34] Less than three months later, on May 27, he and three other marines in his unit were killed in a rocket attack on his position on Hill 55 southwest of Da Nang.

Jimmy Hickey's funeral was a big event in Quincy. He was buried on June 10, the day before his sister graduated from Quincy High School. At the wake, Jimmy lay in an open casket; the fatal wounds were on his back. A group of his friends took up a collection, which they used to buy new vestments for the priest.[35]

Jimmy's uncle Philip Byrnes, described as a "soulful" man who loved his nephew deeply, wrote a poem, which he distributed after the service. He recalled that as a child, his nephew was always claiming he had a magic horse in his room. Evoking themes from the Peter, Paul and Mary 1963 song "Puff, the Magic Dragon," Byrnes reminded all of the little boy who was Jimmy Hickey.

Magic Horse

When he was just a boy he had a magic
    horse.
No one else could see it but it was there,
    of course.

He'd gallop off at night and tie it to his bed,
He knew it would stand guard so nothing
    he must dread.
Years have ways of passing and so do
    Childhood dreams,
As boys to manhood grow almost
    overnight, it seems.
Leaving those he loves the most, leaving
    his magic horse,
Now he goes to search out from life its
    very force.
He must be a Marine though it may bring
    him harm;
Fate will cross his path in the Province of
    Quang Nam.
Now speaks a gentle voice, Jim, we
    mustn't tarry,
For I have come this night to take you
    home to Mary.
But Father I'm so young, I do not
    understand.
He knows, He knows, my son, he bade me
    take your hand.
He took me, too, you know and I cried out
    in pain,
To ask my Father why by men must I be
    slain.
He sacrificed His son that men might learn
    to care,
He led me to my home and I must take
    you there.

He will not let you hurt as I did from the
  cross.
Dear Jim, I'll lead you home upon your
  magic horse.

Written for James P. Hickey
by his uncle, Philip Byrnes

Before Jimmy's death, his father and his uncle had opened a tavern that they called the Magic Horse on Highway 139 in North Abington, Massachusetts. They had hoped that when Jimmy Hickey came home from Vietnam, he would go to work at the tavern and ultimately take it over.[36]

Magic horses — and dragons — may live forever. But little boys do not. In 2014, the city of Quincy dedicated a square in honor of James Hickey. They also named squares after David Pitts and two other Quincy marines who had been killed in Vietnam. By the time of the dedication for Hickey, there were some twenty squares in that city honoring residents killed in Vietnam.

Carol Hickey, Jimmy's mother, had been home with a cousin when two marines and the parish priest, Father Mel Krumdick, came to the door. She never recovered from the news they shared with her that day. Five years later, on Mother's Day, she suffered a fatal accident when she slipped and fell down the steps and broke her neck. Her friends said she "wanted to be with Jimmy."

■ ■ ■ ■

Uniformed delegations were knocking at the doors of other parents and spouses on that Memorial Day weekend. There were funerals around the country, quiet gatherings of family and friends. And obituaries in local papers. Still, while the Vietnam War was on everyone's mind, most Americans had little contact with those who were serving there on the country's behalf. But a month later, there would be a sharper, more personal introduction to the casualties of Vietnam.

The June 27 issue of *Life* magazine had a cover story titled "The Faces of the American Dead in Vietnam: One Week's Toll." The editors chose the week of May 28 through June 3 for their coverage because it included Memorial Day. (The dates were a little misleading since the story's focus was on those men whose names had been released by the Pentagon during this week, which included a number of men who had actually been killed prior to the period. It also did not include many who had been killed on those dates.)

The magazine featured 242 men killed in what they defined as the seven-day period. The article included photos of most of them, more than eleven pages, twenty pictures to a page. These were largely high school graduation pictures or basic training/boot camp pictures, with a few candid shots from the field. Often smiling — but also serious. And young. Many of the dead were not yet old enough to vote or to be served alcohol in most parts of the United States. The captions simply identified them by name, age, rank, and hometown. The close-up cover photo was of William Gearing, a twenty-year-old soldier from Greece, New York. Gearing had been in Vietnam for more than six months when he was killed by a mortar blast near Tam Ky on May 19. Jeremiah June from Birmingham, Alabama, was killed in the same explosion. He was not included in the magazine story.

Forty years later, *Life* editor Ralph Graves still recalled the power of this issue. He admitted that it was not his idea but that of columnist and assistant managing editor Loudon Wainwright, who "had been struck by the fact that week after week during the Vietnam War the Pentagon kept announcing the number of Americans killed, but it was only a number. Wainwright, a deeply sensitive man, said to himself — and eventually to others — these shouldn't be just numbers. These are people. These are real people. *Life* should find a way to say that — and show that."[37]

There had been some concern about whether *Life* editor in chief Hedley Donovan, who was a strong proponent of the war, would approve of the story. Donovan looked at the mock-up of pictures and said, "Run it." He said that he approved because of all the families that had supplied pictures. He did not think *Life* could disappoint them. Graves reported that they had received photos from 217 of the 242 on the list; most of the missing 25 were due to an inability to locate family members. "Only a minute handful of family members said no."[38]

Whether readers were supportive of the story or critical of its perceived antiwar sentiments, the issue captured the attention of Americans around the country. It put a very human face on a distant war. The young men had their own backgrounds and stories, but of course shared one tragic and defining characteristic. *Life* described some of them:

There is a catalogue of fact for every face. One boy had customized his 13-year-old car and planned to buy a ranch. Another man, a combat veteran of the Korean War, leaves seven children. A third had been an organist in his church and wanted to be a singer. One had been sending his pay home to contribute to his brother's college expenses. The mother of one of the dead, whose son was the third of four to serve in the Army, insists with deep pride, "We are a patriotic family willing to pay the price." An aunt who had raised her nephew said of him, "He was really and truly a conscientious objector. He told me it was a terrible thought going into the Army and winding up in Vietnam and shooting people who hadn't done anything to him . . . Such a waste. Such a shame."

One of the soldiers pictured in the story was from Boring, Oregon. The editors reported, "In the state of Oregon a soldier was buried in a grave shared by the body of his brother, who had died in Vietnam two years earlier."[39]

Family members and friends of the dead wrote to *Life*'s editor, and the magazine published their reactions. A mother of one of the soldiers pictured wrote from Placerville, California, that there had been "five deaths in my son's 1966 graduating class." Another wrote of her cousin, who was pictured, "The 'faces' show us that these young men are *all* our cousins, brothers, husbands, and sons." Another was shocked in looking at the pictures to see "the smiling face of someone I used to know. He was only 19 years old. I guess I never really realized that 19-year-olds have to die."

The *Life* feature resonated with those who were uncertain about the war but thought of those fighting in Vietnam as young victims of a cruel and heartless war. Popular criticism of the war had not yet expanded to portray those serving in Vietnam as *perpetrators* of a cruel and heartless war. That would change.

One couple in Montclair, New Jersey, wrote to the editors of *Life* asking why their story focused only on the American dead: "And what of the Vietnamese, Koreans, Australian, and other endless victims of our lunacy?" It turned out that even as the magazine hit the newsstands and mailboxes, a new development was advancing that would begin to bridge the moral distinction.

On June 26, 1969, Army colonel William Wilson, then serving with the inspector general's office in Washington, was concluding his preliminary investigation of an allegation that American soldiers had participated in a massive slaughter of civilians in an area called Pinkville in March 1968. Wilson had reluctantly but unequivocally concluded that the stories were true.[40] In Vietnam, this place of atrocity and horror was called My Lai. By the end of the year, that tragedy would dominate discussions about the war. But in May 1969, it was a more conventional battle, a shockingly conventional battle, up in the A Shau Valley, that would be the focus of attention.

2
DONG AP BIA: BECOMING HAMBURGER HILL

As the federal Memorial Day weekend approached, *Boston Globe* reporter Bud Collins, who had spent time as a correspondent in Vietnam, wrote an opinion piece for the newspaper. Collins noted that "in Massachusetts you can take your pick of Memorial Days, which is convenient. But it's not nearly so convenient as the system in places like the A Shau Valley where every day is Memorial Day."

The A Shau Valley was in the far northern reaches of South Vietnam, south of the bitterly contested Khe Sanh region and just a few miles from the border with Laos. This area had been largely controlled by the North Vietnamese Army after its substantial attacks finally forced the U.S. Special Forces to abandon their isolated A Shau Camp in the spring of 1966.

Over the next few years, the United States and the South Vietnamese attacked North Vietnamese positions in the area on several occasions, and in May 1969 the Military Assistance Command, Vietnam initiated a major offensive there. Operation Apache Snow aimed to wrest control of the valley and its western mountains from North Vietnam. It developed into an eleven-day sustained and vicious battle, particularly on Hill 937, the mountain called Dong Ap Bia.

On May 10, three battalions of the 101st Airborne Division, the 3rd Battalion of the 187th Regiment, the 2nd Battalion of the 501st Regiment, and the 1st Battalion of the 506th Regiment, approximately 1,800 men, along with the 1st Battalion of the 1st ARVN Regiment went into the A Shau Valley. In addition, the 9th Marine Regiment sent units to block the northern end of the valley.

The 187th Regiment would carry the brunt of the fighting on Dong Ap Bia. Soldiers from the 187th who fought there for eleven days would name it and remember it always as "Hamburger Hill," that place where the American attackers were ground up by the enemy defenders. Collins noted that while there were many hills in the valley, "Now there is one they call Hamburger Hill to think about on whatever Memorial Day you reserve to think about such things."[1]

This battle had already become controversial in Massachusetts and nationally. The previous week, ironically on the day American units finally captured the top of the hill, Sena-

98

tor Edward Kennedy of Massachusetts had criticized the entire operation on the floor of the Senate. He argued that the Paris Peace Conference then under way should be the primary American focus, not major new military operations in Vietnam.

I am compelled to speak on this question today for I believe that the level of our military activity in Vietnam runs opposite to our stated intentions and goals in Paris. But more importantly, I feel it is both senseless and irresponsible to continue to send our young men to their deaths to capture hills and positions that have no relation to ending this conflict.

President Nixon has told us, without question, that we seek no military victory, that we seek only peace. How then can we justify sending our boys against a hill a dozen times or more, until soldiers themselves question the madness of the action? The assault on "Hamburger Hill" is only symptomatic of a mentality and a policy that requires immediate attention. American boys are too valuable to be sacrificed for a false sense of military pride.[2]

Kennedy's remarks initiated a major debate. It was not that his criticism of the war was unusual; antiwar sentiments were common by then. But what seemed a new turn, an escalation to some, was the senator's explicit criticism of the military leadership for a battle in which "American boys" would be "sacrificed" due to a "false sense of military pride."

Half a world away and half a day ahead of all of this debate, some of the men of the 101st had been taken off the hill and were unwinding on Eagle Beach. This facility was an in-country R&R center east of Hué on the South China Sea. It was described as a two-hundred-yard strip of white sand beach, with picnic areas, barbecue pits, a post exchange, enlisted men and noncommissioned officer clubs, a miniature-golf course, television, pool tables, and a movie theater. And hot water showers and clean fatigues. The commanding officer of the 101st Division, General Melvin Zais, said of his men relaxing there after they had returned from Operation Apache Snow, "I don't know anybody who deserves it more than you guys humping the hills."[3]

General Zais was also a Bay Stater — a native of New Bedford, Massachusetts. It is not clear whether he knew about Bud Collins's column. But he surely was aware of Senator Kennedy's remarks. He first declined when reporters asked him to respond to Kennedy, saying, "To reply would be engaging in useless dialog." But he went on, "I fight the war to the best of my ability and he performs as a Senator to the best of his, there in Washington. I don't know the conditions surrounding

100

Senator Kennedy's statement. I know for sure he wasn't here."[4]

While his commanding general and his U.S. senator were sparring, another Massachusetts resident, Donald Sullivan, was out on Eagle Beach. Sullivan was the leader of the 2nd Platoon of Charlie Company of the 3rd Battalion of the 187th Regiment, who had just come down from Hamburger Hill. Of the 42 men in his platoon who had landed with him on May 10, there were 18 with him on Eagle Beach; the remainder were in hospitals — or in coffins. He described Eagle Beach as a pleasant interlude at a chaotic place. "We landed and it was a zoo. There were full colonels running around with rations and uniforms and lieutenant colonels, majors, etc., all sorts of people and they could not do enough for us. It was the most incredible thing I ever saw . . . Obviously General Zais and General [Richard] Stilwell [the commanding general in charge of all tactical operations in I Corps, the northernmost military sector of South Vietnam] didn't care what rank you were." Sullivan noted that regardless of position, all were "doing something for these troops that had been up on the hill. I was very impressed with that."[5]

Donald Sullivan was born in Winthrop, Massachusetts, in 1946, and he grew up on the south shore in Weymouth. As a young man, he intended to become a Jesuit priest.

He went to seminary out of high school and after three years transferred to Boston College, from which he graduated in 1967 with a major in economics. When Sullivan received his draft notice in 1967, he visited the army recruiting station in Boston to discuss his options. The recruiter told him that he should become an officer. When he added that this would involve an extra year of obligation, the young graduate asked why he would ever want to agree to that. The recruiter replied, "Well look at it this way. You can either be inside the Officers Club having a martini or outside guarding it."[6] Sullivan opted for OCS and came to Vietnam as a second lieutenant.

It is not clear if there were any martinis on Eagle Beach, but there was a lot of beer. Don Sullivan and others from his 187th Infantry Regiment didn't care. They were alive, and there were showers, clean clothes, hot food, and dry beds. They were basically unaware of — and in truth largely indifferent to — the intense debate back home over their extended battle. The fact that many people in the States even knew that a major battle had taken place by itself was unusual. Most Americans had little knowledge of daily battles and operations in Vietnam. But this encounter was different. Unlike most of the combat operations in Vietnam, the battle on Dong Ap Bia was large scale, sustained, and it came to have a resonant, ominous, unforgettable name:

Hamburger Hill.

While he was at Eagle Beach, Don received a letter from his mother, Helen Sullivan,

Dear Donald,
The news this week is all bad. They are constantly talking about the 3/187th taking horrible casualties attacking a hill. I certainly hope you had more sense than to go up there.[7]

In so many ways, much of the essential and conflicting narratives of the Vietnam War is captured in the interactions of these four Massachusetts natives: the antiwar senator who was critical of the nature of the war, the army general who pointed out that he was just doing what he was assigned to do, the mother who worried about her son in the midst of news of "horrible casualties," and the young soldier who was untouched by all of this political and emotional debate. He was only trying to catch his breath after a costly battle; the casualties his platoon took on the hill were enough to think about. He thought about — and still does forty-five years later — his soldiers. One casualty especially gnawed at him.

Willard Dufresne Jr. was known as "Buck." He was a twenty-two-year-old staff sergeant from Hutchinson, Minnesota. Described as athletic, handsome, an all-around great kid, mischievous, and a natural leader, he had been a member of his high school football team, a student leader, and a member of the National Honor Society. He dropped out of the University of Minnesota in the spring of 1967 when he got married. He knew this likely would result in a draft notice. And it did. He was a good soldier and was selected out of basic training for the army's special NCO Academy in Fort Benning, Georgia. He graduated from the program at the top of his class and was promoted to staff sergeant. Following "Jump School," he was sent to Vietnam, where he joined Charlie Company of the 3rd Battalion of the 187th Airborne. His platoon leader was Second Lieutenant Don Sullivan. Sullivan quickly learned to value Dufresne and his leadership.

On May 14, while Charlie Company was maneuvering to circle over to the north of the North Vietnamese bunkers blocking access to the top of Dong Ap Bia, a grenade wounded several members of the platoon. One, Michael Milner, was seriously wounded, and Dufresne and a medic organized a party to carry him down on a makeshift stretcher to a place where he could be medevaced out. As the group was making their way down the hill, a rocket propelled grenade (RPG) fired by a North Vietnamese soldier struck the group. Milner and two others were killed immediately.

Dufresne knew he was seriously wounded. The blast had torn off a leg and he had other serious injuries. He told Sullivan that he was not going to make it. Sullivan assured him that he would and quietly asked the medic to give him a maximum shot of morphine to ease his pain. As they continued down the hill, the men promised him that a helicopter was coming soon to carry him to a medical station. Dufresne told them, "No, a chariot is coming to get me," and in a voice that the men around him would not forget, the critically injured soldier started to sing, "Swing low, sweet chariot, comin' for to carry me home." He died before the group reached the medevac helicopter. His son was born a few months later. And Don Sullivan bore heavily the memory of this young man, his ability and his promise, and the echo of the song he sang as he was carried "home" that day. Dufresne's sister recalled that her brother had always excelled at everything he did. He seemed so lucky throughout his life that when the family was notified of his death, they could not believe it was true.[8]

Casualty reports for the battle vary because it was hard sometimes to attribute a death or injury to a specific place. It became even harder in this case as major losses in the battalion command operation as well as in company and platoon leadership left reports unfinished and records unfiled. But it is clear that the 3rd Battalion of the 187th had 39 men killed on Dong Ap Bia. In addition, 3 men from the 326th Medical Battalion serving with them died in the operation, as did 1 soldier from the 2nd Battalion 319th artillery. And 23 men in the 1st Battalion of the 506th Regiment died in their coordinated attack on Hills 800 and 900 to the east of Dong Ap Bia. In addition, 23 soldiers in the 501st Battalion were killed in a devastating North Vietnamese assault on their compound at Fire Support Base Airborne just four miles north of Ap Bia. When the operation ended on June 7, 107 Americans had died in Operation Apache Snow — 89 members of the 101st Airborne Division and 18 marines.

For most of the battle, Hamburger Hill had been little noticed in the United States. The Vietnam War was marked by scores of vicious fights daily but few major sustained, multiday battles. Ambushes, platoon- and company-level encounters, often very bloody and relatively brief, describe most of the war. Places like Ia Drang in 1965, Dak To in 1967, Hué during the Tet Offensive in 1968, and the battle for Khe Sanh at the same time were the outliers as substantial *places* where opposing forces fought over several days to control geography. Hamburger Hill would join this exclusive bloodied category. If none of them was of the historic scale of Bastogne or Okinawa, they were the marker battles of the Vietnam War.

For context and calibration — and as an illustration of the scale and complexity of Vietnam combat operations — in the thirty days following the landing of the 101st Airborne on Hamburger Hill on May 10, some 1,592 Americans died in Vietnam. So less than 5 percent of this number died on Dong Ap Bia. The other 95 percent died in small-scale actions in places largely forgotten — except by those who fought there and the families and friends of those who died there. In truth, it is not that the rest of us have forgotten these places but that we didn't ever know them.

The enduring symbolism of the battle for Hamburger Hill cruelly underlines the nature of the Vietnam War. This fight was sustained and on a scale large for Vietnam. But even in this well-known battle, the traditional elements of previous famous battles were missing. Hamburger Hill lacked a clear frontline narrative; it was an operation with a conclusion but no real sense of classic "victory," of victorious elation; there were no widely disseminated tales of combat enriched by popular stories of heroic men described in heroic encounters. The heroism was there, but the tales of it were missing. All of these missing elements, of negative evidence, left the public with a residual sense not of triumph but of "So what?" and "Was it worth it?" There was no flag raising on the top of Dong Ap Bia, no symbolic moment when weary soldiers reached the summit and combat photographers captured their victory with an inspiring, iconic image. The soldiers on Eagle Beach surely had a sense of accomplishment, even success, but the feeling that best described their attitude then and later was the quiet elation, and sometimes the gnawing guilt, of survival, and the private mourning for those who did not survive to experience either elation or guilt.

It was largely after the eleven days of fighting that the battle for Dong Ap Bia became well known in the United States. In mid-May in the middle of the battle, for most Americans it was just another round of combat in another obscure place in South Vietnam. Walter Cronkite on the *CBS Evening News* broadcast of May 15, five days after the operation began, had a brief reference to it: "In Vietnam Allied troops are on the offensive. It was revealed today that 10,000 Americans and South Vietnamese kicked off Saturday in a sweep west of the A Shau Valley. They are attempting to clear the area and cut off infiltration of North Vietnamese from nearby Laos. Tonight American paratroopers are battling for control of a key mountain in the area."

On May 16, *New York Times* correspondent Joseph Treaster reported, "For the fourth time in a year, United States and South Vietnamese troops have begun a search operation throughout the narrow Ashau Valley near the Laotian border in northern South Vietnam." Treaster wrote that the U.S. Command had not announced this assault until the day before "for security reasons" but that American and ARVN troops with "fleets of helicopters" had so far killed 201 North Vietnamese, and 36 Americans had died.

Over the next few days, news accounts of this operation picked up a bit. The battle at Ap Bia became somewhat newsworthy due to the scale of involvement and particularly the extended fighting. On May 17, the Pacific edition of *Stars and Stripes* reported that in this assault, the U.S. and ARVN forces had gone in to the area west of the mountains to block the North Vietnamese Army's access from Laos. Despite heavy air bombardment, the fighting continued. As one officer on the ground told AP reporter Jay Sharbutt, "Those bastards are still fighting."

On May 19, Sharbutt filed a story focusing on the lengthy fight for Dong Ap Bia. This account became an important source and catalyst for the questioning of the operation. Sharbutt quoted a wounded soldier who criticized the 187th 3rd Battalion commanding officer, Lieutenant Colonel Weldon (known by his call sign "Blackjack") Honeycutt: "That damn Blackjack won't stop until he kills every damn one of us." It was Honeycutt's battalion that had carried the fight since May 10 and had taken significant casualties. Sharbutt quoted another soldier, who said that despite all of the air and artillery strikes, "those gooks are still in there fighting." This soldier wondered why they had not just used B-52s to blast the mountain: "I've lost a lot of buddies up there. Not many guys can take it much longer."[9]

Stories with explicit criticism — and names of officers — by men in the field were newsworthy. A May 20 UPI story reported that some GIs were now calling the mountain "Hamburger Hill." The story also reported that the U.S. Command in Saigon announced that 340 Americans were killed in Vietnam the previous week, double the figure of the week before. On that same day, *The New York Times* headlined its front-page dispatch from Vietnam, "G.I.'s in 10th try, fail to rout foe on peak at Ashau."

Sharbutt's account of soldiers criticizing the army command and the stories about the repeated attacks with growing casualties led Senator Kennedy to speak out. There was no indication that his remarks and particularly his criticism of military leadership were a premeditated tactical shift. One of his aides said the senator did not call anyone for advice but just told his staff to draft brief remarks. "It was almost spontaneous, just something he felt inside." *Times* editors sniffed that he "shot from the hip." They did not believe that any "civilian is competent to hand down so dogmatic a judgment on battlefield tactics, especially when the battlefield is 12,000 miles away."[10]

Senator Kennedy was clearly interested in positioning himself as the strongest antiwar option for Democrats preparing to challenge Richard Nixon's reelection bid in 1972. As *Commonweal* puffed, "Squeezed by comrades McGovern and Muskie on the left and Nixon on the right, he must speak loud and constantly to carve out his own constituency."[11] Senators Edmund Muskie and George McGovern were already signaling their intentions to run for the Democratic presidential nomination. More charitably, James Reston of *The New York Times* came to the same conclusion when he wrote that the last of a generation of the Kennedy brothers "is now the head of the clan and aiming to be the head of the party."[12]

Intentionally or spontaneously, Senator Kennedy did broaden the debate on the war. Previously the critics had focused primarily on the geopolitical wisdom of fighting this war, on the casualties and the cost of military engagement, and increasingly on the Vietnamese civilian casualties, the morality of the war. Now the criticism expanded to include tactical wisdom, military judgment, and the competitive egos of commanders. Insisting that a line had been crossed, critics of Kennedy focused less on the wisdom of this combat operation and instead argued that the subject itself was not a proper one. Anonymous military officials in Vietnam said they were only carrying out the American War strategy — to wear the enemy down and disrupt their supplies and communications. They said that if the senator wanted to complain, he should address the White House. And White House press secretary Ron Ziegler insisted that the administration had no reason to challenge General Zais's claim that Dong Ap Bia was a "tremendous, gallant victory." He pointedly reminded the press that "the President does not second guess his field commanders."[13]

On Sunday, May 25, Republican senator John Tower of Texas said that Kennedy had insulted "the finest class of military leadership the world has seen." And Maine Republican senator Margaret Chase Smith said that if the military command determined that the taking of the hill was important to protect soldiers in the valley, then "it serves no useful purpose to second guess that purpose as senators." Democratic senator Harry Byrd said that Kennedy should not try to manage military tactics: "If we try to run the war from the United States Senate, the results may be even more disastrous."[14]

Senator Everett Dirksen of Illinois, the

Republican minority leader, said that fighting war was "a tactical and strategic art." He shared the thoughts of the Roman general Lucius Aemilius Paullus as quoted by Livy: "If, therefore, anyone thinks himself qualified to give advice respecting the war which I am to conduct, which may prove advantageous to the public, let him not refuse his assistance to the state, but let him come with me to Macedonia . . . But if he thinks this too much trouble, and prefers the repose of a city life to the toils of war, let him not, on land, assume the office of a pilot." Senate majority leader Mike Mansfield of Montana defended his Democratic colleague, reminding the critics that senators have a right to say whatever they think is important. They are accountable to their constituents. And he reminded the senators that Vietnam "is a war in which we never should have become engaged."[15]

The debate in Boston and in Washington over Dong Ap Bia was only nominally a disagreement over military tactics. It was fundamentally about the geopolitical presumptions and the overall strategic conduct of the war. And the Nixon administration even then was looking to change the nature of this debate. On June 8, President Nixon announced the policy of Vietnamization, a fundamental shift that would place more of the combat responsibilities on the Army of the Republic of Vietnam and would be accompanied by a drawdown of U.S. forces in Vietnam. There is no evidence that the impact of Hamburger Hill had any role in this strategic shift; planning for it was under way well before the operation. But the fight in the A Shau Valley and the controversy that followed did result in a tactical modification. Over the objections of Creighton Abrams, the commanding general of MACV, and other senior military leaders, Secretary of Defense Melvin Laird imposed greater restrictions on U.S.-led combat missions.[16] There would be no more Hamburger Hill–scale operations. The rules of the engagement and the terms of the debate would not be the same following this battle.

Operation Apache Snow was larger than most other Vietnam War operations, at least in terms of the scale of the air assault. One historian called it "the largest Air Mobile assault operation of the Vietnam War." Despite this, it was pretty routine in terms of its objectives. It aimed to cut off supply lines and support networks. The A Shau Valley was a crucial location. A U.S. Air Force report had observed that "except for the area near the DMZ and along Route 9, the A Shau Valley was the keystone of enemy logistics and troop infiltration in I Corps."[17] And the 101st Division's historian wrote a few weeks following the battle that "the principal objective of the operation was to establish a firm Allied presence in the A Shau and cork up that traditional infiltration route." By August, he would claim that the division had achieved that goal.[18]

Success was an elusive concept in the summer of 1969 — and indeed, throughout the entire Vietnam War. Dong Ap Bia was different from most previous experiences in that the enemy did not withdraw following the initial encounter. There had been little doubt that the North Vietnamese were in these border areas, but their pattern had not been to sustain a fight for control of a location. Normally, they ambushed and otherwise resisted the troops carrying out the assault, hitting them hard sometimes, and then slipped away. North Vietnamese military leaders recognized that the Americans would bring in tremendous firepower, especially air ordnance.

In the case of Dong Ap Bia, according to the North Vietnamese Army accounts, these forces decided to take advantage of their location near large support facilities in Laos. Their goal was "to annihilate an entire American battalion." They planned to accomplish this by developing integrated fortified blocking positions and then drawing the Americans in close. Ever since the battle in the Ia Drang Valley in 1965, the North Vietnamese leadership recognized that keeping their forces close to the Americans, "grabbing them by the belt," was the best way to prevent heavy air and artillery bombardments. The North Vietnamese command determined that Ap Bia would be a place to stay and fight, and they counted on their belief that Americans were "arrogant" and overly confident that they could drive the NVA away.[19]

Apart from presumptions regarding American attitudes, the U.S. Air Force had a similar assessment of the battle site. "For an NVA force willing to face U.S. firepower, Hill 937 was a better place than most to defend. The NVA regiment held high ground ringed on all sides by concentric bunkers with mutual supporting fires. Listening posts down the hill gave early warning, while interconnecting trenches upslope allowed screened reinforcement to the bunker complexes set ever more densely as the summit was neared."[20]

When the 187th moved into the mountains on May 10, the landing zone on the west slope of Dong Ap Bia was prepared with a heavy bombardment. Tactical aircraft engaged in a fifty-minute assault using daisy cutters — fifteen-thousand-pound bombs that destroyed underbrush and trees, as well as any enemy forces unfortunate enough to be near the landing zone. This was followed by eighteen minutes of artillery fire and then a one-minute assault by ARA — aerial rocket artillery, fired by Cobra helicopter gunships under the control of the 101st Artillery unit.[21]

The landings were uncontested — these were not "hot" landing zones. The 3rd Battalion of the 187th, assigned to the Dong Ap Bia assault, set up a command post and a night defensive position. Their four companies as well as battalion command had been airlifted in by late afternoon. The assumption was that the next day, May 11, they would move out in a large "reconnaissance in force" assault and would be on top of the mountain by midafternoon.

On the 11th, when the lead platoon in the assault moved out of a tree line to an open meadow beneath the wooded top of the mountain, they received heavy fire from North Vietnamese in well-fortified bunkers. These emplacements blocked the fingers or ridges that provided access to the top. They would continue to block for the next ten days.

Battalion commander Weldon Honeycutt kept up the assault on the bunker line. On May 14, he tried moving Charlie Company off to the north for a side assault on the emplacements. They were cut down by machine guns and RPGs. This was where Buck Dufresne was killed. The close confines made air and artillery attacks dangerous to the Americans. The soldiers suffered major casualties from friendly fire incidents, especially from ARA attacks. The battalion command post had taken heavy casualties and

117

damage from these gunships on May 11. Two men were killed and 35 wounded, and the operation center basically was shut down. Lieutenant Colonel Honeycutt received shrapnel wounds, but he remained at the post.

The enemy bunkers provided protection from bombs and artillery. But the NVA defenders did not simply hunker down in these facilities. They also went out to counter-attack when U.S. forces withdrew.

The army would later report that tactical air had dropped 1,088.5 tons of bombs, 142.5 tons of napalm, and 31,000 rounds of 20mm shells. Army artillery units fired 18,262 explosive rounds, as well as 513 tons of tear gas and white phosphorous. Colonel J. B. Conmy, commander of the 101st Division's 3rd Brigade Combat Team, said, "This is my third war and I haven't bumped into a fight like this since World War II in Europe. The enemy has stood up and fought and refused to retreat."[22]

They stood and fought despite prolific invitations to defect. Army Psychological Operations, also working with the marines, dropped more than seven million leaflets, including those promoting the *"chieu hoi"* campaign — which promised "open arms" for those who surrendered. PsyOps units also broadcast almost forty-eight hours of loud-speaker promises and threats. Of the handful of enemy soldiers captured, most severely wounded, no NVA soldiers defected or surrendered during the battle.[23]

Of course, by the time the battle ended, more headlines had appeared in U.S. newspapers, and as a result of the information and the controversy, there was greater public interest in the fight. A reporter came up to Don Sullivan at Eagle Beach and asked him if he had really wanted to go up Hamburger Hill. Sullivan replied, "Nobody in their right mind wants to go up a hill where they know somebody is going to be shooting at them. It's not a question of what you want. It's a question of what your duty is." The reporter was not satisfied with the answer — and Sullivan continues to be troubled by the exchange.[24] He thought that this reporter, and others, sought to describe the drama, the dissent, rather than the reality of the experience.

As long as there have been wars, those who have fought in the field have not had the opportunity, or perhaps even the interest, to read or hear contemporary accounts of their fight. Those who send them to war and who debate the wisdom of this are engaged in intellectual or political arguments about the purpose or the morality of the war. These are critical questions that need to be resolved — at best before the troops are dispatched. But once in the field, those at war focus on their limited objectives and their survival.

The actual experience of those on the ground may or may not differ significantly in detail from the account of war that is grist for debate and the building block of the public narrative. The experience is a very personal one. Other than the dramatic, sometimes distorted stories that characterize many public accounts of war, little of the experience is understood. The accounts of the men who fought on Hamburger Hill provide a different narrative or at least a different perspective on the experience, one that touches on the eternal and existential nature of war.

The men who flew in the helicopters to the landing zone on the west slope of the hill on May 10 had no idea what they would encounter there. This is not unusual in combat operations. Alpha Company commander captain Bob Harkins said that "it was no surprise that we were going someplace where there was a whole bunch of bad guys that didn't like us." They all understood they were likely in for a fight — "the hill happened to be incidental because that's where they were."[25]

As the troops landed, the men on the ground were impressed, or at least surprised, by the scale of the operation. Lieutenant Frank Boccia, who then was on his twenty-fifth air assault, "had never seen or heard anything like it. No one had." The Huey helicopters "spread out across the valley like a swarm of giant green dragonflies . . . the spectacle was awesome, frightening, inspiring, and sobering."[26] One officer, a veteran of a number of operations, said he had never seen that many helicopters at one time in his life. Other men described it as "unbelievable" and "massive."[27]

John Snyder of Bravo Company described it as "the biggest movement of troops I had ever experienced and the most helicopters I'd ever seen in one spot. It was kind of awesome, but you knew something big was happening but you didn't know exactly what you were getting into — other than we already knew the A Shau was bad."[28]

The 187th soldiers, called the Rakkasans, were pleased to discover that it was not a hot landing zone. Jumping from a hovering helicopter into hostile fire while the pilot was already maneuvering to leave the area was dangerous. On this landing, the only casualty was a young man who broke his ankle jumping from the helicopter hovering above the elephant grass.[29]

An uncontested landing was obviously preferred. But no one assumed that this meant the operation would be uncontested. The soldiers knew the reputation of this area near Laos. They understood that their command would have sent in an assault force of this size only if a substantial enemy resistance was expected. The evening of May 10 and overnight, some men were uncomfortable. It was very quiet. One soldier said to his platoon leader, "Bad-ass area, ain't it?" Frank Boccia tried to reassure him by noting it was only "another night in Viet Nam." The response was prophetic: "This area . . . it just *feels* different, you know? . . . I just got this feeling someone's fixing to bringing a bag o' shit on our heads."[30]

The unease was widespread. New men had the natural fear of a first landing. For those who had been on these operations before, the feeling was familiar: "You know, you were frightened, but then again, I was always frightened." One young officer who looked around at the surroundings was not optimistic: "I think we're heading towards some pretty big shit."[31]

It probably would not have comforted the men on the ground that night to know that the senior officers in their command had not known what to expect either. They expected a fight, but they did not anticipate that here the North Vietnamese Army would stand and fight them for a prolonged period. American intelligence did not have a good assessment of the extent of the enemy emplacements and the size of the enemy forces. Lieutenant Colonel Weldon Honeycutt was a feisty veteran of the Korean War, and he was prepared to fight. But he acknowledged years later that not only did he not know what to expect, neither did Division Headquarters or MACV: "They had no idea. They were just like us, going in raw." After the battle, he told one soldier that his briefing for the fight "was the most ludicrous thing in the world — a G3 put his hand on a map and that hand covered just about half the province and almost all of the A Shau and said, 'We believe the enemy is here.' "[32]

Company-level briefings had not been very informative. "There was no mention of Dong Ap Bia whatsoever," Frank Boccia said. "There was no particular emphasis of any given terrain feature. We just knew we were going into the A Shau and that we would be seeking out the enemy, wherever he was. And we had no idea who the enemy was." Another soldier recalled, "Somebody should have known what we were going into. For whatever reason, they didn't."[33]

Prior to landing there, Don Sullivan didn't even know that Dong Ap Bia existed. "I had no idea from any of the briefings or anything that we were going to that specific mountain. I had no idea what size unit we expected to encounter. And in fact, other than the fact that we were all carrying much more equipment and ammunition and so forth than we could realistically carry, I just had no idea that we really were heading for a major fight."[34]

They surely were. On the morning of May 11, there were few signs of what was pending. It was hot and humid, and the jungle and the high grasses restricted vision — for the infantry veterans it was business as usual. First thing that morning at a meeting with the company commanders, Honeycutt handed out assignments for an aggressive move up Dong Ap Bia. Bravo Company had the lead, going up the main ridgeline, and the company commander, Charles Littnan, told Frank Boccia that his platoon would take the point: "Go up that hill there, and see what you can find, and then after that there's a ridge that seems to lead in the direction we want. If all goes right, we should be on top of Dong Ap Bia by 1400." Even though the early part of the trail was quiet, it was not reassuring; there were always surprises. Boccia described the walk up the ridge and the approach to a clearing: "From me down to the newest rifleman, the disquieting aura of menace coming from the trees and ridges around us was palpable."[35]

When another platoon was moved into the lead, that platoon leader, Lieutenant Chuck Denholm, discovered that the man he asked to walk point through the clearing was badly frightened. The young soldier's mother had written Lieutenant Denholm recently, begging, "Please don't let my son get hurt. Please, please take care of him. He's all I have." When a few shots were fired from the top of the hill, the young man balled up behind a tree. Denholm angrily sent him to the rear, and another soldier, Aaron Rosenstreich from Norwalk, Connecticut, said, "I'll take the goddamn point." Shortly after that, a North Vietnamese soldier shot and killed Rosenstreich. And the fight began.[36]

As predicted, the Rakkasans would reach the top of Dong Ap Bia by 1400 hours. But it would be 1400 hours ten days later.[37] Captain Littnan's conditional projection, "If all goes right," proved to be more than optimistic. On the morning of May 11, the shooting and the dying began. "Then the screaming started: Yells for help, or a medic, and inarticulate screams of fear and agony . . . I could hear the cries: Medic! Chrissakes — MEDIC! MEDIC!"[38] Seriously wounded or dying soldiers often cried out for their mothers.

May 11 was Mother's Day. Throughout Vietnam, 72 men, 50 of them in army units, died that day. Five members of the 187th were killed on Hamburger Hill. This operation was only one of a number of encounters with hostile forces, so this unfolding battle was not yet a big news story at home. But it was for those who were there. Nineteen-year-old Terry Larsen, from Rockford, Illinois, died that day. His friend and fellow soldier Greg Burnetta was awake all that next night thinking of Terry's mother. She "would be waking up, and the first thing she's going to think about is her son in Vietnam and there's no way in hell she would know yet that he had been killed."[39]

Tom Martin was wounded in the assault that day, and when he was evacuated to the hospital at Camp Evans, he saw a sign on the wall just as he was being wheeled into surgery: MAY 11TH IS MOTHER'S DAY. DID YOU WRITE HOME? He hadn't. "I was really upset about that. What a Mother's Day present I gave my mom."[40]

On that first day, no one could have predicted the duration and the cost of the walk through the meadow and the climb to the top of the hill. It was understandable that the men and their leaders still assumed that the ambush in the field was the standard NVA trail watcher fire and the sniper harassment followed by withdrawal. But some veterans were troubled by several dead North Vietnamese soldiers they came across as they were walking up. All were "clean, new uniforms, fresh haircuts, well fed, so we knew these guys were not guys that had just been sitting around there. These were fresh troops from someplace."[41]

Captain Lee Sanders from Delta Company recalls when they understood that this was not going to end easily or quickly. "And I look up at the hill and there's these little fires all around and I realize right then that these guys are cooking their evening meal and the meal for the next day. And that's the first time I ever seen the NVA dig in and say 'We're here, come get us!' "[42]

And these fresh troops stayed. "We went up that day, thought we got ambushed. We withdrew. We went back up again that same day, probably just within twenty or thirty minutes — got hit again. Withdrew. Spent the night, went up there that night to recover the dead bodies. The next afternoon, we started going up again around 1:30 in the afternoon. We got hit again. At this time, we're going, 'What the hell is going on?' We get to this certain spot and we keep getting hit." As the men kept calling for artillery and air support, the jungle foliage was destroyed and the Rakkasans saw they faced a major embedded bunker system.[43]

Mac Campbell was a marine pilot over at Chu Lai on the coast flying F-4s on close air support missions. He ranged throughout I Corps and supported army and marine units. He was called onto Dong Ap Bia by an army forward air controller and he was one of the first to arrive. Within a few days there were many planes attacking the North Vietnamese positions. Campbell recalled, "They just pounded that hill. I still visualize that hill. We cleared that place."[44]

On the night of May 12, the 6th NVA Regiment launched an assault on Fire Support Base Airborne, just a few miles away from Dong Ap Bia. This was on Dong Ngai, a mountain the 3rd Battalion of the 187th had attacked and just secured in April after a difficult thirteen-day battle. Many of the men who had fought there went into Dong Ap Bia on May 10. Some of them had thought of Dong Ngai as the most difficult fight they had experienced. Until Hamburger Hill.

Fire Base Airborne had been quickly established on Dong Ngai and it was the main installation for Charlie Battery of the 3rd Battalion of the 319th Artillery. They were a major artillery support unit for the assault on Dong Ap Bia. And they were guarded by Alpha Company of the 2nd Battalion of the 501st Infantry Regiment. Shortly after midnight on May 13, North Vietnamese sappers, soldiers carrying explosives, came through the wire at their compound. By morning, the ground was covered with American and North Vietnamese bodies. Twenty-seven U.S. servicemen died that night, including 14 from the artillery unit. It was devastating, and it underlined for all that the North Vietnamese were not going to play "be hit and then run away" in the A Shau Valley.[45] Frank Boccia was over on Dong Ap Bia when he learned of this at a morning briefing. His platoon had fought hard and taken casualties in securing Dong Ngai in April. Now they learned that the base had been "overrun." This, he thought, was "the filthiest word in an infantryman's vocabulary. The 6th NVA at Dong Ngai; the 29th here . . . a regiment here, a regiment there — what had we gotten ourselves into?"[46]

On May 14 on Hamburger Hill, Charlie Company was decimated when they split off to the north and tried to encircle the bunker complex. Bravo Company withdrew from an assault position and spent the afternoon and most of that night trying to get the dead and wounded out of the ravine area where they were hit. By then it was clear that this was a real battle. The next day the NVA blocked another assault, and then they counterattacked. "We went from the hunter to the hunted," Frank Boccia said.[47]

One platoon leader recalled, "The company commanders call their platoon leaders together and give us the order — march for the next day, who's going up first, where you're going. Right then, from that night, you know you go back to your squad, your platoon, and you tell them you want a squad here, second squad there. You give the orders of what we're carrying, what we're taking up, the gas masks and grenades, what order we're going up and what we're going to do when we get there. I thought about that at that time. This is the way that the guys at D-day must have felt . . . I said, 'Oh no. We can't go back up there.'

You get the feeling that one more push and we're going to make it. That's what Honeycutt . . . one more push and we're going to make it this time. But I knew one more push, we might make it, but we're going to lose people."

He had earlier fought farther south, and the "whole mentality until then had been body count. If I lose one man, I want to have minimum ten of the enemy. That was the only way I could justify anything. I wasn't seeing that at all. We go up there and I lose five men and I don't see fifty bodies laying there of NVA, then I'm like, 'Wow. Something's wrong here.' "[48]

Frank Boccia picked up on the hunter/hunted image: "We all had to face the fact that we were no longer the hunters, running down an elusive fox, as we had been throughout our time in the AO [area of operations]. We were now two lions facing each other across a territorial boundary, and we had to accept the fact that the other one might very well have the larger claws and the deeper bite. And, more importantly, it was his territory."[49]

North Vietnamese ambushes and attacks and friendly fire incidents combined to take their toll on the men of the 187th. The latter were especially frustrating for the soldiers. One student of the war wrote that at least 7 of the KIA and 53 of the WIA were the result of friendly fire. And a former artillery com-

130

mander said, "Some of those artillerymen aren't as good as they think."[50]

The proximity of the enemy and the confusion that often followed the loss of a platoon leader or a radio telephone operator, as well as the devastation of the battalion headquarters by friendly fire — all of these made the operation difficult, and chaotic. Three of the 4 company commanders, 3 of the 4 first sergeants, and 10 of the original 14 platoon leaders were either killed or wounded and had to be evacuated. Of the 4 who were there at the end, 2 had been slightly wounded. The command structure was reeling by the time the battle was a few days old. But the surviving men and the replacements carried on.

Most veterans have come to agree that Lieutenant Colonel Honeycutt, who had been wounded himself by shrapnel, kept the battalion together and the aggressive operations moving. There was resentment and anger toward him at the time, but the resentment mellowed over the years. Not even this hands-on peripatetic battalion commander could extend his aggressive energy into the field-level operations. And here, one of the striking things about the battle was that lower-level enlisted men assumed more and more responsibility. "A lot of them had not been out of high school and in the army for a year before they came to Vietnam . . . and here they were taking over tactical operations in the jungle in Vietnam."[51]

Always there was the weariness, along with horror and fear: "You know, you'd go up, you'd battle, see people get killed, see people get wounded. After so many dead, we'd pull back and chow down and reorganize and take care of the wounded and evacuate them, and then next time, the exact same thing. I got pretty tired of that!" They recalled the smell of the dead in jungle heat, the sight of dead friends and of unidentifiable body pieces ripped by Claymore mines or RPGs. They remembered NVA snipers up in the high trees — until there were no trees left. A platoon leader retains an image of the arm on a soldier they were carrying out "dragging on the ground and it was only held on by a tiny piece of skin. I remember walking behind that with that arm bouncing along." He still flinches at the memory of the sight of the first dead Americans he encountered: "Both of them, their pants were split right at the groin and their genitalia were hanging out. I was disgusted by that, disgusted that anybody would leave them there lying like that."[52]

The soldiers were committed to bringing out all of their wounded and the dead. Sometimes this meant exposing themselves again to heavy fire in order to reach the comrades and carry them off the field: "One of the scariest times was going in and getting the wounded out and the dead. Because the amount of fire that was going on . . . well, it's just unimaginable . . . bullets were just trimming the bark off of the trees and the leaves were falling down like it was fall and the wind was blowing and the leaves were just coming off the trees, just from the rifle fire. It was just unimaginable how you walk in there and you pick somebody up and you walk back out with them. There were four of us that done that and none of us got hit. I don't know why or how."[53]

Ken Eichholz, a medic, remembered on May 14 when they were carrying Michael Milner down and the RPG struck the group: "It was just absolute confusion and mayhem . . . but all these guys are laying there and not all of them are quite dead but some of them are." He said they were all weak from dehydration, and in fact, when they started out, one of the men switched sides with him to give him some relief from carrying the poncho. That man died immediately in the explosion. Buck Dufresne would die shortly thereafter.[54]

Frank Boccia came out with Bravo Company to help Charlie Company after they had suffered a major attack:

My God. My God . . . I stared around me in disbelief; Jones and Olson, standing silently beside me, did the same, mouths open and eyes widened.

133

Bodies lay everywhere. For that first mind-freezing moment, it had seemed as if the ground were literally covered with them. There were 20 or 30 of them. In that first, horrified, glance, they'd all appeared dead. I now saw that only some were. The others lay on the ground, unmoving, staring straight up into the sky or off into the distance . . .

There were bodies — a long line of them, stretched out along the bushes to my left. Some were whole, with deep, ragged reddish black shrapnel wounds. Some were in scattered, barely recognizable pieces. One, the last in line, lay staring at the sky with wide-open eyes. One single small hole, hardly more than a reddish bruise, at first glance, marred the fair blond hair above the boy's left ear. He gaped at the sky with mouth open, as if in vast surprise.[55]

It was hard to get helicopters in to medevac out casualties and bodies. The slope of the hill made it difficult for their rotors to cycle, and the heavy fire from the North Vietnamese above them made it more complicated. Some helicopters were lost attempting to land or take off:

I was getting the guys ready to go — we were going over to underneath the helicopter, it was hovering. We were getting ready to put the guys on the jungle penetrator,

134

then all of a sudden a big bang — a noise. I grabbed the patient, the guy who was a lieutenant, I grabbed him, threw him off to the side, and luckily we went the opposite way the helicopter was falling, the medevac was falling. I saw a guy get cut walking up — he was trying to run from the helicopter. He got cut in half by the blade because it was still kind of whirling after it was hit.

Then they opened up on us. They came out. They figured there was a chance to get to us. That's probably one of the scariest times in my life because there was no way to get far enough away from anybody. You were stuck, so you had to stand and fight. While that was going on, I heard guys crying in the helicopter. They were burning to death after it crashed. That was a real bad day.[56]

Sometimes soldiers had to sleep next to body bags with the dead because they were not able to get them out on helicopters. The terrain and the weather and the heavy North Vietnamese fire seriously restricted the ability of the Huey evacuation helicopters to come to the front. So the men had to carry wounded and dead down the hill in order to find secure landing zones. And of course this reduced further the number of soldiers who were available to attack the North Vietnamese.[57]

In this situation was born the legend of "Crazy" Rairdon, also earning the nicknames "Saint" and "Slick" because of his flying through "zero-zero" weather — zero visibility horizontally and vertically — to get the wounded from battle zones. Eric Rairdon was a twenty-year-old pilot of a light observation helicopter. These were small single-pilot, glass-enclosed aircraft that had neither armor nor armament. They were for observation and for ferrying three or four passengers. Lieutenant Colonel Honeycutt liked to fly with Rairdon. The young pilot discovered that he could follow the terrain under the cloud cover and move so quickly that enemy gunners were generally startled, and he could be gone before they could react. He often resupplied forward firebases when the Hueys could not get into an area, and piled into his helicopter — and on its skids — the wounded who required rear-area medical care. And he also brought out the dead. Tom Martin had to hang partially on the helicopter's skids when Rairdon brought him out. He remembers him as a young guy who "risked his life going out when all the other helicopters were grounded because of the bad weather and the dark."[58]

Starting out as a messenger, an observer, and a taxi service, Rairdon became an indispensable part of the operation. "So one day I was up there milling around, kind of waiting for . . . hoping that the clouds would clear

136

off, and I thought to myself, 'You know, I think I could just bring this thing to a hover and I'll just hover up the side of this hill, through the fog. I've got to get to the top, if I just keep going up I'm going to get to the firebase because I know it's at the top of the hill.' So I did that. I hovered up the side of the hill — it was easy to do, leaning out of the OH-6. It was really no different than walking down a crowded street; you don't run into things, you take your time, and pretty soon here comes the perimeter. I see the wire and the perimeter buildings and sandbag huts and stuff they had. I come up over the top and find my helipad and I plop it down and everybody thought that was kind of neat. And it was. It worked out great."[59]

For those who served and survived, he became a crucial part of their own story. He did not slow until he himself was shot through both legs after landing the helicopter to pick up a wounded soldier on May 18 and required hospitalization.

Young medics braved enemy fire to help the wounded and comfort the dying. These soldiers learned to do procedures that they were uncertified — and untrained — to do. One dealt with a soldier with a "sucking chest wound." He had seen a movie in training showing what an MD would do in these circumstances. "So I took my scalpel and cut a hole in the side and I poked a tube through

137

it and then I got all the blood coming out of it and then I saw his chest raised up so I knew he was getting oxygen now." Another medic, a friend of his, was working on an injured soldier when the North Vietnamese started firing at them. He threw himself across the injured body, saving that man as he was killed by the gunfire.[60] Another medic dealing with a sucking chest wound asked the injured soldier if he had any cigarettes — nearly all of them did at that time. He lit two, gave one to the soldier, then pulled the cellophane off the cigarette package, held it over the chest puncture, and told the soldier to take a breath. He did, and his lung reinflated.[61]

Sustaining a fight was especially difficult in the midst of chaos and tragedy. Bravo Company commander Charles Littnan had some men physically stop a young soldier who was racing away from the action, screaming hysterically. He continued to cry, and finally they learned that he had been standing a few feet from a friend when an RPG struck him and blew him to pieces.[62]

Frank Boccia couldn't believe it when he got orders on May 14 to assault the bunkers again. He said to Captain Littnan, "You're shitting me." He wasn't. So when Boccia returned to his men and told them, "Saddle up. We're going back up," some rebelled. One said, "Tell Black Jack to take the fuckin' hill his own damn self." After several men vented, they started gathering their gear to go back out. One "conversationally" asked the platoon leader, "Whatta we do when we get up there, Lieutenant?" Boccia replied, "We kick the fuckers off the hill." After a pause: "Oh. Okay. It's good to have a plan, you know." The men laughed at the exchange, and then they moved up the hill again.[63]

Frustration and fear increased as the battle continued and the casualties mounted. The soldiers watched friends being medevaced out, some dead, and they understandably grew uneasy about another assault. A platoon leader wryly observed, "If they would have said, 'No, I'm not going,' then what could you do? Threaten to send them to Vietnam? There is no threat you could make to those guys." They stayed together and went out again "for their buddy." It had little to do with "duty, honor, country."[64]

At one point, Joel Trautmann's men said they were not going back up again. He admitted being "scared to death of mutiny." He thought that if they did resist, "it would spread like poison through the whole unit." So he picked up his rifle and walked through them as they sat on the ground, saying he was going up the hill. They followed him.[65]

Don Sullivan also faced a revolt. On the last morning, he told the men to saddle up because their platoon, what remained of it, was ordered to lead the assault. His sergeant came back to him and said, "Sir, the men are not going to attack." Sullivan was "stunned" by the news. So he started to pick up his gear. When the sergeant asked him what he was doing, he replied, "I've been ordered to attack the hill. I'm going to attack." The men were troubled at the idea of the lieutenant they had come to respect assaulting the hill alone. They headed over to the tree line where they had left their gear. Grumbling, they were going to join Sullivan.

Just then, the North Vietnamese laid down a mortar attack that struck near their equipment. None of the men were wounded, but some of their gear was struck by shrapnel. As one of the men approached his pack, he noticed it was wet. It turned out that shrapnel had poked holes in a can of C-ration fruit cocktail he had been saving. The sweet juice of fruit cocktail was a great treat in the heat of the jungle, and he had been eagerly anticipating that meal. His can was now drained of juice. The soldier started screaming, "We're going to go up there and get those fuckers! I'm going to kill those bastards!" Sullivan's platoon, depleted and weary, was inspired for what would be the final assault.[66]

The idea of delicacies out on the hill required a new and elastic use of the term. It was a more basic environment than that. Sometimes the men did not receive food and water when they needed it because all supplies depended on the helicopters, which couldn't always fly. In tight times, replenishing ammunition was the top priority. But one company got a very special delivery on the night of May 17: ice cream. Of course it was melted — "It looked like soup by the time we got it" — but no one complained. The army had even brought in some journalists — "the place was loaded with reporters" — to cover the ice-cream feast in the field.[67]

Following daily assaults beginning on May 11, the 187th did take the hill nine days later. There had been a major argument within the U.S. Command over this. Many of the senior brigade and division officers believed that Honeycutt's battalion was too depleted to lead the assault and needed to be replaced. He was insistent that his men could finish the fight — and having come this far and suffered so many losses, they deserved to do that.[68]

By May 17 or 18, the North Vietnamese had realized that their supply lines were cut and they were running low on food, water, and ammunition. They struggled to care for their wounded and get them off the mountain. The NVA command began to withdraw over the night of May 19–20, but the guns at the bunker openings were still manned. When Sullivan's platoon and others attacked the next morning, they still received heavy fire. But they were closer now to the bunker open-

141

ings. They were able to launch and even throw grenades into the apertures.

Johnny Jackson, a young black soldier in the 3rd platoon of Alpha Company, was becoming increasingly frustrated by the NVA fire. Shouting, "Fuck this bullshit!" he ran right at them, alone at first, putting down heavy fire in the slots of bunker after bunker. He didn't stop until he reached the top of the hill.[69]

Army specialist 4th class Edward Merjil, a member of Sullivan's platoon, also led an assault on the bunkers. It is hard to sort out firsts in the chaos of that day, but many, including Don Sullivan, describe him as the first to reach the top of Dong Ap Bia. In fact, Sullivan was preparing to step on top himself, and Merjil asked him to hold back in case there were North Vietnamese soldiers prepared to shoot. Their platoon was so decimated that Merjil said the platoon leader had to be careful. He stepped up and called back to Sullivan that there were a lot of North Vietnamese there, but they were running around and not paying much attention to the American soldier on top of the hill. So Don Sullivan followed Ed Merjil to the top of Dong Ap Bia.[70]

Within a few days, most of the soldiers who fought for the hill had been transported out, and soon all would have a chance to rest at Eagle Beach. There were follow-up fights on some of the nearby ridges, and Americans continued to take some casualties there. But Hill 937, the Crouching Beast, Dong Ap Bia, Hamburger Hill, was secured.

It was a costly victory. The four companies of the 187th that went in on May 10 had casualty rates of from 50 to 75 percent. The numbers of Americans killed in the Dong Ap Bia operation stood out on the MACV reports: 39 or 56 or 66 or 71, depending upon what encounters and what places were being counted. These counts are part of the necessary scorekeeping, the tally of war. But each number came associated with a name and each name represented an experience and every single body bag transported from the hill carried in its wake the emotional casualties of the buddies in the field and the families and friends back home.

By early June, the Americans had withdrawn from the hill, and North Vietnamese units began to return to the bloody ground. General Zais — and his successor, General John Wright — insisted that the battle was never about securing and holding a hill. In fact, Dong Ap Bia had "no tactical significance," but the enemy was there and the objective was to kill and to disrupt the enemy.[71] Terence Smith reported from Saigon that U.S. officials were operating under the policy initiated by President Johnson and left in place by President Nixon: It was a war of attrition and the objective was to place "maximum pressure" on the enemy, to disrupt supplies and communications. General Abrams and the American command could claim that they had done exactly that in the A Shau Valley and especially on Dong Ap Bia.[72]

An anonymous officer quoted in *Stars and Stripes* said that the battle just concluded was "nothing out of the ordinary" and that the casualties on Hamburger Hill were within a range the command considered "light."[73] Back home in New Bedford, General Zais said, "We didn't retreat from that hill. We left it because we had defeated the enemy."[74]

There is no record of any U.S. officials pointing to Khe Sanh as a good example for not trying to maintain an American occupation of the hill. It was. Khe Sanh was less than sixty miles north of Dong Ap Bia. In late 1967 and through the winter of 1968, it had been the scene of a massive siege by North Vietnamese forces on American marines occupying the base there. No one in the command said anything about the analogy, but surely officials recognized by that experience the difficulty of maintaining a permanent American presence at a site just a few miles from Laos and cut off from any means of reinforcement and supply other than by air. Air supply or support could not be counted on with dense jungle, cloud cover, and weather. And those same factors could leave the American forces exposed without one of their major combat advantages, close air support. The United States would avoid such positions in the future.

When *Time* magazine's correspondent John Wilhelm reached the top of Dong Ap Bia, he "found a piece of cardboard and a black 101st neckerchief pinned by a G.I. knife to a blackened tree trunk. 'Hamburger Hill,' a soldier had scrawled on the cardboard, and someone else had added the words, 'Was it worth it?' " That is a question that transcends tactical considerations and requires an assessment of the "value" of a hill and measuring it against the "value" of the lives lost securing it. It is a question framed by fundamental moral — and spiritual — principles and the most basic personal and human considerations. How do we weigh these against the act of gaining some geography?

If Abraham Lincoln asked for a resolution that the dead at Gettysburg shall not have died in vain, how does a society do more than "highly resolve" that won't be the case? One soldier took that equation on directly: "We took the ground, took the high ground, and paid a hell of a price for the high ground . . . We felt like we owned that damned property and we needed to keep it."[75] Most of the men who fought at Hamburger Hill seemed, at the time and still forty-five years later, to be largely indifferent to the decision to withdraw. They fought and they took the top and they didn't care — or no longer cared — what the army did with the hill. As one said, "We went up a lot of hills and a lot of ridgelines and we didn't keep 'em. You just went up, and if you had a fight, you had a fight, and then you went off."[76]

Neil Sheehan is a distinguished correspondent who served in the army in Korea and then covered the war in Vietnam. He wrote of Hamburger Hill a few months following the battle, asking if men who were killed at places like that had questioned their purpose there. "Perhaps there is no difference, but it ought to be one thing to perish on the beaches of Normandy or Iwo Jima in a great cause and another to fall in a rejected and unsung war."[77] At the time, some of the soldiers who fought there were anonymously critical of the basic assumptions and the nature of the battle. A number wrote Senator Kennedy to applaud his comments.[78]

In these debates, there is a danger of evaluating wartime battles only by a "who won" that is determined by the possession of real estate, although such possession is often the immediate objective. And there is an after-the-fact impulse to test it against iconic historical battles. But Hamburger Hill, Dong Ap Bia, can't be reduced so easily to the flag that ultimately flew over the red clay of a desolate jungle hill. Or to the ultimate place of the battle in the ultimate conclusion of a war that doesn't conclude neatly.

Following the battle for Hamburger Hill, Ward Just wrote a thoughtful piece for *The Washington Post*. He said that this battle represented what the war had come to in South Vietnam, "a war without a front." Because of the Sharbutt story, this battle had become well known. But "there were other battles where just as many men died under equally difficult conditions, which no one ever heard about. Who can remember all of them now? No one except the participants. They do not seem to be part of any pattern, except the pattern of death."

Just went on to say that those who argued that Hamburger Hill was "not worth a single dead American" missed the point. For "that is not the way it goes in South Vietnam. It never has. An army is fielded, and if it is a good army, it fights. If it must fight against an entrenched enemy on a hill, then that is what it does. The war does not take place in a classroom or on the pages of a newspaper, and it is not fought by . . . men who read headlines."[79]

As one soldier described it: "We were there to make contact with the enemy, and if we were in a firefight for a day or two or whatever, you moved on and . . . got resupplied and maybe were back in the rear for a few days." He said that this battle was of a greater magnitude, but they moved on, "and then you were back in the jungle doing what you got the big bucks to do, you know."[80]

One veteran of the battle didn't learn that the army had withdrawn from the hill until a few weeks later. He said soldiers in the field never had any information about these things. When you spent weeks or sometimes a month out in the jungle, "watching your uniform rot off your body, your boots rot, having them come out with big bags of replacement uniforms, you can't imagine — we didn't know, we just didn't know what was going on in the world." He said things were ironically simple out there. People hoped to get "canned spiced beef and peaches" in their C rations. "That was a great meal. But that's what you were worried about, and keeping your weapon clean, having enough water, making sure that you kept security and you didn't get your buddies killed somehow by doing something stupid. That's what you were worried about. You really didn't know strategic stuff . . . There's a saying that soldiers were like mushrooms. You know, they fed us shit and kept us in the dark."[81]

The Battle for Dong Ap Bia became an important example in the debate that was being waged in the United States over the Vietnam War. It was a colorful and dramatic and very costly battle, but it was more enduring as a focus for debate than it has been as a piece of military history. It does not figure today in the curriculum at West Point or at the Army War College.[82]

The North Vietnamese did assess the battle. A 2009 monument at the top describes it as "A Victorious Place at Ap Bia Hill." Soldiers who fought there recall looking down from their bunkers every morning to see what the Americans would do — and every morning seeing that the Americans were coming back up the hill. By the eighth day, the NVA knew they would have to withdraw. But their lesson was an extension of the American one: The U.S. Command was surprised that the North Vietnamese stayed and fought. The North Vietnamese soldiers were surprised when they learned that they *could* stay and fight the Americans.[83] Each lesson would influence decisions for the remainder of the war.

Even as a debate topic, the argument over this battle was more fundamentally an argument over the war itself. The question may have been framed as, Why engage in such a nasty fight with an entrenched enemy in order to take a hill from which you withdraw? But this question was a surrogate for the major issue in the United States in the spring of 1969: Should the United States be engaged in this war at all? What were the nature and the strategic objectives of the war? Debates over battlefield decisions now followed.

The battle for Dong Ap Bia and the men who fought — and died — there surely deserved to be more than surrogates for a debate question. But "deserved to be" is not an operational concept in war. Combat is not about fairness and the appropriate application of rules and allocation of credit. Understanding that battle required an understanding of the considerations that brought these American soldiers to the A Shau Valley. And this in turn needed to be preceded by understanding the considerations that brought the United States and more than a half million men to Vietnam in May 1969.

3

PASSING THE TORCH TO
A NEW GENERATION

January 20, 1961, was a bitterly cold day in Washington, DC. The bright sunshine was pleasant but hardly compensated for the 22° temperature. Despite the weather, some fifty thousand Americans gathered at the East Front of the U.S. Capitol for the inauguration of John Fitzgerald Kennedy as the thirty-fifth president of the United States. An estimated million people later stood along the Pennsylvania Avenue parade route.

An eight-inch snowfall the previous night had covered the ground and snarled traffic in a city unaccustomed to such substantial winter challenges. Only about one-third of the ticket holders had made it to the evening preinaugural concert at Constitution Hall. And only sixty of one hundred orchestra members were there. On the morning of the inauguration, the U.S. Army had used flame-throwers to clear snow from some areas of Pennsylvania Avenue.

Marian Anderson sang the National Anthem at the inaugural ceremony, and the president-elect mouthed the words along with her. When Cardinal Richard Cushing delivered the invocation, the Catholic Kennedy blessed himself. There was a small incident at this time, when an electric motor controlling the podium height shorted out and began smoking. Secret Service officials quickly doused the fire and Kennedy looked on "with a broad grin." Robert Frost charmed the crowd when he rose to read from the inaugural poem he had written for the occasion. The bright sun reflecting off his typewritten pages made it impossible for the eighty-six-year-old poet to read, so he recited from memory one of his other poems, "The Gift Outright."[1]

The upbeat, celebratory nature of the day overcame the weather, and the young, energetic president who had campaigned on a pledge to push on to a "new frontier" represented a new era. President Kennedy turned to it in his inaugural address:

Let the word go forth from this time and place, to friend and foe alike, that the torch has been passed to a new generation of Americans — born in this century, tempered by war, disciplined by a hard and bitter peace, proud of our ancient heritage — and unwilling to witness or permit the slow undoing of those human rights to which this nation has always been committed, and to which we are committed today at home and around the world.

Looking back, the occasion seemed to many to herald the legendary decade of the 1960s, a time of profound change and challenge. It was remembered as the time of Camelot in Washington and of youthful idealism and energy across the country. But the herald was in so many ways premature. If it was not truly the fifties, it had not yet become The Sixties. The top hats that the new president and the retiring president, Dwight Eisenhower, wore to the ceremony suggested an earlier time. It was the last inauguration dramatized by men in top hats.

The number-one popular song of January 1961 was "Wonderland by Night" by Bert Kaempfert; the traditional orchestral melody appeared in the Top 25 in other versions by Anita Bryant and Louis Prima. Other Top 5 hits included recordings by Lawrence Welk ("Calcutta"), Ferrante and Teicher (Theme from "Exodus"), and Elvis Presley's "Are You Lonesome Tonight?" The only '60s-era preview in the Top 5 was the rising hit by the Shirelles, "Will You Love Me Tomorrow." The top box office hit was the movie *The Swiss Family Robinson.* The calendar may have turned to a new decade, but the culture and values of the country still echoed the 1950s.

Robert Frost left with President Kennedy a

copy of his undelivered poem. It promised that the day marked the dawning of a new "Augustan" age. And in this age "poetry and power" would coexist. But the poet appended a note to the new president: "Be more Irish than Harvard. Poetry and power is the formula for another Augustan Age. Don't be afraid of power."[2]

The president's inaugural address was more than a salute to the new generation now assuming leadership. It also was a summons to responsibility — and to the responsibility of power. It was muscular: "Let every nation know, whether it wishes us well or ill, that we shall pay any price, bear any burden, meet any hardship, support any friend, oppose any foe to assure the survival and the success of liberty."

And it called out for Americans to stand up to the challenge of their moment on the stage of history: "In the long history of the world, only a few generations have been granted the role of defending freedom in its hour of maximum danger. I do not shrink from this responsibility — I welcome it. I do not believe that any of us would exchange places with any other people or any other generation. The energy, the faith, the devotion which we bring to this endeavor will light our country and all who serve it — and the glow from that fire can truly light the world."

The new president urged Americans to pick

up the burden and to serve: "And so, my fellow Americans: ask not what your country can do for you — ask what you can do for your country." The *New York Times*'s James Reston observed, "The evangelical and transcendental spirit of America has not been better expressed since Woodrow Wilson, and maybe not even since Ralph Waldo Emerson."[3] The columnist's assessment would have an insight that he surely did not intend at the time: If it was a new generation assuming responsibility, it was not a new torch that they would carry.

The president eloquently described a world that was threatening. Indeed, he ominously noted that "in the long history of the world" there were few times more threatening. Essentially the entire address focused on foreign policy — on the challenges that Americans faced and the opportunities they had. In his blessing, Cardinal Cushing prayed for the strength and the grace "to perform with complete vigilance our duty to prevent the spread of totalitarian terror everywhere. To perform with religious fervor our duty to teach, implement and create true freedom as a way of life at home and abroad — for true freedom underlies human dignity and is a holy state of life."[4]

Democrats were ecstatic over the forceful speech and the response to it. *The Denver Post* called it "A Call to Action," and the

Huntington, West Virginia, *Herald-Dispatch* described it as "eloquent and persuasive."[5] Importantly, following a very hard election campaign and an incredibly narrow victory, Republicans applauded the speech. President Dwight Eisenhower said it "was very, very fine," and Republican Senate floor leader Everett Dirksen called it inspiring, "a very compact message of hope." The *Wall Street Journal* editors acknowledged that they were pleasantly surprised, that there was "considerably less naiveté" in Kennedy's speech than there had been in his campaign. They applauded his "Let every nation know" assertion that Americans would stand up to the Communists. The speech would not provide "a banner for a nation tempted to yield to either threats or blandishments."[6]

The president's speech, despite the eloquence of its delivery and its inspiring call to his generation of Americans, represented in its themes the 1950s wicking into the 1960s. Kennedy's postwar world had been a competition between the United States and the Soviet Union. The threat of Josef Stalin, the Berlin blockade, the fall of China to the Communists, the Soviet explosion of an atomic bomb — these were the substantive elements that shaped the fear that marked the late 1940s. Even though the anticommunism of Joseph McCarthy was a grossly exaggerated and cynical political ploy, it worked, at least for a time, because of the perceived reality of the threats. And if the Korean War of the early 1950s in which 36,000 Americans died "stopping communism" was now, for most, a forgotten war, the alert nonetheless persisted.

In the election campaign of 1960, Senator Kennedy and his opponent, Vice President Richard Nixon, had focused often on foreign policy threats. Kennedy pointed to the existence of the Communist regime of Fidel Castro just ninety miles from the United States. He accused the Eisenhower-Nixon administration of allowing American military strength to decline, particularly in areas of technology, so that there was now a missile gap with the Soviet Union, illustrated frighteningly by the Soviets' successful launch of Sputnik 1 in 1957. Kennedy and Nixon argued about who would be stronger in standing up to Communist China, as that nation seemed to be threatening the islands of Quemoy and Matsu between the Chinese mainland and the Nationalist Chinese "temporary" home on Formosa.

Kennedy had laid out his indictment of the Eisenhower-Nixon team and his promise during the campaign when he spoke to the American Legion convention in Miami: "The fundamental problem of our time is the critical situation which has been created by the steady erosion of American power relative to that of the Communists in recent years . . . American strength in relation to that of the Sino-Soviet bloc relatively has been slipping, and communism has been steadily advancing until now it rests 90 miles from this city of Miami." The threat went beyond McCarthy's warning of subversion — in terms of military power, the Communists had advanced while the United States had declined. Senator Kennedy illustrated this in his speech with examples ranging from hydrogen bomb arsenals to missiles to jet plane capacity to submarines to the United States still using the M1 rifle. He noted that while Americans had 17 military ground divisions on active duty worldwide, the Soviets had 150.

Kennedy proposed to the Legion members that the United States needed to push ahead with the Minuteman missile program, the Polaris submarine, and the capacity to airlift our forces around the world "within 24 or 48 hours." He reminded these veterans that the Soviets seldom directly challenged the West by moving their forces across international borders, but they worked with Communists in places ranging from Cuba to Laos to Ghana, Nigeria, and the Congo. "Communist influence, propaganda, and subversion, are moving in Latin America, Africa, and Asia."

The audience applauded the young senator's promise to maintain commitments around the world and his reminder that he, a

World War II naval officer and hero, "never believed in retreating under any kind of fire." As they did again when he said, "I don't want to be the President of a nation perishing under the mushroom cloud of a nuclear warhead, and I intend, if President, or if I continue in the Senate, to build the defenses which this country needs, and which freedom needs."[7]

In 1960, the census revealed that there were some 8.5 million males in the United States between the ages of ten and fourteen. This was essentially the cohort that would provide a substantial number of the young men who would serve in Vietnam. More than two and a half million Americans would be posted in that country, and over 58,000 would die there. The incremental decisions of policy makers, the worldview shared by postwar America, and the political values and calculations that would contribute to this result are the subject of this chapter. And surely many of the forces at work were embedded far longer and deeper than the 1960 election campaign or that January day in Washington, but President Kennedy's inaugural remarks and the values and experiences they represented provide an important insight into them. To understand the generation that fought in Vietnam, it is essential to know the world in which they had grown up — to understand the fears, the obligations, and the confidence in their country that they had learned.

Most students of the Vietnam War agree on some standard historical markers that outline the process, or the rationale, by which Americans found themselves in Vietnam. A series of commitments and decisions made by the presidential administrations of Harry Truman, Dwight Eisenhower, and John Kennedy led the United States to an engagement that none of these presidents fully planned. Nonetheless, each of them should have anticipated that this was a possible consequence of their serial actions. Lyndon Johnson did make plans for an engagement in Vietnam but never truly foresaw where this would go.

When the Japanese occupation forces surrendered in what was called Indochina, then involving much of modern Vietnam, Laos, and Cambodia, in the late summer of 1945, the United States was not eager to see the French reinstall their colonial governments in the region. On September 2, 1945, a Vietnamese nationalist and revolutionary, Ho Chi Minh, and his Viet Minh forces declared the Democratic Republic of Vietnam. France, however, was insistent upon returning to its position of world power following its quick fall to Hitler in World War II and the Nazi occupation of their country for more than four years. By late 1946, following the failure of Indochina negotiations, the French and the Viet Minh were engaged in a battle for the future of Vietnam. Few Americans doubted the ability of the French forces to prevail militarily, but President Harry Truman was not sympathetic to neocolonialism, so he did little at the outset of the conflict to assist the French. By the late 1940s, however, a series of alarming events apart from Southeast Asia caused Americans to think again about the drama playing out in Indochina.[8]

In the winter of 1948–1949, following a Soviet blockade of all rail and road routes into the jointly occupied city of Berlin, the Western allies, led by the United States, began airlifting supplies into Berlin. It was a massive effort, and by the spring the blockade had essentially been broken. Any remnants of the postwar collaboration between East and West now were shattered. On August 29, 1949, the Soviet Union detonated an atomic bomb, elbowing into the exclusive nuclear club with the United States. On October 1, Mao Zedong announced the establishment of the People's Republic of China (PRC), a Communist state replacing one that had been a strong American ally and friend. That government, under Chiang Kai-shek, lost a long and difficult war with Mao's revolutionary army. Chiang finally withdrew from the mainland and set up the government of the

161

Republic of China on the island of Taiwan.

Then in June 1950, the Communist government of North Korea swept across the 38th parallel and occupied Seoul, the capital of South Korea. The artificial boundary marking the "temporary" division of that country that had been negotiated at the end of World War II was militarily breached. President Truman and his advisers considered this an unacceptable challenge, and with American persuasion the United Nations dispatched troops to Korea. The largest burden carried by the UN Command in what would be a three-year war was the American one.

More than 36,000 Americans died in the Korean War, the majority of them as a result of fighting PRC "volunteers" who had come across the Yalu River in the fall of 1950 to join the fight. President Truman and Secretary of State Dean Acheson were very mindful of what their generation considered the Munich precedent: When British prime minister Neville Chamberlain and French prime minister Édouard Daladier met with Hitler at Munich in 1938, they had agreed to the German occupation of parts of Czechoslovakia with an understanding that he would take no more territory. Chamberlain's proclamation of "peace in our time" proved to be a brief time. The following spring, the Nazis occupied the remainder of the country with little resistance. And the "lesson of Munich"

162

for the postwar generation was an understanding not to appease aggressors, for they will only want more. They must be confronted and stopped.

The events from 1948 to 1950 changed markedly the way American policy makers — and American citizens — looked at the world. The implicit threats posed by the Soviet Union and Josef Stalin at the end of World War II and their brutal occupation of Eastern European countries now seemed a pattern of continuing behavior and of explicit challenges. And early in 1950, when the People's Republic of China and the Soviet Union recognized the Democratic Republic of Vietnam, this action, in the context of these troubling explicit challenges, made the French war in Indochina a fight for Western-style democracy an important part of the East-West conflict, rather than a battle to restore a colony. The United States did press the French to provide greater autonomy and independence in Laos, Cambodia, and Vietnam, but there was little American leverage.

Just as the newly inaugurated Dwight Eisenhower oversaw in 1953 the negotiation of a cease-fire in Korea and the restoration of the old 38th parallel boundaries there, the Indochina situation was deteriorating. The French forces established a major garrison in the valley at Dien Bien Phu west of Hanoi, near the border with Laos. They were confident they could defeat the Vietnamese revolutionaries. They did not. In a major military operation, the Viet Minh forces defeated the French and captured the garrison. This embarrassing defeat effectively ended the French colonial empire in Indochina. And the United States increasingly assumed responsibility for France's noncommunist supporters there.

In an international conference held at Geneva in the summer of 1954, the participants developed a plan whereby Vietnam would temporarily be divided, with Ho Chi Minh and the Viet Minh controlling the northern zone and the allies of the last emperor of the Nguyen Dynasty, Bao Dai, in charge of the southern zone. Bao Dai was a playboy and had worked closely with the French colonial administration, including their Vichy counterparts who had cooperated with the Japanese during occupation. The Geneva negotiators agreed there were to be elections held to reunify the country by the summer of 1956. The U.S. delegates and those of Bao Dai's State of Vietnam did not sign the accords — nor did they ever implement the provision for a national election. U.S. and South Vietnamese officials privately admitted that the North Vietnamese leader Ho Chi Minh would win any such election.

When the United States replaced the French as the patron and the defender of the "temporary" government of South Vietnam, a number of cumulative obligations and unplanned consequences followed. In retrospect, these followed naturally but never inevitably. There were many promises to keep and a number of constraints, but there were no points when American leadership was too constrained to be able to choose a different option.

Bao Dai was an embarrassment, "ruling" South Vietnam from Paris with his appointed Prime Minister Ngo Dinh Diem actually looking after the government. In an electoral coup, Diem ousted Bao Dai in 1955 and assumed power as president of the new Republic of Vietnam. Diem was a complicated man, a Catholic from Hué, with a clear vision of a noncommunist Vietnam. After some early hesitancy, the United States threw its support behind Diem. And it proved to be major support: Between 1955 and 1961, the Eisenhower administration provided more than $2 billion of economic and military support to South Vietnam, one of the largest beneficiaries of American foreign aid. In May 1957, President Eisenhower welcomed Diem to the United States.[9]

This visit was a major celebration of a head of state. President Eisenhower met the Diem party at the airport, a courtesy he had extended only once before. The South Vietnamese leader enjoyed a state dinner honoring him and spoke to a joint session of Congress. He had private meetings with the president and top U.S. officials and in New York enjoyed a ticker-tape parade down Broadway. The police department estimated that a quarter of a million people lined the parade route. New York City mayor Robert Wagner presented him with the city's Medal of Honor and observed that "history would judge him one of the great leaders of the century." At a dinner presided over by Henry Luce, Francis Cardinal Spellman gave the invocation and dinner guests included John D. Rockefeller Jr., Eleanor Roosevelt, William Randolph Hearst Jr., and Senators John Kennedy and Mike Mansfield. Diem enjoyed the use of President Eisenhower's plane for his travel within the country and received honorary degrees from Seton Hall University and Michigan State University.

The New York Times described Diem as "an Asian liberator, a man of tenacity of purpose, a stubborn man," whose life was "devoted to his country and his God." The Boston Globe called him "Vietnam's Man of Steel." And the St. Petersburg Times proclaimed him a "nationalist leader, struggling to stand against both the Red tide and reaction." He was described as a "miracle man" and a "savior."[10]

This visit enhanced the image of Diem as a resolute Vietnamese ally of the West. And this was in the context of Vietnam evolving to a position as a key battleground in the great contest between East and West. In a speech at Gettysburg College in April 1959, President Eisenhower warned that "the loss of South Vietnam would set in motion a crumbling process that could, as it progressed, have grave consequences for us and for freedom." Like a set of falling dominoes. This image became a fixed metaphor for the threatening linkages that framed the apocalyptic competition of the postwar world.[11]

So the stakes of the contest in Vietnam had been framed, and the leader the United States would support in that contest had been celebrated when John Kennedy stepped onto the platform to take the oath of office. The new president did not challenge either. Even if he shared the Eisenhower administration's private criticism of the Diem administration, President Kennedy displayed publicly a remarkable and reassuring confidence. He put together a like-minded team to work with him. One scholar noted, "The junior officers of the Second World War were taking over from the generals. The ideal candidate for his administration, it was observed, would have a brilliant academic record, impressive war service, athletic achievement, and a glittering professional career." Observers described their "tough and militant character."[12]

Two-thirds of the Kennedy cabinet and the

senior staff involved with his foreign policy team were veterans of World War II, although there were not many combat veterans. Secretary of the Treasury Douglas Dillon, Secretary of the Interior Stewart Udall, Secretary of Agriculture Orville Freeman, and Assistant Secretary of State for Far Eastern Affairs Roger Hilsman, along with the president, were members of this distinctive group. The veterans of World War II were just beginning to come to Congress. Most of the veterans on the Hill had served in World War I. In the 87th Congress, which convened in 1961, 20 percent of the representatives and 29 percent of the senators were veterans. They had been honed by war and most were eager to build upon what they had learned from their experience. Robert Dallek noted, "In 1961 Americans were fixated on Churchill's observations about Munich: Chamberlain had a choice between war and dishonor; he chose dishonor and got war."[13] They readily accepted the history and the lesson it presented, and no one wanted to repeat the choice and suffer the result.

The new president's description of his generation as "tempered by war, disciplined by a hard and bitter peace" captured the profile of his America. In 1960, of the American males between the ages of thirty-five and thirty-nine, 74 percent were veterans. In December 1960, a Gallup poll reported that

50 percent of Americans thought there was "much danger of war."

The early months of the Kennedy administration did not ease anyone's fears. In its first hundred days, the Kennedy team had to deal with a worsening situation in Laos, where the Communist-supported Pathet Lao seemed on the verge of taking over the government. In early 1961, that country seemed to be the focus of cold war tensions in Indochina, even more than Vietnam, despite the concern that the latter also seemed to be unraveling. Kennedy faced a crisis in the Congo following Patrice Lumumba's death and the growing influence of Soviet sympathizers there in the fight for succession. And the failure of U.S., British, and Soviet negotiations on a nuclear test ban seemed a major setback.

President Kennedy learned on April 12 that the Soviet Union had successfully launched Vostok 1 for a manned orbital flight. Yuri Gagarin had safely returned to his country as a hero and to international recognition of his accomplishment. The Soviet advantage in space now seemed appreciably greater. This was all in the context of what seemed to be a worsening situation in Cuba. In mid-April, following up on a plan developed under the Eisenhower administration, the Central Intelligence Agency launched an attack with a force of anti-Castro Cuban defectors against the island. Kennedy had signed off on the plan but did not authorize U.S. military involvement. The Bay of Pigs was an embarrassing fiasco that resulted in the Castro government executing captured leaders of the invasion as well as many of their followers.

The following year, 1962, proved no safer or better. It may have been the most frightening year of the cold war. The Soviets and the East Germans built a wall dividing East and West Berlin; the temporary 1945 occupation zone divisions had become permanent. And in the fall of 1962, Americans were stunned to learn that the Soviet Union had established intermediate-range nuclear ballistic missiles in Cuba. This was followed by a U.S. naval blockade of Cuba and frightening saber rattling by Nikita Khrushchev — and by Kennedy. In November, the two sides reached an agreement that resulted in the withdrawal of the Russian missiles from Cuba and, more quietly, of U.S. missiles from Turkey and Italy. It proved to be a good resolution, but the conflict that had moved East and West uncomfortably close to war left many feeling uneasy.

All of this provided the context for President Kennedy's actions regarding Vietnam. Early on he had gone along with a compromise in Laos that left the Communists essentially in control in that country. To most American officials, Vietnam seemed a better place to make a stand because of its long coastline and seaports and the fairly stable Diem government with the well-equipped and well-regarded army of South Vietnam. It would turn out that even though the coastline and the ports were as secure as promised, neither the government nor the army was.

American military involvement in Vietnam incrementally brought the United States into what some have described as a quagmire. But that narrative, the official account and the public accounting, which described French withdrawal and the perceived responsibility of American engagement to halt the spread of communism and the fall of dominos, while largely an accurate summary of dominant American views at the time, is also too simple.

A troubling aspect of America's growing engagement in Vietnam was the real difference between public conviction and private reservation. At some level, not cynically judged but realistically described, this disparity perhaps is part of political life. The public statements of politicians rarely convey even a hint of uncertainty, nuance, or ambivalence. The world in which political leaders and those who would be statesmen make decisions is filled with qualifiers. What is harder in the case of considering the escalating American involvement in this war is to reconcile the private skepticism, the genuine ambivalence and uncertainty, the alarming cynicism, the doubts and the outright duplicity with public statements of certainty and resolution. The stakes were more than rhetorical. And the rhetoric of leaders has consequences.

The Eisenhower administration presented a consistent narrative of the need to contain communism and the importance of supporting the Diem regime as a model democratic alternative in Vietnam. They did this while privately backing off from committing American combat troops to Vietnam and despite some doubts about the Diem government and the South Vietnamese Army. The Eisenhower team was publicly resolute and privately "wary of the cost and feasibility of policing the world." And after Diem visited the United States in 1957, he returned to Saigon with statements of public enthusiasm echoing in his head yet with none of the additional commitments that he sought from President Eisenhower in his pocket. By the time of Kennedy's inauguration, "the United States was trapped by the very success of the Eisenhower administration in keeping Diem in power and in promoting his symbolic role."[14]

By most accounts, President Kennedy was privately uneasy about Vietnam. He was increasingly dissatisfied with the Diem regime and was very resistant to the idea of sending U.S. combat troops to Vietnam. The public

Kennedy exhibited little of his private uncertainty — except in his expressed reluctance to send in combat troops. In 1961, the president declined a Pentagon request to send up to 200,000 troops to Vietnam. He invited retired general Douglas MacArthur to meet with senior officials, and when the question of sending infantry forces into Vietnam was raised, MacArthur told them, "There was no end to Asia and even if we poured a million American infantry soldiers into that continent, we would still find ourselves outnumbered on every side." President Kennedy often reminded his Joint Chiefs of Staff of this warning when they discussed introducing ground troops to Vietnam.[15]

On the other hand, Kennedy insisted that he was not going to allow "any country to fall to communism on his watch." He increased the American troops in Vietnam significantly and ratcheted up their advisory role by authorizing Green Berets to engage in counterinsurgency operations. He also approved Americans using napalm bombs with their indiscriminate lethality, and he signed off on Operation Ranch Hand, which would use herbicides to destroy the jungle foliage that provided cover for the NLF forces.[16]

The U.S. Army's Green Berets, the Special Forces, became a special interest of President Kennedy. He believed that in the world of Communist guerrillas and insurgency challenges, these special troops, well trained, tough, and capable of working with local populations, could provide an American edge. In an October 1961 visit to Special Forces at the Special Warfare Center at Fort Bragg, North Carolina, Kennedy was impressed by the troops and he authorized them to wear the green beret as a mark of their distinction — ending an army debate about whether such headgear was appropriate. "If Peace Corps volunteers were supposed to be soldiers of peace," the president said, "the Special Forces were projected as the peace corpsmen of war."[17] In 1962, President Kennedy authorized the establishment of two Navy SEAL teams, reorganizing the older Underwater Demolition Teams. They deployed to Vietnam and served as a counterpart to the Green Berets.

Kennedy's determination that this new generation of Americans would confront the challenges of the world in some new ways was not confined to military organizations. The Peace Corps would be the force of young Americans reaching out a hand to help those in the world who were less fortunate: The world's troubles were their troubles. During the campaign of 1960, in a late-night visit to the University of Michigan, the young senator had challenged the students with his vision:

How many of you who are going to be doctors, are willing to spend your days in Ghana? Technicians or engineers, how many of you are willing to work in the Foreign Service and spend your lives traveling around the world? On your willingness to do that, not merely to serve one year or two years in the service, but on your willingness to contribute part of your life to this country, I think will depend the answer whether a free society can compete. I think it can! And I think Americans are willing to contribute. But the effort must be far greater than we have ever made in the past.[18]

In the late winter of 1961, the new president authorized a test group that would evolve into the Peace Corps, a plan that was enthusiastically received. Polls indicated that 68 percent of the public liked the idea, and an American Council on Education survey showed that 94 percent of college students supported it. It was endorsed by more than 150 educational groups, including the National Student Association. President Kennedy's proposal was approved by Congress in August 1961, after it included a loyalty oath as part of the legislation.[19] This peaceful plan to improve the world had a humanitarian purpose — and it also clearly related to the competition between East and West to gain the confidence of undeveloped nations.

There was another Kennedy initiative that was not conventionally military but was aimed directly at the competition with the Soviet Union. The Soviet spacecraft that carried Yuri Gagarin into orbit concluded a four-year period, beginning with the Sputnik launch, in which the Soviets appeared to be ahead in this important area of science and technology. Kennedy had campaigned on the idea of a "missile gap." Now the gap seemed to be widening. He addressed this in May 1961, in a speech to Congress: "If we are to win the battle that is now going on around the world between freedom and tyranny, the dramatic achievements in space which occurred in recent weeks should have made clear to us all, as did the Sputnik in 1957, the impact of this adventure on the minds of men everywhere, who are attempting to make a determination of which road they should take."

The president offered an audacious challenge: "I believe that this nation should commit itself to achieving the goal, before this decade is out, of landing a man on the moon and returning him safely to the Earth."[20] His commitment to this was based less on science and more on cold war competition and military considerations. Kennedy's science adviser Jerome Wiesner observed that "these rockets were a surrogate for military power." The special presidential commission chaired by Secretary of Defense Robert McNamara and National Aeronautics and Space Administration head James Webb put it succinctly: "The nation needs to make a positive decision to pursue space projects aimed at enhancing national prestige . . . Civilian projects such as lunar and planetary exploration are, in this sense, part of the battle along the fluid front of the Cold War."[21]

The "new generation" of Americans was creative and competitive. The Peace Corps and the Green Berets and the Navy SEALs became enduring and strong institutions. And the space race would result in a historic accomplishment. They all confirmed American resolve, discipline, creativity, and "toughness." Sargent Shriver, the president's brother-in-law and the successful first director of the Peace Corps, had a sign above his desk: GOOD GUYS DON'T WIN BALL GAMES.[22]

In October 1960, in the week in which Senator Kennedy made his resolute address to the American Legion and his imaginative challenge to the students at the University of Michigan, United Artists released the movie *The Magnificent Seven.* An American western, based on the classic Japanese film *Seven Samurai,* this movie starred Yul Brynner, Steve McQueen, Charles Bronson, Robert Vaughn, and James Coburn as part of a group of old gunmen who were recruited to cross into Mexico to protect a Mexican village that was being repeatedly pillaged and extorted by bandits. In a bitter gun battle with the marauding force, the Americans secured the confidence of the villagers, who joined with the seven in the final standoff. They defeated the bandits, although only three of the Americans survived to return across the Rio Grande. They left behind a village that was free and citizens now prepared to keep it that way.

The Magnificent Seven was not a box office success, but it was the top movie in the week of October 23. It was replaced by another Western, which would earn the top weekend box office receipts for the year. John Wayne's *The Alamo* was a fictional account of the 1836 battle for that historic fort in the war between Texas and Mexico. The actor had spent more than a decade seeking to make a film celebrating the sacrifice of brave men there. Wayne himself played the American frontiersman Davy Crockett, who came to Texas with other adventurers to join in the fight. They all died there in the face of a far superior Mexican force, fighting rather than surrendering. Just so there could be no doubt of the heritage that John Wayne sought to rekindle, an advertisement said "THE ALAMO WILL REMIND A FORGETFUL WORLD WHAT KIND OF PEOPLE AMERICANS REALLY ARE . . . savagely cruel against injustice, willing to carry their share of disaster — *and at all times on the side of God-fearing people.*" The critics were not impressed by the lengthy film, but it, or at least its themes, resonated with many in the audience.[23]

The forces of cold war competition and American commitment, of resolve and toughness, would combine to establish the impressive operations that would enable Neil Armstrong to step out onto the moon in July 1969 and would return him and his crew home to heroes' welcome. And, ironically, those very forces would have an unintended parallel consequence: They would result in Americans fighting their way up Hamburger Hill just two months before the moon landing. There would be no heroes' welcome for those who took that step.

In the month he announced the moon initiative, Kennedy authorized a substantial increase in troops in Vietnam. When he entered the White House, there were fewer than 1,000 American military in Vietnam, and they were largely advisers. At the end of 1961, that number was over 3,200, and they were in military uniform. When John Kennedy was assassinated in November 1963, the number was over 16,000. As Kennedy biographer Robert Dallek noted, "Kennedy resisted a large, high-visibility military commitment, but a shadow war was another matter."[24] Americans became more secretive about their activities and their objectives, more engaged in "hiding the truth." There was a fear that knowledge of an enlarged American military role would undermine the image of Diem as having the situation under control and it would also feed the anticolonial themes of the Communist insurgents. James Reston of *The New York Times* called it "an undeclared war in South Vietnam."[25]

President Kennedy had a complicated relationship with the American engagement in Vietnam. He was a cold warrior and he worried about the domino theory. He told the United Nations that if Communists were successful in Laos and Vietnam, "the gates would be opened wide." He also recognized that early setbacks at the Bay of Pigs, an unproductive conference with a clearly condescending Khrushchev at Vienna, and an unsatisfactory compromise in Laos that empowered the Pathet Lao had all left him with a need to show the world — and the American voters — that he could exhibit the very strength that he embraced at his inaugural. He admitted to John Kenneth Galbraith that after the Bay of Pigs and Laos he could not accept any more "defeats."[26]

On the other hand, the Cuban missile crisis had alerted him to the real dangers of cold war brinksmanship. He recognized the consequence of miscalculation. His American University commencement address in June

1963 was a call for a pulling back on nuclear competition. He said that he sought peace, "not a Pax Americana enforced on the world by American weapons of war. Not the peace of the grave or the security of the slave." He wished genuine peace "for all time." And noting the persistence of the cold war threat, he affirmed that "the Communist drive to impose their political and economic system on others is the primary cause of world tension today." It was an important speech.[27]

Yet later that month, in a visit to Bonn, Kennedy affirmed that the United States would "not accept" the "subversion or an attack upon a free country which threatens, in my opinion, the security of other free countries." By late July, the United States, the Soviet Union, and Great Britain had agreed on a ban on atmospheric nuclear testing.[28]

The Kennedy team was increasingly dissatisfied with the Diem regime in Saigon. They were convinced that he and his family were ignoring — if not partaking in — corruption, that the army was demoralized and corrupted, and that the government was not supportive of the very democratic principles that Americans were supposedly supporting there. President Diem's brother Ngo Dinh Nhu, along with his wife, Madame Nhu, were particularly contemptuous of dissidents.

The largely Catholic government insiders had an especially tense relationship with the

181

Vietnamese Buddhists. They had different visions for their country. In the summer of 1963, two Buddhist monks burned themselves to death as a protest against the government. The Diem family engaged in a harsh crackdown on the Buddhist dissidents, raiding pagodas and jailing leaders.[29]

Kennedy was engaged with much more than Vietnam in that crucial summer of 1963. He was pushing ahead with a tax cut proposal he had sent to Congress. He was working hard to stay on top of and ahead of the March on Washington that the Reverend Martin Luther King Jr. had organized for August. He was finishing up the nuclear test-ban treaty. One count indicated that in the six months between May 22 and November 22, none of the telephone messages he decided to record dealt with Vietnam. And of 107 taped meetings, only 14 discussed Vietnam, largely in the period when the Diem regime was foundering.[30]

President Kennedy accepted the recommendation of advisers in Washington and in Saigon, including newly appointed ambassador Henry Cabot Lodge, that the United States should stand aside when South Vietnamese military leaders mounted a coup to remove President Diem. Given America's ties with the government in Saigon, standing aside was the same as supporting the coup. In covert meetings with some of the senior conspirators, the American support became more explicit. Diem and his brother were increasingly intractable in their dealings with the Americans and showed little interest in reform. There even were suggestions they might be open to some sort of agreement with North Vietnam.

On November 1, 1963, the generals led the revolt against the Diem regime. Ambassador Lodge did not offer any help or comment, and Diem and Nhu finally fled the palace. The next day, the brothers came forward, surrendering to the dissident soldiers, expecting to be sent into exile. Instead, following the instructions from the leaders of the coup, they were shot and killed by the soldiers taking them to the military headquarters.[31]

By every account, President Kennedy was stunned by the news of the death of the Ngo brothers. Dwight Eisenhower, on the other hand, privately blamed Kennedy for "the cold-blooded killing of a man who had, after all, shown great courage when he undertook the task" of defeating Communists. A critical scholar concluded that American complicity in the Diem death "marked the end of any pretense that America's main objective was to preserve South Vietnam's right to determine its own political fate." Now, he argued, the United States was responsible for what would happen in the war, and it would be "harder for the Americans to withdraw."[32]

On November 21, as President Kennedy prepared for a trip to Texas, he met with adviser Michael Forrestal, who was going to Cambodia and Vietnam. He told Forrestal that after he returned, he wished to meet with him to talk about what to do next in Vietnam. He wanted a thorough review including a consideration of whether the United States should remain there. Recently, the administration had announced that 1,000 American troops would be withdrawn at the end of the year. This was to be a symbolic assurance that the United States was not looking to escalate the situation and that the administration had confidence in the new government.[33]

Lee Harvey Oswald assassinated President Kennedy in Dallas, and the nation entered a period of deep mourning. The 1,000 troops would be withdrawn from Vietnam — but not for long. In the next year, the U.S. deployment in that country would be increased by nearly 50 percent, and then in 1965, the major escalation of the American involvement in the war would begin.

Over the years, many commentators, Kennedy associates, critics and friends, as well as biographers and other scholars have weighed in on the interesting question of what the president would have done in Vietnam if he had survived. And many point to that last meeting in Washington with Forrestal as evidence that he was not prepared to commit to staying in Vietnam, much less to escalating the American military presence.

One comment from President Kennedy's conversation with Michael Forrestal reveals the complexity of his calculations. He noted that in a year he would be standing for reelection, and that ruled out "any drastic changes in policy, quickly," but he would like to consider alternatives. Earlier in the spring, he had assured Senator Mike Mansfield, an opponent of the expansion of American engagement in Vietnam, that it might be time for a withdrawal, but he had to wait until after the elections because "there would be a wild conservative outcry" against him. And he pointed out to his close aide Kenneth O'Donnell that if he pulled out of Vietnam, there would be "another Joe McCarthy red scare." He said that he might be able to do it after he was reelected, "so we had better be damned sure that I *am* reelected."[34]

It is likely that these qualifiers would have continued had he been reelected. President Kennedy had an astute sense of politics, and his instincts probably would have caused him to be cautious about withdrawing from Vietnam, careful not to appear to be allowing the Communists to take over there, and about the consequences of this internationally and in American domestic politics. Howard Jones concluded, "The Vietnam policy of President Kennedy was complex and deeply ironic. He

185

was a hostage of the Cold War, a captive of history's so-called lessons, an advocate of the domino theory, and an avid proponent of intervention in the name of freedom." The great irony — the tragedy even — was that while he intellectually was open to other considerations, he was also restricted by the prevailing view of the world and of American politics that *he had helped to create.* This was not a story of a helpless victim trapped on the slippery slope of history.

The speech President Kennedy had planned to deliver at the Dallas Trade Mart contained the reminder of the fearful world and the assurance that his administration had strengthened the American military. And, reminding the audience of the responsibility he had described at his inauguration, the president would have concluded his remarks, "We, in this country, in this generation, are — by destiny rather than by choice — the watchmen on the walls of world freedom."[35] This task had not gotten any easier since January 20, 1961. And the Vietnam options, the watchmen's assignment, for Lyndon Johnson had become even more complicated.

In 1961, President Kennedy had sent Vice President Johnson to Vietnam to evaluate the situation. Johnson made a production out of his embrace of Ngo Dinh Diem, the "Churchill of Asia." His report to the president was leaked to the press with his recommendation

186

that "the battle against Communism must be joined in Southeast Asia with strength and determination" or else the United States would be battling on its own coasts. His private recommendations to the president were more restrained. He expressed confidence in Diem but also shared Kennedy's reservations about any American military buildup, "barring an unmistakable and massive invasion of South Viet Nam from without." He pointed to the French experience and worried about America being "bogged down chasing irregulars and guerrillas over the rice fields and jungles of Southeast Asia while our principal enemies China and the Soviet Union stand outside the fray and husband their strength."[36]

Lyndon Johnson was a politician's politician. He understood the ways of Washington politics in his time as well as any other president has. He wanted to accomplish a very aggressive domestic program — exceeding that of his role model, Franklin Roosevelt — whereas his only real priority in world affairs was to protect what he viewed as his country's interests, as well as to enhance his personal image as a tough and determined leader. Alas, his skill in domestic politics had no counterpart in his at times fumbling approach to international politics.

On the weekend following Kennedy's death, Lyndon Johnson kept only one meeting that had been on the president's schedule. He met with a team of advisers for a report from those who had just returned from Vietnam. His cautions about "Americanizing" the war remained. But he also made clear that "I am not going to lose Vietnam" and "I am not going to be the President who saw Southeast Asia go the way that China went." These proclamations said much about Johnson and about the path of the next five years. He did not want an American war. But even more than that, he did not want to be the president who "lost" Vietnam. His genuine cold war ideology and his deeply felt concern about Munich-type concessions were always part of his calculations. His fear of the political fallout from "losing" Vietnam was justified. But finally his personalizing the contest and potential loss would trump even these ideological and intellectual considerations.[37]

As his decisions on Vietnam became more troubling and the options he chose caused more dissent, Lyndon Johnson said to Under Secretary of State George Ball, "George, don't pay any attention to what those little shits on the campuses do. The great beast is the reactionary elements in the country. Those are the people that we have to fear."[38]

There is little doubt that President Johnson was constrained by the choices and the public commitments of his predecessors — and of his own role in framing these. As Fredrik

188

Logevall summarized it in his prizewinning study of the coming of the war, "For more than a dozen years, the United States had committed herself to preserving a non-Communist toehold in Vietnam," a burden that Kennedy had expanded. Kennedy and Johnson both had reservations about the course they were on, but even more than this, both worried that "to alter that course now, even under the cover of a fig-leaf negotiated settlement, could be harmful in terms of 'credibility' — their country's, their party's, their own."[39]

The precedents and constraints were powerful, but they were not determinative; Lyndon Johnson could have made other choices many times. He believed that bluff and bluster were important politically in the United States. As he told his friend Senator Richard Russell, voters in most states, including those in Russell's Georgia, would "forgive you for everything except being weak." And his flippant posing was evident when he told some military officers following Kennedy's death, "Just get me elected, and then you can have your war."[40]

Some of this could be dismissed or overlooked as the posturing and swagger that was part of Johnson's huge personality. But the president misjudged and showed his naïveté about Vietnamese politics when he assumed that bluff and bluster would work there too.

He believed a show of American force and resolve would eventually cause the North Vietnamese to back off from their goals of a united South and North. He acknowledged this show of force would involve some American sacrifice, some lives would be lost, but he was confident this would certainly not be as many as in the Korean War.[41]

It turned out that the North Vietnamese had misjudged the American capacity and resolve as well. At the December 1963 Ninth Plenum in Hanoi, the Central Committee of the Vietnam Workers' Party determined that they would move beyond a strictly guerrilla war approach. In a larger-scale military campaign, they believed that they could defeat Saigon before the United States had an opportunity to intervene in the war. They also would increase conscription and position forces away from the Mekong Delta to places better suited for military operations. The militant sinophiles in the government had pushed aside the Soviet-aligned faction, including Ho Chi Minh.[42]

President Johnson's instincts and convictions, along with his and Hanoi's misjudgment, combined with another development that moved the United States closer to war: the 1964 Republican presidential candidate, Barry Goldwater, and the saber-rattling image that he projected — and the even scarier feckless trigger-happy image that Johnson successfully attributed to him. Lyndon Johnson was able to present himself as a man who would stand up for America but would never involve the United States in a senseless war. This was an image that he continued to cultivate throughout 1965 even as he escalated American military engagement in Vietnam.

In June 1964, Secretary of Defense McNamara admitted to President Johnson that things were not going well in Vietnam and wondered how to share with the public the news that this was becoming more complicated. "Many of us in private would say that things are not good, they've gotten worse. Now while we say this in private and not public, there are facts available that find their way in the press. If we're going to stay in there, if we're going to go up the escalating chain, we're going to have to educate the people, Mr. President. We haven't done so yet." Johnson agreed but said that an election campaign was not a good time.[43] It turned out that there never was a good time.

In the 1964 election campaign, Senator Barry Goldwater of Arizona promised that he would enable conservative Republicans to "take the party back." He was a conservative libertarian who had a far more measured approach to some issues than he had displayed while campaigning. His foreign policy seemed to rest on a frontier glibness. In terms of the

191

Soviet Union, he quipped that it might be wise to "lob" a nuclear weapon into the men's room of the Kremlin. He talked about using low-level atomic weapons to protect South Vietnam. Lyndon Johnson mercilessly painted him as someone who would take us to war while the president would preserve the peace. The Democrats broadcast a stunning campaign ad showing a sweet little girl playing in a field, counting the petals on a daisy. Her count blends into the countdown for a nuclear explosion, which fills the screen with the familiar mushroom cloud. Lyndon Johnson's voice-over: "These are the stakes — to make a world in which all of God's children can live, or to go into the dark. We must either love each other, or we must die." Over a dark screen, the message was simple: "Vote for President Johnson on November 3. The stakes are too high for you to stay home." Republicans protested, and the commercial ran only once. But it was now part of the news and was seared in the voters' minds.[44]

Johnson was able to campaign as a confident president who would show strength but would avoid war. He said of Vietnam, "Some others are eager to enlarge the conflict. They call upon the U.S. to supply American boys to do the job that Asian boys should do." He reassured that under a Johnson administration, "We are not about to send American boys nine or ten thousand miles away from home to do what Asian boys ought to be doing for themselves."[45] He promised this even as he was preparing for war. As early as the spring, he was pressing Secretary of Defense McNamara to get some "military plans for winning that war."[46]

One officer who was up on Tiger Tooth mountain in the far northwestern reaches of South Vietnam with a marine detachment in May 1964 recalled that "the political pressure from the United States was adamant about not causing any disturbance, not causing any war, not causing any firefights . . . They were very, very strict about that and very, very worried about that." He and his small detachment had to be "very careful about the way we did what we did."[47]

President Johnson secured an overwhelming victory over Barry Goldwater. He won more than 61 percent of the popular vote and all of the electoral votes except for Senator Goldwater's home state of Arizona and five states of the Deep South. The latter would prove an ominous trend for Democrats.

There were plenty of ominous trends in Vietnam as well. In August 1964, Lyndon Johnson was able to demonstrate his claim of decisive but measured leadership. On August 2, the U.S. Navy destroyer USS *Maddox* was attacked by three North Vietnamese patrol boats. The navy had been running patrols in the international waters of the Gulf of Tonkin, north of Hon Me Island. This was part of an extended operation that was probing North Vietnam. The *Maddox* returned fire, and four navy F-8 Crusaders flew over and attacked the vessels, destroying one and seriously damaging the other two. The *Maddox* resumed patrols, part of Operation Desoto. On the night of August 4, the *Maddox* and the *Turner Joy* were in international waters off the coast. It was a stormy night with very low visibility. Their radar picked up rapidly approaching vessels. The two destroyers fired nearly four hundred shells and depth charges, and believed they had turned back the assault. Except it turned out there was no assault and there were apparently no North Vietnamese vessels in the area. Some naval officers immediately had doubts about the account of the attack. They shared these doubts with Washington, where they were ignored. Lyndon Johnson and Secretary of Defense McNamara ordered a major American air attack on the North Vietnamese oil storage and port facilities. Two American aircraft were shot down, with one pilot killed and the other captured by the North Vietnamese.[48] Navy pilot Everett Alvarez would spend more than eight years in a North Vietnamese prison.

Americans applauded their president, their commander in chief. No one questioned the explanation of events or the American response. The historian Edwin Moïse noted that the media praised the military, and "nobody in the mainstream press appeared to have the slightest doubt about the competence or the moral correctness of any action the U.S. military had taken in the Gulf of Tonkin." The public joined them — or followed their lead. Before this, 58 percent of Americans disapproved of President Johnson's handling of Vietnam. Following the August incidents and the forceful American response, 85 percent approved of his actions. The only criticism was that he should have retaliated following the first attack.[49]

The *Los Angeles Times* editorialized that "the quick and firm response to the attack, first by the Navy and then by the President, should be warning enough to the Communists not to try such foolishness again." Roscoe Drummond wrote in *The Washington Post* that "events of the past few days will remove Viet Nam as a controversial issue in the campaign — as long as there is no wavering on the part of the Administration. I do not believe there will be."[50]

The president would affirm that, with reluctance — feigned reluctance, as it turned out. He sent Congress a request for authorization for him to take action "to repel any armed attack against the United States and to prevent further aggression" in this area. The first authority was explicitly his as commander in chief. It was the second that would provide a blank check to him. The House unanimously approved the resolution and the Senate voted approval with two dissenting votes, Wayne Morse of Oregon and Ernest Gruening of Alaska. The latter said, "All Vietnam is not worth the life of a single American boy." Neither *The New York Times* nor *The Washington Post* covered his speech. The president assured an uncertain Senator William Fulbright that this resolution would cover only the existing situation. If he saw the need for additional military action, he would come to the Congress again for approval. Of course, the resolution was not written that way — the language provided that the presidential authority would last until he declared the area secured or until Congress repealed it. Johnson told an aide that the resolution was "like grandma's nightshirt — it covered everything."[51]

As a matter of fact, it didn't cover everything — surely not the major escalation of military action that would follow over the next several years. But few challenged this because there was a continuing understanding that the president would do no more than was necessary to contain communism.

On December 18, 1964, at the lighting of the national Christmas tree, President Johnson said that "these are the most hopeful times in all the years since Christ was born in Bethlehem." His optimism and faith were soon challenged. On Christmas Eve, National Liberation Front operatives planted a bomb at the hotel where American officers stayed in Saigon. Two Americans died there. Right after Christmas, the NLF launched a major attack on the settlement of Binh Gia near Saigon. They had sophisticated equipment and killed 200 South Vietnamese soldiers and 5 American military advisers. These deaths would bring the total advisers killed in 1964 to 136. The war was becoming hotter and Americans were becoming more engaged.[52]

In 1965, this engagement ramped up significantly, in terms both of numbers and the nature of American involvement. In this year, the American War began. Right after the Lunar New Year in early February, the NLF attacked the barracks at Camp Holloway near Pleiku. Most soldiers were in their bunks when the assault began — 9 died. President Johnson told the National Security Council and congressional leaders, "We have kept our guns over the mantel and our shells in the cupboard for a long time now. And what was the result? They are killing our men while they sleep in the night. I can't ask our American soldiers out there to fight with one hand tied behind their backs." Within hours, 150 American planes set off on bombing missions directed at North Vietnam. Pleiku was a pretext for a plan that was already in place by the early winter. There was a sense in Washington that some greater U.S. engagement was essential to protect South Vietnam.[53] This was the beginning of Operation Rolling Thunder. It was not a onetime retaliation such as the attacks following the Tonkin Gulf incident; it was a bombing campaign that would continue for several years. Before it was over, three times the tonnage of bombs that had been dropped on Europe in World War II were dropped on North and South Vietnam, Laos, and Cambodia.

Most Americans applauded the president for initiating this action. The *Washington Post* editorial board concluded, "The violent words and violent acts of the last few days disclose with dreadful clarity that South Viet-Nam is not an isolated battlefield but a part of a long war which the Communist world seems determined to continue until every vestige of Western power and influence has been driven from Asia." The *New York Times* editorial team was more troubled: "In Vietnam, the United States is engaged in a war. In any war, attacks are made and men are killed and wounded. The process, inescapably, is one of escalation. As such a war continues, it becomes bigger, costlier, more dangerous. Vietnam is proving no exception." Walter Lippmann, who would be a major critic of the war in Vietnam, saw the Pleiku attack as a provocation that was orchestrated by Peking as a test, one that he worried they would repeat: "The truth is that President Johnson profoundly desires to avoid war but his power to do that is not unlimited. Nor can he be counted on not to be provoked if the provocation is continual and cumulative. There should be no mistake about this anywhere."[54]

The covers of *Time* and *Newsweek* following the Pleiku attack showed the Vietnam conflict. Both contained pictures of flag-draped coffins of the Americans killed at Camp Holloway. *Time* said the Americans should be very clear, "no more misunderstandings." *Newsweek* reminded readers that "Lyndon Johnson is a prudent man, and proud of it. He opposes confrontations in general, and he had been particularly hesitant to have one in Vietnam." But now it was impossible to be patient. Syndicated columnist Roscoe Drummond said it was time to "show muscle." He stressed that the conflict there was not just about Vietnam. The administration needed to demonstrate to the world and to the American people "that the United States is not going to be driven back to Pearl Harbor in the face of expanding Chinese aggression." South Vietnam was "only part of" the American challenge.[55]

New York Times columnist Hanson Baldwin was a strong advocate of American military power. He pointed out that the bombing runs would have a psychological and a political impact, but not necessarily a military one. He argued that Americans should not recognize any enemy sanctuaries, and "selected United States ground units should be used, as needed, in South Vietnam."[56]

On March 8, a month after the attack on the barracks at Pleiku, Americans saw pictures of U.S. Marines going ashore at Da Nang, some 375 miles north of Saigon. Two battalions based in Okinawa came onto the beach in full battle gear and were greeted there by South Vietnamese officials and by young Vietnamese women with flower leis. Washington had sent in the marines to protect the air base at Da Nang. The deployment of combat troops had been predicted and previewed for several weeks. Secretary McNamara had told the House Armed Services Committee that Pleiku proved that the United States was in a struggle, and the challenge had to be met. "If we fail to meet it here and now, we will inevitably have to confront it later under even more disadvantageous conditions. This is the clear lesson of history which we can ignore only at our peril." *Time* magazine swooned that "the most articulate man in Washington was at his most eloquent."[57]

President Johnson was clearly determined to shore up Vietnam militarily by the winter of 1965. But he was cautious about publicly describing the extent or the consequences of this. He was engaged in an intense discussion with Congress to secure passage of some signature pieces of legislation, including Medicare, Medicaid, and Federal Aid to Education. He was also pushing for voting rights legislation to be a companion piece of the Civil Rights bill he had secured in 1964. The Reverend Martin Luther King Jr. had come to visit him at the White House right after the Pleiku attack. King had just been released from a Selma, Alabama, jail and found the president "absorbed" with the response to Pleiku, but he did affirm his support for a voting rights bill.[58]

On March 7, the day before the marines came ashore in Vietnam, John Lewis and Hosea Williams led marchers across the Edmund Pettus Bridge in Selma. There they were met by a huge force led by Dallas County sheriff Jim Clark and the state police. When the marchers refused to disperse, the authorities attacked and beat many of them badly. *Stars and Stripes* had two major headlines on March 9. The top one said "U.S. Marines Land in Vietnam" and right below it was the companion banner, "Police Batter Selma Negroes." John Lewis, recovering from a fractured skull, said, "I don't see how President Johnson can send troops to Vietnam . . . and can't send troops to Selma, Alabama."[59] On March 15, President Johnson spoke to a joint session of Congress and strongly pushed for passage of federal voting rights legislation, ending his emotional speech with a commitment: "We shall overcome."

In the spring of 1965, the administration deployed additional army combat units to Vietnam, and by June, American officials conceded that the troops in the country were no longer in only defensive positions, protecting American air bases and other key "enclaves." They had commenced patrols and offensive operations, essential steps in the defense of critical positions. This coincided with the spring dispatch of some 23,000 American soldiers and marines to the Dominican Republic to protect that nation from what President Johnson warned was a Castro takeover. Along with wide approval, these military actions elicited expressions of concern and of dissent from some Americans.

In July there was still over 60 percent approval for the Johnson administration's conduct in Vietnam, despite the news that 503 Americans had died in the four months since the marines had gone ashore.[60] By early summer there was growing discussion within the administration about the next steps in Vietnam. Clearly the escalation to this point had not been sufficient to turn the tide there. General William Westmoreland, the commander of MACV, pressed hard for more troops.

President Johnson convened a group of senior advisers to discuss the options. Led by President Truman's secretary of state, Dean Acheson, Johnson called them "the Wise Men." But he and everyone else were aware of the sort of recommendations they would make. Following one session, George Ball, who had become the administration dove on Vietnam, confronted Acheson: "You goddamned old bastards, you remind me of nothing so much as a bunch of buzzards sitting on a fence and letting the young men die. You don't know a goddamned thing about what you're talking about." Acheson was shaken by the exchange, but LBJ rejected Ball's advice. He told his advisers, in what would be a dilemma repeated often over the next several years, "Withdrawal would be a disaster, a harsh bombing program would not win and could easily bring a wider war, and standing pat with existing forces . . . was only slow defeat."[61] Johnson would accept McNamara's proposal to increase American forces from less than 25,000 at the beginning of the year to the range of 175,000 to 200,000.

In July 1965, Congress approved the Medicare and Medicaid bills, the voting rights bill, and the housing and urban development bill, including rent subsidies. The House approved the antipoverty bill and voted to repeal Section 14(b) of the Taft-Hartley Act, which had allowed states to outlaw closed union shops. The Senate would fail to repeal the act when it was unable to defeat a Republican filibuster. Nonetheless, this was quite a package of domestic reform, one that moved the Great Society close to Johnson's ambitious goals. It would be enhanced in the early fall when Congress approved a major reform in the immigration laws.

On July 28, the day the House voted on the repeal of the Taft-Hartley section, President Johnson faced a group of two hundred reporters in the East Room of the White House. In his introductory remarks, he announced that he was authorizing an additional 50,000 troops to be sent to Vietnam, bringing the total to 125,000. He said that there would likely be more later — a vague acknowledgment of his commitment to increase the total to 175,000 by the end of the year, with an understanding that more could follow. Johnson was being less than honest in this public forum. As George Herring concluded, "July 28, 1965, might therefore be called the day the United States went to war without knowing it, and it is now clear this was no accident." Johnson had agreed to "an open-ended military commitment in Vietnam."[62] Ironically, tragically, he did this without any real confidence that this decision would result in a satisfactory outcome.

In his press conference, Johnson acknowledged that a deployment of this scale would require more troops, so the monthly draft call would increase from 17,000 to 35,000, "over a period of time." While the armed forces would work to increase enlistments, there would be no call-up of reserve units. Clearly he and others had learned from the experience early in the Korean War that the draft was a politically more palatable way to mobilize than the call-up of reserves, involving older Americans more established in their communities. He hoped that this show of resolve would encourage the Communists to come to the bargaining table — he pleaded with them to do this.[63]

The public largely applauded the president's actions, which they viewed as measured. An Indianapolis school principal said, "The strongest nation must act like the strongest nation." And a La Mirada, California, housewife commented, "That war's been forced on us, but he's been right." One poll revealed that 75 percent of the respondents agreed with the statement, "We have no choice but to send in more troops."[64]

By the summer of 1965, many people shared this view of the inevitability of the war given all of the provocations and commitments that preceded it and the widely shared assumptions that led to this reluctant obligation. But while there were forces and prior decisions that led to this path, history allows more choice than this explanation acknowledges; there was no inevitability here. In the spring, former president Eisenhower had written privately to President Johnson, "You have to go all out because we are not going to be run out of a free country that we helped to establish."[65] It is true that Ike had helped to create this situation, but he had declined in 1954–1955 to choose the option that he pressed on President Johnson.

Fredrik Logevall assessed President Johnson's situation:

The evidence, however, shows that Johnson was not pulled into war by deep structural forces beyond his control; nor was he pulled into it by overzealous advisers from the Kennedy era. He inherited a difficult situation in Vietnam, in large part because of the policy decisions of his predecessor, but he made that situation far worse with his actions, not merely before the November 1964 election but, more important, in the three months thereafter. This period represented the last good chance to withdraw the United States from Vietnam. In those ninety days, Johnson deceived the nation and the Congress about the state of the war and about his plans for it. He, more than his top advisers, feared a premature move to negotiations; he, more than they, ensured that all options to an escalated U.S. involvement were squeezed out of the picture.[66]

It is especially unfortunate that other available choices were not exercised, because presidents Johnson and Kennedy in fact had serious doubts about an expanded American involvement in Vietnam. But these doubts were always privately expressed. As late as June 1965, when the war train was accelerating down the tracks, President Johnson told Secretary of Defense McNamara that it was going to be just as critics had predicted, a difficult war to fight and to win: "I'm very depressed about it. Because I see no program from either Defense or State that gives me much hope of doing anything, except just praying and gasping to hold on during monsoon and hope they'll quit. I don't believe they're *ever* going to quit. And I don't see . . . that we have any . . . plan for a victory — militarily or diplomatically."[67]

President Johnson is often considered a tragic figure, finding himself reluctantly drawn into a war that he realized would be costly and probably unwinnable and would distract everyone from his domestic agenda. In 1970, he admitted to Doris Kearns:

I knew from the start, that I was bound to be crucified either way I moved. If I left the woman I really loved — the Great Society

— in order to get involved with that bitch of a war on the other side of the world, then I would lose everything at home. All my programs. All my hopes to feed the hungry and shelter the homeless. All my dreams to provide education and medical care to the browns and the blacks and the lame and the poor. But if I left that war and let the Communists take over South Vietnam, then I would be seen as a coward and my nation would be seen as an appeaser and we would both find it impossible to accomplish anything for anybody anywhere on the entire globe.[68]

It is hard to join in President Johnson's self-pity. He was not the victim of uncontrollable forces, the resistant and unfortunate tool of history and politics. He not only helped to create the official view of Vietnam, he deliberately engaged in this war. He could have overcome these pressures if he had chosen less aggressive options. He did not.

President Johnson opened his July 28 press conference by reading from a letter he had received from a woman living in the Midwest:

Dear Mr. President:
In my humble way I am writing to you about the crisis in Viet-Nam. I have a son who is now in Viet-Nam. My husband served in World War II. Our country was

at war, but now, this time, it is just something that I don't understand. Why?

The president acknowledged that he had tried to answer this very question many times. He framed his reply again in this public forum, explaining the decision he was announcing that day to send more young Americans to Vietnam.

Why must young Americans, born into a land exultant with hope and with golden promise, toil and suffer and sometimes die in such a remote and distant place?

The answer, like the war itself, is not an easy one, but it echoes clearly from the painful lessons of half a century. Three times in my lifetime, in two World Wars and in Korea, Americans have gone to far lands to fight for freedom. We have learned at a terrible and a brutal cost that retreat does not bring safety and weakness does not bring peace.

It is this lesson that has brought us to Viet-Nam. This is a different kind of war. There are no marching armies or solemn declarations. Some citizens of South Viet-Nam at times, with understandable grievances, have joined in the attack on their own government.

But we must not let this mask the central fact that this is really war. It is guided by

North Viet-Nam and it is spurred by Communist China. Its goal is to conquer the South, to defeat American power, and to extend the Asiatic dominion of communism. There are great stakes in the balance. Most of the noncommunist nations of Asia cannot, by themselves and alone, resist the growing might and the grasping ambition of Asian communism.

Our power, therefore, is a very vital shield. If we are driven from the field in Viet-Nam, then no nation can ever again have the same confidence in American promise, or in American protection.

In each land the forces of independence would be considerably weakened, and an Asia so threatened by Communist domination would certainly imperil the security of the United States itself.

We did not choose to be the guardians at the gate, but there is no one else.

Nor would surrender in Viet-Nam bring peace, because we learned from Hitler at Munich that success only feeds the appetite of aggression. The battle would be renewed in one country and then another country, bringing with it perhaps even larger and crueler conflict, as we have learned from the lessons of history.

Moreover, we are in Viet-Nam to fulfill one of the most solemn pledges of the American Nation.

He reminded his audience that this pledge had been made by three American presidents. "We just cannot now dishonor our word, or abandon our commitment, or leave those who believed us and who trusted us to the terror and repression and murder that would follow." That, he said, "is why we are in Viet-Nam."[69]

At that time and over the years, there was much debate and dissent about the American War in Vietnam. A fundamental flaw in explaining and justifying the war was that it was always necessary to focus upon the need to protect and defend democracy in Vietnam. It would be hard to justify it otherwise. Yet the Vietnam War was not primarily about Vietnam. It was about a global geopolitical contest with communism, it was about America maintaining its international commitments, it was about protecting positions in U.S. domestic politics, and it was about the personalities of American presidents and other leaders. Vietnam happened to be the place where these very complicated forces played out. Yet it was largely impossible to justify the war by discussing these things, except perhaps the international dominos and the Munich obligation. Instead it was essential to describe this war in terms of an obligation to protect democratic values attributed to South Vietnam and to support heroic leaders purportedly defending these values in that place. This facile construct would prove very fragile.

Even though Vietnam was America's third war in twenty years, this one seemed different from the others. Johnson was direct and Americans found him convincing, but he played down the emotions. *Newsweek* wrote of this new war, "It is a strange, almost passionless war that the U.S. fights in Vietnam. There have been no songs written about it, and the chances that any will be seem remote. There are no hot tides of national anger running. There are no scabrous epithets for the enemy, even on the battlefield."[70]

Between the first week of March and the end of July 1965, America went to war. There were no bands and there was no request for sacrifice. President Johnson did not ask for any new taxes to pay for the war and he declined to call up reserves. He urged Americans to go on with their lives. Nonetheless, even without patriotic pleas for sacrifice, few doubted that sacrifice would be involved — that was the inevitable cost of war. Within a few years, the ranks of the early critics and skeptics would grow, as the recognized cost was growing as well. But in 1965, a large majority of Americans seemed to trust the decisions of their president.

Polls indicated that by the 1964–1965 period, Americans increasingly thought Vietnam was a major problem facing the United

States. They had turned their attention to Asia. In 1961, 49 percent of Americans thought that Russia was the "greater threat to world peace" and 32 percent thought it was China. By November 1964, 59 percent believed China was the greater threat and 20 percent thought it was Russia. In September 1965, 75 percent supported President Johnson's holding firm and even extending the war to the north if that seemed necessary. George Gallup reported that support seemed to be growing even as there were public demonstrations against the war. In December, a Harris poll indicated a ten-to-one margin against withdrawal. But Johnson and his team understood how delicate this could prove to be. One staffer wrote, "I have a vague feeling that this support may be more superficial than it is deep and committed (many people probably do not even understand what it is that they are supporting)."[71] It was a prescient comment — but the support would take awhile to unravel. In the meantime, most Americans reluctantly accepted this expanded military initiative, as the obligation that John Kennedy had embraced less than five years earlier. Few — if any — could have anticipated the duration or the cost of this commitment taken on so readily.

Philip Caputo was born in Chicago in 1941.

While a few years older than the baby boomers, Caputo was culturally and politically part of that post–World War II generation. He received a commission in the Marine Corps upon graduation from Loyola University in 1964, and less than a year later, on March 8, 1965, he came ashore at Da Nang as part of the 9th Marine Expeditionary Brigade, the first combat unit to come to Vietnam. He describes his feelings and the mood:

For Americans who did not come of age in the early sixties, it may be hard to grasp what those years were like — the pride and overpowering self-assurance that prevailed. Most of the thirty-five hundred men in our brigade, born during or immediately after World War II, were shaped by that era, the age of Kennedy's Camelot. We went overseas full of illusions, for which the intoxicating atmosphere of those years was as much to blame as our youth.

War is always attractive to young men who know nothing about it, but we had also been seduced into uniform by Kennedy's challenge to "ask what you can do for your country" and by the missionary idealism he had awakened in us. America seemed omnipotent then: the country could still claim it had never lost a war, and we believed we were ordained to play cop to the Communists' robber and spread our own political faith around the world . . . So, when we marched into the rice paddies on that damp March afternoon, we carried, along with our packs and rifles, the implicit convictions that the Viet Cong would be quickly beaten and that we were doing something altogether noble and good.[72]

The torch that John Kennedy had accepted in January 1961 on behalf of his generation had quickly been passed along to the next generation.

4
RECEIVING THE TORCH

By the end of 1965, there were nearly 185,000 American troops serving in Vietnam. Christmas for them was marked by an effort to celebrate a familiar holiday in an unfamiliar place. The juxtapositions were striking. The armed forces newspaper *Stars and Stripes* said that a Christmas truce had been largely sustained: It was "a mostly silent night." It was only mostly silent, though — and then only at night. Eleven Americans died on December 24, including 6 airmen whose AC-47D gunship crashed in Laos. The wreckage would not be discovered and the remains recovered and repatriated until 2012. Overall, 59 Americans were killed in Vietnam between Christmas Eve and New Year's Day. On Christmas Day, a nineteen-year-old marine from Puerto Rico, Fernando Seda, was shot in the head and killed by enemy soldiers in an ambush, when walking on patrol through a rice paddy near Binh Son.[1]

In Saigon on a warm and muggy Christmas

Eve, Francis Cardinal Spellman of New York celebrated Midnight Mass on a soccer field at Tan Son Nhut airfield near Saigon. The liturgy and the carols were familiar. But it surely was not St. Patrick's Cathedral as "floodlights glittered on the gun barrels of men just back from guarding the jet fighters on the Tan Son Nhut runway."[2]

General William Westmoreland, the commanding general of the Military Assistance Command, Vietnam, was in attendance at the Mass, as was South Vietnam prime minister Nguyen Cao Ky. Also joining the congregants was Bob Hope. He had earlier done a show at the base before 8,000 to 10,000 cheering and laughing troops. He told them, "I forgot to burn my draft card, and here I am." He was joined on his USO holiday tour by Les Brown and his Band of Renown, by the comedian Jerry Colonna, and actresses/performers Carroll Baker, Anita Bryant, Joey Heatherton, Kaye Stevens, and Miss America, Dianna Lynn Batts. He had been met at the airport by comedian Martha Raye, who had just landed after doing a show for the 7th Fleet. Carroll Baker said, "Making a tour like this makes you feel worthwhile." Hope carried his customary golf club and wore a pink beret. He had fallen from the stage during a show in Thailand the day before and torn two ligaments in his ankle. He quipped that "I'll do anything for a laugh."[3]

Cardinal Spellman did not aim for a laugh, but he did seek to reassure and to affirm the mission. In his homily, he told the troops that "Christ came into the world to teach the ways of peace." And he acknowledged that these may seem like "strange words to speak to men of the Armed Forces of the United States." He emphatically vowed they were not: "It is because America is dedicated to the cause of peace that such sacrifices as yours are necessary in today's world crisis." Cardinal Spellman had long been an advocate of American support for South Vietnam, and in these messages he increased his own tensions with the Vatican. Pope Paul VI's Christmas message called for peace in Vietnam and noted that "peace needs to be built on a courageous revision of the inadequate ideology of egoism, strife, and national superiority." Cardinal Spellman had been the Church's military vicar to the armed forces since 1939. Upon arrival at the Saigon airport, a reporter asked him about his thoughts on what the United States was doing in Vietnam. He said, "I fully support everything it does." His 1965 Christmas card showed him standing next to a military jet with two officers.[4]

President Lyndon Johnson had affirmed the same principle as the cardinal, the necessity of fighting for peace, when he lit the national Christmas tree a week earlier: "Our sons patrol the hills of Viet-Nam at this hour because we have learned that though men cry 'Peace, Peace,' there is no peace to be gained ever by yielding to aggression." With British prime minister Harold Wilson by his side, Johnson cautioned that "peace is not merely the absence of war. It is that climate in which man may be liberated from the hopelessness that imprisons his spirit." Wilson was an important allied leader, who had been urging caution on any military involvement in Vietnam.[5]

On Christmas day, troops who were not in the field feasted on shrimp cocktail, roast turkey with giblet gravy and corn-bread dressing, mashed potatoes, peas, cranberry sauce, and mincemeat and pumpkin pie. Santa Claus wished them a Merry Christmas at many dining halls and familiar Christmas carols played in the background. In the days before Christmas, an estimated thirty tons of gifts for the troops were arriving daily. When Anita Bryant concluded the Bob Hope Christmas Eve show at Tan Son Nhut by singing "Silent Night," she asked the troops to join her in singing. "It was a difficult time for them. Many had tears in their eyes."[6]

Bob Hope and his troupe continued their tour. A few days after Christmas, they performed in front of 8,000 troops up at An Khe, in east-central Vietnam. These men were largely with the 1st Cavalry Division (Airmobile), and they turned out for the show despite a driving rain. Sitting on or wrapped in ponchos, they enthusiastically welcomed the group. When Hope was speaking, a helicopter flew overhead, with the loud *thump, thump, thump* of the rotor blades that were such a familiar sound in Vietnam. The comedian looked up. "What is that?" he exclaimed. "It's the biggest darn mosquito I've ever seen." The soldiers "roared" at his quip.[7]

The thump of the 1st Cavalry helicopters and the shouts of its men had echoed around the hills and valleys west of An Khe less than six weeks earlier. But the explosive sounds of a major military engagement accompanied these echoes. And then there was no laughter. In mid-November out in the Ia Drang Valley, near the Cambodian border, the Americans and North Vietnamese had gone head-to-head in a major fight in one of the epochal battles of the war, though it was not clear that anyone recognized it as that in December 1965.

But from November 14 to 17, it had been a bloody encounter, initiated by the United States in order to secure Highway 19 all the way west to Cambodia and to cut off north–south movement by the North Vietnamese. The 1st Cavalry had demonstrated a new form of battle mobility in their heavy use of helicopters for airborne assaults and movement of men and supplies. The official early

220

tallies were that the North Vietnamese Army had 1,411 men killed and Americans suffered "moderate to heavy casualties." The Associated Press would describe these as 289 Americans and 741 Army of the Republic of Vietnam dead. But they also reported that there were 3,452 Communist forces killed.[8]

In a preview of a controversy that would mark the next several years, Charles Mohr of *The New York Times* had published a story on November 26 that challenged some of these numbers. In his commentary headlined "War and Misinformation," Mohr said that he and others were convinced that the military command's accounts of enemy deaths were exaggerated — or at least the figures were impossible to verify. He reported that soldiers with the 1st Cavalry unit were joking about Saigon's requests for "the WEG" — wild-eyed guess — body count.

Regardless of the accuracy of the tallies, there was little doubt in Vietnam that this war was starting to look and to feel like a real war. *U.S. News & World Report* framed it as such for the American audience: "In Vietnam: Suddenly It's a Stepped Up War." The editors elaborated by pointing out that the "U.S. war machine is starting to roll in Vietnam," but they also warned that the "Reds show no signs of backing off." This meant "more fighting, less talk of quick victory." One American officer acknowledged that "the war for us is just beginning." Following the major November battles in the Ia Drang Valley and at the area called Zone D thirty miles northeast of Saigon, the Americans were "satisfied, but under no illusion that the critical phase is over — that the Reds will simply give up and go home."[9]

Since 1927, the prestigious mass-circulation news weekly *Time* magazine had been naming a prominent newsmaker as its Man of the Year. For 1965, this recognition went to General William Westmoreland. His four predecessors on the list had been John Kennedy, Pope John XXIII, Martin Luther King Jr., and Lyndon Johnson. It was distinguished company. But General Westmoreland shared the platform with the men serving under him in Vietnam, the "Guardians at the Gate." *Time* publisher Henry R. Luce and his top editorial team had long been advocates of a more aggressive U.S. engagement in Vietnam. Now this was being realized: "It was clear that the U.S. had irrevocably committed itself to the nation's third major war in a quarter century." Here, they pointed out, the enemy did not fit into previous stereotypes of "heel-clicking Junker or sadistic samurai," but rather a "small brown man whose boyish features and emaciated body made him look less like the oppressor than the oppressed."

While *Time* believed that President Johnson had waited too long before acting in Vietnam, now he had "established beyond question the credibility of the U.S. commitment to Asia." But his "We will stand in Viet-Nam" pledge of July 1965 would need to be redeemed by "the American fighting man." *Time* applauded these soldiers: "With courage and a cool professionalism that surprised friend and foe, U.S. troops stood fast and firm in South Viet Nam. In the waning months of 1965 they had helped to stem the tide that had run so long with the Reds." Despite the "baking heat and moldering humidity," the Americans fought. As General Westmoreland said, "If the other guy can live and fight under those conditions, so can we."

Despite the complexity of the war, and the problems of identifying enemy troops and engaging them, the *Time* editors assured readers that "as it has done everywhere else, the G.I.'s heart inevitably goes out to war's forlorn victims." There were stories of soldiers helping at orphanages, of medics providing medical support to civilians, and of men protecting farmers and their crops. The magazine believed that by the end of 1966, with American forces perhaps at 400,000 men, Vietnam could be controlled militarily and the troops could move on to support the pacification program. All of this, they acknowledged, would be hard, the casualty lists would grow, and the costs would increase. They urged President Johnson to be more candid about this war, saying he needed more than "pulpit platitudes." But he did have the right man in charge, General Westmoreland. And he had troops in the field that all Americans could view with pride.[10]

It was a strong and professional military that came to Vietnam in 1965. Most of the men were enlistees rather than draftees, and many of them had served for several years. Their senior NCOs were veterans, as were their field grade officers; in fact, many had served in Korea or even World War II. Perhaps equally important, the first troops deployed to Vietnam in 1965 came in as units that had trained together and had developed a professional cohesion.

Behind them, and over the next several years, the expanding war would require an expanded military force. The younger brothers, cousins, or neighbors, in some cases even the sons and nephews, of this early force would come to fight the war. The Vietnam War would become increasingly the war of the baby boom generation, those born after 1945.

In 1940, there were nearly 48 million Americans age twenty or under. In 1965, there were more than 79 million of this group. The young families that started after World War II would be an important part of an era that reshaped American society. During the 1950s, the number of children entering school increased annually at an unprecedented rate so that schools had difficulty keeping up with the physical space requirements and the number of teachers these new classes needed. Higher education would see the same pattern. In 1946, American colleges and universities enrolled just over 1.5 million students. In 1960, the number was over 3.5 million, all of them pre–baby boomers, and their enrollment was driven by the expanded availability of schools and the increasing demand for a college education. By 1970, this number was nearly 8 million — the 1940s and '50s pattern of the growing desirability and availability of college had met the baby boomers. Whereas in 1940, less than 16 percent of high school graduates attended college, by 1965 nearly half did. Between 1960 and 1964, the undergraduate enrollment in American colleges increased by 38 percent.[11]

Enduring images and stereotypes of this generation abound. The youngsters of the 1940s and '50s grew up in an era of relative prosperity, an expanding economy, growing communications through highway systems, air travel, telephone contact, and television. The period before 1965 saw the beat generation, the rock-and-roll era, and the great movement to improve race relations. From Howdy Doody to *Mad* magazine to Elvis Presley, it was a time of discovery and experiment. And American society self-consciously sought to support this mood. At the White House Conferences on Children and Youth, there was a growing emphasis on children's "rights." The happiness of the nation's youth depended on "relieving feelings of fear, guilt, and jealousy." In a consumerist age, material things were linked to happiness. Some children's advocates insisted that "self-denial was a thing of the past." And counselors such as Dr. Benjamin Spock advocated a "child-centered approach."[12]

But the 1950s in the United States was not simply a happy-go-lucky, self-indulgent, Ozzie and Harriet world. Far from it. The baby boomers grew up in an America of optimism, of expanding aspiration and growing opportunity, a nation of increasing mobility and freedom — but they also grew up in a country marked by tension. The fears and concerns of their parents and grandparents intruded into the lives of the youngsters of the era. And the intrusions were far more intentional, calculated, than accidental. America in the 1950s, cold war America, seemed also to be a time of fear, preparation, and resolution, for both adults and their children.

One scholar recently described this world this way: "Children and teenagers of the postwar era were told that they lived in a country where anything was possible, but while they were encouraged to find self-fulfillment and expression, they were also told that they were responsible for preserving the democratic society in which they lived. They were the country's next generation of military and citizen soldiers. On their shoulders rested preservation of the country's ideals and way of life."[13]

This was a responsibility with a tangible enemy, the Soviet Union and international communism, and a presumption that at some point it would be necessary to confront that enemy's aggression. Indeed, it was a responsibility anchored in the need to defend the United States — and, more broadly, freedom and democracy. For the early part of the cold war years it was more a question of when rather than if this confrontation would take place. And the expectation was that the schools would shoulder a major part of the responsibility for preparing this generation of Americans for their role. There was "a passionate sense of defensive nationalism, and a corresponding dedication to the cult of the nation, for which schools had become the primary temples."[14]

Neil H. McElroy, chairman of the White House Conference on Education, described it this way in 1955: "In this highly technical era, education has become as much a part of our system of defense as the Army, the Navy or the Air Force. We must have good schools, not only because of our ideals, but for survival." Parents and American society did consider schools as the central means to improve the lives of children. Many spokespersons insisted that patriotic obligation and preparation for national challenge were essential corollaries of this improvement.[15] As FBI director J. Edgar Hoover, one of the most admired Americans of the 1950s, put it in a foreword to a book for adolescents, schooling was about more than academic accomplishment: "When a young man files an application with the F.B.I., we do not ask if he was the smartest boy in his class. We want to know if he was truthful, dependable, and if he played the game fair. We want to know if he respects his parents, reveres God, honors his flag and loves his country."[16]

The Communist threat was an integral theme of the early years of many in this generation. Reminders were never far away. In 1951, the popular *Collier's* magazine devoted an entire issue to an imaginary World War III initiated by an attack by the Soviet Union in Yugoslavia that escalated into Eastern Europe. In this account, the Western democracies, including the United States, and then the United Nations joined in the battle against the Russians. The magazine described in detail nuclear bombs that were dropped on U.S. and other major cities and included striking illustrations. The magazine's

World War III was a long, bloody war with millions of casualties, and the United States and the Western democracies were finally victorious. The issue had articles written by various reporters and commentators — for example, Hanson Baldwin, the military correspondent of *The New York Times,* described the fighting of the war. This edition had been secretly prepared and edited over months by Cornelius Ryan. The issue sold nearly 4 million copies, a half million more than *Collier's* normal readership.[17]

Life ran a news story about U.S. cities that had been targeted by the Soviets for bomb attacks. Magazines, newspapers, and radio and television news regularly reported tensions and provocations with the Russians. Americans watched reports of nuclear tests, and there was a great deal of attention paid to bomb shelters. The government encouraged Americans to build and to stock these emergency spaces to survive a nuclear attack. One boy recalled, "When I saw a brochure for a bomb shelter in the mail on the hall table, I couldn't sleep for three nights." A young participant in the 1960 White House Conference on Children and Youth said, "I'm part of a generation that is faced with evidence daily that the H-bomb may drop tomorrow."[18]

During the 1940s and '50s, the work of "civil defense" became a critical public responsibility. When President Truman organized the Federal Civil Defense Administration in 1951, it worked closely with the nation's schools as part of its preparedness campaign. The administration sent out films and printed materials, and provided some budget support. Most schools eagerly joined the civil defense effort, demonstrating their patriotism and affirming, in the age of McCarthyism, that there were no Communists in their schools. Clearly, there was a concern about alarming the students, but the rationale for this readiness program was that it would provide them with a sense of security, not anxiety. "Action, and plans for action, make for the release of tension and a greater feeling of safety." The focus on preparing children rather than frightening them often resulted in a "perverse cheeriness" concerning nuclear attack.[19]

Perhaps this ambivalent tone was nowhere more evident than in a film prepared by the Federal Civil Defense Administration. *Duck and Cover* was distributed to schools and other youth programs in 1951. The cartoon lead for the film was Bert the Turtle, who was quite adept at ducking and covering. The film showed children ducking under their school desks and covering their heads. A sober narrator reminded them that "we all know that an atomic bomb is very dangerous" so it was necessary to be ready instantly to respond to a threat or a blast — just as it was important to be ready to respond to a fire or to look both ways before crossing the street.

The narrator warned that an attack could come at any time. To illustrate this threat, the clip showed children immediately balling up on the ground and covering their heads on a playground and on a street when a bomb flash appeared. The children needed to respond quickly if there was a flash — the movie showed a young boy identified as Tony on a bike in his Cub Scout uniform heading for a meeting. Happily riding but always alert, "Tony knows a bomb may explode any time of the year, day or night." When the flash occurs, Tony swiftly jumps from his bike and ducks and covers at an abutment along the roadway. In another scene, a family ducks and covers when their happy picnic is interrupted by the sudden flash of a nuclear explosion. The theme song for the film was written by the ad agency that developed the successful "See the USA in your Chevrolet" music and campaign. In this civil defense campaign, children learned how to survive a nuclear attack on their own. They would be secure only if they remembered instantly to "Duck and Cover."[20]

The prestigious *Encyclopædia Britannica* also prepared a film in 1951 for distribution to schools, called simply *Atomic Alert*. In the introduction, the narrator points out that "the chance of your being hurt by an atomic bomb is slight, but since there is a chance, you *must* know how to protect yourself . . . We have the national defenses to intercept an enemy, and we all form a team to help each other through emergencies. *You* are on that team." The message was clear. One session with 311 children age ten to seventeen in the New York City region asked the students what the world would be like in ten years. And 70 percent of them agreed that there was a "fairly strong probability" that there would be a war.[21]

As the world moved to the post-Stalin era in the middle 1950s, there was some moderation in the fear of a nuclear attack. But the high-stakes competition with the Soviet Union did not abate. It flared dramatically again following the Soviet launch of Sputnik in 1957. Even as President Eisenhower cautioned that there was "no reason to grow hysterical," many did just that. And the focus was on the schools and the failure of American education to provide a strong — and competitive — grounding in science and mathematics. Americans, it was said, did not fail in space or in missile strategy; instead, they failed in school strategy.

In 1958, *Life* magazine published a series on the "Crisis in Education," focusing on underpaid teachers, even as they pointed out that "some are not worth what they get," and on the underlying postwar philosophy of education. The editors warned that schools had tried hard "to be all things to all children," resulting in too many electives and a focus on school lunch programs, which may make for healthier bodies, but with these priorities, "the minds shift for themselves." They insisted that "the nation's stupid children received far better care than the bright," with the result that "the geniuses of the next decade are even now being allowed to slip back into mediocrity." Not surprisingly, they concluded that the "standards of education are surprisingly low."[22]

Congress responded to the threat of Sputnik with a major focus on the nation's education system. The National Defense Education Act of 1958 provided federal support for public school science programs, established support for teacher training, and invested money in college science education. The legislation established graduate fellowships and federal undergraduate loans and also provided support for foreign language training. There were no precedents for these sweeping peacetime actions. And many supporters pointed out that there was no precedent for the perceived threats and challenges that led to the legislation.

By the late 1950s, there had been a clear shift from the fear of attack at home to the fear of communism securing an advantage in the world. The tone was less sharp, but the urgency may have been even greater. The United States was in a global competition with the Communist world, and one of the key components of our readiness would be the preparation of young Americans for this world and for the contest in which they must be ready to engage.

While the schools moved to more practical preparation for a world of conflict, the nation's religious leaders reminded everyone of the additional stakes in this contest. Literally, this was about the body *and* the soul of mankind. President Harry Truman defined the cold war as a "just" war and proclaimed that in stepping up to defend South Korea in 1950, the United States should "put on the armor of God." This was not simply a geopolitical conflict to Truman. Throughout the late 1940s, he had defined it as a fight with "Godless communism," which was marked by "the responsibility which I believe God intended this great Republic to assume." There was little political debate about the Manichaean terms of the contest. Dwight Eisenhower, not as traditionally religious as Truman, nonetheless at his inauguration spoke of the "lightness against the dark." He said that "the faith we hold belongs not just to us but to the free of all the world." Even Eisenhower's liberal Democratic opponent in the 1952 election, Adlai Stevenson, reminded

234

Americans that the Communists "seek to dethrone God from his central place in the Universe."[23]

Congress joined in this evangelical framing of the cold war. Edward Martin, a Republican congressman from Pennsylvania, affirmed the power of the Bible and the sword, with a modern twist. He insisted that "America should move forward with an atomic bomb in one hand and a cross in the other." In 1954, Congress passed legislation that added "one nation under God" to the Pledge of Allegiance. Senator Homer Ferguson said this action would underline one of the "real differences between the free world and the Communist world." When President Eisenhower signed the legislation on Flag Day, June 14, 1954, he said that now schoolchildren could daily affirm "the dedication of our Nation and our people to the Almighty."[24]

Postwar America was indeed a religious society. Church membership grew from 49 percent of the population in 1940 to 60 percent in 1960. Fundamental Protestantism flourished, though quietly, and the period saw a sharp growth in Catholic congregations and Catholic schools. Men of the cloth joined the political leaders in framing the eternal terms of this global conflict with communism. The Reverend Billy Graham, a young evangelical preacher, did his part as he established his own role in the country. In the fall of 1949 at the Los Angeles revival that established his reputation, Graham argued that "I believe today that the battle is between communism and Christianity! And I believe the only way that we're going to win that battle is for America to turn back to God and back to Christ and back to the Bible at this hour! We need a revival!"[25]

Absolutely no religious leader — and few secular ones — could get ahead of the omnipresent Francis Cardinal Spellman of New York in defining the cold war stakes. When Joseph Cardinal Mindszenty was imprisoned by Communists in Hungary in 1948, Spellman urged Americans to rally in "defense of the rights of God and man against Christ-hating communists whose allegiance is pledged to Satan." Many other religious leaders of all denominations joined him in outrage against the Communist action. For good measure, Spellman threatened to excommunicate any Catholics who belonged to the Communist Party — or who aided them. He reminded his flock that Catholics needed to "help save civilization from the world's most fiendish, ghoulish men of slaughter."[26]

Cardinal Spellman was a participant in the work of one of the most compelling figures in the anticommunist drama of the 1950s, the man who as much as anyone else focused the West's attention on Vietnam, Dr. Tom Dooley.

Vietnam became an arena for the cold war in the 1950s as the French withdrew from their colonial empire there and as the Soviets and the Chinese supported Ho Chi Minh. The arena took on greater symbolic and then substantive importance as the Geneva Conference of 1954 provided for a temporary division in Vietnam and allowed for a period in which Vietnamese could leave either North or South Vietnam and relocate in the other region. Many North Vietnamese Christians, largely Catholic, decided to emigrate. Their decision was encouraged by American CIA operatives in the North who warned them that they would not be safe in Ho Chi Minh's North. A leader in this was the legendary CIA Saigon operative Edward Lansdale, who arranged for messages to be delivered to Catholic churches in the North — including flyers that proclaimed "Christ has gone to the South."

Under the terms of the Geneva Accords, there was a transition period in 1955 when the U.S. Navy was permitted to join other ships at Haiphong Harbor in North Vietnam providing passage to Catholic emigrants. This migration became a major story in the United States, called "Passage to Freedom." *Look* magazine published a photo of Vietnamese kneeling in prayer on a navy ship, "Battered and shunted about by war, they are too weary to resist the reds without us."[27]

The American press picked up the story of the Vietnamese who voted with their feet. *Time* and *Newsweek* described this as a classic example of the conflict between democracy and communism. In March 1955, *Reader's Digest* published William Lederer's article "They'll Remember the *Bayfield*," an account of two thousand North Vietnamese exiles on the navy ship *Bayfield* being transported from Haiphong to Saigon. Most were Catholics, needing medical care, and they were depicted as extremely grateful to the Americans for saving them. An editor prefaced the article: "They sacrificed their homes and all their possessions for one precious thing: the right to worship in the religion of their choice."[28]

Cardinal Spellman met one group of Catholic refugees in Saigon and prayed with them in thanks for their deliverance. Perhaps as many as one million emigrants came to Saigon from the North following the 1954 Geneva agreements. Many were Catholics, and by 1956 the Catholic diocese of Saigon had more members than in Paris or Rome. Seth Jacobs wrote that the Catholic refugees, "starving, tortured, and devout," came to dominate the American image of Vietnam in the 1950s and to exercise "an inflexible claim on America's conscience." Vietnam into the Kennedy years was depicted by "maudlin and macabre refugee narratives of betrayal, suffering, and salvation in a country . . . that had become the testing ground of U.S. cold war credibility."[29]

The young U.S. Navy doctor Tom Dooley became a symbol for this drama — and indeed a central player in it and narrator for it. He worked in Haiphong and Hanoi, enabling Catholic refugees to leave. Always available for interviews, the personable young St. Louis native spoke eloquently about the need to save the Vietnamese from their impending tragedy. The navy started identifying him as a spokesman for their humanitarian efforts. He spoke to navy personnel about the importance of their work. And his description of their efforts evolved from a humanitarian mission to a battle between satanic communism and Catholicism, the latter increasingly a synonym for Christianity, freedom, and democracy. When the period for open emigration ended and Dooley finally had to leave Haiphong, he went to Saigon, where President Diem recognized him with the most distinguished medal he could award to a foreigner, Officier de l'Ordre National de Viet Nam.[30]

Dooley returned to the United States as a hero. *Reader's Digest* worked with him to publish a book on his experience. Released in 1956, *Deliver Us from Evil* was an immediate bestseller; there would be twenty printings of the book. *Reader's Digest* published it simul-

taneously in its condensed book format —
and it was "condensed" less than any book
since the series began in 1922. It was a book
filled with drama, suffering, and hope. Dooley
concluded it by saying of the Vietnamese, "I
had come to know their valiant hearts and
stout spirit. Somehow, over the bitter months,
without knowing how it happened, I had
identified myself with their dream of life in
freedom and their tragic destiny. They had
become my suffering brothers."[31]

Reviewers, critics, commentators, and editors all gushed about the book — and about
this American hero. *The New Yorker, The New
York Times, The Washington Post,* the *New
York Herald Tribune,* and the *San Francisco
Chronicle* were among the publications that
celebrated Dr. Dooley and his account. In
1956, a Gallup poll indicated he was seventh
on their list of ten most admired men. The
Junior Chamber of Commerce designated
him one of their Outstanding Men of 1956.
In that year, the navy quietly discharged him
for alleged "homosexual activity," an allegation that was kept confidential. He moved on
as a civilian doctor-humanitarian, often
compared with Albert Schweitzer. He was a
remarkable self-promoter, and many groups
and individuals supported his work and his
anticommunism, and endorsed his activities.
He returned to Laos late in 1956 to work

with refugees there, operating with a new organization, MEDICO, which the International Rescue Committee had established for his work.

Actually, Dooley was a charlatan — a complicated one, to be sure. There is little dispute that he worked incredibly hard to assist refugees in Vietnam and in Laos. Always available for an interview, his public accounts were stories of tremendous suffering relieved by his love and dedicated care, while many of his private comments on his work were filled with condescension and racism. He played heavily on the ideology of suffering, which found a ready audience in America. And he framed this ideology in its most satanic terms. In his U.S. tour promoting his book, he described chilling accounts of the refugees he had rescued: "What do you do for children who have had chopsticks driven into their ears? Or for old women whose collarbones have been shattered by rifle butts? Or for kids whose ears have been torn off with pincers? How do you treat a priest who has had nails driven into his skull to make a travesty of the Crown of Thorns." None of the people who served with him was ever able to authenticate any of these alarming stories that he claimed personally to have witnessed.[32]

While in Laos, Dr. Dooley developed cancer and he finally returned to the United States for treatment. Doctors were unable to stem the disease, and he died on January 18, 1961, the day after his thirty-fourth birthday. At the time he was the third most admired man in the world — trailing only the pope and President Eisenhower. Francis Cardinal Spellman was his last visitor in the hospital. The cardinal said, "I tried to assure him that in his 34 years he had done what few have done in the allotted Scriptural span." *The New York Times* eulogized him: "His spirit was like a flame in the dark jungle." And the paper echoed a secular variant of Cardinal Spellman's description: "He had so little time, but how superbly he used it!" The *Los Angeles Times* quoted President Eisenhower, "There are few, if any, men who have equaled his exhibition of courage, his self-sacrifice, faith in God, and his readiness to serve his fellow man." A few weeks later, the former president would join President John Kennedy as honorary cochairs of the Tom Dooley Tribute Fund for MEDICO.[33]

Given his prominence in the 1950s, it was striking how quickly Dooley's myth faded from public consciousness. Some of the young men who went to Vietnam to serve explicitly mentioned being inspired by him. But perhaps less tangibly, most of that generation had grown up influenced by the broader narrative of the American role in protecting the democratic values and religious

242

freedom of the people of Vietnam. Politicians who stressed this obligation often had a receptive audience.

In the early 1950s, in Indian Springs, Nevada, out near the nuclear weapons test site, a reporter overheard the conversation among four eight-year-old boys after they had seen a group of marines who had participated in combat test maneuvers during a nuclear detonation. One of the youngsters remarked, "I'm goin' into the Marines." Two of the boys quickly said, "Me, too." But the fourth boy dissented, saying, "Not me." He announced that he was going to be a rodeo rider. "Aw, you mean you're not goin' to fight for your country?" the first boy asked "disgustedly."[34]

A decade later, Scholastic, a major publisher of books and magazines for schools, published a booklet called *What You Should Know About COMMUNISM and Why*. It described for schoolchildren the tyrannical operation of the Communist form of government and warned of the deprivation experienced by anyone who lived under such a system. It said, "Some of you may have a brother or a cousin in the Armed Forces. Most boys probably will spend a part of their lives in the Armed Forces. That, too, is part of the cost of defending our nation against communism." That price was high, "but we would have to pay a much higher price if freedom were to lose its struggle against communism."[35]

Many baby boomers grew up in a world in which they were regularly reminded of the threat the nation faced *and* of their likely obligation to serve in the military to stand up to that threat. In 1965, the Department of Defense released the film *Why Vietnam?* The production used as its narrative background President Johnson's speech of July 28, 1965, in which he announced a sharp increase in the U.S. military deployed to Vietnam. Framed as a response to the mother of a soldier in Vietnam, LBJ laid out the challenge with footage of committed and suffering Vietnamese. And he pointed out that in order to meet the manpower goals, the nation would expand the draft numbers rather than call up Reserves or National Guard forces.[36]

Many top military leaders, including Secretary of Defense Robert McNamara, were not eager to fight a war largely with draftees. They wanted to call up National Guard and Reserve units, but President Johnson recalled the political firestorm that followed the deployment of these troops early in the Korean War. President Eisenhower warned him that "sending conscripted troops to Vietnam would cause a major public relations problem." But Johnson thought that would be the lesser problem and was hopeful that the war could be ended before the political pushback began. He miscalculated, at least on the latter point.[37]

Under the Universal Military Training and Service Act of 1951, which needed to be renewed by act of Congress every four years, all men had to register for the draft at age eighteen. They were eligible to be drafted at eighteen and a half until age twenty-six. There were provisions for deferments, largely educational, but anyone who exercised one of these options could have his draft eligibility extended beyond age twenty-six for the number of years deferred. Local draft boards had great discretion in allowing deferments and other exemptions, but they had to be within the general guidelines of the legislation and of the national Selective Service office, headed by Lieutenant General Lewis Hershey, who had been in charge of this agency since World War II.

There was little controversy surrounding the draft in 1965. Congress had renewed it in 1963 with little debate. President Kennedy had extended deferments to married men, which made draft calls even less controversial. In 1965, a survey found that 61 percent of junior and senior high school students thought the system was fair. Part of this image had to do with the limited numbers of young men being drafted. From 1955 to 1964, about 100,000 men a year were drafted — out of a nineteen to twenty-five-aged population of approximately 8 million males in 1958 and 12 million in 1964.

The influence of the draft extended beyond the actual numbers called up. Many potential draftees decided to enlist instead of waiting for the draft. Some estimates of the pre-Vietnam period were that more than 40 percent of enlistments were draft motivated. These choices were based on personal planning and calculation — and of course the increasing engagement of American forces in combat in Vietnam added a major complication to the calculation. The draft-motivated enlistments increased as more young men chose the navy, the air force, or the marines rather than waiting to be drafted into the army. The first two service branches provided more potential schooling or training options — and less likelihood of combat. But they required a four-year commitment. The marines actually provided a greater likelihood of combat service, and some young men enlisted because of this. Others simply liked the fact that the Marine Corps offered a three-year enlistment choice and even a two-year option in some cases. Army draft calls were for two years, while army enlistment involved a three-year obligation.

In 1964, some 16,835,000 men were in the eighteen-and-a-half-to-twenty-six age cohort. Of these, 2.3 million were veterans and 2.8 million were currently in uniform. There were

2 million already classified 1-A, ready for induction; 4.9 million had education, employment, or other deferments; and 4.1 million were physically or mentally disqualified. One problem with the system was that the initial classification of 1-A was done by local draft boards. About 50 percent of men the local board considered 1-A failed to meet induction standards. So the pool of draft-ready men was not necessarily as large as it appeared.[38]

In August 1965, President Johnson rescinded Kennedy's order placing married men at the bottom of the draft pool, which had effectively exempted them. By early 1966, the Selective Service System took steps to reaffirm the provision that those who had received a deferment could be eligible for the draft after age twenty-six. They also looked at the I-Y group — those who had conditions or test scores that temporarily made them ineligible for the draft. The military did not particularly want either married men or I-Ys, but the numbers had to be met.

The Johnson administration and Selective Service were not willing to eliminate the deferment for college students. This meant that they needed to look elsewhere to be certain the pool of draft-eligible men was adequate to meet growing needs. They decided to go after the I-Y group, essentially overlooking some minor medical issues and, most important, lowering the qualification level on the mental test. The latter had been a major obstacle for young Americans with little education, essentially from the poorest backgrounds. Given the inequity of segregated schools and medical care opportunities, this category included a disproportionate number of African Americans, especially from the rural South.

Georgia senator Richard Russell, the powerful chair of the Armed Services Committee, opposed lowering this bar — partially out of a fear of a military that would be disproportionately African American. Johnson's conversation with Secretary McNamara on this is revealing of the president's attitude — and his cynicism. He would placate Russell by assuring him that this would result in getting some of the young poor blacks out of his hometown of Winder, Georgia.

Looks to me like what it would do for Russell is move all these Nigra boys that are now rejects and sent back on his community, to move them [into the army], clean them up, prepare them to do something, and send them into Detroit . . . You have to tell him . . . "We'll take this Nigra boy in from Johnson City, Texas, and from Winder, Georgia, and we'll get rid of the tapeworms and get the ticks off of him, and teach him to get up at daylight and work till dark and shave and to bathe . . . We'll put some weight on him and keep him out of a charity hospital . . . and keep him from eating off the old man's relief check. And when we turn him out, we'll have him prepared at least to drive a truck or bakery wagon or stand at a gate . . . And he's not going to want to go back to Winder after he's had this taste of life.[39]

Secretary McNamara maintained that the army did not want to be running a rehabilitation program. Johnson insisted that they go ahead with the program, called Project 100,000. They did.

A RAND study several years later assessed how this program had worked. It discovered that 38 percent of those inducted under the 100,000 program were nonwhite, while only 10 percent of the control group of inductees were. Forty-eight percent of the Project 100,000 men were from the South compared to 28 percent of the control group. And their median scores on the Armed Forces Qualification Test were 13.6, compared to control group scores of 56.8. The Project 100,000 inductee read at the 6.4 grade level, compared to the 10.9 level of the control group. And as for their learning new skills, as the president predicted, in fact 37 percent of the Project 100,000 group served in army combat units while 23 percent of the control group did. The RAND study noted that as soldiers, these men did not do as well as men with higher test scores, but they were satisfactory servicemen.[40]

One comprehensive analysis looked at the "Vietnam Generation" — those who were eligible for the draft sometime during the war. There were 26,800,000 men in that group. Of these, 8,720,000 enlisted in the armed services, 2,215,000 were drafted, and 15,980,000 never served. So roughly 40 percent served in the military. Of those who didn't serve, 15,410,000 were deferred, exempted, or disqualified, and 570,000 were classified as "apparent" draft evaders.[41]

Young Americans from all income levels, educational levels, and parts of the country served during the Vietnam War. And this same cross section served in Vietnam — and sacrificed there. But there is little doubt that those serving in Vietnam, particularly enlisted men in combat units, were disproportionately from the poorer strata of American society. A major contributor to this circumstance was the college deferment. Even as higher education was becoming more available to all classes of Americans in the 1960s, this student population remained solidly middle and upper class in the decade. In 1965–1966, only 2 percent of inductees into the army were college graduates. Those with a high school education or less were 85 percent of the total. This was the pattern despite the fact that 40 percent of the college-age group was going to college. In that same year, 16 percent of the men entering the Reserves were college graduates. Reserve or National Guard service basically provided a pass on Vietnam duty with the exception of a few units that were deployed later in the war.[42]

One draftee and Vietnam veteran wrote, "Like many baby boomers, I'd figured that what separated us as soldiers — later veterans — from reservist and protestors and MIAs and deserters and POWs and draft avoiders came down to luck, fate and timing — who you knew, where you lived, when you graduated from high school, how you were raised, how many WW II movies you saw, when you turned 18 . . ." His number came up after graduating from college and losing his deferment.[43] If there was a randomness to it all, it was not an equitable randomness. And this soldier, a college graduate, served in the rear areas in Vietnam.

A Notre Dame study completed at the end of the war is revealing:[44]

LIKELIHOOD OF VIETNAM-ERA SERVICE		
Military service (%)	Vietnam service (%)	Combat service (%)
Low income 40	19	15
Middle income 30	12	7
High income 24	9	7
High school dropouts 42	18	14
High school graduates 45	21	17
College graduates 23	12	9

In 1967, there was a serious effort to remedy what many believed to be the inequity of the draft. President Johnson set up a special presidential commission to look at this issue in preparation for the required congressional action to continue the draft that year. Chaired by Burke Marshall, the former head of the Civil Rights Division in the Justice Department, it was a distinguished group that included Yale president Kingman Brewster; Thomas Gates, head of Morgan Guaranty Trust; Oveta Culp Hobby, editor and chair of the *Houston Post* (she had commanded the Women's Army Corps during World War II and had been the first secretary of the new cabinet-level Department of Health, Education and Welfare under President Eisenhower); Paul Jennings, president of the International Union of Electrical, Radio and Machine Workers; Vernon Jordan of the Voter Education Project; and David Shoup, retired Marine Corps general.

The commission set out to find the means

to provide the manpower required by the military and to do this in a way that was as "consistent as possible with human dignity, individual liberty, fairness to all citizens, and the other principles and traditions of a democratic and free society." Population growth was outstripping military manpower needs. Even with the demands of mobilization for the Vietnam War, the military needed only between one-third and one-half of the two million men who reached draft age every year. Since a substantial part of these requirements were met by voluntary enlistments, only from 10 to 40 percent of the military force needed to be raised by the draft. So the commission recommended a major reorganization of the system. They proposed a centralized national office that could issue "clear and binding policies" on all deferments and exemptions. There should be a reduction in the number and the authority of local draft boards, and women should be eligible to serve on these boards. And the commission urged fixed terms for the members of local boards and suggested that they become more representative of the population. The commission members were particularly troubled by black underrepresentation.

As for the operation of the draft, the commission proposed that the present system of "oldest first" be reversed so that the youngest men, beginning at age nineteen, would be the first call-ups. Even more important, the group recommended that "no further student or occupational deferments should be granted." The exceptions were that those who were currently enrolled be allowed to complete their programs and that students enrolling in ROTC programs be allowed to remain in school. From this now larger eligible pool, they should be inducted in an order "impartially and randomly determined" — a lottery-type system. The commission proposed that enlistment in the Reserves and the National Guard not provide immunity from the draft except in certain restricted circumstances. It also recommended that the military make more service opportunities available for women so that they could meet noncombat needs, and the number of men involuntarily inducted could be reduced further.[45]

This report was an imaginative and comprehensive reform document that would have significantly altered the draft. There seemed little doubt that implementing these recommendations would remove nearly all perceived inequities from the system. But the plan was doomed from the start. Local draft boards fumed about losing control to a centralized agency, as did their many congressional supporters (Senator Richard Russell said of this plan, "I shudder to think of it."). Future college and university students and their parents were alarmed about losing the deferment status. General Hershey pushed back against any modification during the war — he was particularly opposed to the lottery-type selection replacing local draft board discretion, although he later reversed that position.

Lyndon Johnson was supportive of the proposed changes — but then backed away in the face of opposition. And in May 1967, Congress basically ignored the commission's recommendations and renewed the existing selective service system — with the additional restriction that forbade the president from implementing any sort of lottery process. The vote in the Senate was 70 to 2, with Wayne Morse and Ernest Gruening, the 1964 opponents of the Tonkin Gulf Resolution, voting no. In the House, the vote was 362 to 9.[46]

In many ways, the most notable aspect of service in the Vietnam War was the significant number of members of this generation who served. Interviews with individuals who enlisted or were drafted, study of accounts written by them, and a review of the broad scholarly sources that have looked at this process all affirm that they did sign up or answer the call. The reasons varied, to be sure. In his comprehensive study of the war, Christian Appy summarized it this way: "Some men were drafted. Some volunteered. Some went burning for battle. Others entered with great reluctance, feeling dragged down by pressures both obvious and obscure. Some were torn by conflicting emotions, feeling at one moment like a dove, at other times like a hawk. Most entered the military with little reflection, however, believing it a natural and unavoidable part of life."[47]

Of course, each person who enlisted or responded to the draft call had his own deeply personal reasons. But there were patterns that spoke to the roots of this generation of young men. Tim O'Brien grew up in a small town on the Minnesota prairie. Both his mother and his father served in World War II. He received a draft notice just after graduating from Macalester College. He did not agree with the war and did not want to serve. But . . . he wondered if he was right in rejecting his responsibility. "Piled on top of this was the town, my family, my teachers, a whole history of the prairie." He believed he owed them all something. And so he answered the call and was inducted into the army.[48]

Out in the old mining town of Morenci, Arizona, nine young men enlisted in the marines in the summer of 1966. Most of them had just graduated from the local high school. They were tough kids, the sons of miners and millworkers, and their fathers and most of their relatives had served in World War II. The group included three Mexican Americans, two Mormons, a Native American, two local rural kids ("cowboys"), and Stan King, the son of a smelter worker, who had enrolled two years earlier in the University of Arizona. He was not entirely sure he belonged there and was worried about the financial pressure on his parents. He came home and enlisted with the Morenci Marines. These nine men joined the marines because they preferred to be part of a group that wanted to serve rather than with draftees. And they liked the tough image of the Marine Corps.[49]

One of the Morenci Marines said, "We were small-town people, we still believed in mom and apple pie. It was part of my duty as a man, growing up, to join the service. They didn't have to draft us. It was part of what we were supposed to do." As their biographer, Kyle Longley, described it, "One Morenci Vietnam veteran remembered listening to World War II veterans swapping stories about their experiences in the good war at the barbershop." The enlistees spoke of veterans being honored at football games. "This simple ritual exemplified the high visibility that veterans retained in the community, no matter what their social or economic position."[50]

The generational influence was powerful. Dan Shaw, from Dorchester, Massachusetts, put it this way: "I thought I was doing the right thing. I mean, my grandfather went in

1917, my father went in 1942. It was my turn." Bobby Muller joined the marines after graduating from Hofstra in 1968: "You felt an obligation, at least I felt an obligation. When my generation was called, you needed to respond, and you didn't ask why." Herbert Sweat, an African American from Bedford-Stuyvesant in Brooklyn, joined the army shortly after high school graduation: "Military service was simply understood as a rite of passage for young males in his family. His father, his uncles, his cousins, and his brothers all had military service in their backgrounds. They had been in World War II and Korea and deployed to the Dominican Republic. He felt that if he was to earn his lineage, he would have to be part of that tradition."[51]

This was the heritage the baby boomers always confronted. Gary Bray grew up in eastern Oklahoma, where "the men who had served in the military during the war years were regarded as heroes." His uncle had received a Purple Heart at Normandy. When Gary had some questions about what to do with his life, "The army was the only choice that made sense to me."[52] John Nesser went to college in his home state of Wisconsin and in the 1960s developed some real reservations about the war. But he had grown up in a small town, and his Catholic teachings stressed the threat of communism. He learned "duck and cover" and teachers talked about the saintly Tom Dooley. When he was drafted after college graduation in 1968, Nesser went into the army. "My conservative upbringing had instilled in me a strong sense of duty to my country, and I would never have risked the disapproval of my family, especially my dad, who was my model and hero."[53]

Jose Cantu grew up in San Antonio. He said, "I always knew from the start, you know, even when I was a little boy, that I was going to be a marine." His father had fought with the marines in the Pacific during World War II.[54] Another Vietnam marine, Steve Landa, put it this way: "I'm a product of parents from the World War II generation. Okay, it is my duty to serve. Once I knew I was going, I was scared to death but thinking, 'Well, this is what I've got to do.' "[55]

Rick Rajner grew up in Toledo and was influenced by his parochial schools where President Kennedy's picture was displayed. He remembered Kennedy's call to pick up the torch, and he "believed that communism was the enemy of my nation and my faith." His father and all of his uncles served in World War II. The idea of "military obligation" was strong in his home and in his community.[56]

Ron Kovic grew up in the 1950s and was influenced by John Kennedy's inauguration challenge to Americans. His father had served in the navy during World War II. Shortly after Ron graduated from high school in 1964, he joined the marines. He was inspired by what he knew of their heritage, and the night before he left Levittown, New York, to head to Parris Island, he watched television until the station stopped transmitting for the night. They closed with "The Star-Spangled Banner," and Kovic recalled standing and "feeling very patriotic, chills running up and down my spine. I put my hand over my heart and stood right at attention until the screen went blank." Ron Kovic would go to Vietnam in 1965 and later would volunteer for a second tour there. On that second deployment he was seriously injured.[57]

Billy Cizinski grew up in South Boston, the son of European parents — his mother was from Germany and his father from Poland. As a kid, he hated communism, and pledged allegiance to the flag of the United States, and played war games. And then President Kennedy at his inaugural said, "Ask not what your country can do for you." Billy said, "I hated the Reds. I wanted to fight those nasty bastards." He lied about his age and joined the marines at age fifteen in 1965. He was in Vietnam and fought in a firefight at age sixteen and a half in 1967.[58]

Charley Trujillo grew up in the San Joaquin Valley in California. His parents were agricultural workers as was he. Facing the draft, he volunteered. As a young Mexican American, he recalled that this was "part of trying to be an American and patriotic and the whole romantic notion of war. When we got to Vietnam, we wanted to prove that we really were Americans." He served as an NCO in a combat platoon and lost an eye in an ambush. Harlan Pinkerton, from Sand Springs, Oklahoma, grew up in a community that encouraged patriotism: "I was patriotic before patriotism was cool." He joined the air force and flew F-4 missions over South Vietnam out of Cam Ranh Bay. He said that serving in the military "was my responsibility as an American citizen."[59] Wayne Smith grew up in Providence, Rhode Island, and enlisted in the army, but as an African American he knew some members of his community were influenced by Dr. Martin Luther King Jr.'s opposition to the war: "I thought we were going to help free the Vietnamese from Communist aggression. I volunteered. I believed in it. My family was *proud* of me."[60]

Charles Hagel was twenty years old when the Platte County, Nebraska, draft board told him that if he did not re-enroll in college, he was liable to be drafted. He volunteered for the draft and was inducted in 1967. His father had died a few years earlier and Hagel remembered him as a World War II veteran of the South Pacific. His dad and his uncles and their friends were all veterans. Hagel determined that he should follow their lead and accept this responsibility. Later at Fort Dix he stunned other recruits when he asked for his assignment to Germany to be changed to Vietnam. He recalled, "There was a war going on. The right thing, if I was in the army, was to go where the war was." A chaplain at his post counseled him on this decision but Hagel persisted. In an unusual situation, Chuck Hagel's younger brother Tom, who enlisted right after high school, was assigned to the same squad as his brother in Vietnam. On two occasions they were wounded together.[61]

Some families, of course, were uncomfortable with the idea of wartime military service. W. D. "Bill" Ehrhart grew up in Perkasie, Pennsylvania. Every school day began with the Lord's Prayer and the Pledge of Allegiance. His school had atomic bomb drills, "where we would have to sit in rows in the halls, facing the wall and curling up with our heads between our knees and our hands clasped behind our necks." One Memorial Day, he decorated his bike and rode in the parade. The American Legion post fired the twenty-one-gun salute and someone played "Taps." He had nightmares about Sputnik. He and a friend once sneaked into the bedroom of the friend's father to see his Silver Star from World War II. The kids played war — fighting the Japanese, the Germans, or the Communists. In college, he wrote a paper in a journalism class about the protests against Americans being in Vietnam. He pointed out that there was no freedom there and there needed to be. He replied to those who believed Americans "are dying for no good reason" by asking, "What more noble a cause can a man die for, than to die in defense of freedom?" He decided to enlist. And there was "never any doubt" that he would be a marine. He loved their reputation and tradition and their dress blue uniforms. His parents protested the idea — and they had to sign for him since he was seventeen. He said to them, "Is this how you raised me? To let somebody else's kids fight America's wars?" He remembered, "That ended the discussion."[62]

William "Bro" Adams grew up in Birmingham, Michigan. After his father's death, he struggled in college and decided to leave school and join the army. His mother was not happy, but he was inspired by President Kennedy and by Tom Dooley's story to try to make a difference.[63] David Lovelace had finished seminary and was a minister in the United Methodist Church. This position secured him an exemption from military service, but he was bothered by the fact that he was not serving. His wife finally said to him, "If this is what you feel like God wants you to do, quit talking about it and do it." He enlisted at age twenty-nine and served as an army chaplain in Vietnam.[64]

Bill Jevne grew up in a suburb of Minneapolis. He was a college student but was "more than thinking about it [the military]. I think I was assuming that with the draft and everything, I would at some time be going into the military . . . In one way or another, I think all of us, even if we weren't that aware of it, were in a position where we were going to have to decide how we were going to fit that situation into our lives . . . It was patriotism, but it was also wanting the adventure, wanting to test myself, wanting to lead. I think part of it was a drive toward heroism — growing up hearing about World War II and seeing documentaries on TV and everything. I think another thing too — I had a very idealistic view about South Vietnam as being a country ripe for democracy and our job was to make it safe for democracy . . . There was also a lot of talk about 'hearts and minds' — winning the hearts and minds of the people."[65]

Jack McLean was preparing for high school graduation from Andover in 1966 when he surprised everyone by enlisting in the marines. "The prospect of war provided brief flashes of tingling excitement. I was, after all, an eighteen-year-old boy. My whole young life had been filled with endless television shows and movies of cowboys killing Indians, and Americans killing Germans and Japanese. Now it was my turn."[66]

Dick Harris grew up in New Jersey and then his family moved to Pennsylvania. He recalls the "duck and cover" films, but they didn't bother him very much. He was prepared to serve in the military. His father had been in World War II, and he thought, "that's what men did when they grew up." Many young men in his community joined — not necessarily to fight communism but just to take their turn in serving. He did too, as an ROTC graduate.[67]

Jim Sheppard, from Haddonfield, New Jersey, was touched by Kennedy's inspiring inaugural remarks and wanted to help the South Vietnamese remain free and democratic. "My generation was born from the boomerang passion of a world war that was very 'black and white' . . . and supported by all." For his generation, "military service was a proud and eagerly anticipated part of a man's 'rite of passage.' "[68] Frank Grieco, of Clifton, New Jersey, was drafted. His dad had served and "had been badly wounded in World War II." So "there was no way I could say no when they drafted me . . . Back then it was like, you know, what are you going to do? You go."[69]

Tim O'Brien's Iowa boy, Paul Berlin, decided he would serve when he received his draft notice. "He went to the war because it was expected. Because not to go was to risk censure, and to bring embarrassment on his father and his town." Berlin admitted that, "Oh, he would rather have fought with his father in France, knowing certain things certainly, but he couldn't choose his war, nobody could."[70]

Don Sullivan, the Massachusetts soldier who was a platoon leader on Hamburger Hill, remembered Kennedy's words, but he believes his own decision to serve was influenced more by the inspiring story of Tom Dooley than by Kennedy's challenge.[71] Kennedy influenced David Ferriero, who grew up in Beverly, Massachusetts. He watched the growing protests and understood the critics of the war, but "there was still this sense of duty, sense of responsibility for defending your country. That was part of just how I was brought up."[72] Another Massachusetts boy, Mike Wholley, grew up in Methuen, the son of a truck driver. He was admitted to Harvard and joined NROTC there. In his Catholic school, there were air raid drills where the students jumped under their desks and covered up. In the yearbook of his all-boys high school, nearly all the students said their "Future Plans" were either going to "go to college and then go into the military," or else they planned to "go in the military and then continue [their] education." He believed his

Catholic education "focused me on . . . that you need to give back somehow." And he wanted to be a marine and a pilot. He would be.[73] Jack Croall from Quincy, Massachusetts, enlisted in the marines. "We wanted to go over there and we wanted to fight . . . Stop Communism? Too many World War II movies? I don't really know."[74]

In 1966, the Army Green Beret medic staff sergeant Barry Sadler, along with Robin Moore, wrote "The Ballad of the Green Berets." The music follows a military cadence and the lyrics proudly salute the "fearless men who jump and die." These were "America's best." It was the number one song in 1966, ranking ahead of any of the Beatles' or other pop group songs. While most descriptions of the 1960s feature the antiwar young people, this generation was more complicated than that. "The popularity of Sadler's song reminds us that the Vietnam generation may have been one of the most patriotic ever raised. And millions of young men who would eventually turn against the Vietnam War grew up enchanted by military culture."[75] The John Wayne movie *The Green Berets,* based on Robin Moore's book and released in 1968, had commercial success. But even though the drama and action made for an entertaining movie, it was clear by then that many Americans were shifting away from these traditional John Wayne narratives.

Of the men I interviewed, 86 discussed their thoughts about serving in the Vietnam War. Of this group, 56 enlisted and 30 were drafted. And most draftees recalled being willing, if not eager, to serve. Of the entire pool, 59 mentioned some variant of duty, patriotism, fighting communism, or family tradition as an explanation of their willingness to serve. Forty-eight also mentioned personal reasons, which ranged from very practical questions of timing, of the possibility of service leading to some self-improvement, to simply a sense of curiosity or adventure — or a fatalistic concession to inevitability.[76]

David Balazs grew up in the steel town of Ellwood City, Pennsylvania. His father was a steelworker and a high school dropout. Dave was a good student who graduated from college. Then he got a draft notice. When he called his father to tell him, his dad said, "Well, you got a college education — don't waste it. Don't let the army get you. Join the air force or the navy — they got the best deal. Be an officer, you can make more money and you don't have to take orders from as many people." Balazs subsequently told his dad that he had joined the marines. Mr. Balazs replied, "Well, Jesus Christ, I just assumed you had better sense than that." Balazs knew that joining the marines would mean combat service in Vietnam: "I didn't have a death wish. I wasn't that gung-ho, but I was curious. I wanted to see what it was like in the combat zone and Vietnam. I had never done any travel out of the country — I was looking at it like some kind of adventure. And a challenge."[77]

Danny Friedman grew up in Sheepshead Bay, Brooklyn, and went to Hebrew school. He attended Kingsborough Community College but dropped out after three semesters. He realized this would make him eligible for the draft, and he tried to join the National Guard or the air force, but they had long waiting lists. Then he received his draft notice. "I really didn't care. Though I wasn't prepared to enlist, I didn't lose any sleep when I got a draft notice, either. I bought the political philosophy that we were going to have to fight in Vietnam to keep them from fighting on the beaches of California and save the world from Communism. I didn't know a lot about it back in those days, but I bought the line; I bought the political story."[78]

Chris Burns had had deferments for school, but after he graduated he knew the draft was coming. An older friend told him, "Don't run away from it." He assured him it would be a "life-changing experience." Burns respected his friend and enlisted."[79] Lonnie Greckel grew up on a Nebraska farm and, very practically, he said that he knew "I was going to be drafted so I signed up to be drafted a little early."[80] When Steve Hayes, from Wilmington, Delaware, faced the draft, he decided to join the navy. Then he volunteered for Swift Boat duty on Vietnam's waterways, "not for any particularly patriotic reasons, but I thought I'd follow my buddy and have some adventure and get a month's home leave and that sort of thing."[81] Pat Sajak grew up in a Polish neighborhood in Chicago and enlisted "to take charge of my own life and go ahead and join rather than sit around and wait for them to ask me."[82]

Mike Zimmer was living in California when he decided to enlist in the army, and he did this with an understanding that he was going to go into the "medical field." The recruiter had encouraged him to think about X-ray technician school, which Zimmer found attractive. Only later did he realize that he was going to combat-medic training — and then almost inevitably to Vietnam. But, he said, "I was okay with it."[83] Larry Cox, from Mason, Ohio, was nearly twenty-six when he received a draft notice. He thought he was too old to be drafted until he went down to the draft board and learned they were taking him: "I laughed all the way down there and cried all the way back."[84] Obie Holmen was from a small Minnesota town. In college he realized that he wasn't performing as well as he could, so he dropped out to "try to get my act together" and was drafted. He didn't particularly want to serve or to go to Vietnam, but "that was the price I was willing to pay in order to grow up a little bit."[85]

Mark Weston was living in Puerto Rico, where his father was working. He experienced parental pressure different from that of many young men of the period who served in the military. When Mark considered joining the army, his dad said, "That's not our war. It's for somebody else to go fight." But Mark went ahead and enlisted because he was curious. He didn't "understand the politics of it or why people were protesting and wanted to find out what it was all about."[86] Alexander Carver, from Fort Lauderdale, Florida, was commissioned in the army in the summer of 1968. He had mixed emotions: "I was obviously scared to death" but "also felt pretty competent." His parents were of the World War II generation, and "I recognized there's a certain adventure aspect to it, so as afraid as I was, I realized it was probably the greatest adventure I was going to have in my life."[87]

Tom Martin had graduated from college and was teaching school in 1968 when he got his draft notice. He admitted that he still didn't know "what the heck we were doing there" and decided to find out. "So if you are going, let's go now, let's get it over with. It can't be that bad."[88] Mark Baker interviewed a veteran who got his draft notice at the end of the summer of 1968, shortly after he graduated from college. "I went into a state of total panic for days. What the fuck am I going to do?" He looked into options with the navy, air force, and coast guard, but there were none. He was antiwar. He understood that he could pursue some exemption or deferment opportunities to avoid the draft. He even considered filing as a conscientious objector but did not because he really wasn't. "Even in the midst of the terror after the induction notice came, there was a part of me that would lie in bed at night and fantasize about what it would be like if I went." He admitted, "There was something seductive about it, too. I was seduced by World War II and John Wayne movies. When I was in high school, I dreamed of going to Annapolis." He enlisted in the army.[89]

Mac Campbell grew up in Pensacola, Florida, which was a major training base for navy and marine pilots. As a kid, he saw the young pilots driving around in "their brand-new '57 Chevys and convertibles." After graduating from Florida State, he enlisted in the marines with a commitment to become a pilot. He did. And he said he wanted to go to Vietnam. He did that too. Gary Bain also wanted to be a pilot: "By the time I was ten or eleven years old, the only thing I wanted to do in life was be a Marine Corps pilot. I had seen those Blue Angels and other things like that and it just — something happened inside me and that's what I was going to do." Bain served as an enlisted marine and for six years he studied and took tests until he finally qualified for flight school.[90]

Growing up, Kent Hughes had been fascinated by stories of World War II, and as a student at Princeton he had checked with the various ROTC units and others to see about joining. When he spoke to a marine gunnery sergeant who told him, "Buddy, if you want to go to Vietnam, you're talking to the right people," Hughes joined. In fact, in Basic School in early 1968, he and others feared that following Tet, the war would be over before they got to Vietnam. The politics didn't motivate him as much as "the adventure of it all." He would get to Vietnam, as would nearly all of his basic class. About 10 percent of them died there.[91]

John Flanagan was born in 1946 in Brooklyn. "Of course, growing up Catholic, every morning we said the Pledge of Allegiance and prayers; I mean that's just the way it is. You waved flags, you went to parades, you were proud to see your uncles marching in the Veterans Day Parade," and "patriotism is there." He thought he'd probably become a cop. So when he graduated from high school, he knew he faced the draft. After looking at some options, he decided to volunteer: "This way I knew I was going to go soon, but that

273

it would be only for 2 years."[92]

Needless to say, many of the men who served in Vietnam did not want to go there. But a sense of guilt, or pride, or obligation, or family and community concerns won out. Or just a sense that no available options seemed better than going. After Peter Barber graduated from college, he lost his student deferment and then the draft board summoned him. He thought the war "sucked" and he really "wasn't gung-ho." Nevertheless, he decided, "Well, I'm called." So he went.[93]

Robert Ptachik grew up in a middle-class Jewish family in Brooklyn. He was admitted to Brooklyn College in 1963, but he wasn't ready for college. He didn't like it, didn't do well, and dropped out early in his junior year. He thought it was no big deal. Now with no student deferment, he was drafted in August 1966. Even though he was not eager to go, avoiding the draft by running away was not a possibility for him. "I just assumed that if you're asked, you go. Maybe it was my upbringing; I was too sheltered, or it was just not something that I — I even considered. You know, I would just as likely [have] said, 'Well, I'll go to the moon' than go to Canada. I didn't see any other options."[94] So he went into the army and to Vietnam.

Rod Paladino and Tommy Blevins were teammates on their high school wrestling team in Middletown, New Jersey. They went off to separate colleges, and in their second years each decided that it was time to do something else. They joined the marines in 1967. They recognized this would mean a tour in Vietnam, and they were ready to see what that was like. Tommy, a popular, accomplished young man said, "Yeah, I know we'll be going to Vietnam, but I don't want to die there." He did die there, on Memorial Day 1969.[95]

John Chatterton lived in Garden City, New Jersey. In high school in the middle '60s, he thought about the war and was influenced by classmates who were antiwar. Nonetheless, he thought he would volunteer because he was curious to know more about the world and about himself. His father wanted him to go to Yale, and they had a bitter argument. John "asked himself if he could kill a person or fight for a cause he might come to despise. Again, he had no good answer. Then he had an epiphany: he could volunteer as a medic. No matter how ugly things got, as a medic he could help people instead of killing people. He could stay positive and still have a first-person experience with the most important questions in the world." John joined the army and became a medic in Vietnam.[96]

The draft was for men only — and most of the enlistees were men. But a number of women joined the military seeking to do their part. Many of them had a few other options.

Debby Alexander grew up in Stockton, California, and when she graduated from San Francisco State, she described it as a "hotbed" of antiwar activity. The military and other Defense Department recruiters could not come on campus, so she went to see the latter off campus at the federal building and applied for a job with overseas assignment. The earlier requirements of a minimum age of twenty-three with two years of work experience had been dropped, so she was able to join the Special Services branch and within a few weeks was on her way to Vietnam, without any training or experience. They were glad to have her.[97]

Most of the baby boomers did not put on a uniform in the period of the war, and even fewer were deployed in Vietnam. But it nonetheless became an indelible marker for their generation. If only 40 percent of the men who were age eligible for the draft during the war actually served in the armed forces, the primary reason for the other 60 percent not serving was that the lower figure was the number the military needed. But there were reasons why certain categories were screened out. For example, of the 15.4 million who did not serve, more than a third, 6.6 million, were not qualified due to age or, after 1970, their lottery number. This left approximately 8.8 million young men, a number roughly equivalent to the number who served, who were exempted or deferred. Most of these, 5.3 million, were exempted due to physical, mental, psychological, or "moral" reasons. An additional group of 3.5 million had occupational or educational deferments or, the majority, "hardship" deferments — including fatherhood.[98]

Obviously, many eligible men found ways to avoid or to defer and delay service until they were no longer likely to be drafted. But it was more complicated than this. Most college students, at least prior to 1968 or 1969, were in college because they wanted to attend college — military deferments may have influenced the timing and the nature of their decisions, but they seldom drove them. There is some evidence that in 1966 and 1967, graduate school applications increased because enrollment in these programs provided a student deferment. When this option ended in the 1968 school year, there was an increase in college-educated draftees.[99]

Many young men of the 1960s failed the mental and/or medical tests that were a necessary condition of service. Some may have manipulated these screenings. There is ample evidence that young men from higher socioeconomic backgrounds, for example, could get a doctor's letter that identified a medical condition that in the early years would be sufficient to disqualify them for service. Lower-income inductees who depended upon the medical assessments at the induction centers were far less likely to be ruled medically ineligible. Nonetheless, most who failed the tests had genuine physical or intellectual shortcomings.

Even as opposition to the war and the draft increased, overt draft resistance was not as common as it often seemed. It was not criminal to chant "Hell no! We won't go!" But it was criminal to refuse to accept a draft notice. As one draftee said, "It was either go to Canada, go to prison, or go in the army. What choice did I have?"[100] One study of the national draft resistance movement found 210,000 accused draft evaders. Of these, 25,000 were indicted and 8,750 of them were convicted. Four thousand were imprisoned and 4,750 were placed on probation — often requiring some alternative service. These numbers tell only a small part of the broader story, though — opposition to the draft was not criminally consequential, but it was politically significant, and this, in the context of the broader antiwar movement, brought many induction activities to a slowdown.

The most publicized challenge to the draft was that undertaken by Muhammad Ali in the spring of 1967. The young and confident Heavy Weight Champion of the World converted to the Nation of Islam and announced that he had been renamed Muhammad Ali rather than his "slave name" Cassius Clay.

Ali opposed the Vietnam War, and when the draft board reclassified him as 1-A, he refused to serve. Ali considered himself a conscientious objector and further insisted "I ain't got no quarrel with them Vietcong." He was arrested when he refused induction, charged and found guilty of violating the selective service laws. Immediately, the New York State Boxing Commissions stripped him of his title and other state groups followed suit. Ali appealed his conviction and four years later the U.S. Supreme Court held that there had been no serious consideration of his conscientious objector claim and that it must be reconsidered. By then the draft and the war were ending. But Ali had become a hero to many young people, white as well as African American, for challenging what they considered to be an unjust war and his willingness to lose his title over this. The young athlete became the focus of significant criticism from conservative and pro-war voices, as well as continuing insults from racists.[101]

Randy Kehler grew up in Scarsdale, New York. He wasn't particularly alarmed by the "duck and cover" films, and even as a youngster, he always assumed that he would join the military. He attended Phillips Exeter Academy for his final two years of high school and was moved to tears when Hanson Baldwin of *The New York Times* visited the campus and in a public talk warned the students that there was nearly a 100 percent probability that there would be a nuclear war in the next twenty years. He also wept when John Kennedy was assassinated — and he took some time off from his studies at Harvard to work with Rwandan refugees. It was a searing experience for him — including refugee accounts of CIA planes bombing villages with napalm. He returned to the United States resolutely antiwar, and in the fall of 1967 mailed his draft card to the Selective Service saying he would not serve if called. He did not claim conscientious objector status because although he opposed the war in Vietnam, he did not consider himself a pacifist. When he graduated from Harvard, he enrolled in graduate school at Stanford. Active in antiwar activities in the Bay Area, he refused the order to report for induction and was charged in the summer of 1969 with violating the federal law.

His trial was in Cheyenne, Wyoming. He did not challenge the charges but simply said he was justified in refusing to serve. He told the judge that he had learned at home and at church that killing was wrong, and he would not kill. Randy's parents came from Scarsdale for the trial. His father, a conservative Republican, asked to speak to the judge. He said that it was he who should go to prison because he and Mrs. Kehler had raised Randy to be the sort of young man he was.

The judge found Randy guilty and sentenced him to prison for two years, specifically referencing the amount of time he would have had to serve in the army if he had accepted his draft notice. He spent two years in the federal penitentiary in Safford, Arizona. Prior to going to prison, he had spoken to a War Resisters League meeting. At this program was a former marine and a Pentagon researcher named Daniel Ellsberg, who was deeply moved by Kehler's courage. When Ellsberg realized that young men were going to prison because of their deep moral opposition, he resolved to do what he could to stop an "unjust war." He determined that he had "the power and the freedom to act" as resolutely as Randy did.[102]

Matt Shorten, of Garden City, Long Island, was sixteen when his older brother Timothy was killed in Vietnam on March 31, 1968. After graduating from Holy Cross, Timothy had joined the marines and was deployed to Vietnam as a young officer in the summer of 1967. Matt was the youngest of four brothers, and he and his family were at Sunday Mass when an usher asked them to come to the back of the church. Two marines notified them of Timothy's death. Matt probably could have received an exemption from his local draft board due to the family loss, but he chose to file as a conscientious objector. A favorable draft lottery number finally would also protect him. But he became active in antiwar activities at Holy Cross and argued with other students there. He later reflected that he would have come to this view even without Timothy's death. His parents quietly supported him in his challenges of the war and the draft.[103]

Mike Fredrickson grew up in Redwood Falls, Minnesota, the son of a truck driver. He attended Macalester College with Tim O'Brien and received a prestigious Rhodes Scholarship in 1967. His Rhodes group at Oxford provides an interesting profile of a generation dealing with war, with men from around the country including several who graduated from military academies. One new scholar was Charles Abbot, a 1966 graduate of the Naval Academy who was already serving on a destroyer.

The group included, along with Fredrickson, Karl Marlantes, a senior at Yale who would be commissioned in the Marine Corps in the spring at graduation, and Tad Campion, a senior at Dartmouth. The three of them would symbolize the twists of a generation. Both Fredrickson and Marlantes were from rural working-class backgrounds. Both had become convinced the war was wrong and wrestled with what to do. They discussed going to Canada or Sweden. One night they talked, and as Marlantes described it, "I could not desert and go with him to Canada and he could not go with me to war," so they went as friends their separate ways. Marlantes went back and reported for duty as a marine. He would serve in Vietnam and receive two Purple Hearts and the Navy Cross.[104]

Mike Fredrickson agonized greatly over the war and the fact that young men he knew had died there. His "privileged position" was eating at him. He was "copping out" by not taking a stand. So he sent his draft board his draft card and said he opposed the war and would not serve. The next year he went to Toronto, Canada. "I think I thought about everything. I chewed it all over." He worried that he was engaging in an "adolescent act of defiance," and then he got angry about being put in such a position. His mother was frightened about what he was doing and his father said little, but they both supported his decision.[105]

Tad Campion grew up in Bronxville, New York. His uncle was the famous West Point athletic director Russell "Red" Reeder, an army legend who had been wounded at Normandy. Reeder and his father had both graduated from West Point, and Tad Campion visited there regularly and thought he would someday join the military. When he graduated from Dartmouth in 1967, there had already been some antiwar protests on the campus, but he had not really engaged.

Many of his classmates were in ROTC or NROTC, and there was little tension about these choices. When he went to Oxford in the summer of 1967, some of his fellow graduates went into the military. At Oxford, he talked a lot with Fredrickson and Marlantes about the war and their situation, about Marlantes's sense of a "moral obligation" to serve since others were sacrificing so much, and of Fredrickson's deep moral opposition to the war.

The debates at Oxford about the war and the Tet Offensive in the early winter of 1968, with its heavy casualties, convinced Tad Campion that the war was just too costly and too wrong. Three young men he "grew up with" were killed in Vietnam. Two of his Dartmouth classmates, Billy Smoyer and Duncan Sleigh, would die there serving as marine officers. When the Bronxville draft board, responding to a need for more men and the end of graduate school deferments, changed Campion's draft status to 1-A, he left Oxford and came back to the United States and taught in a public school which, because it was designated as a high need school, gave him a draft exemption. He said, "I don't know if I would have had the nerve to go to Canada." The idea of leaving "my country and my home and my family" bothered him deeply. He didn't think he could make a case to qualify as a CO. He did engage with some antiwar

284

activities but never faulted those who decided to serve in the military.[106]

In December 1966, right before Christmas, the American Rhodes Committee had announced the 1967 scholarship winners. Campion, Frederickson, and Marlantes joined others on this list. The story was on page 33 of the December 19 edition of *The New York Times.* On the front page of that same issue was an article about the 1st Cavalry Division engaging in a major fight with a North Vietnamese army battalion near Qui Nhon. The paper reported that 65 of the enemy had been killed, but there was no count of American casualties. At the bottom of the front page was an article about units of the army's 9th Infantry Division arriving in Vietnam. Their deployment increased the total American force in the country to approximately 370,000. In an interview, a young soldier from Pennsylvania admitted that he was "a bit frightened." But he also said that "it's my duty, right, and obligation" to be there. And he predicted that "many more guys" would be joining him. The *Times* reported that 70 percent of this group coming from Fort Riley, Kansas, was composed of draftees.

The stereotype of the opposition to the war coming from a privileged middle class and of support from the war sustained by a conservative working class does not accurately describe the 1960s or the postwar generation. From the beginning, there had been labor union opposition to the war, and by 1968 this became more widespread in blue-collar America. Rhodes Scholars Fredrickson and Marlantes illustrate this. But the other side of this challenge to stereotype is that even though blue-collar Americans were disproportionately on the front lines in Vietnam, they were not the only ones there. College dropouts and college graduates joined them, often as a result of losing deferments but not always as reluctant recruits. They shared the sense of generational responsibility that many had, at least in the early years of the war. And they too were intrigued by the idea of the adventure of it all. This idea seldom lasted more than a few hours for those posted to Vietnam.[107]

General Hershey and the Selective Service System had a major setback in late 1968 when the U.S. Supreme Court ruled that draft boards could not reclassify men based on their protest activity. It was the role of the criminal justice system to prosecute and the courts to determine whether there had been illegal activity and to rule on the punishment. This took away a power that Hershey and some local draft boards had been exercising since 1965. The case involved a divinity student, James Oestereich, who had turned in his draft card as an antiwar protest. His draft board took away his ministerial exemption and reclassified him 1-A. This reclassification was overturned.[108]

One generalization is all-encompassing: From 1965 until the early 1970s, it would have been impossible for anyone in this generation to ignore the war in Vietnam. And the draft personalized their relationship to the war — it hung over not just the men who were draft eligible but also the women who were their classmates, neighbors, and friends — and their wider circle of family and friends. Images of the war were in every living room every evening. The real possibility of serving touched far more than the two and one half million or so young men and women who actually served in Vietnam.

In the fall of 1965, Barry McGuire's version of the song "Eve of Destruction" briefly topped the charts. Peter, Paul and Mary, as well as the Kingston Trio and Johnny Rivers, had popular releases of the folk song "Where Have All the Flowers Gone?" late in 1965, and Phil Ochs's "I Ain't Marching Anymore" became a theme at antiwar rallies.

Beginning in 1965, antiwar demonstrations challenged the war and the assumptions that underlay it. It took a few years for these arguments to persuade a majority of Americans. They more rapidly seemed to persuade young Americans, the boomer generation. Their decade, the '60s, would take on an altogether different and even revolutionary form. And their war, the one for which they had been handed the torch while in their teens, would play a major role in shaping their decade and their generation. But even while this was rapidly evolving, many of them were in Vietnam in a war that also was rapidly evolving.

On January 6, 1967, *Time* magazine named its Man of the Year for 1966. Unlike the previous year, when General Westmoreland had stood as a surrogate for the men serving in the armed forces in Vietnam, this year there were no singular surrogates: the Man of the Year was the "Twenty-five and Under" generation. Called "The Inheritor," this group even explicitly included the women of the generation. Quite a concession for the Man of the Year tradition! The editors focused on the culture, the music, the alleged hedonism, and the intellectual strength of the generation. They acknowledged that some were in Vietnam. "Indeed, Viet Nam has given the young — protesters and participants alike — the opportunity to disprove the doom criers of the 1950s who warned that the next generation would turn out spineless and grey-flannel-souled."

The magazine published in a sidebar excerpts from a letter that student leaders at one hundred colleges and universities had sent to President Johnson. The *Time* editors described it as a letter that politely "questioned the conduct, rationale and very aims of the war in Viet Nam." The students challenged the assumptions that underlay the war and they worried about the effect of military operations in Vietnam. They argued that many of those facing service "are torn by reluctance to participate in a war whose toll keeps escalating, but about whose purpose and value to the U.S." remained unclear.

Time interviewed a twenty-one-year-old soldier of this generation, James Henderson, from Guthrie, Kentucky, who was then serving in Vietnam. Sergeant Henderson disagreed with the protesters: "This is an experience you get a lot out of," he said. "If you live through it."[109]

5

NOT THEIR FATHERS'
WAY OF WAR

By the spring of 1969, when the American War in Vietnam shifted in goals and forms of engagement, it had already lasted longer than U.S. involvement in World War II. It was a war that had its own unique, lethal norms and expectations. These had evolved since the beginning of combat operations in the late winter of 1965. Certainly there is no evidence that anyone in a role of responsibility had planned, calculated, or even anticipated the way this combat deployment would evolve over these first years. In many ways these shortcomings defined, as they were defined by, the nature of the war. But unanticipated developments are the case with all wars.

Philip Caputo, who came ashore with the first marines at Da Nang in March 1965, later reflected on war fighting in Vietnam: "I have found myself wishing that I had been the veteran of a conventional war, with dramatic campaigns and historic battles for subject matter instead of a monotonous succession of ambushes and fire-fights. But there were no Normandies or Gettysburgs for us, no epic clashes that decided the fate of armies or nations."[1]

While those who fought in Vietnam were the sons of World War II veterans, this war's combat operations that began in 1965 were not those of their fathers' war. The Vietnam War had no armies massed in confrontation along front lines. The French, who had fought in Vietnam from 1945 to 1954, enjoyed many advantages over General Võ Nguyên Giáp's forces, but they were continually frustrated by *la guerre sans fronts.*[2]

The Vietnam War was a conflict in which the enemy forces were not always clearly visible and articulated. It was a war marked by political complications, international calculations, and ambiguous and shifting goals that constrained military options. And perhaps most important, it was a war in which America's unequaled military strength was not always determinative. The U.S. military forces surely could win major battles. But the American experience in Vietnam reaffirmed that winning battles does not always translate into winning wars. American officers who met with their former foes after the war insisted that the United States had never lost on the battlefield. The Vietnamese response was that this was "irrelevant." No one could have said this to the Americans following battlefield victories at Normandy or Iwo Jima.[3]

The U.S. military force in Vietnam was formidable, better equipped, and with far more capacity than the Americans of World War II. And the military that fought in Vietnam was prepared for offensive operations that featured devastating ordnance. American troops were well educated, well trained, and highly mobile. In most cases, particularly in the early years of the war, they were led by professional, experienced, and able field officers and NCOs.

The Americans fighting in Vietnam had major firepower advantages and tremendous air transport flexibility and airpower capacity. To the surprise and chagrin of many, these factors were not always sufficient in operations fought against tough, dedicated, and spectral units in Vietnam's highlands and jungles. The American force size and firepower could even be counterproductive in skirmishes fought in the coastal and Delta areas where small villages and farm settlements were adjacent to rice paddies. Collateral damage became a euphemism for civilians whose lives were devastated. Marine veteran William Broyles wrote, "In most wars the soldier knows where the battlefield is. In Vietnam the war was everywhere. In most wars the soldier knows who his enemy is. In

Vietnam it was difficult to tell which Vietnamese were our friends and which our foes, and too easy to give up trying."[4]

The Republic of Vietnam established at the 1954 Geneva Conference was the area south of the 17th parallel, the demilitarized zone. South Vietnam was bordered by the DMZ on the north and by international boundaries with Laos and Cambodia on the west. The country contained about 66,000 square miles of land, roughly the size of Florida. There were more than 1,000 miles of landed border — 46 miles along the DMZ, 248 miles with Laos, and approximately 763 miles with Cambodia. None of these borders was truly neutralized and secure. Certainly Cambodia and Laos provided sanctuaries and supply depots for enemy soldiers. Vietnam was a crescent-shaped country. The coastal plain and the southern Mekong Delta area were rich farming lands, but the interior to the north of the Delta was defined by mountains, highlands, and heavy jungles, with the north–south chain of mountains called the Chaine Annamitique, running from China to the alluvial bottomland of the Mekong Delta.[5]

The U.S. military divided South Vietnam into four Corps Tactical Zones, or simply Corps. The northernmost of these, south of the demilitarized zone and adjacent to Laos was I Corps ("Eye" Corps), containing Da Nang and the ancient capital of Hué. South of this was II Corps, which consisted of the Central Highlands area out to the borders with Laos and Cambodia. This was a large geographical area and it contained one of the major ports, Cam Ranh Bay. The III Corps was the area between Saigon and the Highlands, running out to the Cambodian border and containing 38 percent of the population of South Vietnam. And the IV Corps was the sixteen provinces in the Mekong River Delta. Marked by the Mekong River flowing out of Cambodia and crisscrossed by rivers, streams, and canals, this was the Rice Bowl of Vietnam.

The late journalist Michael Herr wrote in 1968 of looking at the map of Vietnam in his apartment in Saigon. It was an old French map, but now a military overlay was imposed on the geography: "We know that for years now, there has been no country here but the war. The landscape has been converted to terrain, the geography broken down into its more useful components: corps and zones, tactical areas of responsibility, vicinities of operation, outposts, positions, objectives, fields of fire."[6]

When President Lyndon Johnson authorized the introduction of combat troops into Vietnam in 1965 and commenced the Rolling Thunder bombing campaign against targets in North Vietnam, it was clear that he was not looking for a military victory conventionally defined. It was his assumption that the North Vietnamese would see the futility of supporting a war against the powerful American military force and that negotiations would then resolve the conflict in a way that preserved the independence of South Vietnam. His effort to accomplish this limited goal resulted in his raising the stakes incrementally, increasing the force commitment. He was deeply frustrated to discover that Ho Chi Minh and his government were not interested in negotiating while Americans continued their military operations.

In the American War in Vietnam, the policy makers' decisions were marked by incrementalism and ambivalence — and by undisclosed calculations and unspoken plans. Rather than an unequivocal sense of resolution and commitment to a singular military goal, the war's strategic escalations had dual, even conflicting goals. The senior civilian leadership in Washington considered the use of military force as a clear message to cold war foes and allies that the United States would maintain its commitments. Military engagement was a diplomatic tool, a necessary step to the more important goal of negotiating from a position of strength. Demonstrating this resolution with intimidating military strength and a willingness to use it was critical to pressure the enemy. At the same time, military strength was also necessarily tempered and contained due to the diplomatic calibrations of demonstrating to the Soviets and the Chinese that the United States was willing to raise the military pressure — while also taking care not to raise it to the point that either of them determined that they needed to become more involved. President Johnson worried about any repeat of the Korean War experience, where American military operations advanced to the Yalu River, on the border of China, which resulted in China sending troops into Korea.

The United States needed to demonstrate unwavering support for the South Vietnamese government. And it needed to do this in ways that showed full force engagement without allowing the Communists to describe it as an American war fought on behalf of a puppet government. The support also needed to be adjusted and even held back to allow some leverage over the Saigon government. Public affirmations of unwavering military support did not mean that there were not implicit pressures with support withheld as a tool.

There was also the domestic political nuance: President Johnson wanted to show resolve to his anticommunist critics while simultaneously demonstrating full control and restraint to the growing antiwar opposition. It was a challenging exercise that resulted in an incredibly complicated military operation and some duplicity in describing it to various audiences. Vietnam, North and South, became a war zone, to be sure, but also a chessboard for complex now-you-see-it-now-you-don't maneuvering. And military leaders, trained in a focused and linear way for war fighting, had to implement the steps in which war fighting was a means to nonmilitary ends.

When General William Westmoreland assumed command of the Military Assistance Command, Vietnam in June 1964, his was a recently reorganized unit, with increased consolidated authority. Even with this comprehensive oversight, Westmoreland always had to contend with shifting political directives from Washington and fragmented military command structures nurtured by interservice rivalries. Westmoreland was not able to control air force or navy operations in Vietnam's airspace and coastal waters. And he had ongoing tensions with the Marine Corps command in the northernmost I Corps area of South Vietnam.[7]

General Westmoreland served as commanding officer of MACV from 1964 to July 1968. He oversaw the evolution of the U.S. mission from advisory support and training to a primarily combat role with nearly a half million men under his command. He was forced to contend with evolving and sometimes conflicting instructions from the Pentagon. He worked with changing governments with their own political needs in Saigon and struggled to maintain coordination with the South Vietnamese military, primarily the Army of the Republic of Vietnam. During and after the war, Westmoreland became the focus of much of the criticism of U.S. military shortcomings in Vietnam, and of course as the commanding officer, this came with the territory. His performance deserved criticism. But any criticism needs to be tempered by a recognition of the political constraints that framed and limited his options — and by a recognition that his understanding of the military situation and his sense of tactical responses were often more nuanced than the critics acknowledged.[8]

The basic American objectives in Vietnam were to protect and to enhance the support of the Saigon government, to advise and to empower the ARVN forces to carry on the war, to provide protection and support for the Vietnamese living in the villages, and to defend South Vietnam from military aggression from the National Liberation Front and the North Vietnamese Army forces. While these goals were largely constant, none were ever consistently and precisely defined, and there was generally a shifting of priorities.

MACV and General Westmoreland specifically understood and accepted all of these goals. They also recognized that these were not all fundamentally military objectives. It was obvious to most senior officers that this was not a conventional war — it was still commonly referred to as a "guerrilla war." And General Westmoreland, when he served as superintendent at West Point from 1960 to 1963, had mandated that counterinsurgency instruction be part of the core curriculum.[9]

Understanding the nature of the war and its nuances did not mean that it was easy to develop a comprehensive strategy to advance the American military mission. Westmoreland often used a metaphor in describing the war in Vietnam: It was a contest against an alliance of "termites" and "bullies." The "termites" were the National Liberation Front, the guerrilla insurgents who challenged, terrorized, and infiltrated the villages along the coastal plain and Delta region of Vietnam. Their goal was to erode the political leadership and the civic infrastructure of the existing government and to gain through persuasion, reciprocity, or intimidation the loyalty of the civilian population. They were serious threats. But, General Westmoreland observed, out in the nearby jungles and on the hills were the North Vietnamese Army as well as some organized NLF units, the "bullies." These formidable forces did more than gnaw at the infrastructure; they were armed with what the metaphor described as destructive crowbars. Their approach was not subversion but assault. They would come in to destroy the villages whose integrity had been gnawed away by the "termites." General Westmoreland believed that defending the villages against the insurgents, the "termites," should be handled primarily by the Army of the Republic of Vietnam and related civil defense forces. The United States and other allied forces would take on the organized forces in the field, the "bullies."

It was a clear metaphor and description of the two "fronts" in the military conflict. But it broke down the challenges too neatly and viewed the conflict as too easily compartmentalized. General Westmoreland fully understood the need to have the Vietnamese villages secure from subversion and intimidation — but he never wavered in his conviction that the first and the essential step in this was to defeat the standing enemy forces in the field. Only then would the "pacification" objectives work. The NVA and their NLF allies "could not be allowed to roam unopposed through the countryside."[10]

General Westmoreland constructed a three-phase plan. He believed that in 1965 the allied forces would "halt the losing trend" and secure the key areas. In the second phase, in 1966, MACV would move to take the offensive and "destroy enemy forces." Finally, in 1967, the American coalition would secure the defeat of the remaining enemy forces and all of their base area. Then, and only then, could pacification, civic action programs, truly advance because the threat of enemy aggression would have been removed.

One problem with handling the challenges of defeating enemy forces and securing villages sequentially was that the threats were occurring simultaneously, and focusing on one had consequences, often negative and almost always unintended, elsewhere. The American military, through its Special Forces and other small units, was quite capable of operating subtly with a small footprint. As the war continued, however, such operations were not the norm. Frequently, U.S. and ARVN forces cleared out villages in resettlement programs and sometimes destroyed them to make certain that the enemy found no refuge there. Civilian deaths and injuries, even if accidental, and the destruction of homes and property of noncombatants, were not steps toward winning either hearts or minds in pacification programs.

Resettlement as a crude means to "pacification" had a technological partner that also devastated life in many rural villages — and had consequences that persist. In 1962, President Kennedy approved the recommendation of MACV, endorsed by the Pentagon, to implement a defoliation program in South Vietnam. If the NLF guerrillas were hiding back in the triple-canopy jungles and were securing food from nearby farms, this program would deprive them of both the security and the sustenance.

Utilizing a series of herbicides called the "rainbow" chemicals, the most notorious of which was Agent Orange, the American "flexible response" strategy had a destructive new tool. Most of this herbicide was manufactured at the Dow Chemical Company plant in Midland, Michigan, and it was shipped in heavy steel fifty-five-gallon drums to several airfields in Vietnam. From these bases, under Operation Ranch Hand, huge C-123s sprayed the herbicides over jungles, rice paddies, and homes.

By 1967, the Ranch Hand group had partnered with Operation Flyswatter, which was spraying insecticides over large areas near American troops in order to control mosquitoes and reduce malaria. Ranch Hand also partnered with Operation Sherwood Forest, which used napalm and other incendiary bombs in jungle areas to try to destroy them through forest fires. The two operations came to embrace the slogan, "Remember, Only You Can Prevent Forests."

The Americans would spray more than nineteen million gallons of chemicals over two and a half million acres of central and southern Vietnam. Agent Orange was the primary chemical, and it proved to be a deadly toxin. The assurances to President Kennedy that it would be possible to use it in a way that did not harm civilian crops proved false. Agent Orange was not a discrete, subtle tool of pacification, nor did it win hearts and minds. It immediately destroyed the livelihood of hundreds of thousands of Vietnamese. Longer term, it destroyed many lives, American as well as Vietnamese.

In the early years of the use of these chemicals, it is not clear that the policy makers were aware of these dangers. Yet when they started to have reservations, they did not share them with the Americans or the Vietnamese who would have the most contact with the toxins. Just as President Kennedy was authorizing the use of defoliation techniques in Vietnam, Rachel Carson's *Silent Spring* was pointing out the environmental devastation caused by DDT and other chemicals. This began a great debate in the United States, which led — ten years later — to the outlawing of DDT-type insecticides. This debate was delayed in Vietnam as huge areas were devastated and large populations were caught in a chemical health epidemic. The U.S. troops that distributed the chemicals, as well as those on the ground that were in contact with them and the Vietnamese who lived in this toxic world, would deal with the medical consequences for their lifetimes — as would many children born to those contaminated.[11]

So many aspects of the American mission in Vietnam, initiated with a genuine sense of responsibility and even beneficence, had unintended consequences. Few of these were positive. The war-fighting strategy illustrates this process: One objective, one tool, of the comprehensive mission comes to be considered the singular mission. Language can easily move from casual description to explicit objective, especially in complicated organizations. Not long after American military leaders started using "attrition" as a description of their goal of wearing down the enemy's military capacity, accomplishing attrition became a goal. And body counts became the measurable and often the singular means of accounting for progress toward the goal.

In one unit, at Christmas 1969, the company with the highest body count was rewarded with a trip to Cu Chi for the Bob Hope show. And in another area, a battalion commander denied a rifle platoon a morning chopper airlift from a night ambush site, even though the area was known to be booby-trapped, because the platoon had a zero body count.[12]

General Westmoreland knew that the war was about more than body counts. He reminded his command of the need to assist in countering the appeal of insurgents, supporting civic action priorities, working to train and to assist the ARVN forces, and taking actions that would gain political support for the South Vietnamese government. Nonetheless, the threat of enemy forces seemed paramount, and "the lure of battle was ever present in Vietnam and destructive military operations too often nullified social and political progress."[13]

In the early summer of 1965, there was a sense of pessimism among the senior American officials in Saigon. President Johnson's decision in July to expand significantly the size of the American force in the country led to greater optimism. And in November, the Battle at Ia Drang seemed to show the way. Lieutenant Colonel Harold Moore and the 1st Battalion of the 7th Cavalry were lifted by helicopter directly into a North Vietnamese Army staging area. There was a vicious fight marked briefly by a fear that the Americans could be all killed. They fought bravely, and finally the NVA withdrew into Cambodia. The updated count from the field was 75 U.S. soldiers killed and 121 wounded. The NVA reportedly lost 634 soldiers, with another 1,215 "estimated" deaths. General Westmoreland described it as an "unprecedented victory" and pointed to the count of the enemy dead as evidence of this.[14]

In the final analysis, General Westmoreland accepted, or at least tolerated, the consequence of combat operations being reduced to the crude body count. It was a metric that implied a far more accurate assessment of progress — and of bodies actually counted and of their identity — than it ever delivered. And it was a metric that set a tone for the war that reduced all other objectives to a secondary place. MACV and the Pentagon took a number of lessons from Ia Drang. They believed that the kill ratio was very favorable to the United States; they were convinced that the North Vietnamese would not long be able to sustain such heavy and disproportionate losses while the Americans could tolerate them, at least for a time. And time was what they needed to force North Vietnam to withdraw from the field. Second, the U.S. military officials were pleased by helicopters' exceptional mobility and flexibility.

Helicopters as tactical transport and as gunships represented a new method of warfare. President Kennedy had been enthusiastic about this innovation, and in the summer of 1965 Secretary of Defense Robert McNamara had signed off on the organization of air mobile units after successful training and testing. The 1st Air Cavalry Division, the first major mobile force, arrived in Vietnam in August 1965. This innovative battlefield approach seemed to exceed all expectations at the Ia Drang Valley that fall. Now, "freed from the tyranny of terrain," the army could go anywhere. They would have tremendous flexibility to land troops and equipment and to resupply units in the field. And, increasingly, as heavier ordnance was added to helicopter gunships, they could bring lethal firepower into any engagement.[15]

By late 1965, the initial pessimism had been replaced by a spirit of optimism at MACV headquarters. The growing number of troops, numbering 190,000 by year end, the promise of more forces in 1966, and the belief that Ia Drang had not simply been a victory but had been a harbinger and a tactical blueprint on how to proceed, all resulted in a sense of elation over the holiday season. The commanding officers at MACV "hoped that enough military victories of this nature would cause North Vietnam to desist in its war against the South."[16]

The optimism was misplaced, as were some of the lessons and assumptions on which it was based. One of the factors that saved Colonel Moore's battalion was the use, for the first time ever as tactical weapons, of B-52s. These were lethal ordnance delivery vehicles and the North Vietnamese were startled by their high altitude, silent approach, and devastating bomb loads. The planes had been modified to carry over fifty 750-pound demolition bombs. These planes would figure in many subsequent occasions in the war. But it was hard to think of them as a battlefield weapon even as they were used this way. Friendly forces needed to be several miles away to be secure from death and injury from the bombs delivered by the planes. This was not a precise, discriminating weapon.

Second, the helicopter would prove to be a remarkable innovation in the war. But its use as an airmobile transport vehicle had its own consequences, which in so many ways defined the nature of this war. Troops could be delivered to distant locations in the middle of enemy concentrations, as they had been in the Ia Drang Valley. But this meant that troops were now inaccessible by land and surrounded by the enemy. The forces deployed in this way were totally dependent upon the machines that brought them there for delivery of ammunition, equipment, food, water, and other supplies. They were also totally dependent upon helicopters for transporting out wounded and dead servicemen and for bringing in reinforcements.

Dependence upon helicopters also meant dependence upon greater, less controllable factors: visibility and weather patterns; favorable, open, and secure landing zones; limited enemy fire capacity around these landing zones; and the availability of these aircraft. Moreover, the helicopters in turn required massive amounts of readily accessible fuel, a trained maintenance and support system, and security for when they were on or close to the ground and very vulnerable. One estimate was that the 1st Cavalry Division required 2,500 men to provide maintenance and ground security for the division's helicopters.[17]

The troops praised the decisive support of U.S. airpower. Americans did have control of the air over North and South Vietnam. And while the U.S. planes often faced significant rocket defenses and other antiaircraft armaments, these threats were less common in the battlefields of the South. Still, there was plenty of danger there. Between 1965 and 1972, the years of active American combat operations in the South, the United States flew 3.4 million sorties in support of these actions. Not including accidents, there were 2,527 aircraft shot down and 3,034 crew members killed.[18]

In the Johnson years, Operation Rolling Thunder continued to bomb North Vietnam. The missions were always carefully controlled, focusing on military targets and key transportation and communications networks. These were dangerous assignments with heavy antiaircraft fire, and the enemy was remarkably adaptive. Estimates on the number of civilians killed range from 52,000 to 180,000. The campaign had little impact on North Vietnam's willingness to negotiate — and little obvious effect on its capacity to send troops and supplies to the South.[19]

Between 1963 and 1975, Americans flew more than 3 million sorties that dropped over 8 million tons of bombs. Only 8 percent of this was used over North Vietnam. The bulk of it was used in the South and in adjacent areas of Laos and Cambodia, to destroy enemy supply and support units and storage facilities. In South Vietnam, airpower ranging from helicopter gunships to B-52s was on call to clear landing zones, to strike enemy positions or possible enemy positions, and to provide close air support for U.S. forces engaged in a battle with the enemy. Less than 10 percent of the sorties in the South were in direct support of American troops: About 6 percent were from aircraft called in and not planned, about 66 percent were planned strikes on identified enemy locations, and about 25 percent were more spontaneous calls to attack an enemy site.[20]

Providing the operational and security infrastructure for the helicopters and the aircraft was a major issue faced by the large and technologically dependent force deployed to Vietnam. The logistical and support needs for the U.S. military operation were extensive, and the speed and general quality with which they were met was quite remarkable. In 1965, the Americans had difficulty finding port facilities adequate for off-loading growing numbers of troops and supplies, and then had to find secure bases for both. Supporting the troops and equipment required clearing land and building facilities for them. Some combat deployments were delayed due to the lack of facilities. The Americans were introducing the most technologically advanced and supply-line-dependent military force in the history of the world into a rural country with difficult terrain, few modern ports, insufficient roads, and significantly inadequate facilities for aircraft.

Within just a few years, the United States built more than 100 airfields, including 15 that could handle jets; 7 deep-water ports plus wharfing facilities for small craft; storage for 3 billion barrels of petroleum products; permanent billets for 350,000 troops; hospitals with over 8,000 beds; 56 million square feet of covered and open storage areas; 2.5 million cubic feet of cold storage; over 600 miles of improved streets, roads, and highways. By 1969, American facilities treated 4 billion gallons of water annually and produced 25 million kilowatt-hours of electric power per month. The United States maintained over 700 miles of roads and collected and disposed of 350,000 cubic yards of garbage monthly. Many of the fixed-wing aircraft were based in Thailand or were carrier launched. These required a major support structure that was not really tallied as part of the Vietnam infrastructure.[21]

Some of the early construction was done by military crews, by navy Seabees and army, air force, or marine engineers. But the bulk of it was done by American international construction firms: Raymond, Morrison-Knudsen, Brown & Root, and J. A. Jones — generally described collectively as RMK-BRJ. Most of the laborers under U.S. Command were Vietnamese civilians — an estimated 200,000 worked on these projects at one point or another. By 1966, construction materials accounted for some 40 percent of the "military" tonnage arriving in Vietnam. The remainder was war matériel. There were as many bulldozers shipped to Vietnam as there were armored personnel carriers.[22]

One navy officer attached to MACV described the responsibility of monitoring construction projects in 1968. RMK-BRJ had taken over most of the work from the military crews. They worked on cost-plus contracts, and the military slogan was, "Good. Fast. Cheap. Pick any two." It was impossible to have all three and fast and good were the priorities.[23]

Although Ia Drang seemed to demonstrate the American path to victory in Vietnam — disproportionate enemy losses, great troop mobility, and overwhelming air and ground firepower — the battle also contained a few ominous signs. The North Vietnamese slipped back into Cambodia with a new confidence that they could fight against the Americans even if they had to find ways to minimize the U.S. firepower advantage. Perhaps most troubling to the American calculus, the North

Vietnamese were able pretty quickly to replace the troops they had lost in the Ia Drang Valley. And finally, the sense of victory and elation at MACV and in the 1st Cav Division resulted in a sharper focus on battlefield confrontation. American military leaders had always refused to accept that they "could be losing a war to peasant insurgents." (Lyndon Johnson had described Vietnam as a "damn little pissant country.") Now they had demonstrated that they could overwhelm these rudimentary forces: MACV noted that "more enemy were killed and captured in this engagement than in any thus far."[24] A description of a battle became a strategy, and too often a singular one. Pacification programs slipped back further in the active list of military priorities.

Secretary of Defense McNamara visited Vietnam shortly after the Battle of Ia Drang. He was struck by the mood of celebration — and he noted that pacification had stalled and that ARVN desertions had increased. He told reporters before leaving Saigon that "we have stopped losing the war," but he also acknowledged that the NVA and NLF did not seem to have been slowed. He concluded, "It will be a long war."[25]

The North Vietnamese also took stock after Ia Drang and some of the other early contacts with the American forces. North Vietnamese Army general Nguyen Chi Thanh instructed

313

his troops that they needed to "always take control, pick the best location and the most propitious time for battle; force the enemy to fight *our* battle *our* way; always attack and move, concentrate and disperse rhythmically, cover, camouflage, hide, and disguise well, using subterfuge to fool the enemy; fight in close range and fast, fight ferociously, terminate the fight quickly." He believed that U.S. firepower advantage could be negated by engaging in contact for only fifteen to twenty minutes and by following the approach described as "grabbing them by the belt," meaning to fight in very close combat range so air and artillery fire could be used only cautiously to avoid friendly fire casualties. He told the NVA to study the enemy closely and to learn how they operate, to know the topography well, and to always seek to "open fire from a high elevation to overwhelm the enemy."[26]

The correspondent Ward Just spent time in the field with American forces over several years. He concluded that "Vietnam was a country where the enemy fought at times and places of his own choosing when he could manage it, and he managed it quite often." Americans quickly learned that they were fighting well-equipped forces that were disciplined and professional. They were not pajama-clad amateurs.[27]

Early in 1966, MACV reports indicated

314

that the NLF controlled nearly three-quarters of South Vietnam. Nonetheless, there was a sense that Hanoi had lost the initiative. But "in a war without fronts, it was so hard to tell."[28] The war that evolved in Vietnam, from the Ia Drang Valley fight in 1965 to Khe Sanh and Tet in early 1968, fell into a pattern of engage and withdraw. Feint and fight. Wars without front lines still might be fought over geography — but the geographic goals were seldom more than gaining strategic ground to deprive the enemy of holding it. Most such places shifted back and forth. Philip Caputo said, "Men were killed and wounded, and our patrols kept going out to fight in the same places they had fought the week before and the week before that. The situation remained the same. Only the numbers on the colonel's scoreboard changed."[29]

Operation Attleboro in the fall of 1966 symbolizes much of the frustration with this asymmetrical war. This operation aimed to clear the NLF forces out of the III Corps area by the old Michelin rubber plantation up near the Cambodian border, in Tay Ninh province. There were 18 U.S. and 3 ARVN battalions involved, along with 24 artillery batteries. American pilots flew 1,600 sorties and dropped 12,000 tons of ordnance. On one single day, the army artillery units fired 14,000 rounds. Americans would count 1,016 enemy casualties in a successful operation. Military officials were pleased. Some believed that this sort of large multidivisional sweep might provide the key to clearing out enemy forces from some areas. Then when the allied forces withdrew, the NLF forces "quietly returned." Their political power had not diminished; if anything, the villagers were now more resentful of the U.S./Saigon team for the destruction they left behind.[30] There were few hearts and minds won in Tay Ninh.

Official reports on combat operations reveal a war of small-unit operations in which most armed contact was initiated by the NVA or NLF forces. An American staple was the search-and-destroy operation, which generally focused on jungle and/or isolated hill areas. In truth, these "searches" were often more appropriately described as invitations to the enemy to initiate action.

As senior army general William DePuy described it, "The game in the jungle is to send in a small force as bait, let the enemy attack, and be able to react with a larger force in reserve nearby." One analysis reported that the enemy initiated 88 percent of the fighting with the U.S. forces and that nearly half of these contacts began as ambushes. So the men walking on point on patrols understood that rather than advance sentries and trailblazers, they were the "bait," inviting an attack. Even though most patrols were not subject to attacks, this did not ease the tension. There was a "heavy psychological toll. Constant fear and tension pervaded American patrols with potential threats lurking in every hamlet or rice paddy."[31]

During his first tour in Vietnam as an adviser, Colin Powell joined an ARVN unit up in the A Shau Valley. His ARVN counterpart welcomed him and told him it was a "very important outpost." When Captain Powell asked why it was there, he was told, "Outpost is here to protect airfield." And when he inquired about the purpose of the airfield, Captain Hieu told him, "Airfield here to supply outpost." In all the years Powell spent dealing with Vietnam, he said that "Captain Hieu's circular reasoning on that January day in 1963" made the most sense as a description of the mission.[32]

Locating the enemy became the goal, and the understanding was that in most cases the enemy would be located only in places and times of its choosing. One soldier described the experience: "Vietnam was the unexpected war, an alien world ruled by its lack of rules, totally at the mercy of its unexpectedness." Or as Philip Caputo noted, "The war was mostly a matter of enduring weeks of expectant waiting and, at random intervals, of conducting vicious manhunts through jungles and swamps where snipers harassed us constantly and booby traps cut us down one by one."[33]

317

Arguments between the Marine Corps command and MACV illustrate some of the complexity of confronting the multiple priorities of the war. The Marine Corps covered the northern stretch of South Vietnam, with deployment almost entirely in the I Corps area south of the demilitarized zone and bordered on the west by Laos. The marines were centered at Da Nang, where they had first come ashore in March 1965. Much marine activity was southwest of Da Nang, down to the An Hoa basin and including Liberty Bridge, and also north to Hué and on to the DMZ. They built a major air base at Chu Lai to the south and they had a growing presence in Phu Bai to the north. Marine units went out west along Highway 9 just south of the DMZ.

Up in I Corps in their own more independent enclave, marines developed a somewhat different approach to the war. The command surely signed off on the basic MACV objectives — to secure and pacify settled areas, to train and work with ARVN, and to protect the South Vietnamese from assaults from the NVA and NLF. And they understood that they were under MACV command. But they tried to develop their own ordering of priorities. Under General Lewis Walt, commander of the III Marine Amphibious Force (a command that included basically all of the marines in Vietnam), the marines organized a program they called the Combined Action Platoons (CAP). This involved deploying small marine commands, usually all lower grade and younger enlisted men, to stay in villages. There were no officers — generally a sergeant was in charge — and most of the men were nineteen to twenty-one years old. They worked closely with the villagers, assisting them in their work, building roads and wells and schools, and protecting them from the NLF.

General Victor Krulak, the commander of Fleet Marine Force, Pacific, became a spokesman for this program. He insisted that making the villages secure was essential. But he recognized that accomplishing this required stopping the flow of men and materials from the North. Back in Washington, Krulak urged the mining of the port at Haiphong to cut off all supplies, which mostly came on Soviet, Chinese, or Soviet bloc country vessels. The senior civilian leadership balked at such an initiative, fearing that it would lead directly to war with China or the Soviet Union. General Westmoreland insisted that the villages could not be secure until the NVA and NLF units were destroyed, and he continued with the major search-and-destroy programs.[34]

The marines in I Corps also had to continue with their own search-and-destroy missions, and they never had the number of men needed to provide the CAPs. And numbers was one of the Westmoreland/MACV concerns. Despite the rapid buildup of American forces, there were not nearly enough troops in Vietnam to provide an ongoing presence in the villages, to maintain a combat force to engage the enemy, to train and to act as liaisons with the ARVN forces, and to sustain the U.S. military infrastructure. At their peak in the summer of 1969, there were 1,895 marines in I Corps serving in 114 Combined Action Platoons. These covered about 20 percent of the villages in the I Corps area. By one estimate, there were between 2,100 and 2,552 villages — and another 10,000 to 12,000 hamlets — in South Vietnam. One critic has argued that the marines exaggerated their success with this program while also noting that the army command, recognizing the importance of village security, did try to experiment with similar types of programs, but the scale was simply beyond the capacity of the force.[35]

Even though there were many instances and some remarkable stories of U.S. servicemen working closely with and in support of Vietnamese civilians, it is hard to find anyone who argues that the various programs described collectively as pacification were successful over a large area. The American military continued to focus primarily on engagement with enemy forces in I Corps, the Highlands, the Delta, or pockets of major concentrations, largely NLF forces, nearer the coastal villages and population centers. Focusing on the war in the field resulted in not just ignoring other critical U.S. priorities; it also often was counterproductive. One marine officer, not part of a CAP unit, acknowledged that the more he and his platoon went out into the villages as part of patrols, the more the people turned against them.[36]

The heavy use of airpower — bombs, rockets, heavy machine-gun fire, phosphorous explosives, and napalm — seldom won hearts or minds from nearby civilians, who watched their fields, their villages, their homes and possessions, and often their family members and friends, destroyed and killed in these assaults. A pointed NLF inquiry in contested villages asked, "If the Americans are such great friends of the Vietnamese," then how is it that "their planes and helicopters destroy whole villages and kill many innocent people when there are only a couple of VC there?"[37] As early as 1965, General Westmoreland assured the Joint Chiefs of Staff that his command understood the problems of noncombatant casualties caused by U.S. troops. But he pointed out that the necessary first step was for the forces to set up a shield to protect the villages. As Gregory Daddis concluded in his recent study of Westmoreland, "A big

321

reason that MACV could not win over the populace was fomented, at least in part, by the disruptive force of American air strikes across Vietnam."[38]

Many of the villagers were indeed sympathetic to the NLF forces, but as often as not this was because they were related to them by blood and community ties rather than ideology. The allied forces did not engage in subtlety in trying to convert them. An example was the village of Ben Suc, about thirty miles northwest of Saigon, in the area called the Iron Triangle that was the center of much of the NLF activity. During Operation Cedar Falls in 1967, the village was evacuated and destroyed. Nearly 6,000 people were relocated. Then the NLF returned to the area after the Americans left.[39]

In 1969, the village of Phu Hoa Dong north of Saigon was fully encircled by U.S. and ARVN troops in order to engage in a search for NLF. The operation was successful in terms of capturing and killing the enemy. The American commander said that the local VC network "had been knocked for a loop" and that "it will be months before they recover from this one." Villagers were not so sure of this. This was the fourth such operation in fifteen months, and they knew that when the Americans left, the NLF would come back. In this operation, twenty houses were destroyed. The United States promised to replace them — but that would take months. During this period of cordon and search, all activity stopped. One junior American officer, when looking at the deserted central market, said, "They say this village is 80 per cent VC supporters. By the time we finish this it will be 95 per cent."[40]

The NLF approach was more than friendship and promise, exploiting American miscues. They also used intimidation and assassination to secure control of contested villages. Their terror tactics were effective, and many villagers felt that they were caught between two opposing forces. And those who determined that American support was preferable were often vulnerable to NLF reprisals.[41]

James Trullinger, in his study of the village of My Thuy Phuong, south of Hué, discovered that here the individuals who supported the Saigon government "were the *same individuals,* or from the *same families,* who had been active supporters of the Diem regime, and before that of the French." They tended to be large landholders or successful tradesmen, and half of them were Catholics. They were only about 3–5 percent of the population in this village. The NLF continued to promise the villagers "a better life." The models they presented were villagers who were more representative of the large majority of the population. And even though most residents were pessimistic about the delivery of the promise, they determined that it was a more likely outcome than it would be if they threw in with the Americans and their "puppets."[42]

Similarly, in Long An in the Mekong Delta south of Saigon, the South Vietnamese government failed repeatedly to find ways to assist the local population. Their heavy-handed counterinsurgency approach was counterproductive. And the Americanized war with its massive use of airpower and large operations resulted in tremendous dislocation and suffering. NLF Party officials were able effectively to appeal to the civilians in this environment.[43] In addition, the Americans were limited because very few of their own military spoke Vietnamese.

Neil Sheehan reported on a U.S./ARVN operation in Binh Dinh province on the coastal plain in central South Vietnam in early 1966. The allies reported on enemy dead and captured weapons. They did not point out the destruction from air attacks and artillery barrages. Sheehan noted that 1,000 homes were estimated to have been destroyed and that the coconut tree groves that were the major source of local income were now a desolated patch of trees that had been snapped in two by bombardment. One village had 100 killed and 90 taken to hospitals. The estimates were that 5,000 people were now refugees. The Saigon officials who met with the refugees told them that this was in response to even greater atrocities that the NLF had committed with their bombing in Saigon. An American who was nearby asked, "What's the point of telling somebody who has just lost his relatives about a bomb atrocity in Saigon?" Sheehan noted, "Most of these peasants have never been to Saigon. They do not know exactly where it is or who is in power there."[44]

Colin Powell described burning down a temporarily abandoned Montagnard village during his tour as an adviser. He said that the goal of burning homes and destroying crops was to deprive the NLF forces of food. As for the villagers, "The strategy was to win their hearts and minds by making them dependent on the government." He knew that "these mountain people wished they had never heard of the ARVN, the Viet Cong, or the Americans."[45]

Perhaps one of the most horrible, and indiscriminate, of these operations was that undertaken by the army's 9th Division in the Mekong Delta as part of Operation Speedy Express in the spring of 1969. In a culture that emphasized body counts, this operation was an obsessive example. Major General Julian Ewell claimed a kill ratio of 134 to 1. It is not known how many Vietnamese were killed, but many were civilians. This was a heavily NLF area, but it was also the home to many Vietnamese who were not engaged in the war. There were 3,181 air strikes during the operation, and one local hospital treated 1,182 civilians with war wounds. The army later claimed that 10,089 enemy soldiers were killed during the operation. Most estimate that at least 5,000 of these were civilian noncombatants.[46]

Protecting civilians by relocating them was one option that the Saigon government exercised and it was not a politically productive step. By mid-1968, an estimated million and a half villagers had been moved to cities, where they lived often in slumlike conditions. The forced relocation was just a fraction of the dislocation. Some estimated that more than one-third of the 17 million people in South Vietnam were forced to move because of the war.[47]

Sometimes the slums developed in traditional villages. An account of Tan An Hoi, just twenty miles from Saigon, described a place with 15,000 Americans nearby at the large base at Cu Chi. The village "leads a schizophrenic existence of listless government by day, Communist harassment by night, and not even the most optimistic observers can foresee a day when the resistance might cease." Shacks outside the base advertised laundry service and subtly offered prostitution. "Dozens of 'Lucky' and 'Playboy' tailors, 'Peppermint Twists,' 'Oscar,' 'Sam' and 'Melody' laundries sell pot and women." One officer described it as "the saddest thing I have ever seen. It's worse than Tijuana or Juarez. The filth, the bawdiness, the degradation . . ."[48]

While some Americans exploited the civilians, others were warned to distrust them. In 1966, the army's 1st Division issued a "Lessons Learned" report to its men on engaging with the Vietnamese. "Females actively support VC activities and have been encountered in battle. Also young children have been used to hurl grenades into vehicles or commit other acts of sabotage. These tactics present problems for Americans who are not usually wary or alert for encounters of this nature." Another warning to the troops was unambiguous: "Do not trust children at any time. They may be VC agents."[49]

Even though some sympathized with the plight of civilians who suffered at the hands of armed forces on both sides, distrust and indifference and racist condescension were part of the attitudes of many Americans who served in Vietnam. They wondered why they were there fighting for people who seemed indifferent or even hostile toward them. One soldier said, "I think one of the biggest disappointments over there was the attitude of the Vietnamese peasants. None of them seemed to give a shit about us. The feeling was mutual. We didn't even think they were people."[50] This contempt escalated to distrust and often hostility when some of the Americans concluded that South Vietnamese civilians were accomplices in the attacks by NLF forces. The emotions of war are not only fear and courage and brotherhood. They also include hatred and a desire for revenge. These may begin with a specific and tragic interaction with a specific enemy soldier, but they can develop into a broader hatred.

Philip Caputo discussed the destruction of a village from which some NLF soldiers had attacked a marine platoon. Apparently no villagers were hurt during the retributive attack, but their animals were shot and their houses burned down. Caputo watched a woman in the smoldering ashes. "She is on her knees, bowing up and down and keening in the ashes of what was once her home. I harden my heart against her cries. You let the VC use your village for an ambush site, I think, and now you're paying the price. It is then that I realize that the destruction of Giao-Tri was more than an act of madness committed in the heat of battle. It was an act of retribution as well. These villagers aided the VC, and we taught them a lesson. We are learning to hate." Philip Caputo ended his tour in Vietnam when two men in his platoon killed two suspected NLF soldiers. It was not clear that they actually were part of the NLF, and the killings appeared intentional. Caputo took the blame for it and, finally, when the first of his men was acquitted in a court-martial, the charges against the others were dropped with Caputo receiving a reprimand.[51]

The worst cases of criminal misconduct went beyond hate. *Time* magazine reported on the first war crimes case of the war, in which two soldiers from the 1st Infantry Division were found guilty of "bringing discredit upon the armed forces" in a 1967 court-martial. They had cut the ears off of three dead enemy soldiers to keep as trophies. One reporter, CBS newsman Don Webster, who had recorded this, said of them, "You must understand the emotional state of some of these men and their anger and sorrow at the loss of their buddies."[52]

Vietnamese fear of the Americans was based on the experience of too many of them. In My Thuy Phuong, the villagers watched the Americans shoot their water buffalo for sport. They warned children not to run out to the trucks hauling U.S. troops to beg for gifts after some marines threw C ration cans from the trucks, using them as missiles rather than gifts. One woman saw her son grabbed at by men on a truck. He fell under the wheels and the truck stopped, but too late. The boy had already been crushed to death.[53]

Attacks on U.S. forces from anywhere in or around a village could result in indiscriminate fire in return. Bob Kerrey's group of SEALs killed as many as 20 unarmed civilians in the village of Thanh Phong. While some of the details remain unclear, there is little doubt that these were women and children, and that Kerrey had ordered his men to fire. Kerrey said the incident would "haunt" him. The haunting would become public as well as private.[54]

In 1966, five soldiers from the 8th Cavalry of the 1st Cav Division were preparing to go out on a patrol in the Bong Son Valley in the Central Highlands. One of the leaders of the group decided to kidnap a young Vietnamese woman, Phan Thi Mao, and take her with them. Four of them raped and murdered her. The fifth man reported them. He had trouble initially getting the army to take it seriously, but finally the men involved were court-martialed and found guilty. All four received prison sentences that were subsequently reduced.[55]

There are many examples of criminal behavior by U.S. troops during the Vietnam War. The My Lai Massacre in March 1968 has become the symbol of this. My Lai may have been uniquely horrible, but the attitudes of some, and the conduct displayed in that village on that day, were not unique. Nick Turse and others have argued that it was more than not unique — it was representative. I disagree. The nature of the war resulted in some instances of indiscriminate killing and, perhaps even worse, an indifference by some of those involved. And there clearly were atrocities and acts of homicide. There are cases of army units engaging in a campaign against civilians — the most notorious of these was the 101st Airborne Tiger Force, which used torture and murder to intimidate Communists and their supporters. Despite clear evidence of their crimes, the army never pursued them. These atrocities were documented in accounts published in 2003 in the *Toledo Blade.* However, these incidents do not make such conduct uniform or universal. Americans serving in Vietnam often became frustrated by the nature of the war, and for some, this resulted in a hatred for the Vietnamese. This hatred could have been the greater for some due to racism. Yet these attitudes were not representative and those who held them did not necessarily engage in criminal conduct.[56] They were not psychopaths unleashed on the civilian population.

American attitudes toward their ARVN allies were often more condescending and even contemptuous than what they sometimes felt toward the villagers. The army's 1st Division officers who warned men to be cautious of civilians, including women and children, hoped to use ARVN forces as intermediaries in these dealings. They then decided this would not work because the ARVN troops were not dependable. A wartime survey of servicemen in Vietnam discovered that they did not think of themselves as fighting for Vietnam because they considered South Vietnam a "worthless country." The antagonism was most pointed when directed against their ARVN allies: "Disparaging remarks about the fighting qualities of the South Vietnamese forces are endemic." Ironically, the men interviewed had more respect for their Vietnamese enemies: "Why do our Vietnamese fight so lousy and theirs fight so good?" was the question.[57]

Senior American military leaders had major misgivings about the ARVN forces. They questioned their field leadership and even their commitment to the goal of defeating the enemy. There was a sense that they had failed to quell the NLF rebellion, despite a decade of American training and heavy infusions of U.S. military equipment. So the U.S. military was not at all willing to depend upon them now.

As the training programs continued, the collaborative operations became more symbolic. This resulted in a greater American military independence, which involved ignoring one of the mission priorities. The American military attitude too often became condescending. Language was always a barrier, and few Americans devoted themselves to lifting it. Particularly in the early years of the war, very few American servicemen knew Vietnamese and the command did not seem to attach a priority to learning it. One senior Vietnamese officer said, "I know of no single instance in which a U.S. advisor effectively discussed professional matters with his counterpart in Vietnamese." And in the field, this went from ignorance to indifference to patronizing; from this point the attitudes frequently expressed were contempt, racist contempt. It was not unusual for American troops to dismiss their South Vietnamese allies as "little people," "gooks," or "Marvin the Arvin." The ARVN soldiers excelled in battle a number of times, but they also failed often. As young conscripts from poor families, poorly supported, poorly led, struggling to maintain enthusiasm for the government, they had a difficult task, and the Americans were increasingly of little help.[58]

Great debates about the causes of the American War in Vietnam, about its objectives and the conduct — political, military, and moral — marked the entire history of the experience. These increased and expanded throughout the first years of the war. Simultaneously, hundreds of thousands of men and women were coming into Vietnam or processing out to return home, passing through Saigon, Long Binh, or Da Nang. And increasing numbers were being processed out on medical evacuation flights to Okinawa, Japan, or the United States. And of course still others were being processed out by Mortuary Services contractors. The experience of those who served and those who sacrificed was obviously framed by political, diplomatic, and policy decisions made in Washington and by strategic choices and tactical moves determined in Saigon. These civilian and military decision makers shaped the war. Those out in the field experienced it.

Absent major determinative battles, the war in Vietnam nevertheless had heavy casualties. Some 2,594,000 American men and women served in Vietnam throughout the entire war. (This does not include the number of air force personnel who served elsewhere in support of the war, notably Thailand, or the sailors who served in navy vessels in coastal waters.) Of these, 8.2 percent (about 213,000) were major casualties, either killed or wounded and hospitalized. The army had 7.78 percent of its soldiers in-country who were such casualties, and the marines suffered 16.9 percent.

These casualties followed a pretty clear pattern as the war went on. Over the course of the war, more Americans were killed in Vietnam in May than in any other month. Looking at the years of heaviest casualties, 1965–1971, 12 percent of the American deaths occurred in May. The spring was often a time when major operations and offensives were carried out. Looking in detail at these May killed-in-action data reveals some important patterns. For example, in May 1965, the median age of the Americans killed was twenty-nine; 62 percent of them were married. This reflected the seniority of the advisers who were still an important part of the troops deployed. It also reflected the fact that a large number of the men killed in May 1965 were on aircraft. Ground units were still deploying and had not yet initiated any major operations. Over 25 percent of the dead were crew members or passengers on fixed-wing aircraft or on helicopters. Thirty-nine percent of the deaths in May 1965 were members of the air force. None of the men killed in May 1965 were draftees.[59]

This would change dramatically over the next few years. The casualties increased sharply. The 89 men killed in May 1965 became 591 in 1966; 1,396 in 1967; and 2,416 in 1968. This was the highest monthly figure of the entire war, and it represented the dramatic annual increases in the cost of this war. In 1965, 1,928 American servicemen were killed in Vietnam. In 1966, this was 6,350; in 1967, 11,363; and in 1968, 16,899. Nearly a ninefold increase in three years.

Although none of the men killed in May 1965 were draftees, in 1966, more than 15 percent were, and this proportion more than doubled in 1967 and 1968, to 31 percent. By May 1969, this percentage had grown to 42. Perhaps it is most revealing to look at the army only, because that branch of the military had most of the draftees. The marines had a small number, and the air force and navy had no draftees. In May 1967, 1968, and 1969, over half of the army enlisted dead were draftees. In 1966, it had been less than one-quarter.

The median age of the May killed in action dropped from twenty-nine in May 1965 to twenty years of age in May 1967 — and it shifted upward to twenty-one in 1968, where it remained for the duration of the war. The men on patrols out in the jungle, serving with army or marine infantry units, were young and, by most assessments, working class. And at first they were disproportionately African American. In May 1966, nearly 18 percent of the men killed in Vietnam were black. In the subsequent May casualty lists, the number would never be this high again, but it would not drop below 11 percent until 1972. In May 1968, nearly 14 percent of the servicemen killed were black. Latino servicemen were not recorded by the Pentagon as a distinct group in this period. One study looking at Spanish surnames from the five southwestern states determined that 18.2 percent of the men killed from these states were Latino. In these states this group was over-represented in the killed-in-action figures.[60]

William Broyles described the marines he met when he arrived on Hill 10, southwest of Da Nang in the fall of 1969: "I have fifty-eight men. Only twenty have high school diplomas. About ten of them are over twenty-one. Reading through their record books almost made me cry. Over and over they read — address of father: unknown; education, one or two years of high school; occupation: laborer, pecan sheller, gas station attendant, Job Corps. Kids with no place to go. No place but here."[61]

Christian Appy's classic study of the men who served in Vietnam as well as other analyses and observations confirm that the men who were in combat units — and who were disproportionately casualties — were from blue-collar backgrounds.[62] And by no means were all or even most of them there reluctantly. The 9 young men from the mining town of Morenci, Arizona, who joined the marines together in 1966 wanted to go to war. They all went to Vietnam, and 6 of them died there, including 3 in the late spring of 1968. The close-knit community experienced a continuing sense of mourning and of funeral processions — and of Marine Corps Honor Guards firing salutes beside the graves of the fallen young men.[63]

The nature of death also reveals something of the nature of the war in Vietnam. In 1966–

1968, more than half of the men killed died as a result of small-arms fire or artillery, rockets, and mortar rounds. The small-arms fire was clearly a sign of encounters on field operations, as likely were most of the deaths from the explosives. In these years among the May casualties, there was a sharp increase in deaths resulting from "other explosive devices" and "multiple fragmentation wounds." These would also have reflected field operations with Claymore and other mines and related explosive discharges. The aggregated statistics for the war reveal that 73 percent of the deaths resulting from hostile action were from small-arms fire, grenades, mines, or multiple fragmentation wounds. All related to direct combat actions. Despite the increasing lethality of explosives, the most deadly wound continued to be gunshot.[64]

There are no good figures on the number of men killed by so-called friendly fire incidents. Most of these resulted from artillery or mortar rounds or air strikes that were not on target. But the targeting itself was complicated by the proximity of the enemy soldiers to the American forces. One pilot on a helicopter gunship found it sometimes "unnerving" because the American troops would ask for the rockets to come in closer to them. "In the jungle areas, we could not see the action at all. We knew from the tops of the jungle where the rounds were hitting, but it was almost impossible for us to ever actually see the units themselves."[65]

Jim Webb, a marine platoon leader in the Dodge City area southwest of Da Nang in the spring of 1969, notes that "almost every Marine who has ever fought in close combat can relay stories of short rounds, stray rounds, misdirected shots, accidental discharges, and other chaos resulting from friendly fire." Rounds would "wander from their intended targets" due to a variety of factors, including "map error" and "human error." It was pretty basic: "Things could go wrong, and often did."[66]

Even as the number of men and women deployed to Vietnam grew to and then beyond a half million, the concerns continued about having an adequate force to meet all of the assignments and responsibilities that went with a modern military. Part of this problem stemmed from the scale of noncombat assignments. In 1967, this became the source of a major disagreement at the Pentagon, when it became clear that of the 464,000 troops then in Vietnam, only about 70,000 were serving as combat troops. Secretary McNamara pushed back on this number and the military chiefs agreed to reassign more of the men to combat roles.[67]

Shifting assignments was not easy. For example, the army base at Long Binh, twenty-one miles from Saigon, was the largest U.S.

military installation outside of the continental United States. At one point there were 60,000 men and women stationed there, which exceeded the number of U.S. Army soldiers in all combat assignments in the country. Long Binh was the major replacement and processing center for Vietnam, the logistics center for the war, and the headquarters of MACV. It was a key administrative and records center, often called Pentagon East.

There were 3,500 buildings and 180 miles of roads on the base. It had one of Vietnam's largest hospitals and a large Graves Registration center. The base contained the major stockade in Vietnam, called by the soldiers Long Binh Jail, or LBJ. Long Binh also had swimming pools and miniature golf courses and skeet ranges and fishing ponds and go-kart tracks and movie theaters and basketball and tennis courts and baseball/softball fields. There was a "war museum" on the base so that people stationed there could see mock-ups of villages and related combat settings that would inform them of what it was like out in the bush.[68]

Long Binh was the most extreme example of the massive operation providing support for the troops in the field — and for those who were supporting the troops in the field. Beer, fresh food, including ice cream — massive American dairies located in Vietnam could produce over two million gallons a month — were available. The United States spent about $220 million annually feeding the troops in Vietnam. A rations were fresh foods supplemented with frozen, canned, or dehydrated foods. C rations were canned ready-to-eat foods in the field. The military food and mess supply operation tried to get A ration meals to the field whenever possible. This was complicated and depended upon helicopter availability and field accessibility. The ice cream didn't always get out into the field.

At the major bases — and many of the minor ones — open mess clubs served alcohol and food, had live entertainment, including go-go dancers and slot machines. By 1969, 7,200 part-time and 1,320 full-time U.S. military ran more than 2,000 mess clubs around the country. These clubs employed tens of thousands of Vietnamese as cooks, bartenders, dishwashers, waitstaff, and the like. In 1969, the army's open messes generated over $177 million in revenue and over $22 million in profit. Air force, navy, and marine clubs also did well.[69]

By 1971, Special Services had built 1,339 athletic facilities in Vietnam. These were mainly fields and outdoor courts as well as gymnasiums and indoor facilities in places with troop concentrations. For example, Pleiku, with 5,400 military personnel, had two baseball fields, two football fields, nine volleyball courts, seven basketball courts, one tennis court, one badminton court, seven multiuse courts, and a weight room. Special Services operated forty-eight swimming pools in twenty-two locations. There also were pools on bases that were not run by Special Services. And there were beaches on coastal bases that were maintained by the military — Cam Ranh Bay, for example, had three separate beaches. And books were available. There were thirty-seven fixed libraries on military bases by 1970, supplemented by a major interlibrary loan program.[70]

Debby Alexander arrived in Vietnam to work in Special Services. She had no prior training and she received none there. She was posted out at Soc Trang — she and another young woman in Special Services and several hundred men were stationed at this large airfield. They ran the Service Club, providing activities for enlisted men, bingo on Sundays and something every night. They ran a library and provided arts and crafts training and showed movies, raffled off cartons of cigarettes, and organized floor shows with Filipino talent. She served at a number of bases over the next year — and came to know a number of men who were killed while out on a mission.[71]

In many regards, such an infrastructure may have been an inevitable cost of modern warfare — or at least warfare as the United States fought and managed, supplied, and recorded it at this time. Flying, maintaining, and protecting aircraft, providing and staffing a complicated supply system, delivering food, ammunition, and supplies to hundreds of bases and units, trying to provide many of the recreational and social options and comforts of home, providing health care at field clinics, small hospitals, and major medical and recuperation facilities, and then assuring security at all points in the chain, monitoring and accounting and managing the entire operation — all of this required a large force. There was a tension over this, and not only in Washington. The men in the field, the grunts, referred to those who worked back at the bases as REMFs (rear echelon mother fuckers).

One soldier whose unit served on Hamburger Hill said that he and his buddies sometimes wondered, "How the hell did we end up out here in the jungle every day and living out here like animals for weeks, sometimes, a month?" They were out there with their uniforms "rotting off" while some "guys are back in the rear, living a life similar to what we had in the States, you know? But I guess that's just the way it was."[72]

The antagonism could be serious. Shortly after Second Lieutenant William Broyles reported to his marine infantry platoon near

Da Nang, he was on night radio watch when he received a call saying that the marine command base in Da Nang was under rocket attack. He was ordered to move the platoon across the river to try to intercept the NVA rocket team. The radio operator shouted out to the platoon, "They're rocketing Da Nang." Broyles was surprised by the reaction to the news that other marines were under attack. "The response was not what I expected. The response was — cheers. All around the perimeter my fellow marines, the descendants of the heroes of Guadalcanal and Iwo Jima, were shouting with joy." And "Get those REMFs!" was at the core of the cheering. Broyles's squad leader told the new lieutenant that he should forget about ordering the men to cross the river at night: "Ain't no way we gonna move this platoon, at night, off this hill, cross that river, and go diddy-bopping through that jungle trying to find some gook rocketmen. We gonna get our asses kicked — and you know it. And all for some REMFs." The platoon waited until daylight to cross the river.[73]

Military assessments indicated that the morale was lower among soldiers in the rear echelons. The highest rates of criminal conduct, drug use, and absenteeism without authorization were in the bases rear of the combat areas. There was more black market activity there, more opportunities for escapism. It seemed that the men out in hostile territory had less time to think about — or at least to pursue — these activities. Survival was their priority.[74]

When the first combat troops came to Vietnam in 1965, they came as units. Generally they arrived by ship and had trained together, developed close friendships, and worked with veteran NCOs and officers, including veterans of Korea and of World War II. This would change within a year as the military adopted rotation systems. Individual deployments would be for one year — except for marines, who served a thirteen-month tour of duty in Vietnam. There was little doubt that group cohesion suffered as a result of this turnover. Units contained men with altogether different levels of experience, and veterans were concerned about the safety of the FNGs (fuckin' new guys) as well as their own safety with the inexperienced replacements. Casualties tended to be higher among the newest men in combat units. And as unit cohesion suffered, so did unit competence, effectiveness, and efficiency. An "army of amateurs," some called it.

Infantry veteran Chuck Hagel recalled in 2002, "The rotation problem was bigger than we could have imagined and didn't quite even understand it when we were going through it. As I look back on it now, it's — it was the worst thing that could possibly happen. You had guys rotating in and out daily. You would break the continuity of leadership. You'd break the continuity of confidence, of teamwork."[75]

On the other hand, one study based on extended interviews with officers who served in Vietnam as platoon leaders or company commanders found that the rotation system was very effective in addressing individual morale. Everyone knew when he would be going home.[76]

Early in 1968, the routine shifted dramatically. The previous year had been marked by a greater number of U.S. operations. MACV remained focused on population security and was increasingly aggressive in seeking out enemy troops. The idea of "social policy" was still on the to-do list. This was even as the United States reorganized its pacification program in a new agency, Civil Operations and Revolutionary Development Support (CORDS). There had developed a strong group encouraging a far greater priority for counterinsurgency operations. Military and CIA officials including John Paul Vann and Edward Lansdale, State Department officers Richard Holbrooke and Robert Komer of the National Security Council, and Rufus Phillips of the Agency for International Development had been pushing for some new initiative to emphasize counterinsurgency. Finally in 1967, President Johnson agreed to transfer the old Office of Civil Operations into the new CORDS agency. Komer would be the director and would report to MACV, working directly with Westmoreland. CORDS did have some greater success than the other disorganized elements of counterinsurgency. Due to health issues, Robert Komer was replaced by William Colby as director in 1968.[77]

Colby oversaw a more successful program. Washington was increasingly interested in pacification and counterinsurgency. And Colby's long service as a CIA officer influenced his approach to the program. He came to be convinced that it was necessary to counter the NLF cadres in the contested villages. And the CIA Phoenix Program became a signature piece of this effort. Operating under CORDS, Phoenix and its South Vietnamese government partner, Phung Hoang, worked with Provincial Reconnaissance Units to "neutralize" NLF leaders. Working largely with South Vietnamese operatives, in some cases using torture and assassination, this program oversaw the killing of some 20,000 alleged Communist leaders in the villages (some estimates are twice this number). Phoenix/ Phung Hoang significantly reduced the influence and the numbers of Communist shadow government officials — even as it also likely increased the fear and distrust of the South Vietnamese government or the Americans in the villages.[78]

One military historian said that any sense of progress in winning hearts and minds was misplaced. "What brought about the perception that the countryside had become pacified was the fact that large numbers of civilians were forcibly removed from contested hamlets and villages and resettled in areas controlled by the government." Rather than convincing people to come over to the government side, "It was the hard hand of war, of death and destruction brought about by military operations . . . In order to survive, many villagers simply left the war zones, moving closer to government facilities, which would at least provide safety from American air and ground attacks." Some participants used the metaphor "draining the pond," likely playing off Mao Zedong's dictum that the "guerrilla must move amongst the people as a fish swims in the sea." Resettlement, Phoenix/Phung Hoang, and Operation Ranch Hand addressed a part of the problem — empty the ominous sea.[79]

In November 1967, over a period of less than three weeks, the army's 173rd Airborne Brigade fought a major battle at Dak To in the Central Highlands near the borders of South Vietnam, Laos, and Cambodia. They defeated the North Vietnamese regulars of the 1st Infantry Division who had been staging there — or at least they forced them to withdraw from the contested Hill 875. The 173rd lost 208 men and 645 wounded in this battle — their twelve rifle companies had 51 percent killed or wounded in one month. One estimate was that 60 of the dead, 29 percent, had been killed by friendly fire. The 173rd never again operated in Vietnam as a complete unit. General Westmoreland was in Washington at the time, and he said that the battle there was "the beginning of a great defeat for the enemy." He observed that the war was now swinging in the direction of the Americans and the South Vietnamese and that it was possible that the withdrawal of U.S. forces could begin "within two years or less."[80]

General Westmoreland had been summoned back to Washington as part of a Johnson administration campaign "to prove that no stalemate existed in Vietnam." All of the major players were urged to look for examples of real progress. Dak To became such an example. At the National Press Club, General Westmoreland acknowledged that the war's progress could not easily be portrayed on maps, but he wanted to emphasize "the most optimistic appraisal of the way the war was going" that he had ever comfortably made. He did not say there was a light at the end of a tunnel, but he came close when he concluded that the war was at a phase "when the end begins to come into view." He was confident that his policy was now moving toward a successful resolution. Victory "lies within our grasp."[81]

General Westmoreland expressed only one concern about the Vietnam prospects: He worried not about the military situation in that country but about the political situation in the United States. He cautioned against "political pressures" in America to "throw in the towel."[82]

Over in Vietnam, the war did seem to be taking some positive turns and, defined strictly in military terms, perhaps "victory" would be within the grasp of the American and South Vietnamese forces. But as their senior civilian and military officials would repeatedly be reminded, the American War in Vietnam never could be reduced to or defined strictly in military terms.

At the end of 1967, the American troop levels in Vietnam had reached a new high, with 486,000 men and women in uniform serving. There was a mood of optimism. In spite of ominous signs that the Communist forces might be planning something, there was a general sense of confidence that the allied forces were now able to handle any initiatives the Communists undertook — and, indeed, to turn these into victories, as they had recently at Dak To. And as they had throughout the war by inviting — challenging — the enemy to attack first so that the Americans could respond with overpowering force.

In Hanoi, the Vietnamese Communist Party officials also recognized that the Americans were inflicting heavy losses on the NVA and NLF forces. The war was proving to be costly to them. So some of the top officials pushed hard for a more aggressive strategy marked by a major offensive. General Võ Nguyên Giáp pressed back against this initiative. He believed it would be premature and likely would fail given the U.S. advantages in mobility and firepower. He believed in a protracted guerrilla war. He was not persuasive, and the Communist military command went ahead with planning for a major offensive on January 31, 1968, during the Tet holiday.[83]

Late in 1967, General Westmoreland and his top advisers expected that any major NVA offensive would likely originate in the northwestern hill country of South Vietnam, in areas adjacent to Laos. Increasingly, there were signs that the NVA was massing in Laos in the area just south of the DMZ. The expectation was that they would attack the airfield and base camp at Khe Sanh, just seven miles from Laos and fourteen miles south of the DMZ.

General Westmoreland decided to increase the marine presence at Khe Sanh. He did this over the objections of the senior marine commanders in Vietnam, including General Lewis Walt, and in their Pacific command, notably General Victor Krulak. The marines believed that Khe Sanh was not strategically important and that any troops stationed there would be isolated and vulnerable. General Westmoreland held that the NVA was hoping to initiate an attack at Khe Sanh that would annihilate the defenders and would repeat the defeat of the French at Dien Bien Phu fourteen years earlier. He would lure them into doing just that — and then with the firepower available to the Americans, he would destroy them.[84]

When the North Vietnamese began an assault on the 26th Marines on January 17, 1968, all predictions, best and worst, seemed affirmed — the marines were concerned about their vulnerability and MACV was confident that they had figured out the Communist plan. There were 6,000 marines at the outpost, a sizable force. They were surrounded by some 20,000 North Vietnamese (some estimates put that number as high as 40,000). The defenders were subjected to heavy artillery shelling, mortar attacks, sappers, and gunfire. They were totally dependent upon helicopters and cargo planes for supplies. The dramatic siege of Khe Sanh became an important staple of television footage from Vietnam. President Johnson watched it closely and worried about it. Westmoreland believed that the major assault there would come after the Tet Lunar New Year holidays in late January. The influential columnist Joseph Alsop predicted that the siege "may turn out to be a major turning point" of the war.[85]

The major attack did come in the middle of the Tet holiday — and the presumed cease-fire. But it did not focus only or even primarily on Khe Sanh. The joint NVA/NLF forces mounted coordinated attacks throughout South Vietnam. Following some premature attacks on several cities on January 30, the next day at 3:00 A.M., some 80,000 Communist troops assaulted more than three-quarters of the provincial capitals in South Vietnam, nearly all of the large cities, and the major U.S. military bases. It now seemed apparent that the NVA activities out at Khe Sanh and at Dak To, although serious initiatives, were also diversionary attacks to draw more American troops out to the hill country and away from the cities. Indeed, for the first few days of Tet, the leadership at MACV was convinced. General Westmoreland was warning two days after the attacks that the enemy's "main effort" was yet to come and it would be at Khe Sanh.[86]

There was a major and a symbolically significant fight in Saigon itself, with suicide squads attacking the presidential palace, the ARVN general staff compound, the main radio station, the massive Tan Son Nhut airfield, and even coming onto the grounds of the American embassy. The three-line headline in *The New York Times* was "Foe Invades U.S. Saigon Embassy; Raiders Wiped Out After 6 Hours; Vietcong Widen Attack on Cities." Fighting in Saigon continued for several days.[87] On February 2, the *Times* had at the top of the front page a photo of ARVN general Nguyen Ngoc Loan, with a pistol to the head of a man identified as a "Vietcong terrorist," preparing to execute him on the street. The photographs by Eddie Adams, an AP photographer in Saigon, appeared throughout the world in many publications and television broadcasts, and later won the Pulitzer Prize.

The major battle was in the ancient city of Hué. Throughout most of the month of February, this was a vicious fight with marines and soldiers in house-to-house fighting. The battle lasted twenty-five days, and much of the city was reduced to rubble — some 40 percent of the houses were destroyed or badly damaged. Of the city's 140,000 residents, 116,000 were now homeless. There were 221 Americans killed and 1,364 wounded in the battle. The ARVN had 38 dead and 1,800 wounded. Estimates on the number of Communist soldiers killed were 5,000 in the city and another 3,000 outside Hué. And nearly 5,800 civilians were listed as killed or missing

— nearly 3,000 of these dead were found in mass graves after being executed by the Communists. These were soldiers but also civil servants, merchants, teachers, clergy, and other community leaders.

MACV and the entire military command in Vietnam were shaken by the scale of the attacks, but they responded promptly and effectively to the offensive. They quickly assessed that they had won an important victory — or series of victories. There is little doubt that the allied command had turned back the assault. The Communists lost. The popular uprising that they had expected never happened. In mounting such a wide-scale attack, they had spread their forces far too thinly, except possibly in Hué and Saigon. The combined Communist armies lost at least 40,000 soldiers — and some estimates place the figure much higher. The National Liberation Front, the Viet Cong, never really recovered from Tet as an effective, comprehensive military force. On the other hand, the ARVN forces performed much better in the face of this challenge than some observers had expected. General Westmoreland told reporters in Vietnam that the enemy had suffered a defeat comparable to the Battle of the Bulge in World War II. They had put a large share of their forces in the battles and achieved some "tactical surprise," but they failed. The United States would need more troops to take advantage of this, he pointed out.[88]

In early April, the siege of Khe Sanh was broken. Operation Pegasus with a joint army-marine force had broken through. The North Vietnamese withdrew. The marines had lost 199 killed and 830 wounded in this siege, and the Pegasus forces had 92 killed and 629 wounded. Americans estimated that the Communists had lost between 10,000 and 15,000 men. The United States had launched 158,891 artillery rounds and performed more than 21,000 bombing sorties, including massive B-52 attacks in defense of the enclave. It was not another Dien Bien Phu.[89]

James Reston wrote in his *New York Times* column after Tet that there had been a "troubled silence" in Washington. He said that up until the Tet Offensive, "in a curious way, the capital knew in its mind what the facts were in Vietnam but this week it began to realize in its heart just how complicated they were." *The Washington Post* wrote of the "Maze of Uncertainties" that remained after Tet.[90]

In mid-February, Walter Cronkite of the *CBS Evening News,* probably the most trusted newsman in the country, left his desk in New York and went to Vietnam to see for himself what was happening. He joined the marines who were still fighting in Hué. Back in New York later that month, he spoke from his chair about his experience. He said it was hard to know how to call the results of Tet, and he feared that Khe Sanh could still fall, a "tragedy of our own stubbornness there." He went on to admit that "we have been too often disappointed by the optimism of the American leaders, both in Vietnam and Washington, to have faith any longer in the silver linings they find in the darkest clouds." It seemed to him "more certain than ever that the bloody experience of Vietnam is to end in a stalemate." He concluded that "it is increasingly clear to this reporter that the only rational way out then will be to negotiate, not as victors, but as an honorable people who lived up to their pledge to defend democracy, and did the best they could." Following the broadcast, President Johnson said to his press secretary, "If I've lost Cronkite, I've lost middle America."[91]

A number of commentators, military and civilian, later complained that a major factor in losing the Vietnam War was the hostile coverage by the American media. They insisted that the war was reported negatively, none of the American military accomplishments were recognized, and these critical stories caused public opinion to turn against the war. "Our worst enemy seems to be the press," President Nixon argued in 1971. An army general said that the Communists were defeated, but this fact was not reported by media "unquestionably influenced by Communist propaganda." General Westmoreland maintained that the correspondents were young, a majority under the age of twenty-nine, and that "for the most part they had little or no experience as war correspondents."[92]

As with virtually all aspects of this war, issues concerning reportage were far too complicated to be explained by simple slogans or assertions. The news media that covered the war were diverse and evolving, not easily summarized with a few generalizations. The main voices were a professional lot. The reporters were young — but not nearly as young as the men who were fighting the war. Looking at the group of 5,098 correspondents accredited at one time or another by MACV in Saigon, their average age was just under thirty-six. About 21 percent were under the age of twenty-six. The aggregations can be hard to summarize. The number of accredited journalists in the country probably peaked in the spring of 1968 at 586, however less than half of these were Americans — there was always a sizable international group covering the war. And not all accredited "reporters" actually were reporters — the rules required drivers, interpreters, staff, clerical support, and all working in the news media to receive accreditation. Nearly half of the Americans accredited as journalists at that time spent fewer than thirty-one days in the country — they were there to do a feature on a hometown unit or on some occasion. Because of the size of their crews, television media teams dominated in numbers accredited. Over the course of the war, 238 people employed by the three national networks were in Vietnam. *The New York Times* had the highest newspaper numbers in terms of reporters and support staff — 46 who served in the country over the course of the war.[93]

Early in the war, prior to 1964, reporters like Malcolm Browne, Neil Sheehan, Homer Bigart, and David Halberstam had great difficulty covering the war. They basically accepted the anticommunist assumptions that resulted in the American adviser program there, but they were unable to get much information about its operation. The American command was close-mouthed and the Diem administration was downright hostile to them. So they worked with midlevel officers — the Sheehan and Halberstam relationship with John Paul Vann was the most consequential of these connections.

By late in the Kennedy administration, it was clear to most American officials that the system was not working well — depriving journalists of information only encouraged them to go find their own sources, which might not be as accurate and certainly could be less flattering. As one government official wrote in late 1964, "You can't prevent stories by not providing information . . . Whenever we have taken pains to keep the press abreast of what is happening it has worked to our advantage." So MACV developed its system of accreditation and adopted the policy of "maximum candor." No modern American war has provided journalists with so much freedom and so few constraints.[94]

Reporters in Vietnam had to agree to a set of restrictions that finally were pretty commonsensical and not overly restrictive: not to reveal future plans, size of units, information on unit designations and movements during an operation, amount of fuel and ordnance on hand, casualties during an operation and names of casualties following a fight, etc. These were not limiting in their effects. Basically the reporters were free to go wherever they wanted, except they had to travel in military helicopters and vehicles when they went into the countryside. And the military tended to accommodate their travel requests. There were planes of all sizes and many helicopters flying all over South Vietnam regularly, and there was usually space available for another passenger. This mobility was less useful in trying to anticipate a battle. Reporters had the freedom to go, but they had to determine where to go. And this mobility was even more complicated for television crews. A TV sound camera weighed twenty-four pounds, and all of the supporting equipment added another six hundred pounds or so. TV correspondents sometimes complained about the inability of television to cover the breaking news stories — and of course even when they could, there was a lag in shipping film back to New York for broadcast.[95]

When reporters wanted to cover field action, they were supposed to have someone accompany them on their trip. Most reporters said that this was seldom the case with most units. The journalists pretty much went where they wanted and had no one monitoring their interviews or their filming. As Bob Hager of NBC News described it, "We were so uncensored, so loose. We could move ourselves without prearrangement — just sort of go to a firebase and try to hitchhike a ride with a helicopter." Another NBC journalist, Kenley Jones, could not recall an occasion when someone said, "You can't film that." He said the entire relationship was "fairly lax." Terence Smith of *The New York Times* agreed that as long as reporters followed the basic rules, "you were entirely free to go anywhere and write anything — talk to any member of the U.S. or the South Vietnamese military. You were not censored. You didn't have to submit your copy to anyone."[96]

Being free to move around and to cover action was a great opportunity for reporters. But this war was a series of spontaneous skirmishes, patrols and ambushes, unexpected rocket and mortar attacks. The media had to move around, assess situations, and hope to be in the right place. And despite the large number of accredited reporters, few of them were actually in the field regularly, and they could not possibly anticipate and cover the sudden and deadly flare-ups that marked combat in Vietnam. Clarence Wyatt estimated that there may have been no more than thirty or forty reporters in the field at any one time covering the war for national U.S. news organizations. They could hurry over to a base camp and interview men following a firefight, but they were seldom able to time their trips to be with them during the action. Television crews found it particularly difficult to move quickly to the field.

The news media was largely supportive — or at least uncritical — of the troops fighting the war. And they followed the rules pretty carefully — from 1965 to 1972, MACV revoked or suspended credentials of fewer than a dozen individuals. Most members of the press had an adversarial relationship with the official MACV media people in Saigon — they were dismissive of the daily briefings, calling them "The Five O'Clock Follies" for the military officials' stubborn insistence on sharing only official accounts. If some of the journalists were increasingly critical of the assumptions underlying the war or the conduct of the war, they were cautious — and their organizations back in the United States were more cautious.[97]

Most analyses found the press coverage sympathetic to the men in the field. As one described it, "In the early period of the war reporters lauded the efficiency, teamwork, and might of the American armed forces." By 1970 or so, this had shifted as the stories focused more on the drawdown of troops, declining morale, and a concern about deteriorating military discipline. But in the first half of the war this was not the story. *Newsweek,* often more critical of the war, in 1967 criticized the press: "Never in the history of warfare has so much information been inflicted upon so many." They described a "moral schizophrenia" in the United States, a country that was prosperous and serene being subjected daily to reports that caused its citizens to be "steeped in, immersed in, awash in or adrift in the horrors of battle."Yet *Newsweek* learned through a Harris survey they commissioned that over 70 percent of Americans were satisfied by television and newspaper coverage of the war — while 62 percent were satisfied by newsmagazines. Their analysis revealed that "TV has encouraged a decisive majority of viewers to support the war."[98] Despite this, it is critical to note that there was film from Vietnam and casualty numbers on the newscasts nearly every night. It is possible that the nonstop coverage contributed to Americans becoming more pessimistic about the war.

In the fall of 1967, Vice President Hubert Humphrey visited Vietnam. In a session with a group of reporters at Chu Lai, he asked them for a favor: "When you speak to the American people give the benefit of the doubt to our side. I don't think that's asking too much. We're in this together." A veteran newsman responded, "Benefit of the doubt? Hell, what do they think we've been doing for the past six years?"[99]

Fighting the American War in Vietnam was complicated. The tactical objectives on the ground and the strategic goals in Washington and Saigon were rarely tangible or measurable. As a result, covering this war and telling the story in brief daily summaries back home was more than complicated. Most press coverage, certainly prior to Tet, was largely favorable. Horrifying stories such as Morley Safer's CBS broadcast in 1965 showing marines using Zippo lighters to burn down the village at Cam Ne, and the NBC broadcast and the Eddie Adams photo of Colonel Nguyen Ngoc Loan holding a pistol to the head of his NLF captive and then shooting him during Tet, got a great deal of attention.

As they should have. It is true that due to television, the war in Vietnam was America's first living room war — but only in the sense of pretty general, even superficial, coverage. Most television news from Vietnam was "American boys in action" stories, and reports that started with a day's roundup read by the anchor showing a battle map, followed by reports of casualties reported by MACV. The weekly MACV reports on Thursday always had a score card. And the Americans always had the best score on these reports and thus on the visuals. There was little coverage of the Vietnamese people or Vietnamese politics. The New York television network producers wanted "bang-bang" action stories, even if these seldom provided a good insight into the war.[100]

The early reports on Tet certainly were more negative than the results of the fighting merited. But the fact that the battles were fought after months, or years, of reassurances by the most senior military and civilian officials in Saigon and Washington that the fight was gone from the enemy was itself newsworthy. And Walter Cronkite's reflections on Tet as necessitating a reassessment of American strategy and goals were powerful and persuasive to many. But on ABC-TV, Howard K. Smith was equally persuasive to some: "There exists only one real alternative. That is to escalate, but this time on an overwhelming scale." Smith proposed bombing the port of Haiphong until it was no longer usable. He would bomb the dikes in North Vietnam to reduce their agricultural capability, and he would send 400,000 more troops into Vietnam with authorization to begin hot pursuit of the enemy into Laos and Cambodia. Television anchors did not speak with a single voice or share a singular message.[101] If the war in Vietnam began a long drawdown following Tet, the media covered this and the changes in-country that followed it. They did not cause these developments.

Immediately after the Tet Offensive began, in February 1968, Louis Harris reported that some 74 percent of those polled said they were supportive of the war — this was up from 61 percent in December. But the overall support for Lyndon Johnson declined. Between November 1967, during the administration's campaign insisting the war was going well, and late February 1968, support for the president's handling of the war declined from 51 to 32 percent. In the six weeks following Tet, one in five Americans reported having switched from a "hawk," supportive of the war, to a "dove," supporting peace.[102]

In March 1968, President Johnson convened his informal group of senior advisers, the Wise Men. These included Dean Acheson, Henry Cabot Lodge, McGeorge Bundy, Douglas Dillon, Abe Fortas, Averell Harriman, and retired generals Omar Bradley, Maxwell Taylor, and Matthew Ridgway. He had met with this same group the previous November and they had urged him to stay the course in Vietnam.

On March 25, after two days of briefings and meetings, the Wise Men recommended to LBJ that the time had come to reduce the American role in Vietnam. The administration should not deploy the additional troops that General Westmoreland and the Joint Chiefs of Staff had requested; bombing of the North should be halted; and the United States should take steps to negotiate a settlement. The president was shocked. He noted that "the establishment bastards have bailed out." On March 31, after nearly losing the New Hampshire primary to antiwar candidate Senator Eugene McCarthy, President Johnson spoke to the nation. He said that he was going to work for peace. He ordered a partial bombing halt and vowed that he would be willing to negotiate anyplace.

Then he stunned everyone:

With America's sons in the fields far away, with America's future under challenge right here at home, with our hopes and the world's hopes for peace in the balance every day, I do not believe that I should devote an hour or a day of my time to any personal partisan causes or to any duties other than the awesome duties of this office — the Presidency of your country.

Accordingly, I shall not seek, and I will not accept, the nomination of my party for another term as your President.

But let men everywhere know, however, that a strong, a confident, and a vigilant America stands ready tonight to seek an honorable peace — and stands ready tonight to defend an honored cause — whatever the price, whatever the burden, whatever the sacrifice that duty may require.[103]

March had been a highly eventful month. On March 1, Clark Clifford, a Washington lawyer and an important adviser to Democratic presidents beginning with Harry Truman, had replaced Robert McNamara as secretary of defense. Secretary McNamara had three months earlier announced to the president that he thought the war had proved to be a mistake, and they agreed that he should step down. On March 22, President Johnson announced that General Westmoreland would assume the role of army chief of staff and General Creighton Abrams would replace him as head of MACV. That month, 1,767 Americans died in Vietnam.

Fifty-one men died in Vietnam on March 31, 1968, the day of the president's address. Eleven of those who died on that day were under twenty years of age. These deaths brought the total killed in Vietnam in the first quarter of 1968 to 5,571. Since March 1965, when the marines came ashore at Da Nang, 25,140 had died. If the focus up to this point had been on "winning" the war, or at least on attrition of enemy forces, now it would shift to include more actively searching for ways to negotiate a settlement. And in that process the baby boom generation would still step up to "defend an honored cause." Before this period of negotiation concluded, 32,454 more men and women would die.

TRANSITIONS:
THE VIETNAM WAR IN AMERICA

January 20, 1969, was a chilly day in Washington, with the temperature in the midthirties. The previous day's rain had let up by morning, but rain and sleet would return in the afternoon. But at midday, between the storms, on the East Portico of the U.S. Capitol, Chief Justice Earl Warren administered the oath of office to Richard Milhous Nixon as president of the United States. Mr. Nixon placed his hand on two family Bibles held by his wife, Patricia.

It was an ecumenical occasion. The Right Reverend Charles Ewbank Tucker, presiding bishop of the African Methodist Episcopal Zion Church, delivered the Invocation. Rabbi Edgar F. Magnin, Archbishop Iakovos of the Greek Orthodox Church, and Reverend Billy Graham offered prayers. Archbishop Terence Cooke of New York delivered the closing Benediction. The Marine Corps Band played "God Bless America" and the Mormon Tabernacle Choir joined them for "The Star

Spangled Banner" and also performed "This Is My Country." Senator Everett Dirksen of Illinois presided and administered the vice presidential oath of office to Spiro Agnew, governor of Maryland.

Lyndon Johnson appeared relaxed as he watched over the peaceful transfer of power. The official platform group was a familiar one. In 1961, Vice President Nixon had handed over his office to Senator Johnson. Now eight years later, President Johnson was stepping back as Mr. Nixon succeeded him in the presidency. Columnist Tom Wicker would write in *The New York Times* the next day that with the cast of participants presiding over the occasion and with the music and the themes of the day, it was "almost as if the sixties had never happened . . ."

But they had happened. It had been a decade of assassinations and riots and demonstrations and political tension and Great Society reforms and movement toward true civil rights. And a decade defined by war. Moreover, the decade of the '60s was far from over. The Reverend Billy Graham touched on the mood of many that day when he said, "We have sown to the wind and are now reaping a whirlwind of crime, division, and rebellion."

Whereas President Kennedy in 1961 had appealed to greatness and challenged Americans to embrace their unique and historic responsibility, President Nixon now urged citizens to "lower our voices," to stop shouting at each other and begin to learn from each other. He observed that the country was "torn by division" and was "rich in goods, but ragged in spirit . . ." The president asked:

What kind of a nation we will be, what kind of a world we will live in, whether we shape the future in the image of our hopes, is ours to determine by our actions and our choices.

The greatest honor history can bestow is the title of peacemaker. This honor now beckons America — the chance to help lead the world at last out of the valley of turmoil and onto that high ground of peace that man has dreamed of since the dawn of civilization.

A number of protesters had come to Washington, and some demonstrators threw debris and beer cans at the presidential caravan, but the DC police and the regular army soldiers on duty kept the peace. And most commentators applauded the president's modest demand on the citizenry to lower their voices as well as his own ambition to be a peacemaker. It had been a long eight years from the happy, euphoric Kennedy ceremony. And in many ways it had been a longer year since the January 1968 Tet Offensive. That event had shocked so many that it accelerated the process of debating and rethinking the American role in Vietnam. Many described it as a watershed moment in the war. But as the historian Ronald Spector asked, If it was that, why did the war continue until 1973 and why did casualties continue to mount in Vietnam? This disconnect was part of the cruel drama of the momentum of a war that was touched only slowly by the debates and policy shifts at home.

On January 20, 1969, a day that was ending in Vietnam just as the inaugural ceremonies began, 30 American servicemen died. And as Washington celebrants moved through sleet and rain to six inaugural balls that evening, it was already the morning of January 21 in Vietnam, and American servicemen were setting out for patrols in the steamy morning heat. Forty-eight young Americans would die in Vietnam that day. Diego Amador was an eighteen-year-old marine from Chicago. He and two other men in his platoon were killed by friendly fire when American artillery rounds supporting them in a firefight near Thuong Duc landed too close to their position. Friendly fire is a warmly deceptive military description of errant ordnance that mistakenly kills friendly forces; the term could represent a tragic metaphor for the war.

There is little doubt that Vietnam was the priority item for the president and for the nation. On January 21, President Nixon asked his national security adviser, Henry Kissinger, to request the secretaries of defense and state and the director of the Central Intelligence Agency to initiate a comprehensive review of the situation in Vietnam and the options there. Dr. Kissinger responded immediately with National Security Study Memorandum 1, "Situation in Vietnam." He informed the recipients of this document that the president wanted their reports by February 10. This was an urgent matter.

The Vietnam War had hung heavily over the low-key inaugural ceremony. It surely had been on everyone's mind. But if it was the uninvited guest, it was also the unacknowledged presence, referred to but never spoken. President Nixon did not mention Vietnam in his inaugural remarks. None of the speakers did. Nor did the president make reference to the young men then serving there. The program was too carefully controlled and calculated for this to have been an oversight. There was a delicacy, or an incongruity, to all of this. For Vietnam had certainly held the central place in the political debate of the past year and it had provided the focus for the protests in the streets and on the campuses. These debates had often been angry and emotional. But even in these instances, in the United States the Vietnam War was enveloped in a narrative that was removed from the experience of those on the ground there.

In the seven months following Tet, through late August 1968, it seemed as if the republic itself was going to be torn apart. President Lyndon Johnson surprised everyone on March 31 when he effectively resigned from his office. Within a week, James Earl Ray assassinated Martin Luther King Jr. in Memphis, where he was assisting black sanitation workers in a strike for equitable wages. Two months after that, Sirhan Sirhan shot and killed Robert Kennedy in a hotel kitchen in Los Angeles, where he had delivered a campaign speech for the presidency. And at the end of August, antiwar demonstrators and the Chicago police clashed in the streets of Chicago during the Democratic National Convention. If Vietnam was the driving force in much of this dispute, it was more of a background — the palpable drama was right at home.

The policy focus for much of the debate over the Vietnam War was on the bombing of North Vietnam. This was a lesser part of the overall American war effort, but it was emotionally symbolic and substantively critical. All signals were that North Vietnam would not consent to any sort of a negotiation while the United States was bombing their sovereign country. On March 31, when he announced he would not run for another term, President Johnson also initiated a halt in the bombing of the North in the area north of the 20th parallel. Some viewed this as an important concession, while others, including the North Vietnamese, found it inadequate, and so the cessation of bombing became the major debating point of the period up until the November election. In April, the North Vietnamese did agree to meet, and the next month in Paris, representatives began to discuss the rules they would follow in setting the terms for their deliberations. The South Vietnamese government was apprehensive about these conversations because they feared the United States was looking for a way to withdraw and that the government of the South would not be protected.

During this debate, with the focus on Paris and the disagreements about a total bombing halt in North Vietnam, the war in South Vietnam picked up even more. Army chief of staff Earle Wheeler and MACV commander William Westmoreland requested over 200,000 more troops for direct assignment to Vietnam or in reserve for possible deployment. The request surprised many and led the Wise Men and others to recommend to President Johnson that the expansion of troops had to stop. LBJ finally did approve the deployment of some 22,000 additional troops.

While escalation was slowing, combat activities were not. Even as he initiated a qualified bombing halt, President Johnson authorized the largest ground operation of the war. He continued his fight-and-talk strategy — wanting to be able to leave Vietnam but not wanting to lose Vietnam. On April 1, General Westmoreland directed the commanders to "maintain maximum pressure on the enemy in the south." In the two months following President Johnson's March 31 speech, nearly 4,000 Americans died in Vietnam and more than 20,000 were hospitalized. President Johnson also pressed for an increase in pacification programs — Operation Phoenix expanded in this period — and he authorized increased bombing in the South. The number of B-52 missions in South Vietnam in 1968 were triple those of 1967. And even as MACV insisted that the enemy forces were reeling following their major Tet defeats, the Communists initiated major attacks in May and again in August.

President Johnson had an important piece of unfinished business: how to pay for the war. He had always insisted on what was called the "guns and butter" approach: America was wealthy enough to pay for a war without domestic sacrifices. He did not want to request additional taxes for fear that the uncertainty about the extent and duration of the war would become evident, and because he did not want Congress to respond by cutting domestic spending. By late 1967, necessity trumped and he had requested a 10 percent surcharge on business and personal taxes. Congress ignored him. But by early 1968, the economy had slowed measurably and inflation was increasing. There was a run on gold reserves. In his speech he had pressed Congress to authorize the tax hike, and, by twisting arms, in June the now lame-duck president got the tax authority — along with some unwanted domestic spending cuts.

When Lyndon Johnson made his announcement, Washington was uneasy. Clark Clifford, the newly appointed secretary of defense and longtime Democratic counselor, "felt the government itself might come apart at the seams." His apprehension was justified. Things would get worse.

Martin Luther King's death stunned the nation. Black America was devastated. There were riots in 110 cities. Thirty-nine died and 2,500 were injured, and large areas in a number of cities experienced major fires. The worst were in Baltimore and Washington. In the nation's capital, rioters came within two blocks of the White House. Over 14,000 federal troops were mobilized in the city.

Now race and "law and order" would join Vietnam as themes in the election year debate. To many, the three issues were linked. Within a ten-week period, Vietnamese Communist forces were on the grounds of the American embassy in Saigon, and military forces had to set up a protective line at the White House. Dr. King had understood their connection. Exactly one year before his murder, Dr. King had spoken at Riverside Church in New York City and sharply criticized the war in Vietnam. He did not like what it was demanding of young Americans, black as well as white. And he was deeply troubled by the casualties among Vietnamese civilians. At his funeral at Ebenezer Baptist Church in Atlanta on April 7, his position in opposition to the war was one of the things mentioned — following his own instructions.

The antiwar movement was growing and becoming more vocal. In October 1967, 100,000 antiwar demonstrators had gathered at the Lincoln Memorial and 30,000 marched on the Pentagon, where there were brutal scuffles with police and hundreds were arrested. One report indicated that in the first half of the 1967–1968 academic year, there were 71 demonstrations on 62 campuses. In the spring of 1968, many campuses erupted in protest, largely following Dr. King's death, with 221 demonstrations on 101 campuses. There was a weeklong occupation of the president's office at Columbia University. This protest combined antiwar themes with opposition to the university's plans to build a gymnasium in a Harlem neighborhood. There was tension among black and white demonstrators. After a tear gas assault, the police arrested 700. There was a bombing in Berkeley and an ROTC building was burned at Stanford.

Over the summer, Democrats fought over their nominee to replace Lyndon Johnson. The antiwar Democrats had difficulty agreeing on a candidate to challenge Vice President Hubert Humphrey. The death of Robert Kennedy had left his liberal antiwar coalition stunned. Eugene McCarthy was the only clear alternative to Hubert Humphrey. He was a genuine hero to many in the antiwar movement, especially the middle-class campus groups. Nonetheless, the Kennedy people as well as others believed Senator McCarthy did not engage issues of race and poverty sufficiently to represent the party.

As Democratic Party activists were debating the available candidates, a new group, the Youth International Party, the Yippies, were organized by Abbie Hoffman and Jerry Rubin and threatened to tie up the city of Chicago, which was hosting the convention. Some gleefully threatened to contaminate the city water supply with LSD. David Dellinger's National Mobilization Committee to End the War in Vietnam also convened a number of antiwar groups that would come to demonstrate in Chicago. And Tom Hayden and the Students for a Democratic Society made plans to come to the convention. Mayor Richard J. Daley announced that the city would issue no parade permits and would maintain open streets and law and order. Some 10,000 protesters gathered, and the city had 23,000 police and National Guardsmen on duty.

The confrontations at Grant Park and in front of the Hilton Hotel on August 28 became the major news of the convention that nominated Hubert Humphrey for president and Maine senator Edmund Muskie for vice president. On live television, Americans saw police attacking the demonstrators who had refused to disperse. Tear gas hovered over the center of the city. A later commission would conclude there was a "police riot" in Chicago. Shortly after the convention, the Republican nominee, Richard Nixon, visited Chicago, where he criticized the demonstrators. Claiming to speak on behalf of the "forgotten Americans," he stressed "law and order," which would become a major theme of Nixon and Spiro Agnew. It was a popular position; even as antiwar sentiment grew, the protesters made many Americans uncomfortable.

Alabamian George Wallace entered the race as a third-party candidate, heading the American Independent Party. The former Democratic governor had challenged President Johnson in the 1964 primaries and had run a surprisingly strong race in northern urban blue-collar neighborhoods. His campaigns built upon race and racism and their surrogate theme of states' rights. By mid-1968 he too began to stress law and order. With the Vietnam War a critical part of the election, Governor Wallace, having no foreign policy experience, selected retired Air Force general Curtis LeMay as his running mate. When asked about Vietnam at his introductory news conference, General LeMay allowed that it might be necessary to turn to nuclear weapons. (He had earlier written that if North Vietnam did not pull back, it might be necessary to bomb them back to the "Stone Age.") Governor Wallace interrupted him and shortly sent him to Vietnam on an inspection trip. Support for the tandem declined in October and November.

Hubert Humphrey was a cold war anticommunist liberal. His credentials were of the sort that would stand him well in his party — or at least they did before 1968. Even as Humphrey had developed some reservations about the Vietnam policy, Lyndon Johnson had kept him in line. In the summer of 1968, Johnson refused to allow Humphrey much room, while the president was developing a closer relationship with Richard Nixon, nurtured by frequent telephone calls. Nixon and Johnson were using each other. In late September, Vice President Humphrey symbolically seemed to establish his independence when at Salt Lake City he delivered a speech saying, "I would stop the bombing of the North as an acceptable risk for peace." It was not as dramatic a break as it seemed, but it was important. The protesters, who had made it difficult for Humphrey to deliver speeches, stepped back — and also began to focus more attention on Nixon and Wallace.

During the last weeks of the campaign, polls indicated that support for Humphrey was surging, as he and Nixon were disagreeing over who could better deliver peace through negotiations — and maintain the credibility of the United States. Proclamations of decisiveness were accompanied by vague, indecisive policy proposals that promised positive results with unclear methods. Richard Nixon turned this into a campaign position. He assured voters that he had a plan to end the war, one that he couldn't describe because it might interfere with President Johnson's efforts to advance negotiations and because it also would tip Nixon's hand, which he reminded people was a strategic error for a negotiator.

By the fall of 1968, a majority of Americans agreed that Vietnam was the nation's major problem — as they had pretty consistently affirmed for the previous three years. Increasingly, there was a mood that it was time to do something about this problem — and some emerging if vague consensus on what this might be. In May, 41 percent of those polled by George Gallup had said they were "hawks" and an equivalent number described themselves as "doves." Just a year earlier, the self-identified hawks had dominated 49 percent to 35 percent. Gallup's polls indicated that by a margin of 64 percent to 26 percent, Americans approved of the bombing halt that President Johnson had announced back in March. In that same month, by a margin of 69 percent to 21 percent, Gallup's sample agreed with an approach whereby the United States would withdraw troops and leave the South Vietnamese to carry on the fighting — with American supplies and economic support. In August and October 1968 polls, those surveyed indicated by consistent margins of 66 percent to 18 percent that they would be more likely to support a candidate who would turn over more of the fighting to the South Vietnamese and begin to withdraw American troops.

It was clear by 1968 that the cold war consensus that had supported American engagement in Vietnam had eroded. In many ways the polls were ahead of the candidates — or at least were ahead of any explicit plans the candidates articulated. The presidential contenders had no chance to try to explore positions in a presidential debate format since Nixon would not agree to engage in debates.

Nixon's Vietnam strategy, as previewed in the election campaign, had several components: Encourage the South Vietnamese to assume more responsibility for the combat operations in the South, begin to draw down or at least draw back U.S. troops, keep the pressure on the North Vietnamese and try to negotiate a treaty with them, and try to solicit Soviet help in accomplishing this. It appealed to many, even if it was not fully articulated. Nixon also proposed ending the draft at the conclusion of the war and moving to a volunteer army.

Importantly, the only candidates who talked of a traditional military victory in Vietnam were George Wallace and Curtis LeMay. And the pledges of these two men were more rhetorical than a practical plan for how to accomplish this. Governor Wallace insisted that the military should be encouraged to use "all of the military ability we have, including air and naval power" to secure victory — but he took the nuclear option off the table. On November 2, *The Saturday Evening Post* editorialized that only Wallace suggested he would increase the fighting. The editors concluded that Humphrey and Nixon seemed to combine a stay-the-course policy with one of negotiated withdrawal. And "each candidate seems to be basing his campaign on the assumption that nobody really believes what he is saying." Since 1965, the sharp anticommunist, win-the-war-quickly rhetoric had cooled as the problems became more clear and confidence in a quick resolution waned. For most Americans in the fall of 1968, the ambivalent 1965 goals in Vietnam had been reduced to how best to extricate America from the war.

During the fall, *Life* magazine sent its Vietnam correspondents around the country, where they interviewed some 300 men and women in the service about the election and the war. Acknowledging that many of the men and women they interviewed were not yet twenty-one and therefore ineligible to vote, they learned that these citizens were well informed about the election — if not at all convinced that its results would make any difference. Most strongly opposed any bombing halt because they believed that it was essential to keep the pressure on the enemy — and to complicate enemy efforts to keep pressure on the American troops. They still talked about the need to stand up to communism in Vietnam to prevent the fight from moving to American streets. There seemed to be a preference for Richard Nixon as a new face — they knew little about the "old Nixon." And there was a strong affection for Bobby Kennedy — and surprising sympathy for Lyndon Johnson. But finally they were focused on their task: "The only thing anyone here is rabid about is getting out alive."

The Nixon team had worried through the campaign about what they called an October surprise. They feared that President Johnson might have some new initiative that would throw off their momentum. They were right. On October 31, Johnson announced a full bombing halt in the North and said that negotiations to end the war would begin immediately in Paris. Hanoi had finally agreed to allow South Vietnam to participate in the talks in exchange for the bombing halt. The news of peace talks had the potential to influence the election results. Except that the convening of the talks was delayed when South Vietnam refused to join. Johnson was furious. And he was more than furious when he learned, through FBI wiretaps, that the Nixon team, working with Anna Chennault, had urged the Saigon government not to participate. Mrs. Chennault was the Chinese-born widow of the American World War II hero Army Air Force general Claire Chennault. She was a wealthy businesswoman and a Republican Party loyalist. She had assured South Vietnamese President Nguyen Van Thieu that South Vietnam would have far greater success in negotiations convened by the Nixon administration. Lyndon Johnson threatened to go public with information that he considered treasonous. But he finally pulled back — doing so would have involved admitting that he was tapping the phones of the Nixon team.

On November 5, 1968, American voters

elected Richard Milhous Nixon as the thirty-seventh president of the United States. Mr. Nixon received a plurality, 43.4 percent of the popular vote to Hubert Humphrey's 42.7 percent and George Wallace's 13.5 percent. Nixon enjoyed a half-million-vote edge out of nearly 73 million cast. But he won a more significant electoral college victory with 301 electors to Humphrey's 191 and Wallace's 46.

The election returns almost certainly demonstrated that the nation was ready to do something about the Vietnam War. But neither the campaign nor the election provided a policy direction — except that it was pretty clear that an increase in troop levels and an escalation of the ground war were not an option. As far as most Americans were concerned, that phase of the war seemed to be drawing down. Notwithstanding this, in Vietnam that phase of the war continued unabated. As the American election results came in late on the night of November 5, it was midday the next day in Vietnam. On November 6, 33 Americans died in Vietnam. As Richard Nixon assembled his transition team to prepare for the transfer of power, part of this package was the assumption of responsibility for the war in Vietnam.

6

THE AMERICAN WAR
IN VIETNAM

May 1969 was a typically hot and muggy month in Saigon. Except for the weather, however, it did not seem normal — or at least it did not meet expectations of a city at war. As a young soldier wrote of arriving for his tour of duty, "I don't know why, but I figured the runways in Saigon would be under attack, and we'd have to dodge antiaircraft fire. Instead, our arrival was tranquil and fairly pleasant."[1] Now, in fact, planes landing at Tan Son Nhut airfield in Saigon very seldom had to avoid antiaircraft fire. But expectations had been set of a country at war.

Secretary of State William Rogers and Mrs. Rogers, along with an official delegation, arrived on May 14 at Tan Son Nhut for twenty-four hours of meetings, briefings, and social gatherings. Mrs. Rogers's briefing book included warnings about water and food and the heat. Obviously high security would be in place for such a senior delegation, but nonetheless, there was little mention of the fact that they were actually visiting a war zone. Instead, they were told to be prepared for high humidity and rainfall.[2]

The *New York Times* columnist Tom Wicker filed a story from Saigon on May 14, reporting on his first visit to the South Vietnamese capital in two years. In 1967, the mood was of an aggressive and optimistic military engagement. "Then, the emphasis was on war; now there is more talk of peace." The streets now were dominated by motor scooters, with "huge American trucks rolling through the city, laden with men or materiel," and "G.I.s no longer crowd the sidewalks." He did note the continuing signs of war — of wary defenses around the city, particularly near the public buildings. There were gun emplacements and sandbagged buildings, and concertina wire was all over. Nonetheless, Wicker concluded that "the big American moment is past and the sense of the place now is that no one is reaching anymore for that coonskin on the wall."[3]

Several hours after Wicker filed his story, President Richard Nixon made a prime-time nationally televised address regarding the war. His report followed nearly four months of White House–organized studies of the Vietnam situation and a steady stream of interim statements, speculation, and calculated leaks about the future of the American engagement in the war. Increasingly, most of these stories predicted a drawing down of the American military involvement, a greater dependence on the South Vietnamese military forces, and a renewed effort to advance the peace talks that were under way in Paris. These had been part of the public discussion since the previous year. The president confirmed all of these themes in his address. He urged that North Vietnam and the United States agree to remove all troops. And he promised that a South Vietnam, free of all foreign forces, could determine by popular vote the form of government it wished to have and whether that government should adopt a position of neutrality or even agree to reunification with North Vietnam. In many ways the most important statement was one that seemed almost incidental: "We have ruled out attempting to impose a purely military solution on the battlefield."[4]

The day before, on May 13, President Nixon had asked Congress for authorization to establish a draft lottery as a means of instituting a fairer system of conscripting young men for military service. He also promised that after the war, he would recommend an all-volunteer military. In fact, in March he had already asked Thomas Gates, a former secretary of defense, to chair a committee to study the feasibility of such an approach to maintaining a strong military force.[5]

Even as protests intensified on campuses across the country, most commentators observed that the Nixon administration was moving to conclude the war. There were debates about whether these moves were signs of statesmanship or of cynical and political manipulation, and about motives and objectives. But the fact was that things seemed to be moving. Witness Wicker's observation. U.S. news accounts regarding the war increasingly focused on the peace talks in Paris more than on military action in Vietnam.

On June 8, President Nixon affirmed this new momentum following a meeting with South Vietnamese president Nguyen Van Thieu on Midway Island. The two leaders agreed upon a transfer of more combat responsibility to the South Vietnamese military and the beginning of a drawdown of American combat units. At the conclusion of the meeting, President Thieu emphasized to the press that "it is a constant duty of Vietnamese people to take over more responsibility and to alleviate the burden of U.S. people to support us to defend the freedom in Vietnam." President Nixon described the process of this transfer, Vietnamization, to a welcoming crowd of executive branch officers and congressional leaders on the South Lawn of the White House on June 10.

In retrospect, it is clear that the thirty days

prior to the Midway Island announcements was a period of major transition in the Vietnam War. The transition had really begun in January 1968, when the Tet Offensive seemed to rattle the confidence of the U.S. public and the political leadership in a military resolution in Vietnam. This was ironic, given that the Communist offensive failed and the ARVN forces in the northern sectors had handled their responsibilities well. Nonetheless, the forward momentum, the optimistic sense of a war that was succeeding, seemed to falter following these major unexpected assaults. Even though Tet was a watershed moment, the changes came at a slow pace. Tet initiated a process that was underlined by President Johnson's March 31 announcement of a bombing halt and his declaration that he would not stand for reelection, and it continued through the inauguration of Richard Nixon the following January. This period of adjustment was marked by a shift in the American debate and an alteration in the American expectations. It was not yet marked by a shift in the war on the ground.

Richard Nixon's assertion that the United States did not seek a military victory and later his announcement of Vietnamization would be the transition markers. They were underplayed at the time because in many ways they seemed to represent a natural evolution of the war. In fact, Johnson had never set a military victory as the U.S. objective — even if he did shout out about coonskins on the wall. But Nixon's explicit disavowal of military victory as a goal was a significant step. In the summer, the Pacific edition of *Stars and Stripes,* which was circulated on American military bases in Vietnam, proclaimed that " 'Vietnamization' is now the word." The article pointed out that General Abrams was informed that the goal was no longer military victory — Americans would Vietnamize the war "as fast as possible while holding U.S. casualties as low as possible."[6] As the historian of MACV concluded, "Once begun, American withdrawals took on a momentum of their own, each increment following the previous one in steady succession. Domestic political pressures, far more than MACV's evaluation criteria, dictated the pace, as Nixon and the Democrats tried to outbid each other on withdrawal size and timing."[7]

Despite this transition in objectives and rhetoric, it is important not to infuse May 1969 with an image of political leaders clamoring to join arms with John Lennon and Yoko Ono in a chorus of "Give Peace a Chance." The political momentum had swung and, with it, public opinion and public attention refocused. In many regards this was what the Nixon team sought. In the United States, the "Vietnam War" had perhaps always been more of a distant saga that was a cold war chess piece and a focus for debate than it was a combat narrative. In a war without front lines there was little dramatic news from the front to narrate. If the men in the field sometimes found their days routine, it is not surprising that these routine days seldom found their way into a television broadcast or a news account.

News coverage of Vietnam at that time focused on negotiations in Paris or announcements in Washington or protests at Dartmouth, Columbia, Madison, or Berkeley, or even a visiting journalist's observations of a shifting Saigon. These things may have described the direction of the war, and by spring they had become part of the daily drama of what was called the "War." But they did not capture the actual experience, and the war had become a distant, abstracted part of a political and cultural drama.

By the spring of 1969, the actual American combat war in Vietnam, with the exception of some dramatic encounters and some human interest stories, had slipped even further back in the news. Yet it was still very real on the ground. Most Americans had no true concept of that distant reality. And the American command in Saigon and in Washington largely did not try to publicize it beyond general patriotic tales of American youth doing their duty — with little cost. There was little interest or incentive in describing the growing bloody American tally. A MACV Saigon communiqué on May 14 reported that 4 Americans died that day in scattered actions. It would have been cruel and even obscene for anyone to say "only 4." These were, after all, real deaths of real people. But it would not be surprising that most Americans, at least those with no friends or loved ones on the ground, thought of this as at best a largely inconsequential minidrama. Except that actually 66 Americans had been killed that day in fierce actions ranging from the canals of the Mekong Delta to the slopes of Hamburger Hill. Recent transitions such as the shift in military objectives had delayed effects. While these worked their way to the battlefield, the baby boom generation was still at war.

On May 10, the Nixons hosted a party at the White House for their daughter Tricia, with music provided by the Monkees, the Temptations, and Helen Reddy. That same day in Vietnam, helicopters transported the men of the 187th Airborne onto the west slope of Dong Ap Bia. A month later, on June 8, President Thieu and President Nixon agreed that the South Vietnamese were prepared to assume a greater combat role. The previous day, out in the rugged Central Highlands north of Dak To, a group of 7 army engineers sweeping the road for mines were attacked by North Vietnamese regulars.

The men of the 299th Engineering Battalion were guarded by 25 South Vietnamese regular army troops. When the attack began, the ARVN men huddled in a ditch while the engineers tried to fight back. Two American soldiers were killed. Prizewinning photojournalist Larry Burrows of *Life* magazine photographed the skirmish. He wrote that it was not possible to generalize from this experience about the ability and commitment of the South Vietnamese. "But in the eyes of the American troops standing silently around the tailgate of the truck which brought the broken, bleeding bodies of their buddies back to Dakto, you could see what *they* felt. At that moment I was ready to agree."[8]

Ironically, as Americans focused more and more on the peace offensive and an impending drawdown, in May 1969 the number of American troops in Vietnam reached a high of nearly 540,000 men and women. In the thirty days between May 10 and June 8, 1,592 Americans died in Vietnam, an average of 53 a day. Sixty-three men had died on May 10, and on June 8, 39 men and 1 woman were killed. Sharon Lane was an army surgical nurse killed in a mortar attack on the 312th Evacuation Hospital at Chu Lai. From Canton, Ohio, First Lieutenant Lane had been in Vietnam for six weeks. She was the first woman killed as a result of a combat attack. And the son of Gloria Stewart and the stepson of actor Jimmy Stewart, Marine lieutenant Ron McLean, was also killed on June 8 in a vicious firefight up near the Demilitarized Zone where he was out with a six-man reconnaissance team. He was awarded the Silver Star for his actions to shield and save some of his wounded men.

During this month of debate and announcement in Washington, it was hard to find any real change on the ground in Vietnam — unless it was an increase in conflict. The American War would not end until the last troops were withdrawn in 1973. The Vietnam War would not end until North Vietnamese troops occupied Saigon in April 1975. And over those years, even as President Nixon was drawing down the ground war, he was expanding significantly the air war in North Vietnam and in Laos and Cambodia. In the spring of 1970, he would send U.S. troops into Cambodia. But May and June 1969 were marked by the last echoes of the major war and of the understanding and rationale for it. Following this period, attention focused on the drawdown and negotiations with no goal of military victory, and these themes changed the dynamics of the war.

In ironic contrast to this shift, in May, in all regions of South Vietnam the war continued, almost indifferent to the proclamations in Washington and the negotiations in Paris. Throughout the country there were clashes, each area marked by its own unique type of fighting. With the exception of some dramatic and sustained encounters such as Dong Ap Bia, most of these battles seemed noteworthy only when aggregated. For example, the *Los Angeles Times* reported that the 430 Americans killed the week of May 11 was more than double the toll of the previous week. They attributed this to a renewed Communist offensive — but not to any concentrated assaults. Most of the dead and 2,185 wounded "resulted from the pinprick mortar and rocket bombardment of sprawling American camps and bases scattered along the length of South Vietnam." There were 200 such attacks on the night of May 11 alone. At the same time, MACV had not yet drawn back on its war-fighting style — and General Abrams had not significantly modified the Westmoreland approach to the war. In April, he had told his commanders that when the U.S. forces maintained the initiative, "our kill ratio is spectacular."[9]

In the Mekong Delta during this period, there were several ongoing operations, including Speedy Express with its heavy civilian casualties — and with its limited impact on true control of the region. Operation Montana Raider involved major American offensive operations with M48 tanks from the 1st Cavalry Division and the 11th Armored Regiment. The NVA defenders used mines to halt the tanks, and they damaged 352 vehicles in a month. Army and navy patrols along the waterways regularly elicited ambushes — which is exactly what they sought in order to respond with heavy firepower.

The areas east of Saigon, as well as the region to the north and west extending out to Cambodia, witnessed regular Communist attacks. By the spring of 1969, increasing numbers of regular NVA soldiers were in this part of the country. For example, on May 19, around 1,500 Communists attacked an American and South Vietnamese base area near Xuan Loc. This sizable assault received front-page coverage in *The New York Times* and *The Washington Post.* [10] And despite Tom Wicker's observation that Saigon was no longer bearing the look of war, that city was subjected to increasing numbers of rocket attacks — more harassing than consequential, they still were regular reminders of war. The Cholon district was often attacked by mortars and rockets.

The Central Highlands was an intense war zone — from the Kontum–Pleiku–Dak To areas east to An Khe and on to the coastal plains. North Vietnamese regulars were able to slip across the border areas of Laos and Cambodia, and they also used artillery and rocket attacks from within these presumed sanctuaries. The base and small airfield at Dak To was under siege from early May until

July 1969, with bulldozer drivers, mechanics, and other support troops of the 299th Combat Engineers left to defend the area following the withdrawal of the 4th Infantry Division. Some of the men who remained there considered themselves bait for enemy attacks.

The northern I Corps area was regularly the hottest combat ground and remained so in the late spring. Over half of the American ground casualties in the war occurred there.[11] In this intense spring season, operations spanned from the 101st Airborne's Operation Apache Snow out in the A Shau Valley to the 7th Marines in Operation Oklahoma Hills, which aimed at clearing NVA units out of the area southwest of Da Nang, particularly focusing on the Happy Valley and Charlie Ridge locations. The 4th and the 9th Marines sent units into the Rockpile area south of the DMZ in Operation Herkimer Mountain.

For the men serving out in the bush, combat was not measured by battalion-level operations with intriguing and catchy names. Vietnam was more personal than that. All wars finally are personal in terms of being reduced to individual experience. But each war — and each individual experience — is different, based on environment, scale, nature of operations. And surely Vietnam was different. Out in the field, Vietnam was a cauldron of heat and humidity. It was about walking through swamps and rice paddies and streams — and elephant grass that had sharp edges that cut up clothes and bodies. It was rain and mud and rats and mosquitoes and snakes and leeches and ants. It was about being wet, infected, and dirty.

The army recommended that men carry between forty-four and forty-eight pounds of equipment. The average soldier carried sixty pounds, and some had much more than that. By the spring of 1969, they had camouflage tropical uniforms — much lighter than the earlier fatigues. They had baggy pants and a bush shirt that was worn outside the pants. Many wore no shirts in the heat. The old steel helmets were discarded and replaced by "boonie" hats — floppy with wide brims. Their tropical combat boots were quick-drying combinations of leather and nylon, with insoles that gave some protection against sharp punji sticks. They carried ponchos for protection from the rain — but some learned not to wear them at night out on patrol. When these rubber garments got wet, they would shine, obviously undesirable at night in the jungle. The men wore their nylon liners at night — they didn't really keep them dry but at least they didn't shine.[12]

One soldier spent the summer with a platoon on patrols on Dam Trao, a large lake in the coastal area of Binh Dinh. They had rubber boats with mounted M60 machine guns on them and army-issued life vests. When the enemy fired at them — which was often — there was little comfort in being offshore in a rubber boat with machine-gun fire around them. Despite this vulnerability out on the water, they never wore their life vests because "the army in all its wisdom had issued bright orange ones."[13]

In the early years of the war, the standard infantry weapon was the M14, a .30 caliber rifle. It was heavy (10 pounds) and not useful for close-range firefights in the jungle. By late 1965, MACV decided to adopt the M16 — a smaller and lighter weapon with a twenty-round magazine that fired a 5.56 mm bullet. This rifle was made for close-range fighting. The only problem was that it wasn't made for Vietnam — the moisture and dirt caused it to malfunction regularly, and maintenance was very difficult in the jungle. By 1969, the military had worked through these problems with better lubricants, issuing more appropriate cleaning equipment, and refitting the weapons with chrome chambers that reduced jamming.

Adapting. This was the word that fit the experience. Adapting, however, to an experience that was never constant. The uniforms, the boots, and the rifles — all adapted, and all further altered in the field. For the men on the ground, "adapting" described their lives: learning to survive in the environment

403

for which not even the best training could have fully prepared them, adjusting to circumstances and to equipment, confronting the reality of the war, with civilians often in the middle of combat areas, dealing with the common shock of encountering the often hostile attitudes of the South Vietnamese, civilian and military, all of this in the context of changing expectations from Washington. For the men on the ground in this complicated war at this complicated time, this was "Nam." Marine platoon leader James Webb wrote, "By 1969 our salty, sometimes wise-ass Marines took small precautions and countermeasures every day that were not even in the mind-set of those who had been on the battlefield four years before."[14]

By the spring, little of the sense of mission that was common in the earlier years of the war remained. Few of that late 1960s generation spoke of an ideological or global battle against Communists or about protecting the shore of California in the jungles of Vietnam. Though some did. One marine thought then and later that "we were fighting for human rights."[15] For most, however, the sense of fear and of responsibility of the duck and cover days or the challenge and heady obligation of Tom Dooley or of JFK had lost its resonance. Not surprisingly, as American domestic enthusiasm and optimism for the war waned, these attitudes declined in Vietnam as well.

On the other hand, among the military serving there in the spring of '69, there was strikingly less evidence of the sharp opposition to the war that had come to be more prominent back in the States. Within a year or so, as the drawdown changed the scope of the war, this mood of futility and of opposition would increase. In early 1969, however, there was more of a practical focus on endurance and survival.[16]

One soldier who was involved in the fighting at Dak To and came home in May 1969 did notice some differences among the soldiers by that time. "It had become accepted that people would write the peace sign on their helmets or on their trucks. That was almost in a joking fashion more than anything else. It was accepted because it was everybody's right to be able to say what they wanted to say." On the other hand, they really didn't talk too much about this, because "we had a job to do."[17]

Not all arrivals were as tranquil as those at Tan Son Nhut airfield in Saigon. When one marine got off the plane in Da Nang, "just the smell of all that jet fuel and stuff, I can just remember. I was like, 'Holy shit, what did you just do?' . . . the sight and the smell and the flames and stuff in the distance and explosions and jets taking off. It was pretty surrealistic." In this environment, "You know what we talked about? We talked about watching out for each other and making it home." He learned as he was leaving Vietnam that one of his best friends, with whom he had enlisted, had been killed up on Mutter's Ridge."[18]

A soldier who was haunted by his experience upon arrival in the post-Tet Vietnam said, "When I got off the plane, I saw all these other guys that served a year, getting on the plane. I thought they'd be laughing and happy as us new recruits were coming in. They just looked at us with sadness . . . They looked at us like, you guys have no idea what you're going to go through and that type of thing. It was kind of scary, looking at them." Another soldier agreed: "Many of them had the thousand-yard stares." A marine described seeing someone he'd been in boot camp with not long before: "He was infantry and went through hell. I ran into him on some LZ [landing zone] and he had aged 10 years and had the classic battlefield stare about him. He had been a fun guy and now talked like someone who just lost a child."[19]

The first things most noticed on their arrival were the heat and the smell of the country — the heat was constant; the smell varied from place to place. Some men talked of "stepping into a sauna" or "walking into a blast furnace." One recalled that "the sweat just popped." The smell was of native foods and fires and of American military contributions: "sweat, shit, jet fuel, and fish sauce all mixed together." At American bases, fifty-five-gallon drums sat under outhouses, and when they filled they were pulled aside, drenched with kerosene, and burned. The smell of burning excrement was everywhere, and it was unforgettable.[20]

Coming into Vietnam for a tour meant a sharp focusing of attention and emotions. Typically the replacements spent a week or so in orientation and then were assigned to their units. One marine coming into Da Nang said that in orientation "you get used to the heat," although some never got used to it. And at the rear bases where they had orientation, "they need someone to burn the crappers in the rear so the new guys get all that until you get assigned."[21]

On the bus ride to his assigned station, a soldier had lasting impressions of the "condition of the bus and the deplorable surroundings": "The bus windows are broken, and the steel bars in front of the windows don't afford proper protection from bullets and items thrown at the bus. We pass through populated areas that are completely destroyed by bombs. The Vietnamese people give us a cold stare when we pass, as if we're responsible for their plight. The children either beg or scream obscenities at those on the bus . . . The trip is depressing and I feel afraid. I begin to wonder if I can really handle this war. My manhood is challenged. I've been in Vietnam only an hour, yet I feel as though I've aged a year. I can't imagine how I'll change after a year here when I have such strong feelings after one hour."[22]

A young New Jersey marine wrote in his journal upon arrival in Vietnam in 1969, "We're all scared. One can easily see this emotion in the eyes of each individual." And he acknowledged that, "as of now, fear is in me." He died just a few weeks later from a fever he contracted while on a patrol in the northern part of I Corps.[23]

An eighteen-year-old Mexican American marine described his arrival: "The first day I was in Vietnam, I saw four bodies. That was the first time I had ever seen death right there, and I swallowed real hard because I had just kissed my mom four days ago, and here I was looking at this stuff." For him, war was just something you dreamed of coming on the plane: "You saw John Wayne doing it, but when you're actually there, everybody else with you is just like you — there's no John Waynes."[24]

An army company commander arriving with his men was angered by a colonel who gave the new officers an "unsentimental lecture on the facts of life in the war zone." The colonel told them that "enlisted men could not be trusted." They were "nothing but sons of bitches." The new officer was stunned, and wondered, "Aren't those the guys pulling the triggers and doing the fighting and dying?"[25]

Ironically, Vietnam, an intimidating experience of smells, explosions, and death, a place that was the focus of much of the world's attention, was also reduced to a very personal and constrained existence for those who were there. If back in the States it was a big-screen moral and political saga, in-country, especially for those out in the field, it was a very focused view of a very existential world: "You're not thinking about the war and whether it's right or wrong, or whether it's moral or not, or the right thing to be or even the smart thing to do. You're thinking more about your own hide and your own position in life and the fact that you're going to a war zone. So your world becomes smaller in a way. You think less geopolitically than you do in terms of your own day-to-day life."[26]

The striking thing about the accounts and the memories of the men who were out in combat zones at this time is how little attention they paid to the debate and the announcement of fundamental political decisions back home. One soldier who had been opposed to the war before he went into the army said that in Vietnam the soldiers didn't really talk that much about the politics. "We didn't sit around at night saying, 'Oh, what a lousy war.' Even though we knew as much about what was going on as anybody, we really didn't have much of the anger that has been described by others in 1969." Another young soldier said that most of the men he was with didn't do a lot of complaining about the war. One man, who had been antiwar before he was drafted and continued to hold that view in Vietnam, said that he and his company commander were the only ones who cast absentee votes in the 1968 presidential election (though he acknowledged that most of the men in his company were not yet old enough to vote). An army chaplain noted that "their drive was to get out of there, 'do our job and get outta here.' "[27]

An antiwar college dropout who was drafted and volunteered for the Rangers — and heavy combat duty — faced field operations with "a certain inevitability, a certain fatalism, a certain pessimism — but it was very personal. It really wasn't political at all." He acknowledged not thinking about the politics but knowing that the confrontations were "going to be hell and we may not survive it. So it was much more a personal level than a political level." Years later he reflected on his tour in Vietnam by considering "the sheer irrationality of it all — not to the point of being surreal but in many ways that me and my fellow soldiers, our sole motivation was to survive and get home."[28]

Another marine wasn't sure what to think

about the protesters: "I think even after being in Vietnam, I really had no good perspective on what the hell was going on over there. I was in survival mode for thirteen months when I was in country."[29] One twenty-year-old draftee from the Bay Area was a gunner on a helicopter. He too had encountered a lot of antiwar protests back home, but he didn't think about this activity when he was in Vietnam. His mother sent him an article from the San Francisco paper saying that "the Hell's Angels want to come to Vietnam and they were going to end the war in a couple weeks. I told my mom, 'Go ahead and send them.' " And a marine from Indiana said that the protesters should "come over here and bat the bullets down with their signs and see what happens."[30]

Sustaining morale in this environment with young troops was always a challenge. As one young soldier said, "We were disgruntled when we were humping, tired, sleepy, hungry, hot, cold, sick, and wet or when things do not go right for us. Overall combat is miserable and nerve racking. We did not discuss much about politics because we were young and did not know much about the issues or platforms of certain parties."[31]

A soldier who served there in the summer of 1969 described it succinctly: "This is hell. Besides killing and maybe being killed there are many other things that make life almost unbearable. Leeches that suck our blood, insects of all kinds, snakes, spiders . . . The heat, the rain and mud. The long marches with heavy pack, going two or three weeks without a bath, wearing the same clothes for weeks at a time, not having a place to sit down or even lie down except in six inches of mud."[32]

An infantryman who served in the Mekong Delta wrote, "The hot weather, mud, and constant wetness from sweeping filthy rice paddies are reducing my stamina. I am tormented daily by the native pests, including mosquitoes, rats, red ants, and leeches. The mosquitoes are terrible. At night the repellant lasts less than twenty minutes before the pests fly in your ears, nose, and mouth . . . My body is covered with infections from cuts incurred in the field. They won't heal because I'm in water each day for hours at a time. The bottoms of my feet are full of small holes, and I develop a mild case of immersion foot. The ringworm around my waist and ankles is unmanageable because my belt and boots remain wet most of the day. I get very little rest and sometimes suffer from battle fatigue when I deal with booby traps, firefights, suicide missions, and the trauma associated with friends getting wounded or killed."[33]

Christian Appy reminds us that morale is about more than survival. Maintaining a high level of morale depends upon a belief that an organization is engaged in an "important and justifiable cause." There is little doubt that the conviction of the value of this engagement had faded sharply by 1969 — perhaps more slowly among troops in Vietnam than among many Americans back home. But it had faded. Surviving the tour became the obsession, and troops kept a close tally on how long they had remaining — looking for that stage when they would be "short-timers" and then get home alive.[34] "Everyone was scared to death they would get killed during the last month, the last week, the last day. Everyone knew exactly how many days they had left in-country, sometimes down to the minute."[35]

They all understood the task, and this understanding and this task were basically reduced to survival — survival of self and of comrades in the field. There had never been marching bands. Now there were no pledges of "victory." *New York Times* reporter B. Drummond Ayres explained that "the farther out in the field that you got, the tougher the fighting got but the more people hang together and hung together just because everybody knew that you were fighting to stay alive, not necessarily just to kill as many Viet Cong and NVA as you could." He observed an attitude of, "Yeah, people back home really don't like it and I don't like it either

413

but, you know, I'm here . . . I wish I didn't have this to put up with, but we're in it together so we have to hang together or we're all going to die together."[36]

For one young officer, the whole focus was on the task. Among the junior officers, "no one wanted to be there, of course, except for people looking for a career advancement in the military, and I surely was not."[37] A more senior officer and combat veteran, on his second tour in 1969, put it bluntly about his men: "I really didn't care whether he was in favor of the war or against the war. You know, we're all here trying to stay alive." A marine platoon leader quickly recognized that he only had one task: "to keep other marines alive." Another young marine officer put it this way: "We pretty much lived in trenches, and if you weren't in a trench, you were on a patrol every day. All I was thinking about at the time was bringing the same number of guys back that went out with me."[38]

Karl Marlantes experienced combat as a time when he would be "in a white heat of total rationality, completely devoid of passion." In firefights, he "had a single overwhelming concern, to get the job done with minimal casualties to my side and stay alive doing it." Getting ready, getting "up my nerve to cross the final line of departure before an assault," he would then turn "into a computer that was going so fast you would be afraid it'd burn itself up."[39]

A navy corpsman who saw heavy combat action with the marines said the men were pretty focused and didn't really talk about U.S. politics. "I don't remember much conversation about anything going on at home. What I remember more than anything was us just being there to take care of ourselves. I don't remember patriotism, I don't remember, you know, fighting for the good of the USA. I don't remember protests, I don't remember any of that stuff. But what I do remember is that the only thing we were concerned with was us staying alive every day." A soldier in the 11th Light Infantry Brigade said, "While there, I did not think in global political terms. I did not debate in my mind communism versus capitalism. My men and I rarely discussed the war in general. We were doing a nasty job and nobody, and I mean nobody, liked it. There were no grand patriotic swells of enthusiasm for the war, for the fight. There was only us and them with an unspoken firm belief on our part that it was going to be them taking the beating . . . We made the tremendous efforts, we fought and died and kept going."[40]

A grandson of Mexican immigrants joined the army at age seventeen. On his second tour in 1969, all he and his men were thinking about was "surviving. You're thinking about, you know, hopefully getting out alive and unscratched." While the politics of the war was troubling, "you're kind of a little disgruntled because of the things that . . . the higher-ups will have you do or whatever, but you're just mostly thinking of survival and getting out of there and hopefully nobody else gets killed or wounded."[41]

A young helicopter pilot explained that "even though we realized what we were doing, we didn't like the political atmosphere of it, let's say, and what was going on, but we knew we had to help the guys in the field and we would do anything to help them. We didn't really care about the politics of what was happening because we weren't really part of it over there." Their days were pretty basic: "Okay, who are we going to help today and how are we going to do it? Where's the bad guys? Where's their antiaircraft? Where's their gun positions and how do we get around them so we can help out the grunts?"[42]

A twenty-five-year-old college graduate who was drafted and deployed to Vietnam said that "the war was hugely unpopular and . . . there were very few people that really felt comfortable about being there. In fact, I can't remember anybody." But he also noted that they didn't talk about the war very much. He just kept thinking, "I hope I get to come home."[43] Another college graduate had joined the marines to see if he had what it took to be an officer. He did, and went up to

I Corps, where he said they had little knowledge or interest in what was happening back in Washington. "We were more dealing with day-to-day life and death, you know, situations than we were talking about politics. We talked more about the usual stuff that guys in their . . . teens and early twenties will talk about. R&R, drinks, and ladies, and . . . things like that."[44] An enlisted man had some of the same memories: "What we talked about was going home. We talked about girlfriends. I can't even think of anybody who was even married."[45]

In contrast, a nineteen-year-old draftee from Alabama said that the men with whom he served did talk about the war, but "just occasionally in a political sense of, 'Hey, I wonder when somebody in Washington is going to figure this out and get us out of here?' " He even wrote his congressman and was promised that they were looking at the war. The congressman assured him, "We're really supporting you guys on the ground." A twenty-four-year-old draftee from Wisconsin said, "In 1969, all of us were just hanging our head and saying, 'This isn't gonna work. It hasn't worked since the early '60s. It's not gonna work now.' " On the other hand, "You were kind of caught up in the day-to-day stuff, and, you know, like, there wasn't much we could do about it," so they seldom talked about it.[46]

A soldier who had been on Hamburger Hill described the situation in combat zones: "Never mind 'duty, honor, country' and all that stuff. Everybody over there did everything they did — even in regular day-to-day humdrum stuff, they did it for their buddy . . . if nothing else than self-preservation. They knew that they had to do their job and take care of their buddy and that their buddy would do the same thing for them."[47]

"Buddy." This was a common term. It may not have described a long-standing friendship, but in this environment it was emotionally far closer. A buddy had shared an intense and deeply personal experience with you, and the relationship was about deep trust and mutual dependence. The historian Christian Appy pointed out that under the circumstances in which the war was fought in the later years of the conflict, with less support from home, the men in Vietnam may have bonded even more.[48]

An army doctor was impressed by the men he treated in hospitals, some of them seriously injured or dying. They wanted to know how some other men in their platoon did, "caring about others more than they cared about themselves." Perhaps, he thought, that is what soldiers had done in all wars, looked after each other. "But the basic fact [was] that they didn't cower. They didn't avoid their responsibilities. They basically followed orders even though the real gut feeling was, 'Really we probably shouldn't be here anymore. But we are. Let's try to stay alive and let's do the best we can to take care of ourselves and our brothers.' That's what happened. That's what I saw."[49]

In many ways, what is remarkable about this generation is how close they were to each other in combat, and this was true even though they seldom knew the men in their units that well. Unlike the first two to three years of the ground war, when entire units were deployed together, by 1969 the troops basically had all come in as individual replacements. The bonding was not always marked by personal friendships. Some men said that they seldom knew the last names of their buddies.

Rotations and transfers, as well as medical evacuations and sometimes deaths, kept stirring up the mix. Men never quite knew some of those who came in and left. Those who got sick or wounded or killed were taken out, and normally no one would hear of them again. "We were all rotating . . . We'd go in and you'd have two [days] or three sixty-five [days]. And some guys would be going a month later, two months; other guys would be coming in . . ." One helicopter pilot said, "You'd see somebody and you might talk to them for a little while, but I don't recall ever having the kind of friendship or personal acquaintance with any of those guys so I could give you names."[50]

"That was one of the things over there — you didn't get real close with people . . . Most people just wanted to put it in the back of their head and move on with life." One soldier described it this way: "We didn't get close to each other that much because we didn't want to go through the losing someone and getting . . . it's a crazy life out there."[51] A veteran recalled later visiting the Wall to look for those with whom he had served, but he had trouble because he often did not know their names: "We all used nicknames. It was how you protected yourself from getting too emotional with people."[52]

The rhythms and the casualties of war took their tolls. "I'd tend to say that not many of our guys went a whole year over there. They got wounded, killed, and didn't have a lot of time. I don't think I could remember maybe five or ten guys . . . that spent the year with me over there. So many of them got wounded and even killed. We had a lot of woundings going on. Guys came and went." Obviously this sort of constant rotation occurred only in the most actively engaged combat units. Vietnam was not conducive to stateside-style friendships. "This wasn't like an everyday thing at work that people go through in life. You don't have time to sit around and shoot the shit and talk about all the things in life we want to do or did do or whatever. This was a staying-alive thing. I took that very seriously, myself." When the troops came out of the field and went to a base camp for some R&R, then they could talk. "Basically it was a three-day drunk." Here the men could "drink beer and tell lies."[53]

A Dak To veteran who lost several men in his unit never got to know too many people other than the soldier he shared a tent with, who was killed in action. "You got to understand, with that rotation, units didn't go in and out as a unit. It was just constant change. It was just constant rotations." Nevertheless, the deaths and injuries caused him to draw back: "After the first couple, you become sort of numb and you don't really want to get too close to anybody."[54]

Men needed to learn how to cope with death and to move on, and almost always they had to move on quickly. One medic was on his first patrol when the helicopter he was on lifted off with six wounded and two dead soldiers: "my whole body shook and retched. Unnoticed by all around me, I dissolved into heavy waves of uncontrollable weeping."[55] There was little time for weeping in Vietnam. Out in the field, the men knew that the next incident, the next occasion to weep, would involve them if they were not alert and ready. One man lost his best friend. He was still alive when they placed him on the medevac helicopter, but he had a serious head injury from an exploded booby trap. Later that day when the unit returned to base camp, they found the medevaced soldier's duffel bag sitting there all packed, with a "KIA" tag on it. That was the only way this soldier knew his friend was dead. But "there was no time to grieve. You know, it was just business as usual. Next morning you get up and go back to search and destroy."[56]

A soldier in the 458th Transportation Company, on a river patrol boat (PBR), talked about his good friend, Anthony (Tony) Sestito, who was part of the MATS (Military Assistance, Tactical Support) team. He arrived at the ambush scene just after Tony was killed. Tony was serving with a group of about eight South Vietnamese troops. They were monitoring a mangrove swamp "completely occupied by the VC." Sestito and his team went into the area to check on the effectiveness of an artillery attack they had requested. A Boston Whaler dropped them off and almost immediately they were hit by enemy fire that quickly killed them all. "Tony had been shot through the chest. I was already on my way into the fray . . . and I recognized Tony's boots. He was on the bottom of the pile. And it was a sad state of affairs . . . He was down with one round, one round to the chest. And his guys — and they were good guys — they all died right around him."[57]

Soon after he arrived in Vietnam, one marine learned that a dear friend had been killed. "Obviously it hit me like a ton of bricks and really, it honestly changed my life . . . what was clear to me was that all my ideals and my images prior to that moment were pretty immature and naïve. What came to me was I had really almost gotten there like I played on hockey teams and football teams — in a spirit similar to that. This was something really different." This same officer attended a meeting, along with a few other new lieutenants, with their regimental commander during orientation before they went to the field. The senior officer said, "Lieutenants, there's one thing I want you to never do out there in the field. I never want you to cry. There's going to be a lot of times when you're going to want to, but don't cry."[58]

An army chaplain was on a riverboat on the Mekong when a nearby boat was ambushed by the NLF. They had no body bags, so they wrapped what he described as "mangled" remains of three men in ponchos. After doing this, he was covered "with their blood and body fluids." A helicopter came in to remove the three bodies, but when landing, its prop wash blew the poncho off one of the dead sailors. The survivors all looked at their coxswain missing half of his head. After the helicopter left, the remaining members of the crew "washed the blood and bile away from the boats." The chaplain observed that it was almost as if the events had not happened. He knew that back in the States a tragedy like this would have resulted in immediate mourning: "Empathy would pour in from every imaginable source." But not in Vietnam. "There's no time. This in itself is tragic. We have to survive. Another fight may occur at any minute. Energy is now focused on what may happen and not on what has just happened a few minutes ago."[59]

Distancing was a way of coping with the trauma of sudden loss. One soldier didn't know the name of a man in his unit who was killed: "I didn't know many people's names at that time. I mean, I knew them by somebody saying it or whatever, but I was so new that I hadn't got to know anybody." When casualties were taken off the field, usually their unit didn't even learn about it: "When somebody got hit and left the field, you didn't know what happened to him . . . You know, you knew the guy was gone, but it wasn't something that you really wanted to know, to have on your shoulders . . . thinking about." A marine said, "You know, the sad part about it is . . . one of your buddies goes down, you have to keep moving. You go over and you look down at them and you touch them, and if they tell you to move out, you gotta go. And let the corpsman or whoever else is working there get them on a bird and get

424

them out of there."[60]

Still, genuine friendships did develop because of often horrible shared experiences and the recognition of mutual dependence. "Liking" someone as a friend paled beside these bonding and binding forces. One soldier put it this way: "Maybe we didn't get to know each other as well as we might have if we were all together back in the States before coming to Vietnam, but I think the flip side of it is a lot of guys got to know each other probably better in combat than they would have in peacetime . . . The perspective is everybody's watching everybody else." Another added, "You really have to have faith in who you're dealing with on a day-to-day basis so you both could get home and you both could get through the day. The days were arduous."[61]

The men frequently described the green replacement as the "fuckin' new guy," but it was a term used descriptively or teasingly rather than tauntingly. An FNG was cause for concern, however, because of the increased risk of casualties due to inexperience. Rocky Bleier was one of the FNGs: "Now all of a sudden you're in this situation as a new guy, you don't know anybody and the only thing that you have in common is that experience of that day or that period of time. So you don't know names or backgrounds, you don't know how they live. In that realm, the only commonality you have with each other is knowing that you're supposed to take care of each other, knowing that you've got their back."[62]

Frederick Downs joined his unit up at Pleiku, a new lieutenant in-country for only a few days. "I stood there in sparkling crisp fatigues, brand-new boots, new rifle, clean shaven, fresh haircut. I even smelled clean. My helmet camouflage cover didn't have a mark on it, nor did I. The two men opposite me were filthy. Their fatigues were torn, and they had scratches all over their skin, two or three days' growth of beard, and dark circles under their eyes. They looked tired, and they smelled to high heaven."[63]

New guys were not only unfamiliar with the pattern of war, they were also very nervous. A soldier was digging in for a night defensive position when all of a sudden one of the men "empties his whole M16 clip into the hole. Everybody's going, 'Christ!' Everybody hits the dirt; we think we're being attacked. The guy yells, 'Snake! Snake!' And everybody goes, 'Oh my God.'" Actually the "snake" was a large worm. "He freakin' emptied his whole M16 clip on a worm because the freakin' worms were huge out there." Then the men had to move to a different nighttime position because the gunshots had revealed their location. "Everybody was pissed at him. He was a new guy. You know the old term was FNG for the new guys. That FNG making us move a klick."[64]

If ignoring the American political changes and adapting to the environment of combat in Vietnam were characteristics of this group, so was a sense of fear and foreboding. They never forgot they were in a war zone. "I was obviously scared to death," one soldier admitted. Another agreed: "We all thought we were going to die; I thought I would never come back alive." Another was "mostly afraid of losing my arms, legs, or getting really disfigured. I wasn't concerned about dying."[65]

One army Ranger described the first hostile firefight: "The immediate emotion was one of exhilaration; really, the adrenaline was pumping and the realization that I was actually in life-and-death combat was an extremely exhilarating initial emotion." This was followed shortly by "some of the deepest dread that I ever remember." When he had to help carry a dead soldier back to a landing zone for the helicopters to evacuate the remains, he thought about facing the possibility of this fate for the next year. "I went from exhilaration to utter despair in the course of about twelve hours."[66]

One soldier remembers his introduction to the world of snipers and ambushes, riding down a back road and always expecting an attack or at least a few warning shots. The first time they were fired upon, "I got a little bit anxious until I saw that nobody else did anything. And then they basically told me that that guy was a notoriously bad shot. They figured he was, like, six or seven hundred yards away from us, and he'd never, ever hit anything, so they never shot back at him because we were afraid that he'd be replaced by somebody who could shoot."[67]

The adrenaline high from combat was not unusual — although it was not sustainable. One soldier said, "I think when you're nineteen, twenty, and twenty-one years old and you're single, there is quite the adrenaline rush in war."[68] The first close call or observing a friend die, or just the monotony of heat and jungle and the physical and mental toll of patrol after patrol generally tamped back any positive emotional rush.

Chuck Hagel recalled his experience with many firefights and skirmishes, then long periods of monotony. "We were out in the field and sweating," and "breaking jungle for 16 hours a day with a machete and always thinking that you might be in the gun sights of a sniper up in a tree or always knowing that there was a grenade hanging on that tree or always knowing that you could be walking right into an ambush, which we did." He stressed the "mental pressure" as much as the "blood and gore that you see" as being incredibly debilitating.[69]

When one marine learned that a friend had

been killed, he got advice from a veteran: "What he was saying was that you can't let these things bother you. You've gotta keep going, because . . . there's gonna be a lot more and you can't let that keep pulling you back. You've gotta, you know, you've got to deal with it and move on."[70] It wasn't easy. Another marine was on a patrol out in a "very beautiful" triple-canopy jungle. They were ambushed, and a man "who I just loved with all my heart was walking point and he got cut down by a machine gun." This platoon leader was so shocked by this that "almost all I could think about was, 'I can't do this anymore. I got to find some way to get out.' " This was the same man whose regimental commander had warned during orientation that there might be plenty of occasions when they would feel like crying, but it was essential not to.[71]

When they looked at an ominous landing zone or an area their patrol was about to enter, many veterans thought that everyone was about to die. More pungently, a veteran of the siege of Dak To, contemplating what they faced, saw that a tough veteran, "the ultimate mean-ass soldier," was scared by it all. And "then I started realizing — I said, 'We're really in deep shit here.' "[72]

Most combat veterans of any war observe that there are two types of people — those who admit fear and those who deny it. Either way, the constant is fear. The military historian S. L. A. Marshall noted that "the battlefield is a place of terror" and it probably always has been and always will be — even as conditions and means of killing change.[73] In Vietnam there was little sense of control of environment or of circumstances. There wasn't on Iwo Jima either, of course, but in Vietnam, for the grunts there was the constant anticipation and unpredictability. This was a war with an enemy that basically chose the times and duration and means of contact.

One soldier described the constant patrols. "But going back into the bush was . . . it was being out there in the middle of nowhere. You depended on yourself. Sometimes you went to places that didn't have artillery support or sometimes you went to places that the choppers weren't even going to be able to get to because of the weather." Occasionally the patrols would run out of food when the weather prevented helicopters from resupplying them. He said that every time they were ready to get on a helicopter and head out on a new operation, "It means your whole butt would start to pucker because you knew you were going back out into the same thing."[74]

Ambushes were common, always at an unexpected moment but nonetheless generally sought as a means to engage the enemy in a fight where American firepower could dominate. Except that booby traps and mines rather than an enemy force often awaited these patrols seeking to find the enemy. One man landed in a helicopter in a rice paddy when a booby-trapped artillery round killed several men, including some of his best friends. He described it as "the coward's way to fight, but there's nothing we can do about it."[75]

Marine lieutenant Lewis Puller Jr. inadvertently detonated a booby trap howitzer round and then flew through the air with "the acrid smell of cordite in my nostrils . . . I felt as if I had been airborne forever. Colors and sound became muted . . . all movement seemed to me to be in slow motion." He said that at the time "I had no idea that the pink mist that engulfed me had been caused by the vaporization of most of my right and left legs." But as he smelled his own charred flesh, he "knew that I had finished serving my time in the hell of Vietnam."[76]

A marine was on patrol on Mutter's Ridge near the DMZ. His platoon got ambushed when some booby traps went off. A Chinese mine killed or wounded most of the men who were walking ahead of him. They had a firefight with the North Vietnamese, and when the medevac helicopters came in to bring out the dead and wounded, the rotor wash pushed back all of the elephant grass the marines were using as cover, and more were shot. The platoon set up for the night with a plan to get the rest of the dead out the next day. They were ambushed overnight.[77]

Getting the dead out was always a priority after the wounded were taken care of. One army officer is still troubled forty-five years later about an attack in May 1969 that caused his unit to evacuate and leave the dead out on the field for a while and focus on getting the wounded out — and drawing back temporarily from the attack. They had to fire white phosphorous over their own troops in order to create a smoke cover to get the men who were still alive out. Fourteen men were killed in that action. On another occasion, there was a delay evacuating a wounded marine because he had a live RPG lodged in his chest. They kept him alive overnight and managed to cut some incisions and use a rope to pull out the unexploded ordnance.[78]

The normal fears of the battlefield and the deep obligations to their brothers in arms naturally created conflicts. A young marine who had just turned eighteen was on patrol when the men on point encountered some North Vietnamese. The marines fired — and discovered they were facing perhaps a company-size enemy unit. The NVA quickly shot the lead Americans, and the others kept their heads down. "I was going, 'Let's get the hell out of here. These guys are dead. There's no way they're living through that.' The squad leader said, 'We don't leave marines.' It hit me like a rock in the face, and I said, 'Yeah, you're right.' I never ever felt that way again." When they went up the next morning to look for the marines they presumed were dead, he volunteered to go first. As it turned out, some had survived.[79]

Serving out in the field commonly meant days of routine and frustration broken by moments of terror. "You would go out with 100 guys and march around all day . . . You were looking for footprints — footprints of enemy soldiers, you knew what their footprints looked like and what kind of boots they wore." Occasionally the Americans set up an ambush, "but as often as not, they [the enemy] would take and seize the initiative and decide when the time was right." Jan Scruggs was wounded when his unit tried to leave a jungle location at night following a lengthy fight with enemy forces. The Americans tried to walk alongside tanks, but the NVA outflanked them and hit them with small-arms fire and RPGs.[80]

For some, there were more days of action than routine. An eighteen-year-old marine who had already done many missions, described his first daytime patrol as the radio-man. Their point man was leading, when suddenly they heard a loud explosion toward the front and saw a cloud of smoke, like a mushroom going straight up in the sky. They lost their point man that day but couldn't find him. The marine thought, Where is his weapon, flak jacket? All they found was a boot with nothing in it. He had "vaporized." The radio operator realized, "This is Vietnam." But the worst night of his life was his third patrol, a nighttime patrol: The radio was heavy, "like a bag of bricks." Going through the rice paddies was difficult because they could be deep — up to his chest. He had to walk on his toes sometimes to keep the radio dry. When they set up Claymore mines, they had to sit and wait for activity. Bugs bit, it was hot, the radio was heavy. They couldn't move while the bugs were biting, couldn't swat them. It was hard for him to take. No one showed up that night, but he couldn't sleep, it was so quiet, there was an orchestra of bugs. Even though there was no action, he was scared, sweating, his back was sore, he worried about the radio not working.[81]

As a patrol leader, one soldier usually had five to twelve men with him: "What I thought about was what that copse of trees over there might be hiding. I looked for good cover, high ground, trails, signs. I listened for noises, I strained to hear even in my sleep. I sat under the cover and shade of bushes and trees and scoured valleys below me for movement. I devoured my contour maps with my eyes and tried to figure where the NVA were likely to be. I watched what my men were doing non-stop. I slowly walked thru the jungle hunting

NVA, hunting the ones that were trying to kill us. And they were out there for sure. We had seen them and met them numerous times. They were moving from the Ho Chi Minh Trail east to the populated coastal regions . . . Because the terrain was so mountainous and so covered with dense vegetation, we all travelled in single file, both them and us. By July, twice I had met their point men in the triple canopy and killed them at a range of 10–14 feet, winning the fast draw contest by about a second or less. Seeing them first, correctly assessing who/ what they were and shooting them dead. A miss or a slow response would have killed me. Again, not valorous, not funny, not nice. But I was alive . . . We endured sniper attacks, far ambushes, near ambushes, little fire fights, big fire fights, rocketing, mortaring, booby traps, night actions, near capture, near annihilation."[82]

Even though patrols were always preparing for an ambush, some ambushes were unanticipated. One platoon that was doing "mop-up" duty around Hamburger Hill after the battle walked down an A Shau Valley ridgeline on a "pretty quiet" operation. Suddenly, "all hell broke loose." There was rifle and machine-gun fire and rocket-propelled grenades. The men ran for some cover, and one of them shouted, "We're going to die here!" A few weeks earlier, the men in his platoon had set up an ambush. During the night they withdrew from the site because they feared the noise had given away their position. When they returned in the pouring rain to the main body of their platoon, they were alarmed when they learned one of the men was missing. They hurried back to the ambush site and found the "missing" soldier under a poncho to cover him from the rain, sleeping soundly. This soldier who slept so easily would be the one to die so quickly in the ambush on the ridgeline.[83]

One soldier "humped the hills" for months looking for enemy, destroying bunkers, but with little action. Their casualties largely were the result of men stepping on mines. Then one day in late March 1969, while he and several other soldiers stood around talking, they were hit by a mortar round. Eight men were killed that day, and his spine was severed. Ironically, he felt no pain. The mortar attack continued for several hours before the helicopters were able to medevac them off the hill.[84]

Not all ambushes were marked by the sound and tracers of lethal weapons, the sudden devastation of a mortar or a rocket, or the technology of hidden mines. Men on jungle trails were always alert for covered punji sticks. This sharpened piece of wood or bamboo, generally infected with feces or urine and hidden in a hole covered with grass

436

or leaves, was a common ageless weapon. One soldier who stepped off the pathway in order to avoid possible mines slipped and fell onto a punji stick, which punctured his knee. He tried to shrug it off and keep going, but a few days later his knee had swollen up so much from infection that it was impossible to pull his eighteen-inch pant leg above it. He spent some extended time in the hospital for treatment of the infection.[85]

The soldiers' assignments varied. For some time, an army Scout platoon was using armored personnel carriers to provide security to convoys traveling between the Mang Yang Pass and the An Khe Pass up in the II Corps area. Their battles were with North Vietnamese Army regulars seeking to ambush or to disrupt travel. Then the unit moved to the coastal plain, where their enemy was the NLF. Here the skirmishes were limited — the enemy used sniper fire and booby traps. Finally, on an assault against some suspected enemy concentrations, the Scouts dismounted and walked. They found themselves in an area where the grass was knee high. The platoon leader realized that the "area was covered with punji sticks." He ordered his men to be very cautious just as he stepped on one. He sat down to try to withdraw it from his foot and ankle — and sat on another punji stick. He needed to be evacuated. That night, three of his men were killed and several were wounded in an ambush.[86] It was hard to fight land mines and booby traps and punji sticks and even ambushes in which the enemy fired on the patrols and then quickly faded back into the bush.

Combat experience, regardless of the amount of action, took its toll. During his last two months in Vietnam, one soldier "was so spent and so scared, so manic . . . I could not relax my vigilance enough to take a normal bowel movement some days . . . I made a tremendous effort to put my patrol in the right place, not get lost and to stay out of trouble . . . It was ungodly hot and I always had a dry mouth and found it hard to swallow. We were so exhausted and it was so hot that it was an effort to chew and swallow food. Chewing would make you sweat. I took small bites so that chewing would not move my head around and disrupt my vision . . . I could not sleep at night, not soundly. We sometimes got hit at night and that was terrifying. Sometimes we set ambushes at night and that, too, was terrifying . . . I was losing a lot of weight due to the heat, the constant moving with 60–100 pounds of gear on my back, poor food and the stress, the sniper contacts and the occasional fire fight. We were all dead tired all the time but that was our normal condition. We didn't get many stand downs, unit rests, in the rear. They often left us out in the field for 60 to 90 days at a time especially in late 1968 and early 1969 when they expected another Tet offensive like the year before."[87]

Helicopters and their crews were always vulnerable — perhaps none more so than the "dustoff," medical evacuation helicopter teams hovering over areas that were almost by definition hostile. They had little protection, just some armor plating and ceramic pieces on the floor. Every man in one 48-person unit was wounded over the course of a year.[88]

A marine pilot described missions to pick up the wounded: "There was no Technicolor at all, it was all black and white — maybe shades of greys and blacks. We'd fly in the mission and get the guys." Because the enemy knew that the pilots seldom came in to pick up wounded if there was shooting, they would hold their fire to lure them in, "and about the time we were going to flare to land on the ground, then they'd open up again. And you were already there so you just stayed there until they got everybody loaded up and you could hear 'em [bullets] going through your helicopter." They were "sitting duck[s]."[89]

Even heavily armed Cobra attack helicopters were not secure from ground fire — or from the weather. One crew working in the Delta near Quon Loi had to return to base, and because of a monsoon, they had to fly at treetop level, following beacon signals. They inadvertently flew over an NVA regiment, and their helicopter was shot down. All 3 of the crew were killed.[90] The enemy attacks on helicopters were themselves often the result of calculated ambushes rather than random encounters. They would set up three antiaircraft positions in an area the pilots called a "box." Then they would use different ruses to lure the helicopters into these ambushes — there was no escape route that was not within easy range of enemy fire.[91]

Johnny Bryant was a pilot on an army attack helicopter. In January 1969, his copter was struck by ground fire near Cu Chi. They crashed, and he crawled away from the site with a fractured back. Then he saw that his copilot was slumped in the helicopter as flames were starting to flare. Aware of the volatile fuel aboard, he crawled back and managed to save his friend before the helicopter exploded. Awarded the Distinguished Flying Cross, he was hospitalized for several months but kept insisting that he wanted to go back and to fly again. He did, and on May 22, 1969, Captain Bryant and Major Robert Arnold were killed when their AH Cobra crashed during a night mission in the mountains northwest of Dinh Quan. Major Arnold was on his second tour and had won several medals for his actions. He left a wife and two daughters back in Indianapolis. Bryant left a wife and a son in Maryville, Tennessee.[92]

Fought in a distant place, with small-unit action, seldom marked by dramatic battles, and increasingly unpopular at home, it should not be surprising that the Vietnam War had few popular combat heroes publicized by the military and celebrated by the public — traditional heroes dramatically leading successful, perhaps solitary, assaults on enemy positions. There was no celebrated Sergeant York or Audie Murphy, nor was there a John Wayne fictional hero, his 1968 Vietnam movie *The Green Berets* failing to generate popular enthusiasm for the war. But the absence of popular heroes is not the same as the absence of heroes.

If we define heroism as courageous and unselfish conduct, putting oneself at lethal risk in life-threatening circumstances in order to protect comrades or to accomplish a military objective, Vietnam surely had as many heroes as any other war. But they were seldom recognized, except by those with whom they served. Even while acknowledging the legitimate debate about the war, veterans often expressed their frustration that so much of the coverage in the U.S. media was on the protesters rather than on stories of sacrifice.

The Vietnam War narrative did not allow much room for celebrating traditional military accomplishments, perhaps because it was

441

not militarily a traditional war. Vietnam had no flag raising following battlefield "victories." Indeed, there were no flag raisings allowed on the battlefield in order to underline that this was not an American war. There was no dramatic breakout such as the long siege at Bastogne over Christmas of 1944. (Except, perhaps the breaking of the siege at Khe Sanh, which seemed anticlimactic after Tet.) There was no stirring advance such as the first troops crossing the Rhine. (Except, perhaps ironically, the seizing of the top of Hamburger Hill on May 20, 1969, which became the focus of criticism and of defensiveness rather than a moment of national elation.)

Many men found the heroism just a routine part of the war they were fighting — not routine in the sense that all were heroic, but in the sense of being fairly common. One said, "When you want to focus on who did the work and so on, those machine gunners carrying those guns, and anytime something happened, they were the most at risk, except for when somebody got hurt and somebody said 'medic.' And those kids got up and they just went and did what they had to do. Didn't matter what was going on, they got up and they ran and they literally saved lives."[93] Another singled out the medics: "If you want to talk about the heroes, medics are heroes . . . Those guys really had to deal with things in danger probably most of the time or more than most anybody in combat. And they're noncombatant. They're just there caring for those who are hurt."[94]

The men who were in the field commonly cite as heroic those individuals who put themselves at risk to save other men. They often mention the medics or the corpsmen or the helicopter pilots, typically the medevac crews, who braved heavy fire to try to save men on the ground. One pilot turned down a medal for his attack on an enemy position: "I don't want a medal for that. If I save somebody's life, you can give me a medal for it." Within the culture of those serving in Vietnam, there was a sense of not wanting medals for what they did — often because they had negative views regarding the war or were embarrassed to be recognized. One helicopter pilot who had been shot down and had a foot amputated said he didn't want a medal. "Take that medal and shove it. I don't want it. I want my foot back!"[95]

The awarding of medals is a time-honored means for the military — and the nation — to honor those who exhibit courage and heroism in pursuit of a national objective or on behalf of others who are engaged in that mission. Often there is politics involved — many noted the disproportionate number of medals presented to officers and others, while more deserving ones were ignored. Frequently this was because of race or other factors — or in Vietnam because the men did not know the name of the person who was killed or injured while exhibiting courage and heroism. A recent example of correcting for prejudicial procedures was the awarding of the Medal of Honor to Santiago Erevia on March 18, 2014, for heroic actions in attacking enemy bunkers — on May 21, 1969! The Pentagon had reviewed the case and determined that Erevia had been ignored because he was Hispanic.

Ironically, given the Pentagon's penchant for keeping statistical records on most things, good comprehensive statistics for most medals are not available. But during the thirty days before June 8, 1969, 8 men received the Medal of Honor, 5 of them posthumously. These were genuinely earned and fully deserved. Notably, 5 of these medals were awarded for actions in defense of other men and/or rescuing wounded men. Three involved men absorbing a grenade blast or other explosive charge in order to shield others.

Donald Sullivan, the young army officer who fought throughout the entire Hamburger Hill battle and reached the top of the hill on May 20, remains convinced that the army and the Pentagon balked at recognizing men for medals there because of opposition from Senator Ted Kennedy. Sullivan himself received the prestigious Silver Star for his heroic conduct during this battle.[96]

Looking at the 1,592 men who died during the thirty days from May 10 to June 8, 1969, 258 of them received posthumous medals — an impressive number that included, in addition to the 5 Medals of Honor, 7 Distinguished Service Crosses and 76 Silver Stars.

Vietnam had its share of valor — and horror. It was impossible to fight or ever to anticipate the randomness, the cruelty, of war. One soldier had seen some unusual deaths in his work with Graves Registration: A man shot off his own finger to avoid going on a patrol. But the bullet ricocheted and hit an eighteen-year-old in the throat and killed him. One marine on guard duty threw a grenade into the dark where he had heard noises. The grenade hit a tree trunk and bounced back and killed him. Another man threw a grenade into a cave where it was suspected there were enemy troops. He was not satisfied that he threw it far enough, so he reached for it to throw again just as it exploded. A helicopter went to rescue men in the water who had been on another helicopter that was shot down. When the rescue craft came in, the down blast from the propellers was so strong that all of the men in the water were pushed underwater and drowned.[97]

Needless to say, even though this book focuses on the American experience, the cruelty and the randomness and the horror of war were suffered by the Vietnamese in ways and in numbers that will never be fully tallied but that obviously exceeded the American numbers. And while many of these tragedies were part of the incidental, the accidental, the collateral damages of any war, many others were not. Many Americans who served in Vietnam brought with them a set of negative racial stereotypes and, for too many, a set of racist assumptions. "Gooks," "dinks," and "slants" were common epithets that represented racial contempt rather than a hatred restricted to the enemy. They were used for all Vietnamese — NVA, VC, ARVN, and civilians. This condescension toward the Vietnamese could quickly become a callous disregard for them, and in some cases a hostility. If those who engaged in hostile conduct were in a small minority, there is little doubt that their conduct complicated any effort to win either hearts or minds.

Rocky Bleier's platoon patrolled near Vietnamese villages and farms. On one patrol through an area where there were suspected NLF, they came to some "hootches," the Americans' name for the bamboo-and-straw dwellings of many rural Vietnamese, and after searching the shelters, they burned them down. Women screamed at them. He said, "It was absurd. There were no VC anywhere." When a fifty-year-old man appeared — he had no weapon and posed no threat — "one of our young kids, an eighteen- or nineteen-year-old, rushed up to him, kneed him in the groin, and cracked his skull with the butt of an M-16." The man was in agony. The kid screamed, "You motherfucking, slant-eyed dink. You're the reason we're over here."[98]

On another patrol they opened up with massive firepower on a suspected hootch. Then Bleier heard someone "shrieking," and two women, two old men, and some children came out of the area by the destroyed building. They had been saved by a bunker but now they were all "crying and screaming." One of the women "rushed up to our lieutenant and stood toe to toe, looking up at him. Her face was contorted in rage as she cursed him at the absolute top of her voice. He tried apologizing in Vietnamese, but it was of no use."[99]

Frederick Downs had similar experiences. "The first time I saw a Vietnamese family go into hysterics when their hootch was set on fire, I was unsure whether burning down their home would accomplish our mission. The mission was to deny the enemy the use of the hootches, to destroy any food we found, and to teach the people a lesson about supporting the enemy." Even though he was troubled by this, Downs "quickly got used to it and accepted that this was one way to win the war." On one search-and-destroy mission, "The few Vietnamese we found in the area were women, children, and old men who had been left behind. When we started to burn their particular hootch, they would start wailing, crying, and pulling at our clothes. We didn't harm the people, but the orders were to destroy all the dwellings, so we did."[100]

Often this conduct was defensive, when Vietnamese civilians turned on them. One night after an assault, one of the NLF soldiers who was killed was a young man who spent the days on the base working as a barber cutting the American soldiers' hair. Vietnamese youngsters sold the Americans bottles of Coca-Cola along the road, and some men discovered ground-up glass in the drinks. A chaplain's assistant recalled that some of the local civilians who worked in the American barracks up on LZ Baldy embedded razor blades in bars of soap so that the Americans were badly cut when they washed.[101]

As one soldier put it, "We didn't trust each other. They didn't trust us. We didn't trust them." He did not witness any atrocities, but he was convinced these tragedies didn't happen more often because the American small-unit leaders kept things under control. He was sure there were men in his platoon who "were ready to do things that were illegal or whatever, and we wouldn't let them." But it was dangerous when "you got a nineteen-year-old kid with an automatic weapon and hand grenades." He viewed the Vietnamese distrust of Americans as an understandable result of their experience. "We'd come into a village and round everybody up, search the village." He could not imagine anybody doing that back in his hometown.[102]

The newsman Robert Hager described "the way our guys would treat the local populace" when they entered a village. The Americans would "just round them up and throw them into the center . . . Round everybody up and question them, roust them out of their hootches, women and children, and then to make it look good they'd give them some shots and we'd pass out some rations to them, [though] I'm sure they didn't understand American food." He found it "kind of brutal," certainly in terms of the public relations impact. The American troops were even harsher in their treatment of Vietnamese civilians when they suspected there were NLF there. "It does go to show how troops can be innocently dehumanized by the pressures of war."[103]

One man didn't remember anyone abusing Vietnamese civilians. But he did mention a relationship in which the American military clearly dominated: "We may have pushed them around or . . . and they were afraid. We were armed, they weren't. They lived between two worlds . . . They were in fear of the Vietcong and they feared us, too, you know."[104]

Destroying Vietnamese homes intentionally was too common to be dismissed. This was part of the war. But also part of the war were the countless occasions when the American troops tried to reach out with food, medicine and medical care, and other forms of support. These were substantial but seldom dramatic — and American actions such as those described by Downs and Bleier overwhelmed the charitable acts in the local narratives. One soldier was in a heavily contested area near the Cambodian border, where the men tried to work with the civilians. But the latter were "as often as not, afraid." The overall relationship was "difficult, tense, resistant."[105]

Americans did try to buffer civilians. When the North Vietnamese Army approached the village of An Hoa southwest of Da Nang, a group of villagers gathered in a field hoping to get out of the area before it was occupied. The marines sent an H-53 helicopter down to evacuate them, and people ran up the ramp to get on board as soon as it landed. When the pilot asked the crew chief how many were on board, he said, "I stopped at 100. I didn't even count the babies." The helicopter was rated to carry 38 equipped marines. It managed to take off, and the people were taken up to Da Nang. "Their smiles when they got off that thing were just amazing."[106]

An army lieutenant who spent a lot of time in the villages said, "We tried to do everything we could to support the Vietnamese civilians." Some men taught in the school, and some rebuilt levies and a schoolhouse." When Saigon got word of their efforts, they decided to focus on it. General Abrams led a contingent up to the village: "It was like the MUNI bus lines — we had helicopters coming and going, VIPs bumping into trees. It was almost comedy."[107]

There were not many instances of comedy, of course. One army doctor treated Vietnamese civilian casualties in the hospital at Long Binh. He couldn't tell if their response was gratitude for the treatment or resentment for the war that had caused them to need treatment. The doctor also set up clinics in villages. They even did minor operations there. One woman was brought into the main hospital. She was eight and a half months pregnant and had been shot by an NLF soldier because her family was supportive of the Saigon government. The doctor did a cesarean section and delivered a healthy baby girl. The mother recovered from a wound in her spleen, and they managed to make a crib and get some infant formula from Saigon for the baby. The army nurses in the ICU took pride in taking care of her. The mother returned to the village and left the baby behind — she did not want the child. Eventually a career sergeant at the hospital and his wife back in the States arranged to adopt the baby and bring her home with him.[108]

A navy officer who served on the hospital ship *Repose* that was stationed off the coast of Da Nang recalled civilians coming out to the ship in little fishing sampans. "They'd bring out their babies and hold them up, and we would hoist them up and treat them." The navy doctors treated congenital problems, but the "most upsetting were the kids who were injured" as a result of the war.[109]

One soldier who spent two tours in Vietnam reflected on the civilians he encountered: "All they wanted to do was be able to farm their rice, live a peaceful life — and they were peaceful people — hard, industrious working people." He said that the Americans too often "treated them like dogs, unfortunately, but that was the nature of war." He was convinced that most of the people in rural Vietnam really didn't care who ruled the country. "They just wanted to live in peace and just go on with life." A television reporter who covered Vietnam agreed: "These rural people tending their rice paddies and the fear in which they lived their daily lives because of what was going on all around them — didn't understand democracy from communism." Another echoed these sentiments: "The people I saw, they didn't want the North, they didn't want the South, they didn't want us . . . they didn't want anything except to raise their families in peace."[110]

Perhaps this attitude of fear, hatred, and indifference, of simply wishing to be left alone, was what most surprised the Americans who came to Vietnam in this period. Most still understood the American mission as one of protecting the South Vietnamese population from the Communist takeover of their country, a protection they believed was dearly wanted by the Vietnamese. It was this presumption that best explained why they were there. Yet the civilians sometimes said to them, "You people — you know, 'you Americans — You're actually making it worse and you should actually go home.' "[111]

In the fall of 1968, a young marine pilot from Dallas wrote to his sister about the moral and intellectual complexity of the war. Flying an A-4E Skyhawk he was going out an average of two missions a day from his base at Chu Lai. He provided air support in an area ranging from the DMZ down to An Hoa and Kham Duc — including at least one night mission into North Vietnam. He reported that he was "yet to be shot at. Not bad!" Life back on the base was often boring but he and some other marines supported some Vietnamese children in a nearby village. He spoke of one orphaned boy whose parents were killed by NLF — "he deserves a break."

The marines made provision for him to go to school. Phillip Barger said that he didn't mind "hosing down" NVA or NLF forces but he recognized that some of the "farmers by day fighters-by-night" Vietnamese were not easily sorted out. So he wondered what the United States was doing in a civil war. He was not comfortable with it all. "I would just like something more definite in the way of a rationale for killing people. And it's not to be found." On November 11, 1968, three weeks after writing this letter, Dennis Barger was hit by "hostile ground fire" west of Dong Ha while he was on a close air support mission. His plane crashed and he died.[112]

When their inspirational, idealistic understanding of the mission faltered in the face not of just the absence of expressions of gratitude but ones of hostility, the servicemen and -women wondered what they were doing there. So many American casualties were the result of mines, ambushes, and booby traps. "The Vietnamese people knew where those things were occurring, but they weren't telling us," a marine said. "That didn't seem like the kind of reaction you would expect from a people you were there fighting for."[113] His was a common observation. They were frustrated, disappointed, and often angry that the people in the countryside did not warn them about a trap or an ambush.

There was even greater disappointment with the South Vietnamese military, the ARVN. One soldier who was a college graduate and went to Vietnam at age twenty-five thought he understood the rationale for the war — until he arrived there. He was particularly frustrated by the way that the ARVN troops "time and time again" did not succeed in simple missions. "Their will was not in the battle or the fight. Our will, after a small taste of the Vietnam experience, then changed to survival and getting home."[114]

One veteran observed, "I have probably relaxed on this over the years, and the word 'hate' sounds not quite right, but at that particular time in my life, I grew to hate the South Vietnamese. I saw them run in battle. I saw them scam all the time. They were the worst soldiers in the world." Another was in a village that was harassed at night by NLF — killing officials or taking rice or kidnapping young men. "There was an ARVN compound maybe five hundred meters down the road, but the sun would go down and the moon would come up and the ARVNs would not be out to help those people at all." Another saw ARVN forces running away when there was a skirmish, and some of the men in his unit were so frustrated that they fired at them rather than at the enemy. Another said of ARVN that the men in his unit just didn't trust them. "We'd be out there humping and taking casualties, and they'd be bopping around . . . They'd get attacked and just drop their weapons and run. It was just boggling."[115]

The core principle of Vietnamization was that the South Vietnamese Army would assume responsibility for carrying out the war and they would do it successfully. This was based on high expectations in Washington and it was derailed by low expectations in Vietnam. If the low expectations were based on experience and observation, the Americans had helped to shape these experiences. The American military never had confidence in the South Vietnamese military. This was unfortunate, because some ARVN units and their soldiers performed bravely and successfully. This was particularly true in I Corps, where they were generally distant from their home villages and where they often served in units with good professional leadership.

The ARVN forces were never as well trained and surely never as well equipped as the U.S. military. This was partially the U.S. military's fault because they never trusted them enough to give them the support they needed. Nor did they ever trust them enough to give them the responsibility that would have buttressed their confidence. These attitudes were consequential even though the failing of ARVN was largely the fault of a corrupt government system in Vietnam that resulted in officers

456

who commanded units based on any of a number of "qualifications" and contributions, none of which were military. The inevitable result was a conscripted army of young men who had no confidence in the government and no commitment to securing it.

Terence Smith was in Vietnam at this time, working for *The New York Times*. He described the ARVN being marked by weak commanders and "intense politics" at the top levels. Americans were "disappointed again and again" by their conduct. ARVN, he observed, "did not have much discipline in their ranks. They very rarely carried the battle to the enemy. They were poorly paid, partially trained soldiers who were unsure of themselves and what their future might hold."[116]

One of the negative consequences of the American troop buildup that began in 1965 was that MACV shifted away from its earlier focus on training and supporting the South Vietnamese forces and came to depend upon them far less to carry the fight. Four years later, it was difficult, indeed impossible, to base Vietnamization on this record of American indifference and continuing symbolic statements of no confidence. Many ARVN units had performed much better and deserved much more. Charles Edwards was an army helicopter pilot who had two tours in Vietnam. During his first tour, he was motivated to help the Vietnamese fight communism. When he returned in 1968, he thought that the South Vietnamese military was "basically relying tremendously on American units to take the fight to the enemy."[117]

Living out in the bush, participating in the ambush patrol and the ambushed patrol, joining the helicopter assaults, providing the defense against nighttime raids — these experiences were not widely shared among the Americans deployed in the country. It is likely that of the 540,000 men and women in Vietnam in the spring of 1969, fewer than 100,000 were in combat units. It was not a representative force with a cross section of America on the front. While there were many college graduates and college dropouts among these combat troops, not simply among the officers, the grunts on the ground were basically blue collar in background.

Increasingly, the frontline troops were draftees. Even so, the draftees had more years of education and scored higher on aptitude tests than did the enlistees. It is impossible to get full profiles of the combat troops, but one study calculated that 90 percent of the draftees were sent to Vietnam by 1969 — and by 1970 they filled 70 percent of the combat slots. The vast majority of those had not chosen to go into combat units — of every 100,000 army combat assignments, only 4 percent had selected these fields as their first choice of Military Occupational Specialty. In 1963, 23 percent of those in combat specialties were draftees. The marines were somewhat different. They had few draftees and still depended on enlistments. And most who chose the Marine Corps did so understanding that this would mean infantry duty as a grunt — almost certainly in Vietnam.[118]

Christian Appy called Vietnam "the blue-collar war," and aptly so. His study remains the most comprehensive and convincing analysis of the Vietnam army. D. Michael Shafer also summarized some compelling studies. He learned that young men from South Boston were twenty times more likely to die in Vietnam than were students from Harvard and MIT. James Fallows and his Harvard friends gained deferments while the young men from Chelsea, "white proles of Boston," did not. The men killed in Vietnam who were from Salt Lake City were disproportionately from poorer neighborhoods. In Wisconsin, poor and working-class young men were two times more likely to die in Vietnam than would have been projected from their share of the population. And young men from poor neighborhoods in Chicago were three times more likely to die in the war than were those from wealthy neighborhoods — and those from neighborhoods with low educational levels were four times more likely to die than were those who came from neighborhoods with high education levels.[119]

The men in Vietnam may have been apart from American culture, but they were still a part of it. And it was a part of them — its tensions, its values, its rhythms. As Philip Caputo observed at the time of the landing of the first combat troops in Da Nang in 1965, "When we marched into the rice paddies on that damp March afternoon, we carried, along with our packs and rifles, the implicit convictions that the Viet Cong would be quickly beaten and that we were doing something altogether noble and good."[120] That sense of optimism and confidence had eroded by 1969, even as the troops came in and slogged around with packs and rifles. But many troops also brought with them more negative baggage from American society of the late 1960s — racial tensions and the growth of a drug culture.

Racial conflict in Vietnam increased as the war went on — and it grew as these tensions flared in American society. If much of what happened in Vietnam was filtered in the telling in the United States, American culture and politics and attitudes, as well as tensions, accompanied the men to Vietnam. The young black officer Colin Powell, deploying in 1962 as an adviser, recalled the "unnerving" drive with his wife to Fort Bragg, North Carolina.[121] Ironically, early in the war there was less evidence of racial conflict in Vietnam. Of course, "less evidence" does not mean it was not there. It was. But the growth of the civil rights movement in America and its increasing impatience and episodes of militancy accompanied the expansion of the war. As Lyndon Johnson was ordering the first combat marines into Vietnam in March 1965, young black demonstrators were beaten on the Edmund Pettus Bridge in Selma, Alabama. As LBJ was addressing post-Tet Vietnam and withdrawing from the presidential race, Martin Luther King Jr. was assassinated. The troops in the field didn't spend too much time talking about American politics, but they did talk about race in America. They discussed it and they lived the tensions that followed it.

White racist assumptions carried over to Vietnam. Early in the war there were disproportionate black combat deaths, but this difference moderated by the late 1960s. Yet in terms of military specialties, choice assignments, and promotion and medal opportunities, the disparities continued — and they were pronounced. African American servicemen noticed and resented these things. A white officer on Hamburger Hill said of Johnny Jackson, the young black soldier who successfully charged the last resisters and rushed the top of Dong Ap Bia on May 20, that if he had been a white soldier he would have received the Medal of Honor.[122]

Time magazine did a cover story in May 1967 about "The Negro in Vietnam," which included several stories about black soldiers, their professionalism and their courage. But it gushed too much in proclaiming that these men were fighting an additional battle, proving their "manhood" against the "matriarchal dominance of the Negro ghetto back home." They were shattering "stereotypes of racial inferiority" in a place where the "only color out here is olive drab." The editors hoped that the nation could learn from this that "democracy can work as well in the cities and fields of America as in the foxholes of Viet Nam." It was an upbeat story that did profile some of the professional black soldiers. But it didn't truly capture the black experience then, only touching on tensions, "racist graffiti from both sides" and fights along the "night-town" streets of Saigon, and describing the black bar area of Saigon, called Soulsville, as a "self-segregated" area.[123]

Wallace Terry, a black journalist, Vietnam correspondent, and the editor of the *Time* article, later produced an oral history of the black experience in Vietnam. He found that the early military units deployed had black career soldiers who believed that military service offered them opportunities that were not available in most places in America. As the army came to have more draftees, American tensions played out. Increasingly, young black men were strongly influenced by the flaring of tensions in Watts and Harlem. In cities across the country and at crossroads in the rural South, many were angry about the assassination of Martin Luther King Jr. and were inspired by Muhammad Ali's refusal to serve in Vietnam. Terry wrote that these new soldiers "were filled with a new sense of black pride and purpose." They did not overlook racial unfairness and racist behavior. They called for unity among the black troops.[124]

The prevailing popular view of the troops on the ground includes powerful images of tensions between black and white servicemen. This view is somewhat accurate — even though, as with most stereotypes, it fails to capture nuance and complexity. Within the U.S. military camps and bases were other armed camps, divided along racial lines. The symbols of this were the Confederate flag displayed, usually tauntingly, and meant to be just that, by white servicemen. These flag wavers were primarily, but not only, Southerners. And confronting this were signs of black brotherhood — also taunting, whether intended or not, of Black Power salutes and daps, and of the closed groups of black servicemen. When these men gathered to talk, to laugh, to sing, their gatherings often were defined by and immediately identifiable by race. Even though white servicemen also had their closed groups, it was their black counterparts who seemed to garner attention.[125]

One of the nuances of this situation had to do with the experience of the men who were in the bush fighting the battles. Vietnam was the first American war where combat units were fully integrated (the last part of the Korean War had made major steps in this direction). But in Vietnam, "fully integrated" could mean that the units were sometimes disproportionately black. Nonetheless, there were few stories focusing on race out in the bush in hostile situations. By most accounts, the men were mutually dependent.

Full integration was sometimes greatly exaggerated. The senior ranks were not. But ironically, back in the States, especially at military bases in the South, the racial barriers and indignities were more pronounced. Bruce Saunders was by all accounts a remarkable young lieutenant, a black man, who was killed at Fire Base Airborne in the brutal night attack on May 13, 1969, in which 27 men were killed. He conducted himself bravely. Just a year before this, at Fort Benning, he and his wife, Deborah, could not always go with the other young officers in their unit. They still faced WHITE ONLY and BLACK ENTRANCE signs.[126]

Most men observed tensions at the rear areas, but they noted that "it wasn't pronounced out in the bush . . . You need everybody. You gotta be operating like one." If everybody seemed to divide into racial groups in the rear, in the field "everybody had to go to their own squad" and do their jobs. The hostility and even dislike perhaps remained, but the tension seldom got to the point in the field that it did in the rear — "You had to get along."[127] Colin Powell noticed more racial tension when he returned for a second tour in the summer of 1968 — except out in the field, where men "did not have time to be hostile toward each other." Back in the rear, it was different. There was clearly racial friction, and young blacks, "particularly draftees, saw the war, not surprisingly, as even less their fight than the whites did." A Mexican American soldier observed the racial tension in the rear area. Much of it was talk — taunting — but it did not carry out to the field, where "everybody would talk to each other. And during the battles or firefights, they would help each other."[128]

One white soldier who had grown up in Orange, New Jersey, in a largely black community with black friends, encountered racial tensions when he went into the army: "The Southern guys, they'd make stupid remarks," but once they got to Vietnam, at least out in the field with infantry groups, "that shit all stopped. I don't think there was a color line — not in an infantry group, at least. We're too busy having to look after each other to look at each other's color. If I was somewhere and I needed to be dragged out, it was just as likely that a black guy would drag me out as a white guy, and vice versa." Another (white) soldier agreed: "In the field, we were all brothers out there. Just watching out for one another." Another, who talked of "bad" tensions in the rear, said in the field "everyone was subject to being killed so everybody had to pull together."[129]

It might seem oxymoronic to consider combat situations as inducing reduced tensions. And it would also exaggerate somewhat this particular situation. The brotherhood of men under fire in Vietnam was not quite a Kumbaya moment. Obviously, race was not left at the base camps. But out in the field, there was an understanding of mutual interdependence. And no one was likely to make a racist comment to a black infantryman carrying an M16. Certainly race provided a bonding element for black soldiers in an environment where personnel were turning over all of the time. And by the late '60s, this bonding became stronger because these soldiers knew they were going to go home and resolved to make a difference.

A black GI said that "the buddy system has to happen. You start realizing that you can't get through not communicating. Guys started opening up." He was welcomed warmly and protectively by other blacks when he arrived in his infantry unit. And they maintained a closeness through it all. But this young man realized, "I'm stuck out here in the boonies, and the white guy from the South is stuck out here, and it's life and death, we'd better begin to erase all this coloration immediately." They may not have erased "all this coloration," but they managed to suppress it in times of mutual need, and some developed close friendships. As he prepared to leave his unit after some fierce battles, he noted that out there "you couldn't think just white or just black — you had to think for everybody."[130]

If the Vietnam War included images of black and white tension, perhaps even more powerful is the stereotyped view of Vietnam as a center of freewheeling drug culture. The exaggerated view of addicted servicemen is one of the enduring myths of the war. Certainly there were drugs in Vietnam in the spring of 1969, although their use was not as widespread as in the early '70s. And even in the later years, it was not as widespread as the folklore argues. In 1969, as with racial tensions, the drug use that did occur more commonly flared back at the major bases and the base camps rather than out in the bush. And it was confined to these areas for some of the same reasons that racial conflict was sharper there. The stakes were too high out in the field for it to have been otherwise.[131]

Many men acknowledged drug use in Vietnam, largely marijuana, but few of them affirmed that their units used it in the field. As one said of Hamburger Hill, "You had to have your head about you." Others said "when you went out in the field, you pretty much stayed straight." Being stoned in the field "would have been suicide."[132]

A soldier remembered, "The bond was the people in your squad and the people in your platoon. You didn't want to be a slacker for them." Another, "We were long range. We didn't have time for drugs . . . We couldn't afford to be high as kites and be climbing mountains and stuff. I mean, we were always in a precarious type of situation." Out on patrols in the jungle, there was no smoking in most units, not even the ubiquitous cigarettes. There would be breaks in which smoking was allowed — but no marijuana. "Never ever did I see any" in the field.[133]

A point man on patrols made it clear to the men in his unit that "if you're on drugs or even drinking and you're out in the field, you're not going to be behind me because my life is depending on you." He was certain that "we didn't have any problems like that." There was drug use back at the base camps, but not among the men who "were actually doing the fighting."[134]

It should go without saying that not every

man followed these rules, One sergeant described the "best point man" in the country — a young soldier who "was a hippie; he wore the beads under his shirt." The sergeant defended him when a colonel pressed him on regulation uniform. He knew that the man loved marijuana, but he "promised me he would not use it in the field." It was not clear if he always kept his promise, but "as long as he performed his job out in the field, I didn't say anything to him."[135]

Drugs were widely available in the urban areas and at the major bases. The men in the field pointed to those stationed permanently on the rear bases, the REMFs, as the drug users. There was heroin and cocaine as well as plentiful supplies of marijuana. By 1969, it was fairly common for grunts to use marijuana when they came in from the field. According to one marine, when they came back to a base camp, they'd go to a bunker and it would be divided — on one side the men smoking pot and on the other "the Budweiser crew."[136]

Alcohol was widely available and was the drug of choice for many men. Beer — warm beer — was often delivered to base camps along with ammunition, food, and mail. And of course alcohol did not carry the same stigma either in the States or in Vietnam. One soldier said that when they came back to base camp, he would have eight or so beers. A soldier who served with the river patrol boats on the Delta knew one man, "a Jersey guy" who was a "pothead." He smoked marijuana "24/7." He also knew men "who were drinking Jack Daniel's for breakfast."[137]

An army helicopter pilot said that "drug use was strictly prohibited," but "we didn't consider alcohol as a drug causing a problem." He had no knowledge of any pilots flying drunk, but "some of them had to have a couple shots in the morning to get going, to go back out again." And a marine jet pilot at Chu Lai said that when the club opened at 5:00 P.M., all the pilots who were not on duty would be there. The men generally avoided drinking too much, but when they got up in the dark to prepare for the next day's flights, "the first thing you thought about was getting in that airplane and getting that oxygen mask on to try to help clear your head."[138]

Another element of American culture that the Vietnam '69ers, the baby boomers, brought with them to their war was popular music. Tensions played out even here; some wanted to hear '60s rock, others preferred Motown, and many were fans of country. Popular music was everywhere — played on tape decks or on turntables at base camps, performed by regular USO troupes or Special Services groups of Vietnamese or Filipinos playing at field sites and clubs, and on the ubiquitous American Forces Vietnam Network. Sometimes, accompanied by one of the group with a guitar, the men would sing. There was a powerful moment when the marines were besieged at Khe Sanh and the nation worried if they would survive. A television crew captured some of them with a guitarist singing the Pete Seeger antiwar ballad "Where Have All the Flowers Gone?"[139]

Pat Sajak, who would go on to have a successful career as a television host, was a young Chicagoan who dropped out of college and enlisted in the army in 1968 as a twenty-two-year-old facing the draft. He had worked for a college radio station and his army assignment was with the finance section at Long Binh. He managed to secure an appointment as a disc jockey on the American Forces Vietnam Network, a role he held through the end of 1969. He succeeded by a couple of years Adrian Cronauer, the author of and central character in *Good Morning, Vietnam,* a popular movie starring Robin Williams as Cronauer.

Sajak did not know about Cronauer when he took over as the morning DJ on the network that broadcast to all American military installations in Vietnam. The network's role was to perform the same music the men could expect to hear back home "wherever you were from." Because the morning show had an older audience — as opposed to the late-night programs — the

DJs stayed away from some of the hardest rock. But he played what they wanted to hear. It was American Top 20 music. And American Top 20 music by 1969 was the music of the baby boom generation.

Sajak said that the men who called and wrote basically wanted a reminder of home. "It was not as if we were trying to romanticize the war or romanticize the military. We were just trying to duplicate what they would have heard at home." There was little censorship of their choices — although the station prohibited the Kenny Rogers song "Ruby, Don't Take Your Love to Town," because of the line that pleaded with Ruby, "It wasn't me that started that ol' crazy Asian war," even though the singer was proud to serve, and now "I'm not the man I used to be." Apparently the censors found this story too depressing for young servicemen. Sajak also said that they were not permitted to play the song from the musical *Hair* that included a parody of the national anthem. Other than that, they were pretty free to play what they wanted — except in the summer of 1969, they were asked not to play "Give Peace a Chance." Sajak played this John Lennon song as he was finishing his last show on his last day before he left Vietnam.[140]

One soldier spent a day riding with a door gunner on Huey flights that were picking up and dropping off rifle platoons for daylight patrols. The gunner shared his radio-equipped helmet with the soldier. They were tuned into AFVN Radio: "It was surreal flying missions while listening to the Beatles."[141]

A recent study analyzed playlists and interviewed and surveyed veterans to try to determine the most popular songs for the men and women serving in Vietnam. Often these were songs that evoked a feeling or experience. The same as their counterparts back in the States, they liked the Beatles and Creedence Clearwater Revival. Favorite songs ranged from Johnny Cash's "Ring of Fire" to James Brown's "Say It Loud — I'm Black and I'm Proud" and Nancy Sinatra's "These Boots Are Made for Walkin'." Sentimental songs such as Porter Wagoner's "Green, Green Grass of Home," Otis Redding's "The Dock of the Bay," and Peter, Paul and Mary's "Leaving on a Jet Plane" were very popular. As were Jimi Hendrix's "Purple Haze" and Creedence Clearwater's "Fortunate Son." The consensus top songs were also popular in the States, but with a special message in Vietnam. The number one choice among those who served there was the Animals' "We Gotta Get Out of This Place," and right behind it was Country Joe and the Fish's "I Feel like I'm Fixin' to Die."[142]

In the summer of 1969, the Americans initiated an offensive operation to blunt the

473

North Vietnamese movement into the area west of Da Nang. It was the first major assault after the United States had announced a drawdown and a transfer in military responsibilities to the South Vietnamese. Even with this action, the war was shifting — and there was no longer any presumption of "winning." A slogan echoed across the jungles and rice paddies that had been heard during the last battles at Pork Chop Hill and Old Baldy in Korea, as that war negotiated down to conclusion: "Who wants to be the last to die?" or "Who wants to die for a tie?" Or as one soldier was quoted as saying of his generation's war, "Fuck it, it don't mean nothin'."[143]

7
GETTING OUT OF THIS PLACE

"At times I wish we never would have grown up," wrote Sandy Boyer of her older brother Larry. Larry Boyer died on May 25, 1969, while on a patrol up on Mutter's Ridge, a steep, dark, forebidding hill in the northern reaches of South Vietnam, near the Demilitarized Zone.[1]

Sandy's brother was just ten days away from his twenty-third birthday. Larry Boyer was from Ellwood City, Pennsylvania, and had been in Vietnam for four months when he was killed by small-arms fire during Operation Herkimer Mountain. His good friend Byrle "Beetle" Bailey, from Omaha, Nebraska, was killed in the same incident. Bailey had just turned nineteen. Boyer was the squad leader and Bailey was walking point when they came across some Vietnamese words carved into the bark of a tree. Right beyond that, near the top of the ridgeline, they made a sharp turn on the trail and ran into a North Vietnamese Army outpost.

Bailey was killed at nearly point-blank range, and when Larry Boyer ran up, he was shot and killed. Navy corpsman William Denholm scampered in to try to aid them, only to discover it was too late. Denholm was shot in the arm while trying to assist them. Following a firefight, the NVA withdrew and the bodies were placed under a tree. Shortly thereafter, they were carried out by helicopter. The carving on the tree they had passed was later interpreted as a birthday greeting to Ho Chi Minh. He had celebrated his seventy-ninth birthday the previous week.

Larry Boyer was considered an all-around great kid growing up. Described as good-looking and generous, he was a very good baseball player and his father helped coach one of the teams on which he played. His dad still bore a large scar from a bullet wound he had suffered during World War II. Larry Boyer talked about playing baseball professionally, and many thought he had the talent to do that. He had a baseball scholarship to Marietta College in Ohio, where he played shortstop and had professional scouts watching him. Early in 1967, after two and a half years in college, Larry Boyer dropped out and enlisted in the marines. He felt that he had a responsibility to serve. He also got married before he shipped out to Vietnam.[2]

Bailey and Boyer were among the 43 Americans killed in Vietnam on May 25, 1969. Of these, 37 were born in 1946 or later. Of the others, four were senior NCOs and 2 were young officers born in 1945. It was now clearly the baby boomers' war. Despite Sandy Boyer's regrets about the consequences of doing so, they had grown up. Over 80 percent of those killed in May were born in 1946 or later — the baby boomer cohort. This percentage had risen over the 50 percent mark in 1967. The postwar generation assumed the burden of the Vietnam War. By May 1969, it was a war in transition — although few in Vietnam would have recognized this at that time. What was clear was that the enthusiasm — even more important, perhaps, the *optimism* — of the spring of 1965 had eroded. The war that had been widely embraced as an American responsibility to the world and a necessary step in the country's own defense had become a political burden from which an exit needed to be found through negotiations rather than military means. In the meantime, the military effort needed to be sustained while being reduced. This meant a steady stream of young Americans were deployed to Vietnam — and several streams were coming home. The numbers in the latter group would increasingly exceed those in the former.

In the first four years of the war, the ramp-up years, as the numbers of troops had increased in Vietnam, the logistics of bringing men home became more complicated. In many ways it was more challenging than the rather straightforward pipelines that brought replacements into the country. Basically, there were three ways to leave Vietnam. The largest number of troops came home on charter planes as part of regular rotation. By May 1969, more than 40,000 a month were rotating out of the country, around 1,300 a day. The second-largest group that month, 4,334, came out on medical flights. And finally, 1,455 men came home in body bags in the hold of the charter flights or in designated cargo planes heading for Oakland, California, or Dover, Delaware.

Certainly, the troops deploying to Vietnam were nervous and uncertain. After all, they were going to a war zone. But there is at least anecdotal evidence that the men and women waiting to rotate home at the end of their tours had some apprehension as well. For many, "reentry was surreal, jarring, and difficult . . . I think it was quite common for Vietnam veterans to feel an unfathomable anger after we came home. We had risked our lives for nothing, and of course many lost theirs."[3] In addition to the common wartime nervousness about adjusting to home and family and the uncertainty about next steps in their civilian lives, there was by 1969 also a concern about confrontation. The American public's support for the war had soured even more, and in Vietnam many heard that the antagonism now was also directed toward those who served there. One returnee's "biggest fear was coming home, because we knew that if the war wasn't popular, we weren't going to be popular. That was a tough time. Nobody knew how to handle that." A soldier warned, "You don't want to go through California." This was the state where protesters were allegedly spitting on returning veterans. On the other hand, some soldiers weren't concerned because, after all, "their brothers and sisters and friends were all going to these antiwar protests."[4]

Getting out of Vietnam and heading home trumped all apprehensions. They were living the line of their favorite song, the Animals' "We Gotta Get Out of This Place." Other than career military, or some for whom an extended tour would result in a shortened enlistment or a desired assignment, there is little evidence of anyone wanting to stay in the country. On the other hand, the big moment for which they had been counting down days was subdued for most. The process of going home was bureaucratic rather than ceremonial. There was an isolating randomness to it all. Typically, the returnees didn't know anyone else on their plane. They were quiet and tired — and eager to get off the ground. And on the return flight there was little opportunity for the extended withdrawal with others that troop ships had provided in World War II and in the Korean War. One day men were out in the bush and two days later they were flying out of Tan Son Nhut or Da Nang and less than twenty-four hours after that they were in Seattle or San Francisco or Los Angeles. One marine returning home from his first deployment didn't know anyone else on the plane and they didn't even talk on the whole ride home.[5]

Jack McLean had engaged in some intense combat up near Landing Zone Loon. One day, after his company boarded helicopters for another jungle landing, he caught a mail helicopter back to Dong Ha and then on to Da Nang for the trip home. "I was so very sad. I was so very happy. Mostly, I felt very alone." When he finally got off the plane back at Travis Air Force Base in California several days later, everyone pushed off in different directions, saying good-bye to those they met on the plane. But he knew "the real parting had occurred days before, in the field, when the extraordinary Charlie Company bonds that had been forged over the past year had been broken — most forever."[6]

Of course, for some there was a sense of elation, of conclusion. A flight attendant on one of the charter flights leaving Vietnam wrote of a young soldier in her diary: "the first guy in line at the gate, dressed in camouflage, heavy boots, jumping up and down and waving his process papers like he couldn't wait to get to the john." He had "the biggest smile on any face in all of Asia." He kissed her hand ten times before climbing the steps to the cabin — and also kissed the bottom step of the ramp going up to the plane. The flight attendedant noted that he still smelled of the jungle. He said softly, "I'm goin' home." She learned that home was a small town in Alabama.[7]

An army chaplain rotating out wondered if one last mortar shell would hit the plane. "I try to will the pilot to gun the engines so we can leave this dirty dangerous place called Vietnam." Upon liftoff, "One hundred and seventy-five GIs let out wild cheers. The tour in hell is finally finished. We're on the way back to a world of hot dogs, mom and apple pie." This chaplain's perspective surely was neither uniquely spiritual nor was it unique.[8]

Soldiers had been prepped for their reentry into what they called "the World." Their official briefings were rarely up-to-date or helpful. The army distributed to returning veterans a publication they called *Tour 365: For Soldiers Going Home.* The magazine was updated periodically, and the "Mid-Year 1969" edition had a cover note from MACV commander General Creighton Abrams saying the soldiers completing their tour of duty "know the difficult tasks inherent in fighting to protect the freedom of peace-loving people against Communist invaders." He reminded them that they understood the task "better than many of our countrymen." Quoting all of the presidents from Dwight Eisenhower to Richard Nixon to affirm the consistency of the American assignment, General Abrams said that "people at home will want to hear your story of the war." And, the commanding general instructed, "Tell it."

The publication was glossy, with high-quality color photographs of landmarks and peaceful people. There was a review of the American engagement, with subsections. The period from 1961 to 1964 was called "The Darkest Era." But then the war turned around and "1967 saw the Free World Forces tighten the screw on the enemy." The magazine described Tet as a major Communist effort in which the enemies were "deprived of their every major goal, with the possible exception of publicity." Now, in 1969, the soldiers were assured that "substantive negotiations" at Paris were possible.

Tour 365 also reminded the soldiers of what were described as "The Pleasant Moments." The returning soldier had been, "much more than his counterparts in any other war," the "beneficiary of a myriad of programs designed to maintain his morale and improve his general welfare." There were striking photographs of R&R at beaches, "with bikini-clad 'birds' " along with great sightseeing and food in Thailand, Singapore, Australia, and Tokyo. They had enjoyed correspondence courses and other educational opportunities and recreational facilities and USO shows and DoD Special Services programs, led by Bob Hope's tour with his "beautiful girls to brighten the Christmas season." The soldiers had access to post exchanges with bargain luxuries and great snack bars and clubs with cold beverages, as well as movies and other entertainment. There is no record of what soldiers still carrying the red dirt of the A Shau Valley or the caked mud of the Mekong Delta thought of all of this.

The publication confirmed that those who had completed a tour in Vietnam surely had sacrificed: "From Valley Forge to Dak To, American soldiers have endured the hardships of a thousand battles. In Vietnam, however, unprecedented morale and welfare opportunities help make the burdens of war at least a little more bearable." The back cover of the magazine showed a line of men getting on a TWA jet with an attractive young flight attendant standing at the bottom of the stairs to greet them.

Lieutenant General Frank Mildren, deputy commanding general of the U.S. Army, Vietnam, added a note to this publication reminding the men how much Vietnam and the United States were in their debt. He said their family and friends were proud of them, and they "will look to you as an authority on what is happening in the Republic of Vietnam. This magazine, a history of this country and the year you have spent here, may help you to tell your story." It turned out that most at home did not want to hear the "story," and not many of those who returned wanted to tell it.

The informal network of those who had returned to the United States had a different theme to brief the returnees. Warnings about a hostile reception and advice not to wear a uniform after landing were common. One army nurse was warned not to go out into the streets with her uniform on, which "made us feel worthless." In fact, she had no difficult encounters. At her home in upstate New York, her parents had a WELCOME HOME sign on the garage. A marine officer connecting to a flight back to Boston said that as soon as the stewardess saw him in uniform, she moved him "right up to first class." And in Boston he had a "nice homecoming." A navy corpsman received a first-class upgrade as well by a grateful stewardess. At the Los Angeles airport, some people shouted at a returning soldier. Before going home the next day, he flew to Lewiston, Idaho, where he spent the night at a hotel. When he entered the hotel dining room in uniform, he received a warm welcome: "I couldn't buy a drink. I couldn't buy my own dinner." Another said,

"Most people didn't care a whit if you had served. I was never insulted, but I was never thanked, either." A fellow returnee agreed: He acknowledged that he had no unpleasant incidents, "but nobody ever said, 'Welcome home,' or 'Thank you for your service and time and what you did for us in Vietnam.' "[9]

Despite the warnings and the initial tension, most of the returnees had no real problems at the airports. Often there were protesters, but there were few serious encounters. One soldier noted that the antagonism was directed toward the government and its policies rather than "with us guys who were over there." The navy corpsman who had been touched by the first-class upgrade from the stewardess said this was the only time that anyone other than family members greeted him as a "returning hero." They were warned not to wear uniforms when they got home because "you're just asking for trouble." On the other hand, the airlines gave discounts only to those in uniform. He wore his and said he had no problems.[10]

The absence of gratitude often escalated to a more subtle indifference or, perhaps more accurately, a discomfort in discussing or even acknowledging the experience. Everyone wanted to move on. This often included the closest family members. One marine's family was "overjoyed" to see him home, but "they didn't dare ask me questions or anything. I didn't get debriefed. I wasn't in touch with anybody that I could really talk about the war with, but I was with people that loved me and accepted me." For another, who had been wounded on Hamburger Hill, the Vietnam experience was a "nonsubject." After seven months in a hospital, "nobody asked questions about it. And I don't think it was out of meanness. I think it was probably just awkwardness on their part."[11]

For one army nurse, it was only when she returned home that she had "problems dealing with my having been in Vietnam," because she had no warning about the attitudes of most people. She didn't encounter hostility but rather people who were "absolutely, totally indifferent." Her church organized a potluck supper to welcome her home, but even on this occasion, "there were very few people that mentioned anything about Vietnam. They didn't want to know anything about it." A soldier who had been drafted after he graduated from college said that while there were no unpleasant incidents, there was little warmth or interest. "My friends had all gone to grad school. They didn't quite know what to make of it. Nobody wanted to talk about it. I didn't talk about it for a long time."[12]

One marine said, "You have survived your journey to war, and are ready to begin your journey from war . . . However, it is a very different you who are leaving. You are absolutely not the same person who started your journey to war months earlier . . . You are now back in the World, but without a real home, even in your home town. You are there, but your soul isn't. And oh, the survivor's guilt. Strangely, you miss and want to be back with your Marine unit, even if it means going back to the hell hole that is the Nam."[13]

Families and friends ignoring Vietnam was often the result of a tacit mutual agreement: Let's forget about this last year. Most men were not eager to discuss the war experience with those who had not been there. They were not sure how to describe or explain it — and, in fact, many veterans have spent years trying to make sense of their experiences. One said, "For the most part, other than my family, nobody knew I was in Vietnam. I didn't talk about it and I didn't tell them." Another admitted, "I went in a hole. I didn't tell people I'd been there. I didn't talk about it. I certainly wasn't ashamed that I'd been there, but I certainly didn't broadcast it." A third offered his solution: "The only way to survive was to grow your hair as fast as you could, lose your tan, and don't tell anybody where you'd been the last few years."[14]

There has been a great debate about the level of hostility the returning soldiers encountered at airports and elsewhere. Although many experienced no antagonism, some recalled very unpleasant incidents. Protesters did come to the gates of the major airports. One medic mentioned "jeers and threats" at Los Angeles International. An army nurse described her sadness and pain when she realized that many were making more than antiwar statements; they were directing "venom" toward the returnees. The parents and three sisters of a sailor who was a riverboat veteran on the Mekong Delta met him with WELCOME HOME signs while protesters were shouting that he was a "baby killer" and a "baby burner." A navy officer who arrived at San Diego heard people screaming. He looked behind him to try to figure out who it was they were yelling at, and he realized they were yelling at him.[15]

A twenty-year-old marine experienced "cold indifference or muted hostility" from all but airline crew members. At Chicago O'Hare and then at a train station, there was open anger and shouts of "baby-killer." After arriving in Milwaukee by train and hauling his duffel bag a couple of blocks to the bus station, "I heard a horn blow and turned expecting more crap. I saw a truck driver smile and wave to me. I actually nearly cried then. That returning home experience marked me for life."[16]

Some veterans reported that they were spat upon. One recalled several men and one woman shouting and spitting at them at Seattle-Tacoma airport. A chaplain in uniform reported being spat upon. A wounded veteran came into New York and rode in an ambulance to St. Albans Hospital. The ambulance had screens on the windows to protect against thrown objects, and when he left the hospital someone spat at him. His father showed him a WELCOME HOME sign they had removed from the house because people were vandalizing it. Most people didn't know what to say to him. And others were "real assholes." He just started hanging out "with the hippies."[17]

An army medic who was a veteran of the costly assault on Dak To in May 1969 wasn't a victim of spitting, but people said "snarky things, just talkin' out their ass." He was amused by it all because "I was a hippie before I went in . . . a long-haired, you know, pot-smoking party guy." And now, because he had short hair and a uniform, people were calling him names. He had trouble getting a job — some potential employers even told him, "We don't hire Vietnam veterans." So he bought a van and hung a hammock in the back and just traveled around the country.[18]

A combat veteran came into Travis Air Force Base in the Bay Area and went to see some friends enrolled in the university at Berkeley. While they were there, Governor Ronald Reagan sent the State Police and the

National Guard to remove the protesters at People's Park. The authorities used tear gas against the demonstrators. Just two weeks earlier, this soldier had been on a difficult mission and the Americans had used CS gas to clear the area. That smell and that experience stayed with him. So as soon as he saw the canisters, he told his friends he was "getting out of here!"[19]

One soldier encountered hostile protesters in the Jack London section of San Francisco. Another soldier had no problems with protesters until he was back home and was in a bar where his brother was bragging about his service in Vietnam. When the veteran went to the restroom, three men beat him up.[20]

Even nonviolent hostility left its mark. One serviceman tried to cash a U.S. government check at a New York bank. They refused to cash it. "I am sure part of that was that I was a soldier and that the people behind the counter didn't have a very high regard for soldiers." An Indiana marine married his high school sweetheart in 1970, six months after he returned. This was in Crawfordsville, where "you could not get any more Middle America, more patriotic." The minister at the local Methodist church initially refused to marry the couple if the groom wore his uniform, but finally relented: "I think that says more about how the attitude in the country had changed in those few years toward the war."[21]

Even as the war angered or numbed the country and its capacity to welcome veterans home, some veterans found each other. One soldier who arrived at the San Francisco airport had to wait overnight for a flight to the East Coast. He was wandering around the airport in dress uniform with a rucksack and an SKS — a Soviet carbine — souvenir. He was apprehensive about encountering protesters when he saw walking "toward me was somebody in a field jacket — beard, beads, peace symbols — and we're just walking toward each other." He expected a difficult confrontation. "I'm deciding what I'm going to do if this son of a bitch starts giving me some shit — and the guy, as we get closer, he ambles over to me and we stop, stood there looking at each other. He says, 'Welcome home. I was over there in '66–'67 with the 173rd.' We shook hands, and he went on his way and I went on mine."[22]

As those men and women returned to the States and had their separate encounters, there was another group coming home, less visibly, on medical transport planes. In May 1969, nearly 10 percent of the returnees, 4,334 Americans, were flown out of Vietnam to various hospitals: some in Asia, with the primary places being the U.S. Army Hospital at Camp Zama and the Naval Hospital in

Yokosuka, both in Japan; others to the Tripler Hospital in Hawaii; and many, often the most seriously wounded, directly to hospitals in the States. Patients sent to Japan were expected to return to duty within sixty days. The May medical evacuation totals were the highest monthly figures for the entire war.

Wartime medicine was about far more than dramatic treatment of serious battlefield injuries. In 1969, only 19 percent of the hospitalizations in Vietnam were for battle wounds and injuries. Approximately two-thirds of the patients were suffering from diseases and other medical problems. This was common in wartime, and by then the disease problem had been reduced in Vietnam. During World War II, 85 percent of the hospitalizations in the Southwest Pacific theater was due to disease. The major problems in Vietnam were fevers of "undetermined origin." The second major illness was malaria. The mosquito-borne disease was in some places epidemic, despite preventive medications. It was critical to control the high fevers that accompany malaria. Men were being sent back to the States in comas, in near-vegetative states, due to prolonged high temperatures. A third category was called "neuropsychiatric conditions." This was considered a nonbattle injury, though of course it was often directly the result of battlefield experiences. Throughout most of the period, diagnoses of these neuropsychiatric conditions in Vietnam had been more or less the same as for the army worldwide. However, in 1968 and 1969, while these hospitalizations increased throughout the army, they did so far more rapidly in Vietnam than anywhere else. These diagnoses doubled there between 1965 and 1970.[23]

Diseases were more common than battlefield wounds, but they were typically less debilitating. In 1969, battlefield injuries resulted in hospital stays some two and a half times longer than the periods required for diseases. In Vietnam, battlefield wounds and disease often went together. Vietnam was considered medically a "dirty" war in terms of infected wounds suffered in highly contaminated places, including rice paddies, waterways, humid jungles filled with insects, and hidden infected punji sticks. Nonetheless, the medical support system in Vietnam saved many more of the wounded than were saved in World War II or the Korean War. One of the reasons for this was the nature of wounds. In Vietnam, more of the wounds were from small arms, booby traps, and mines; in the earlier two conflicts, a higher proportion were from artillery and other high-explosive projectiles.

But there was also a shift in this ordnance of death and injury during the Vietnam War. Small-arms fire wounds decreased from 42.7

percent in June 1966 to 16 percent in June 1970. Concurrently, there was a sharp increase in injuries caused by mines and booby traps, from 49.6 percent to 80 percent. This was a result of more U.S. offensive operations — and more carefully contrived ambushes for the units involved in them. Importantly, small-arms fire remained the most lethal on the battlefield. Down through 1970, small-arms fire caused 51 percent of the deaths in Vietnam. In World War II, this figure was 32 percent. The head and upper torso were favored targets for enemy soldiers firing rifles. A high-caliber bullet striking the human body in these places typically resulted in death.[24]

Men suffering battlefield injuries were saved in Vietnam due to several factors that had little to do with ordnance: good battlefield medicine, readily available whole blood in the field preserved in Styrofoam containers, rapid evacuation protocols, and excellent forward hospitals and surgical procedures. The immediate battlefield treatment was critical. One medic acknowledged that "while everyone was down trying to kill everyone else, I was the one up looking around for spare body parts. This bit of cynicism might be funny if it weren't so tragically true."[25]

The army medics and navy corpsmen serving with marines had to do preventive support in the field — checking for blisters and other sores, dispensing salt tablets, urging men to change into dry socks. Some soldiers gave up wearing socks and the mesh combat boot insoles because they trapped dirt and mud, and retained water. They tried to air out their feet as much as possible when they were not on patrol. Some gave up wearing GI cotton underwear in the field in order to keep dry and ventilated. One said, "We didn't wear underwear because you couldn't or else it would rot."[26]

During and after any firefight, army medics and navy corpsmen had a major, and dangerous, assignment in assessing conditions and stabilizing wounds, stopping bleeding, trying to comfort those with intense pain, and getting the wounded out of there. Their role was instinctively to triage the wounded. Medics acknowledged administering morphine against the guidelines when there had been loss of limbs and sedating men who were suffering great pain. Most of the time no one monitored the doses closely, especially in the midst of heavy casualties. At one hospital, when a helicopter came in with numbers of wounded, a medic gave morphine syrettes containing a half gram of the powerful drug to anyone who was screaming. One soldier's pant leg had four needles stuck through it. "I wondered if anybody could even *survive* two full grams of morphine. In training we were instructed to administer no more than two doses."[27]

An army medic who served on Hamburger Hill said that each medic carried five one-quarter-gram morphine syrettes. He kept his in his left front pocket so that everyone would know where it was. He gave additional morphine to those he did not think would survive to "keep them comfortable." Dying men often asked, "Where's my wife?" or "Where's my mom?" He always told them that she was on her way. He learned early that no matter how bloodied and torn someone was, it was important to "make sure you have a smile on your face, because that guy is going to look straight in your eyes, and if you're smiling, he thinks he's going to be okay." Often dying men asked, "I'm not going to make it, am I?" He tried to reassure them — and then administered more morphine.[28]

A medic at Dak To described the carnage when the bunker was hit by an NVA rocket. There were a few survivors whose concussions had "just knocked them senseless." He observed a new medic trying to start an air hole in the neck, called a cricothyroidotomy, with a ballpoint pen. It wasn't working. Then he realized that the man was dead. Their biggest difficulty was sorting out torn bodies, matching limbs and torsos and heads, in order to wrap them up and get them evacuated. One soldier has never forgotten the overwhelming sensation: "I didn't know you could smell blood. I don't mean burnt blood. I mean blood. You could smell it. It has a salty, ocean — I can't really describe it, but it smells."[29]

The trauma of these experiences became part of the enduring memory and agony of those who survived. At a forward medical station on Landing Zone Baldy, a medic saw "everything — arms, legs blown off, brains falling out of their head. It's everything you can imagine — numerous bullet wounds, fragmentation grenade . . . booby traps — the worst thing." He noted the contagious effect of bloody trauma: Often those who were not injured but saw a buddy "blown up next to them" were "just hysterical because they're just young kids. You have to take care of them as well as the wounded." A nurse at the 71st Evacuation Hospital at Pleiku cared for one man who was deeply depressed. "It was like every time I looked into his eyes, they were like pools getting deeper and deeper." She learned about his experience: "They had called in artillery and they had called it in wrong. It ended up right on top of their own people. He went to grab his friend and his friend's head rolled off." She said that some of the men who came there were very troubled and violent, and "you had to drug them right up to the limit. You couldn't get to them."[30]

In a nighttime ambush, a young farm boy

from Illinois, Terry Dean Miller, was killed. A soldier from Montana, Miller's friend, was with him and had to wait until morning to evacuate the body. So his friend sat there holding his dead friend all night. Another soldier there said the friend "was just absolutely covered in blood and flies, and he just sat there on the ground, staring at the ground. He never acknowledged anybody walking by."[31]

Traumatic brain injuries and psychological trauma were common, but few knew how to deal with them. These conditions would flare once the shock of the experience and the sedating effects of the morphine wore off. One nurse said that in her hospital, many were ready physically to return to their units, but a large proportion were "scared of the war and hated the way they were treated." One man shot himself in the foot to avoid going back out, but he was recuperating — and he was hostile to everyone. A young soldier with fragmentation wounds was healing quickly, but he was "battle-fatigued." He walked widely around corners and often walked backward. He kept saying, "I can't go back. I just can't go back there. There's no way I can face it." The nurse said the non-medical military were not very sympathetic: "They don't believe there's anything psychological that can be going on. They don't believe that somebody could be mentally ill."[32]

The clinical condition post-traumatic stress disorder was not identified until the late 1970s. In 1969, people still talked about shell shock or combat fatigue or battle fatigue. And soon they would be describing many forms of depression or antisocial attitudes as part of what was called the Vietnam Syndrome. But few men in the field — and even fewer commanders out there — thought of aversion to combat as being a clinical condition but rather dismissed it as a character flaw. Concussion or other moderate brain injuries were things to be "shaken off."

One forward observer spent a lot of time in outposts in the jungle. When a mortar struck near him at a post beyond the Cambodian border, it "rattled my brain a little bit." Afterward, he had trouble writing down coordinates and doing the calculations necessary to direct air or artillery fire. His immediate chain of command told him he was fine and to stop complaining. Finally, a medic insisted that he be sent to a hospital for evaluation. There they determined that he was a "paranoid schizophrenic with homicidal and suicidal tendencies." He was shocked, and it took many years for medicine to catch up with his condition involving traumatic brain injury and PTSD.[33]

A chaplain helping the medics after an

ambush on the Mekong River wrote, "Everyone wants water. How do I tell a man with his guts hanging out his side that he can't have water?" The whole place was "a scene from a horror movie. Blood is everywhere . . . One soldier has part of his brain hanging out through a huge hole near his ear. He is still alive and might even survive but he will probably be in a vegetative state." Another man had a slight wound but was "more injured in his soul. He just looks through me as he seems to be staring out into space. Another sits in a corner simply singing hymns in a low voice, while sitting in his and other's blood."[34]

Following a devastating rocket attack on an artillery battery near Dak To, one soldier saw his best friend all charred and trying to breathe. He saw his platoon leader, or the top half of him. The rest was severed, "like a deflated person laying there." And then he encountered a head, "perfectly cut." He recognized him, "just a young kid, just turned twenty-one a couple of months before that . . . He had big blue eyes and curly blond hair . . . A Shirley Temple man." The head seemed so normal, "it was like you couldn't believe that anything was wrong with him other than there was just a head there." Another soldier who survived the attack described the lone head: The face "looked shocked, like you could imagine in a horror movie." He thought the young soldier looked like "he knew almost what was going to happen when it happened."[35]

A medevac pilot flying dustoff missions to evacuate the wounded said that by the late '60s, the extensive field hospital network was so efficient that most flights could deliver a patient to these facilities in around ten minutes. The helicopters had a medic on board who could start IVs and administer morphine. But these responses were less critical on the short flights. The medics kept the men alive. And following every flight they would get out their water cans with hand pumps and clean out the inside of the aircraft because "the blood and guts and brains and everything else would get all over the place back there."[36]

A marine medevac pilot related, "We took off one time — this is just vivid in my mind — we got out, wc had about 4 guys laying in the belly of that thing. We got airborne and got leveled out and the crew chief called me and he said, 'Lieutenant, can you do a hard right turn and then put it into unbalanced flight?' I said, 'Yeah, what's the problem?' He says, 'We got 2 inches of blood in the bottom of this.' So we were able to angle the helicopter to get all that out."

He noted that there were always nagging questions after they had raced from the battlefield with injured marines: "Could I have gotten there quicker? Could we fit more people on? Could we have done this or that? . . . and then we were looking at the 'Golden Hour,' they called it. If you could get them back to a Med Base, they had a 90 percent chance of surviving. Then you're all set to go and you can hear the [microphone] click on and the guy will say, 'You can return to base' — the medevac is now a routine medevac, which meant that he had passed away. So here you are — you got these emotions working against each other. You got all this adrenaline, you got this sorrow thing going on and you got this thing, 'Why couldn't I have gotten there quicker?' "[37]

The medical helicopter pilots preferred not to fly out the men who were dead on the same flight with the wounded. But they had little choice sometimes. The pilot Eric Rairdon on Hamburger Hill, who had limited capacity on his light observation helicopter, determined that he would first fly out the seriously wounded, then the other wounded, and then come back for the dead. He knew that the soldiers would not leave the dead behind and "that's not good for them to be carrying their buddies around."[38]

One doctor who served as chief of surgery at Long Binh concluded that there was a sort of "biological predeterminism" at work: "The bad injuries don't make it. If they survive enough to be evacuated and fly for ten,

502

fifteen, twenty minutes and they're still alive, then you've got a chance to save them. In a sense they're preselected when they hit the emergency room." The exceptions were the head injuries. "Once the soldier arrived alive, they're young, healthy guys; with resuscitation and appropriate surgery, the vast majority of them were saved." Most wounds in his experience were fragmentation wounds of some sort — RPGs or other shrapnel. He was certain that one of the problems in Vietnam was that it was so hot the soldiers would not wear their flak jackets out in the field, so they took more torso wounds.[39]

Army nurses found themselves literally on the front line of the medical care system. According to Department of Defense figures, 7,500 women served in Vietnam in the military and most were nurses. Eight nurses, including 2 male nurses, died in Vietnam, mainly from plane and helicopter crashes and illness. Sharon Lane was the only one killed by direct enemy fire, on June 8, 1969.[40]

Lane was twenty-five years old and was stationed at 312th Evacuation Hospital at Chu Lai. A native of Canton, Ohio, she had been in Vietnam for six weeks. She had completed nursing school in 1965 and enlisted in the army in the spring of 1968. After training and a brief domestic assignment, she requested assignment to Vietnam. On June 8, she finished a turn in surgery at the 312th, and then moved to the 4th Ward, which treated Vietnamese patients. She was in the ward when it was struck by a rocket. She was hit by flying shrapnel in the neck and throat and died quickly.[41]

One army nurse said the news of Sharon Lane's death was one of those moments she would never forget. It reminded her of learning of JFK's death: "I had the same recall to Sharon's death because I think by June of '69, the war itself to me was so tragic and so horrific for the men." But the death of a nurse "just personalized it for me that we lost an army nurse — a woman — and I just felt so sad for her and for her family."[42]

One nurse at the 91st Evacuation Hospital saw an eighteen-year-old coming out of surgery. He was the only survivor of a mine that destroyed an APC. He was "crying for his mother. I felt so helpless. I was barely older than he was and he's crying 'Mommy! Mommy! Mommy!' " She didn't know what to do, so she "just held him." After spending some time in Vietnam, she thought of writing her mother to see if she could find "one whole eighteen-year-old." She wasn't sure there were any left. "We had too many bodies lying in those beds minus arms and legs, genitals, and faces, and things like that can't be put back together again."[43]

A nurse at the Naval Hospital at Da Nang noticed that "nights were especially difficult because this was the time when people who were wounded would be very frightened — moaning and groaning and calling out." Sometimes she would hold them and "they'd be hanging on — 'Oh, I don't want to die.' " But they did. A veteran nurse finally saw "so much suffering and so much dying that I was numb. You go to work, you do your job, you do the best you can. Numb doesn't mean you're not compassionate or caring, but you don't have an emotional reaction to anything anymore. I'd seen it all."[44]

A navy corpsman who had spent time in the field with marine units described the horror and the suffering and the trauma: "Nothing before or since has made me question virtually everything I learned in academics and religion" as did his medical duty in Vietnam. Another medic referred to the 28th Evacuation Hospital as "a butcher shop. Dried blood was hardened on everything. On the ground and the wooden boxes. On every litter and every soldier. All over the fronts of our shirts and pants, forearms, necks, and faces."[45]

A conscientious objector agreed to serve, despite his Quaker father's objections, as long as he did not have to carry a weapon. The young soldier knew that if he refused to serve, then some other young man would have to go in his place. He became a combat medic. "For myself I just saw my job as trying to keep these boys alive. That was everything for me. When we made contact, someone was always hit early and it was my job to move. I was life and if I moved we would be OK. Which of course didn't always work and that's the dirty trick and heartbreak of being a medic and what breaks you in the end. You can't win."[46]

Iran Brown, called Ira, was a young black marine from North Carolina. He was on Hill 55 southwest of Da Nang and was out on patrols regularly. On the night of May 29, 1969, they had a major firefight with North Vietnamese regulars. Three marines were killed and Brown was wounded. Twenty-four marines, including Brown, were evacuated that night to various nearby medical facilities. The evacuees included the navy corpsman Michael Kuklenski, who was awarded a Silver Star for his bravery and support for the marines that night. Badly wounded himself, he crawled out to assist the other wounded marines. Kuklenski knew Brown, and in their conversations over the previous days, he'd learned how badly Ira Brown wanted to go home. The night before this firefight, Brown said that he had been wounded three times and normally that would be sufficient to rotate out. But he was still there. He said, "The only way I'm ever going to see my mama again is if I die . . . Doc, the next time I get hit — even if it's a hangnail — I'm

506

just going to die because that's the only way I'm going to get home." He died in the hospital that night. The medical staff there were surprised — they had not identified his wounds as life-threatening.[47]

Emerson Martin, a Navajo from Gallup, New Mexico, died in the same battle in which Brown suffered his fatal wounds. Martin was greatly admired in his unit. When their outpost was attacked by the NVA, he successfully detonated two Claymore mines, inflicting heavy casualties on the enemy. One marine who was there saw that when Martin ran out of ammunition, he had disabled his weapon "and had thrown it so they [the enemy] couldn't use it, and then he took a grenade and put a grenade under it and it blew the bipods off in the front and put shrapnel all through the machine gun." As he moved toward the perimeter, Emerson was seriously wounded by fragments from enemy grenades. When the enemy ran toward his position, he stood up and said, "Fuck Ho Chi Minh" just as they shot and killed him. He was awarded the Silver Star for his actions that night. Native Americans were by one estimate over 2 percent of the men who served in Vietnam — despite being less than 1 percent of the U.S. population. They largely served in combat units, and at least 250 of them died there.[48]

At one of the evacuation hospitals, a nurse

treated a patient whose lower body had been largely blown away but who was surviving through "mast-trousers," a pumping device that continued the blood flow. It was at best a crude temporary expedient. At the hospital they had to deflate the mechanism to check his injuries. He asked the nurse to hold his hand, saying, "I think I'm going to die and I don't want to be alone." She held his hand, crying, and he died within seconds. She had to pry her hand lose because he had held onto her so tightly. She accompanied the body to Graves Registration. "I just couldn't let him go alone."[49]

Monsoon rains frequently flooded the hospitals, bringing rats and snakes in with the water. A nurse said, "We were so pumped up when we went to Vietnam, so patriotic, so full of American idealism." That enthusiasm lasted "about two days . . . Our guys would go in to a hill or a village, get the hell beat out of them, and then we would receive the casualties. The next day they would be pulled out of there. Then they'd go back another week; we'd take more casualties . . . Marines were getting shot, they were getting mutilated, and there was no purpose; there was no rhyme nor reason to it."[50]

A National Guard medic who served at the 27th Surgical Hospital at Chu Lai said sometimes it was so crowded it was "like opening night at Fenway Park." There were "people on stretchers everywhere." And men would be asking, "Am I going to lose my arm? Am I going to lose my leg?" When someone died, he thought, "God, he's got a family. Family is going to be notified by the army." Shortly after he arrived at the hospital, he ran out to help unload a medevac helicopter. The crew there gave him "a steel pot helmet covered with a poncho." As he walked away, the helicopter blades blew the poncho away and inside the helmet he saw only "an ear and a hand and some dog tags. I just grabbed the poncho and got sick to my stomach."[51]

A badly wounded soldier was waiting to be taken to Japan for further treatment. "Finally," he said, "the attendants load me on a large military transport. I lie on the lowest cot, which is attached to a make-shift wall support in the plane. The cots are three tiers high and extend the length of the cargo plan. I look down the aisle of the plane and notice a number of intravenous bottles and tubes attached to each patient. It's overwhelming to see all these wounded men in such a deplorable state."[52]

Memories of the scenes in the hospitals could also be traumatic. A pilot who was hospitalized after being shot down, described the scene: "I saw enough carnage in that hospital to last me fifty lifetimes. It was just horrible. The irony of it — the guitar players missing fingers and guys shot through the spine and flip-flopping them like pancakes every few hours — guys without their legs, football stars. Just horrible." A soldier who had been wounded and was recovering in a hospital, helped to deliver mail to men in the burn unit: "You had to walk by these guys who were literally cooked. I mean cooked. The smell of that and the sight of that and guys screaming because they're being dipped in Betadine Solution or whatever it was — that was horrible. It was probably every bit as bad as anything that I saw when I was actually in the field."[53]

In the thirty days prior to June 8, 1969, about 3.5 percent of those who returned from Vietnam came in aluminum shipping crates. In that period, 1,591 American servicemen and 1 servicewoman died in Vietnam. This understates those who were killed in the theater of operation. In the early morning hours of June 3, during an operation in the South China Sea, the navy destroyer the USS *Frank E. Evans* collided with an Australian Navy aircraft carrier, and the front section of the *Evans* sank within minutes in 1,100 fathoms of water. Seventy-four men were lost. These included three brothers, Gary (age twenty-two), Gregory (twenty-one), and Kelly (nineteen) from Niobrara, Nebraska. The Sage brothers had requested that they serve together.[54]

The 1,592 dead came from all fifty states plus Puerto Rico, Guam, and Washington, DC. In fact, 14 were from Puerto Rico. The most were from California, with 172. New York counted 118, Michigan 94, Texas 86, and Ohio and Pennsylvania had 75 each. The killed in action included 97 eighteen-year-olds, 214 nineteen-year-olds, and 421 twenty-year-olds. One hundred forty-four were over age twenty-five — 83 percent of those killed were baby boomers.[55]

The postwar generation that served in Vietnam in 1969 was basically born in the presidency of Harry Truman (1945–1953). But there were a few casualties who were Eisenhower babies. Dan Bullock was one of these. The youngest serviceman to die in Vietnam, Bullock, a black marine, was fifteen years old when he was killed on June 7, 1969. Born in North Carolina, he was eleven when his mother died, and his father soon remarried and moved to Brooklyn. He did not like the city, and at age fourteen, with an altered birth certificate, Bullock, who was large for his age, joined the marines. He started boot camp at Parris Island in September 1968, and by May 1969 he was in Vietnam. Stationed at An Hoa, on the night of June 6 he was on guard duty on the perimeter. During an NVA attack, Bullock was killed in a firefight. A marine who served with him said, "He did everything we did except he was killed the first time in combat." *Newsweek* magazine, in its profile section, included brief stories on Dan Bullock and Sharon Lane.[56]

Body bags and ponchos covered the dead, rendering them almost anonymous, abstracting them as numbers rather than young men. The mangling nature of lethal ordnance, the missing body parts and faces all amplified the distancing. But it was hard to separate oneself from the cost of it all when bags containing bodies were lined up and stacked up for processing. The industrial scale of "processing" did not negate the individuality of human tragedy. In his powerful novel *The Quiet American,* capturing the war shifting from the French to the Americans in the middle 1950s, Graham Greene described a bombing in a Saigon square that left many dead. His main character, Fowler, was stunned by the attack and looked closely at some of the bodies. He reflected, "Suffering is not increased by numbers; one body can contain all the suffering the world can feel." One naval officer out on the hospital ship *Repose* off of I Corps was overwhelmed by "the body bags lined up on the ship to be sent back to the U.S. with eighteen- and nineteen-year-old kids in them." It was a haunting sight — "the carnage of those young people in this completely surreal environment."[57]

Soldiers regretted that there was no time to memorialize the lost men. And there wasn't, at least not out in the bush. Memorials could come back at base camps later. If it was often impossible to grieve in the field, it was also impossible not to grieve the loss of a friend — or even those who were not close friends but were part of a unit. One chaplain wrote, "Today I conduct the memorial service for K. He hadn't been in the unit long enough to make friends." But they all gathered for K, who had been shot by a sniper while walking across a bamboo bridge.[58]

Sometimes the cruel sequencing of war made grieving difficult. Tom Martin, a young schoolteacher in New Jersey, was drafted and found himself in the assault on Dong Ap Bia. He was wounded by friendly fire on May 11, and a week later he was in Japan recuperating. On that day, a good friend of his, Lenny Hickson, was killed on the hill. A Navajo Indian from Window Rock, Arizona, Hickson with his brother and sister were the first Navajo triplets to survive birth. His niece described him as the "shining star" of the family, "the one the relatives wanted to take care of, very athletic, handsome, charismatic, funny . . . When he signed up, he went to do his part, and although a fear nicked at his spirit, he went. He became one of the best soldiers — ever — according to his army buddies. They said he was young. He was strong.

He was handsome. He was the platoon's combat star, and without knowing it, he trained all his life to go to war. The heartache of his twenty-two years of life is just that — he only got twenty-two years."

His death was devastating to his family and to the people on his reservation. And it was devastating to Tom Martin. He wrote to Lenny Hickson's parents, a letter subsequently published in the *Navajo Times,* about Lenny, "a buddy of mine in Vietnam." He told them how Lenny helped him to "adjust to the world of the jungle," sacrificing his own rest to help Tom. The two of them often did night guard duty together, keeping each other awake when both of them were so tired. Lenny was an M60 machine gunner, requiring him to carry not only the twenty-five-pound gun but also extra rounds of ammunition. While most carried two hundred rounds, and a few could take the extra weight of four hundred rounds, Lenny carried eight hundred rounds. When Tom Martin was wounded, Lenny Hickson ran out of his own cover to help his friend. "What a privilege to have known such a man."[59]

Memorial services were typically held when the units returned to a fire support base or elsewhere in the rear area. They followed a standard protocol: Someone would read the name or names of the men who had been killed, with a rifle stuck in the ground with its bayonet and a pair of boots for each of the dead. Sometimes the CO or another man from the unit offered a few words. A chaplain would make a few comments: "We give him to God and pray for them. We'd pray for their families . . . very brief — always very brief." There was customarily a calling of the roll of the dead. This chaplain said that "the men usually didn't want to talk much about it. They showed great respect and all. But you know, going through their mind — they were thinking, 'I'll probably be the next one.'" And another chaplain underlined why caution was so necessary. Following one of his memorial services, as the company was moving out to the perimeter, one man stepped on a mine and was "blown to bits. One leg is located about fifty yards from the site of explosion. His other leg is never found."[60]

On May 31, the marines from Battalion Landing Team 1/26th had returned to the USS *Iwo Jima* and held a memorial service aboard ship. They had lost 21 marines and 2 navy corpsmen; all but one of the dead had been killed in Operation Pipestone Canyon. The program included a number of readings from the Psalms and from the New Testament. There was the roll call of the dead, a moment of silence, and the playing of "Taps." The service ended with Ecclesiastes: "For everything there is a season . . . a time for war, and a time for peace."[61]

The chaplains who served in Vietnam — sometimes called sky pilots — found themselves often presiding over these memorial services. One estimate is that in the spring of 1969, there were 476 military ministers serving. In the second quarter of that year, they held 37,612 religious services for 907,122 attendees. Chaplains were attached to specific units, but they also moved around the country to minister to units wherever they were stationed. They were disproportionately men from more conservative Protestant denominations, and there were shortages of Catholic chaplains and particularly of Jewish chaplains, as well as representatives of black Protestant churches. So the chaplains were fully ecumenical, serving men of whatever faith. Sixteen chaplains died in Vietnam. Three received the Medal of Honor, two of them posthumously, for their work assisting wounded men on the battlefield.[62]

The chaplains often found themselves in or near firefights. One said that the men in battle stayed away from him because they insisted he brought in more enemy fire — they called him "the right reverend magnet-ass." Yet another chaplain was popular in the field. He joked that he never worried about getting hurt "because there were too many guys lying on top of me or near me." They assumed that they would be safe next to the chaplain![63]

Sometimes chaplains had to preside over

services for one of their own. One chaplain, army lieutenant colonel Don Bartley, died instantly along with 5 other men when the vehicle in which they were riding struck a mine southwest of Da Nang. By all accounts he was a remarkable man. He had helped to oversee the building of four chapels on some desolate bases in South Vietnam. The most prominent of these was his home base on Landing Zone Baldy. When he was killed, just three weeks before he was to return home, he was on an assignment to help a crew film a series on the service of chaplains in Vietnam. He wanted to include the navy chaplains who were serving marines. Three sailors and 2 marines died with him that day.

Bartley's death was a shock to those who knew him. Chaplain Bartley's aide said, "Oh, for a long time I thought he was the only chaplain ever to be killed. Of course, I know a whole lot different. But he was the best chaplain that was ever killed. Yes, I figured if anybody was safe, it was him . . . it just seemed as though he was magic. He was going to be spared. The morning he left, I just had a feeling that that was all going to change. Then when I heard the news — yeah. Then I questioned everything. I really hadn't questioned all of the other guys I had seen die. But then I questioned everything when I knew that he was gone."[64]

The rifle with fixed bayonet, the helmet,

and the boots — the traditional markers of field memorials — were poignant symbols and reminders. But there were no bodies or graves to provide personal focus for the services held in Vietnam. That war broke with the historic process followed in all previous American wars of burying the war dead in temporary cemeteries near the field where they fell, and then subsequently moving them to a permanent cemetery — either in their hometowns, in a national cemetery, or, in the cases of World Wars I and II, in American military cemeteries overseas. The ground in Vietnam was never truly secure enough, except on the major bases, to provide a protected place for a temporary cemetery. And in any event, the efficient and massive air transport system allowed the dead to be shipped home for burial.

When the ground war ratcheted up in 1965, MACV established a Graves Registration program and a system of collection points. By 1966, command of this operation was shifted from the air force to the army. Tan Son Nhut Air Base was the site for the mortuary used for embalming remains for shipment home. By 1967, it was clear that the Tan Son Nhut mortuary needed to be expanded, and that same year another mortuary was established at Da Nang to handle the dead from the I Corps region. The collection points expanded as the war casualties increased. At their peak, there were 22 body collection points with the capacity to store 750 refrigerated remains. The system required all remains to be at the mortuaries within two days of recovery. The army staffed and controlled Graves Registration activities for all of the services, while the embalming responsibilities of the Mortuary Services division were handled by civilians under contract with the Department of Defense.[65]

The most important challenge facing the Graves Registration/ Mortuary Services command was identification of the remains. Early in the war, identification was considered to be validated when two men who served in the unit of the deceased, along with the dog tags when available, provided positive identifications. An embarrassing error demonstrated the fallacy of this system. In November 1967, Quinn Tichenor of Louisville, Kentucky, was killed near Que Son when his unit engaged the enemy and lost 12 men. Two men from his unit told Graves Registration, "That's Quinn." Unfortunately there was a John Quinn in the unit and he was the one listed as KIA and his family in Texas was notified. Except John Quinn was alive and still with the unit — so the Quinn family had the good news of learning this, but only after undergoing several traumatic days of believing that John was dead. The Tichenor family of Louisville was then notified of Quinn

Tichenor's death.[66]

Following the Quinn/Tichenor confusion, the command moved to a system that required the use of fingerprints and dental records. Identification by members of the deceased's unit were still critical, but they were no longer sufficient. For example, when Phillip Burfoot was killed on June 7, 1969, near Dak To, in the incident that Larry Burrows described where the ARVN soldiers did not assist in repulsing the ambush, the men serving with Burfoot in the 299th Engineering Battalion identified him by the leather medicine bag this Native American soldier always wore around his neck. But this was not considered sufficient for full identification.[67]

The celebrated dog tags were not sufficient either, largely because less than 50 percent of the remains still had these identifications when they were recovered. The Graves Registration and Mortuary Affairs operations also matched remains with "recorded characteristics of race, height, hair color, tattoos, scars, healed fractures, injuries, cause of death, markings on clothing and jewelry."[68]

Working in Graves Registration was emotionally difficult, but everyone who was there volunteered to serve. Often shunned by other soldiers, they were committed to identifying bodies, handling them with respect and dignity, and returning them to their loved ones. It was a cruel task, sorting body parts, confronting the charred remains of young men, handling bloated bodies that had been in the water, and enduring the stench and the blood and brains and body fluids draining all over them. No matter how often they showered and cleaned, the men in the chow halls would move away if they sat near them — the stench of death never seemed to go away.[69]

The first task of the Graves Registration staff was to check the bodies carefully for any unexploded ordnance still in a body cavity. Or for bodies that had been in the field for a time, it was not uncommon to find that the enemy had placed a booby trap inside the remains, to be detonated by an unsuspecting person in the body removal process.

Graves Registration personnel sorted through any personal effects that were on the body, looking for identification materials. And they sent to the armory any weapons or ammunition. They, and sometimes others who went through the deceased's possessions from the base camps, disposed of anything that could be embarrassing — pornography, drugs, etc. — before these items were sent back to the family. There would be a full inventory of all possessions — excepting those things discreetly removed. But this process of inventory also added a very personal dimension, a very human story, to the often unrecognizable remains: pictures of parents, of young women, girlfriends or sisters or maybe spouses, and sometimes of babies "that the deceased would never meet."[70]

Some bodies had few marks on them — a piece of shrapnel cutting through an artery caused a quick death. Clifford Taira, from Honolulu, was born on the 4th of July, 1948, and was described as a handsome, muscular young man. He told a friend while they were on Ala Moana Beach before they left for Vietnam that he might not return. He was killed in his first action, and it was hard for anyone to identify the wound that caused his death.[71]

Other bodies were mangled and commingled parts — like a bowling ball, as one described a compressed mass of humans. One told of 4 men killed by a powerful booby trap. There were only thirty to forty pounds of recovered body parts. Death by burns was terrible — and everyone said the worst were the helicopter crews. The intense heat of burning fuel and the magnesium in their helmets melted plastics onto their bodies. The bodies would be shrunken, "like little tiny midgets." Sometimes in the gallows humor that was a necessary part of coping with this gruesome assignment, the burn victims were described as "crispy critters." The bodies that had been in the water for an extended period, called "floaters," were filled with water and gases, just "oozing" fluids. Those and bodies that had been in the jungle were often crawling with maggots.

The Graves Registration staff tried to clean up all the bodies and worked to establish a preliminary identification through material in wallets, dog tags, input from men in the unit of the deceased, and fingerprints. The head of the collection point at Quang Tri estimated that his unit identified "at least 95 percent" of the bodies they processed. The Graves Registration crews placed the remains in body bags and tried to get them quickly to Da Nang or Tan Son Nhut mortuaries for body preparation and further forensic tests for identification. In some of the field collection points, there was inadequate water to take daily showers, so the smell of death was pervasive. It was hard to clean out the facilities — if they were not able to hose them down, they covered them with chemicals to kill the bacteria and the smell.

The morticians were thorough, very proud of what they were able to do. The embalmed bodies were placed in aluminum transport cases, which were stacked on pallets for shipment to the United States. Once in the States, at either of the two mortuary centers in Oakland, California, or Dover, Delaware, the bodies were further prepared, including putting a uniform on them if there were enough remains to cover. The bodies were placed in new caskets. These enclosed a metal sealer that had glass on the top half. If the remains were not suitable for viewing, the glass was sprayed with gray paint. The caskets were ready to be transported to the next of kin. Then the aluminum shipping containers were cleaned out, sanitized, and returned to Vietnam for the next set of remains.

While the bodies of the war dead were being identified and prepared in Vietnam, the process of notifying families was under way back in the States. It was a methodical process that was marked by caution — no one wanted a repeat of the Quinn/Tichenor incident. And no one wanted to return to the impersonal and clumsy procedures that had been used in the early years of the war. These involved a telegraph message beginning with the cold news that the "Secretary regrets to inform you . . ." This was the World War II and Korean War method of notifying next of kin. Following the battle in the Ia Drang Valley in the fall of 1965, most of the dead were with the 1st Cavalry Division, based out of Fort Benning, Georgia. Many spouses and families lived nearby in Columbus. There, on November 18, 1965, Yellow Cab drivers drove around delivering telegrams. There were stories of drunken taxi drivers, of telegrams improperly delivered, and in all instances the absence of any warmth or ability to explain or comfort.[72]

In 1966, the Department of Defense insti-
tuted a new procedure — families would be
personally notified by a visit from military officials. This was a marked improvement, if
there can be such a thing under these circumstances. Those military officials had a very
troubling duty. They typically were stationed
at nearby bases, recruiting stations, or perhaps serving on a nearby ROTC faculty. Usually they were themselves Vietnam veterans.
Harry Spiller, a marine combat veteran who
then assumed notification duty as part of his
recruiting station assignment in Missouri,
told a new man in his office about these calls
on next of kin that you "never get used to it.
The more you make, the worse they get."

Spiller was a marine still in his teens when
he had gone ashore with some of the first
ground troops in April 1965. He had numerous combat encounters, and when he returned to the States, he was assigned to
recruiting duty in Cape Girardeau, Missouri,
in 1967. He juggled the tasks of encouraging
high school boys to consider enlisting following their graduation — and telling families
that their son or husband or brother was dead
or wounded. By the time he left the post, he'd
notified the parents of three young men he
had recruited, that their sons were dead. And
he informed the parents of another of his
recruits that their son was wounded. His
black humor line was, "You enlist one and

you plant one." But he did not find it a humorous task. The obligation included accompanying the returned body and helping with the funeral arrangements. By the time he left the post, he was drinking and having great difficulty with the assignment.[73]

Spiller dealt with tears and trauma, with hurt and anger. Most people realized what was happening as soon as he drove up to their house and got out of the car, always accompanied by another marine and sometimes with a local priest or minister. His message was, "As a Representative of the President of the United States and the Commandant of the Marine Corps, it is my duty to inform" the parents or spouse that their marine "had been killed in action in the Republic of South Vietnam in the defense of the United States of America."

Few were able to hear the entire message. One mother of a young marine kept crying, "Not my baby." She fainted at the funeral, and at the cemetery when they fired the traditional graveside rifle salute, two other women fainted. Another mother fell to the floor in a faint when she was notified. The marines revived her and carried her to a couch and put a cold washcloth on her forehead. When she revived, she cried, "Bring him back! Please Jesus, bring him back." The marines stayed with her for three hours. Spiller found the parents of one marine working at the local glove factory. When he told them that their son had been killed, they sat and cried, and then after a bit the father asked him about the return of the body. Spiller said that their son had been hit directly by a rocket. "Sir, there are no remains." The parents then cried "uncontrollably" and each of them collapsed to the floor. A mother in Kennett, Missouri, answered the door and was stunned to see the marines there. She stood inside the glass storm door with her hands over her mouth, crying. They opened the door, and she grabbed one by the arm and started screaming. At the funeral of her only son two weeks later, she "had to be pulled off the casket. It took three people to subdue her."[74]

On one occasion when Spiller came to tell a family their son had been killed by a booby trap, the father opened the door and innocently, pleasantly asked, "May I help you, Sergeant?" When the marine informed him that his son was dead, the father screamed and ran into the house and came back with a gun. He shouted, "You son-of-a-bitch! I'll get you for this." His wife persuaded him to give her the gun and the marines unloaded it. The father continued, "Fucking senseless war! Senseless shit! And look at our pretty, little sergeant all dressed up in his uniform. Why the fuck don't they send you over there?" Another father, a Missouri farmer, when told that his son had died from friendly fire, angrily challenged Spiller as his wife sobbed beside him: "I thought the Marines were good fighters. Supposed to know what's going on. Killed by his own goddamned men." The mother tried to comfort her husband as she cried, "Honey, don't get mad at them. They're only doing their job."[75]

One afternoon Spiller was talking to two high school students about joining the marines. He had just come from the funeral home, where he had accompanied the remains of a marine and tried to console the parents. He asked the two boys if they knew the dead marine. They said they did, so he encouraged them to visit the funeral home and look at the casket, and then to come back if they still wanted to join. They did as he suggested and returned and said they still wanted to enlist. When he asked them why, they said that the marine had "died for his country. We want to fight for our country, too. Die for it if necessary." They admitted that their parents were not too "thrilled about it" but wouldn't stop them.[76]

One senior army enlisted man who had this duty, described telling a nineteen-year-old woman that she was a widow. These occasions were often met by silence, "the deadening part, when you can't say anything more and you can't walk away, so you just stand there and wait for the tears to come." By the time the notification team knocked on the door, it often wasn't necessary to tell the next of kin anything: "When they see the staff car pull up with two uniformed men, they know." An army officer working out of Fort Benning on this duty said, "You feel like hell when you go out and you feel like hell when you come back." A navy chaplain at Marine Corps Recruit Depot San Diego said that "some get hysterical, some are calm, some are bitter and blame you or the Marine Corps and some take it as the will of God." At many posts men on this duty were rotated off after a week. "A week of that is about all the human heart can endure."[77]

One veteran of the Battle at Khe Sanh had this duty after he returned to the navy base in Rhode Island. He dealt mainly with parents, since most of the marines were young and unmarried. Whenever he went out on a notification assignment, he tried to get a clergyman to join him. But the official car was always a giveaway. When they came into a town in their government sedan, people followed them. One time they found a grandmother, the only remaining relative, when she was walking home from work. They got her in the car and told her there. Out on Cape Cod they went to notify a family of the death of their son, and a group followed them to the parents' house. When they were inside with the family, the angry crowd tried to tip over the sedan. At the subsequent funeral, so many people tried to touch the casket at the cemetery that the straps broke and the casket and several bystanders fell into the grave site.

At one house, when the officers, accompanied by the local parish priest, knocked on the door, the man who opened it, "a big guy," didn't say anything but "grabbed me by the shirt and basically tried to beat the shit out of me." He had the officer "pinned under the piano in the living room." The priest helped get them settled down. But then the dead marine's mother came home from work, and when she saw the official car, she "literally lost it and crashed into the sedan." The parents later asked when the body would be returned, and the officers told her it would be in a week or ten days. This was in early December, and the priest unthinkingly said that it would be just in time for Christmas. The father once more erupted in anger and physically attacked the marine officer a second time.[78]

Of course there was no way for any family truly to be prepared for the abrupt visit of men in military uniform. One pregnant spouse of a soldier was living with her parents when she saw the car drive in and shortly heard the knock on the door. She opened it praying that her husband had been wounded rather than killed. When she asked the soldiers, "How bad is it?" they read to her the note that began, "We regret to inform you . . ." Her parents became "hysterical" and she just began shaking. She ran to her room and threw herself on the bed sobbing and "gasping for air."[79]

When army chaplain Don Bartley was killed, his family was living in Virginia. His fifteen-year-old son was out fishing, and when he returned home he saw a number of cars. The minister came out to meet him and told him that his father had been "hurt." He went into the house and saw his mother and others crying. They told him his dad was dead. He ran out and climbed up a nearby cliff where he just sat and looked over the land. He used to enjoy sharing this view with his father. Allen Collins was fourteen when the car pulled up to his house in Alabama and two soldiers asked him where his parents were. When they came home, they learned of his brother Jerome's death and just sat and cried. His mother said, "It's the will of God." Allen left the house and walked down the path to a dock on the river, where he sat and cried.[80]

Thomas Crawford was nine years old when he saw his mother get out of a car with a marine. He thought it was his father, a gunnery sergeant, back from Vietnam. He went running to the car screaming, "Hey, Dad!" Then he saw that the marine was not his father. He went into the house with his mother and two marines. One of them took him in the next room and said, "Your father was killed, you're the man of the house now. You got fifteen minutes to cry; you have things you have to be responsible for, you have to take care of your mom and brothers." His father, a highly respected marine, had been killed in Operation Meade River.[81]

Harry Breski was thirteen, and on the last day of school he stopped by a friend's house. They had just finished eighth grade and were playing music. He heard a tune about a lost brother and he ran home. His parents were out on an errand and he was sitting on the porch when the car pulled up. The two soldiers came to the porch but didn't want to talk and said they would wait to see his parents. Harry wanted to talk to them, however, and he told them all about his brother, an army helicopter pilot. He showed them his brother Joe's picture and asked if they knew him. He was so proud of his brother. After fifteen minutes or so, his mother arrived home, and the soldiers told her that her son had been shot down in Vietnam and was missing. Harry Breski ran to a corner of the room and cried.

The next day when he returned to the house, he heard his mom and dad crying. They had just learned that the army had found and identified Joe Breski's body. He was killed on June 6, 1969. By all accounts an exceptional pilot, Breski had flown his helicopter out of the base area at Quon Loi in the Delta. The command said an attack was imminent, and they wanted to get the craft off the ground and out of there. It was monsoonlike weather, and Breski had to circle back toward the base, at which time the North Vietnamese shot him down. His dad said he would never forget that date because exactly twenty-five years earlier he had gone ashore at Normandy.[82]

Doug Sommer had been shot and killed while crossing a field on the mop-up operation following the battle of Hamburger Hill. The men with him identified him, and there was no doubt that he died of a gunshot wound to the head. One of those men is still haunted by Sommer's death. There was no vegetation left in the field except for one stump. "Myself, I had this strange feeling come over me that death was in the air. Something was going to happen. And I just felt this could be the end of it." Doug's family lived in Kearns, Utah. A Mormon, Doug had dropped out of high school and joined the army because he was upset that some of the other Mormon kids were going on missionary work and not going to Vietnam. He thought everyone had a duty to go. He and his sixteen-year-old brother Brad were the youngest of seven children. Brad was home when the army representatives came to say that Doug was "missing." A few days later the car returned, and when the two soldiers came to the door, his mother grabbed Brad and started crying before they had even opened the door. She cried, "You're not going to get another one. You're not going to get anybody else!"[83]

Terry Dean Miller, a soldier in the 506th Infantry of the 101st Airborne Division, was an Illinois farm boy. His brother Daryl was eighteen and was ready to go out in the field and continue the cultivation for planting. His parents were in town running errands. A car came, and two soldiers were there with his dad's cousin. They had stopped at his farm first. They asked for his parents and would tell Daryl nothing. He kept asking, "It's Terry, isn't it? Something's happened to Terry." They told him they could not say anything until they met his parents. He went to the field because his dad wanted to get the cultivating done but found this waiting too tense, and he came back when he saw that his parents had returned. His mother was sitting there saying that everyone thinks this won't happen to them. "It happens to other people, but then when it hits home, then you just don't know. God's got a plan for everybody, I guess." Daryl went to get his sister Brenda at church, where she was helping in a vacation Bible school. He told her, "You have to come with me right now" but said nothing on the way home. Their dad told her about her brother and she just sat and hugged her parents.[84]

Richard Cyran was a twenty-one-year-old soldier who was killed along with 7 other men by a rocket attack near Tay Ninh on June 6. He was from Clifton, New Jersey, and his family was notified of his death on June 12. His mother had recently undergone a double mastectomy and returned from the hospital at around 11:00 that morning. The army representatives arrived at noon. They had earlier gone to the home of the parish priest to ask him to join them in the call. Coincidentally, Richard's sister Josephine was working there in a hot lunch program at the parochial school. The priest suggested she go home. She arrived home to find her recuperating mother in bed weeping. Her father tried to deal with things but fainted several times. Ricky Cyran was buried at St. Michael's cemetery on June 21. Josephine was six months pregnant at the time. Her son was born prematurely the next month and died three days later. In August, her mother died.[85]

Gladys Grubb was the twenty-year-old wife of Steve Grubb. When he died, the army went to her listed address, at her mother's house in Faber, Virginia. They learned that Gladys was working in Richmond and, telling her mother nothing, they went to Richmond and informed Gladys that her husband was missing. A week later they returned to tell her Steve was dead. She never understood the two stages in the notification. It was common because sometimes the army knew someone was no longer with his unit but they did not yet have a positive identification of the remains. Steve had apparently died of a heart attack in the 67th Evacuation Hospital where he had been taken with injuries suffered from the detonation of a Claymore mine. Two other soldiers died on the same day as a result of the explosion. Gladys Grubb was the youngest of thirteen children, and her sister did not leave her alone for the week between these two official visits.[86]

In all of these cases, the families were notified when the remains of their loved one would be returned. The families could meet the airplane flying their sons or husbands to a nearby major airport. In many small towns, the funerals for these dead servicemen were major events. Terry Miller's family went to St. Louis but had to deal with a twelve-hour delay in the delivery of the body. Sandy Boyer went to Cleveland with her parents to receive Larry's body. It came in the cargo hold of a United Airlines plane and they were able to go to the tarmac to pick up the body. When Sandy saw the United plane, she said to her parents, "We are united."[87]

Tommy Blevins was a young Middletown, New Jersey, star athlete who joined the

536

marines knowing he would go to Vietnam. He was ready but had said that he did not want to die there. Before he went out on an operation on May 31, 1969, he told a friend that he was not going to survive this one. His friend asked the platoon leader to leave him behind, but there were not enough marines to fill in. So Tommy went out and was killed — trying to save some of his own men. In Middletown, a large convoy of automobiles accompanied the hearse in his funeral procession.[88]

Military escorts always accompanied the bodies. In Oakland, California, the unit that provided this coverage for many of the western states had at its peak about 55 men, and they might accompany several hundred bodies a month. In some small towns, the streets would be lined with flags and local veterans, and fraternal groups would help organize a funeral. One town in California had lost 17 men in Vietnam, and a local restaurant refused service to the escort. In some larger cities, such as San Jose and Santa Barbara, some called out to the escorts that they were "killers."[89]

Generally, the military discouraged families from viewing the remains, but the option was theirs. Joe Breski's dad wanted to see his son's body. This veteran of Normandy and the Battle of the Bulge insisted he could do it. The funeral director asked Mr. Breski if his son had any body scars. The grieving father said no, then asked why he asked this question. The funeral director said that a body scar would be the only way he could recognize this young soldier killed in a helicopter crash. The father agreed not to view the body. Doug Sommer's family was also advised not to look at the body. The funeral director said "he was in the jungle for a little while," but he did confirm a scar on the back of the remains. The Boyers did not look at Larry's body because he had been shot in the head. When Terry Dean Miller's dad said he wanted to see his son's body, the funeral director relented but strongly suggested that he not bring Mrs. Miller. The experience was "very hard" on Mr. Miller. Allen Collins looked in the open casket with the body covered with a clear glass, and said Jerome looked "just like him when he left." Gladys Grubb did view and touch her husband's body. "To this day I thank God that I was able to realize it was him, because until I actually saw the body, I held out hope."[90]

In January 1968, just before the Tet Offensive and the heavy losses that came with that series of battles, the Department of Defense increased the allowance provided to families to cover the burial of the dead servicemen. On February 1, this payment increased from $200 to $500 when the family buried the remains in a private cemetery.

The military provided mortuary services. They did not increase the existing $75 allowance for families that chose to have the remains buried in a national cemetery.[91] The military escort, men stationed locally, also provided the traditional military funeral rituals at graveside: the playing of "Taps," the folding and presentation to a next of kin of the flag covering the coffin, and the rifle salute.

Lenny Hickson had a Catholic funeral at Window Rock on the Navajo reservation. His parents then asked a traditional medicine man to do a blessing of Lenny. One of Lenny's triplet sisters threw herself on the coffin, begging them to bury her with her brother.[92]

Not everyone was able to hold a funeral. As of March 2016, there were still 1,590 American military personnel listed as missing and unaccounted for in Southeast Asia. In addition, there were 31 civilians. Fifteen men were listed as missing in the thirty days from May 10 to June 8, 1969. Not surprisingly, most of those still classified as missing were on aircraft that were shot down or crashed and the presumed remains were not found. Some were on missions in Laos and Cambodia. And of course there were those who could not be identified following an explosion. For example, on May 25, a North Vietnamese shell hit an ammo pit filled with mortar rounds at a marine base west of Con Thien. Fifteen marines died in the explosions, and 2 men known to be there, Monek Weitz and Leroy Williams, were never found and there were no identifiable remains. They were finally declared dead, remains not recovered.[93]

More complicated perhaps were the missing who were not clearly part of an aircraft crash or the victims of an explosion. Nineteen-year-old Gregory Benton had been in Vietnam for about ten weeks with the 1st Battalion, 9th Marines. They were engaged in Operation Apache Snow above the Da Krong River along the Laotian border. On May 23, during a fight with North Vietnamese soldiers, 2 marines were killed — they died instantly. Benton was with them when they were killed, as well as a fourth marine, who was wounded. The men in the unit saw that Benton was "notably disturbed" and needed to lean against a tree to stand upright. When a helicopter came to remove the bodies, Benton was observed near the landing zone. No one ever saw him again. The marines searched for him until dark and were unable to find any sign of him or any of his gear. They initiated a search of all of the sick bays and hospitals in the area as well as the hospital ships USS *Sanctuary* and *Repose.* An investigation determined that he "was physically and/or mentally ill" after seeing his friends die and he had "wandered out into the brush." Follow-up searches then and subsequently in 1993, including areas in Laos, did not locate him. In 1978, the Department of Defense officially designated Benton as killed in action. This was part of a decision made that year to declare all of the men missing in action as presumed dead in order to provide death payments to families and to try to bring some small measure of closure to these situations.[94]

Charles Dale and David Demmon were in an OV-1C Mohawk turboprop armed observation plane that went down somewhere over the U Minh Forest in June 1965. This was a forbidding area, home of National Liberation Front units, that was often called the "forest of darkness." Their remains were never located, and in 1978 they were declared dead. The families held memorial services, but Dale's mother would write several years later, "You can't kill your own son in your mind. I can never stop thinking, 'My God, if he's alive, what must he be going through?' " She thought it would be easier to accept her son's death if his remains had been found and returned.[95]

One additional group was the prisoners of war. These were largely in North Vietnam and were primarily pilots and crew of aircraft. There were 771 Americans captured and imprisoned during the war — and of these,

113 died in captivity and 658 were released to U.S. control — including 591 who were part of the major repatriation negotiated in Paris and who were freed in Operation Homecoming in March 1973. During the spring of 1969, a dramatic escape was engineered at the Cu Loc prison near Hanoi, called the "Zoo" by the prisoners there. Despite misgivings by many prisoners fearing the retribution that might follow, on the night of May 10, two air force prisoners, Ed Atterberry and John Dramesi, climbed over a wall as part of a well-planned escape, but then had to move through the Vietnamese countryside. The men were captured the next morning and were tortured. Dramesi survived and was released in 1973. Atterberry died on May 18 — the North Vietnamese said he died of pneumonia and a "virus." Other prisoners said the torture was so severe they could hear it blocks away. All of the prisoners at the complex were punished, and some who were considered accomplices also were tortured. No one tried to escape again.[96]

Between May 10 and June 8, there were 5 Americans taken prisoner — all of them in South Vietnam. Juan Jacquez, Lenard Daugherty, and Thomas Horio were captured at a listening post near Pleiku. After spending time at a place called Camp 101 in Cambodia, in the fall of 1969 they were marched up the Ho Chi Minh Trail and arrived at a North

Vietnamese prison in April 1970. One American, and perhaps more, died on this months-long trek. Horio, Jacquez, and Daugherty were released in March 1973. Jessie Harris was with the 501st Infantry and was captured on June 8; after 135 days in captivity, he was released in October 1969 as part of a calculated NLF prisoner release program.

Larry Aiken, a black soldier, was a twenty-year-old draftee who lived with his mother in Jamaica, Queens. On May 13, 1969, he was captured by an NLF group and taken prisoner during a battle at Nui Yon Hill. He was held at a local complex near Tam Ky and was spotted there by a Vietnamese civilian, who alerted Americans. On July 10, the United States initiated a raid to free him, but in the skirmish, the Vietnamese captors clubbed him in the head with a rifle butt. Unconscious, he was rushed to an American hospital at Chu Lai, where he died on July 25 without regaining consciousness.[97]

In July 1969, the first troops returned home as part of the drawdown marking Vietnamization. Unlike the individual returns, this involved a unit returning as a group. There was a parade in Seattle marking the return of the 3rd Battalion of the 60th Infantry Division to Fort Lewis. They were welcomed home "by bands, beauty queens, flowery oratory, and some tears." Children of base personnel were there with WELCOME HOME signs. There were protesters as well. A band played "When Johnny Comes Marching Home." And a woman "circled around the troops showing a picture of her son and asking if they knew him." She told them he had written on July 14, 1968, sending the picture and writing on the back that he would be home soon. He was killed the next day.[98] She hoped to learn from them more about her son, Robert Hickox. None of the men she approached knew him.

There was a sense by the summer of 1969 that the war was changing if not ending. With the drawdown and the drawing back begun, the accounting for the war and the assessment of results had commenced in earnest. When President Nixon made a surprise visit to Vietnam in July, he said at Di An, "I think history will record that this may have been one of America's finest hours, because we took a difficult task and succeeded." Most critics were dismissive of the Churchillian description of the American hour. And "success" was elusive and still to be determined. It was clear that the goal was shifting. Max Frankel, a reporter for *The New York Times*, filed a report from Saigon pointing out that this presidential visit had none of the "come home with that coonskin on the wall" language of LBJ in 1966. One of the president's aides told him that "in a normal war the military factors are always dominant, but this is not a normal war."[99]

The men in the field certainly didn't need to be told that. Among the files of official photographs of President Nixon's visit is a picture of him standing on the hood of a jeep, wearing a suit and white shirt and tie, and reaching up to shake the hands of a soldier who is leaning over from an armored personnel carrier to greet the commander in chief. Spray-painted on the side of the military vehicle, just next to the hands locked in a handshake, were the words MAGICAL MYS-TERY TOUR.[100]

8

DUCK AND COVER

On May 4, 1972, President Nixon's national security adviser, Henry Kissinger, wrote to the U.S. ambassador to South Vietnam, Ellsworth Bunker. He expressed the White House's frustration with General Creighton Abrams and the Military Assistance Command, Vietnam. Kissinger asserted, "It must be clear to him that we are playing the most complex game with the Soviets involving matters which extend far beyond the battle in Vietnam as crucial as it is." Kissinger's reprimand was in response to General Abrams's request to divert some bombing raids to South Vietnam when the president had ordered a heavier campaign against the north.[1]

As they always had been, the combat operations in South Vietnam were only parts of a global strategic contest. With the critical exception of fewer American casualties, the last years of the American War in Vietnam were not unlike the first years: broad political calculations that used military force as one of several tools rather than as a primary implement and an American civilian leadership that was not locked in on a singular, measurable military strategy but instead was engaged in a process of improvisation while juggling the pressures of domestic politics and working the various postures and expectations of global politics. And this evolving drama continued to take place in a context in which the Vietnamese casualties, South and North, mounted and the Vietnamese interests became less determinative.

In the spring of 1972, the Nixon administration was engaged in delicate negotiations with the Soviet Union, which had followed a historic presidential trip to China. The White House had nearly completed the drawdown of American troops in Vietnam and was working to conclude a treaty with the North Vietnamese. The Hanoi government was not willing to make any concessions, and in fact had that spring initiated a major multifront offensive in South Vietnam, called by Americans the Easter Offensive, commencing just before Easter weekend. These were all complicated moving parts, and the White House looked at them in the context of President Nixon's reelection campaign. The new American bombing campaign, called Linebacker, was aimed at the North and sought unambiguously to signal Hanoi not to challenge the Nixon administration, while also assuring the South Vietnamese government and military officials that they could count on the United States.

The ground war in Vietnam that spring had an intensity that matched that of Tet. But this bloody campaign had seldom seemed less relevant to the strategic planning in Washington. It was the South Vietnamese military defending against these assaults on the ground. Americans were involved primarily as advisers. Beginning on March 30, 1972, North Vietnamese divisions swept across the Demilitarized Zone and attacked ARVN forces there, finally taking Quang Tri. They also attacked in the Central Highlands and moved toward the city of Kontum. The battle for Kontum was particularly lengthy and costly. It was a critical garrison that was key to controlling central Vietnam. On May 7, the North Vietnamese intensified their assault on the outpost at Polei Kleng to mark the date of the 1954 victory at Dien Bien Phu. The South Vietnamese defenders and their families finally had to withdraw two days later. One account said that they were attacked in crossing the Dak Polo River and the water there was "running red with blood." A few days later, an American adviser at Kontum said, "We were being attacked from three directions and needed immediate help." Within a few weeks, Lieutenant Colonel Tom

McKenna would describe what he and the few Americans at the post then thought was a last stand: "We would have to fend for ourselves. We would come out shooting, but this gunfight would probably end like the climax of *Butch Cassidy and the Sundance Kid.*" *Stars and Stripes* reported in mid-May that "everything above the South Vietnamese capital seemed fraught with desperation and crisis."[2]

Additional North Vietnamese troops came in from Cambodia to Binh Long Province and sought to capture An Loc, about sixty-five miles north of Saigon. This was the largest offensive operation since the Korean War, "stunning in its scope and ferocity." The South Vietnamese government, MACV, and the officials in Washington recognized it was a major challenge. Each saw it in a different way, however, and responded differently, as Henry Kissinger's complaint to Ambassador Bunker emphasized.[3]

On April 7, Frank Brochetti was serving as a radiotelephone operator at the 3rd Regional Assistance Command site at Nui Ba Den, Black Virgin Mountain. The twenty-year-old had dropped out of college and, facing a high draft lottery number, enlisted in the army. He was part of the last group of Americans serving in Vietnam — and was now confronting the Easter Offensive. The North Vietnamese regulars had pushed out of Cambodia and were heading toward Tay Ninh and An Loc — and potentially Saigon. Brochetti wrote to his girlfriend back home in Pennsylvania, "Things are really getting bad over here." The North Vietnamese had large units and heavy ordnance and "the South Vietnamese have proved they are not capable of holding their own." He knew that with an election coming up, "Nixon can't afford . . . to send troops back in," so they were on their own. Brochetti was getting "a little jumpy." He wished that he could be back on a Florida spring break with his girlfriend, lying on the beach with her, but "somebody has to be here playing army." Just a week earlier he had assured his brother that he doubted that the enemy forces would "make it up our way."

Yet they did. Four years earlier, there had been an attack on the outpost, and 24 Americans died in what some called a massacre. On April 8, 1972, enemy forces again assaulted the radio relay post on top of the mountain. They brought rockets, RPGs, and small-arms fire, followed by sappers through the wire. Frank grabbed his weapon and rushed out to engage the attackers. An army Cobra helicopter pilot providing some fire support said as they approached the mountain in the predawn dark that "the top of the mountain was burning like a huge beacon in the night." Even after Brochetti was seriously wounded by a grenade, he continued to fight until he, along with another soldier, was killed by heavy enemy fire. Army captain Johnnie Ray, from Port Arthur, Texas, was wounded by a grenade in the assault and captured by the North Vietnamese. He joined 6 other Americans imprisoned near Snuol, Cambodia, and finally was repatriated in 1973.

Frank Brochetti's parents received a posthumous Silver Star in July 1972, recognizing the bravery of their son on that mountain as the war was ending. In the letter he wrote to his girlfriend, Patti, the day before he died, Frank attached a poem, "I shall pass this way but once." He included the line, "Remember me, is all I ask."[4]

It was the accounts of these embattled forces — and the consequences for South Vietnamese politics — that resulted in General Abrams's delayed implementation of the presidential order to send more bombers to the North. His MACV leadership was concerned about enemy successes in An Loc, Hué, and Kontum. South Vietnam president Nguyen Van Thieu had urged MACV to give "top priority" to support the defense of these positions. The White House had little choice but to defer the expanded bombing campaign in North Vietnam, but not without reminding the military command in Saigon that the actual "battle" in Vietnam, "as crucial as it is," was but a piece in this wider geopolitical drama, this "most complex game."[5]

So the war that began as a chess piece on a global board would, not surprisingly, end as one. To understand how inconsequential ground combat action in Vietnam had become in this strategic contest, it is critical to understand the calculations and the moves of the Nixon-Kissinger team.

When the American War in Vietnam was over finally, the cold war seemed less threatening. The debate continues whether the major U.S. military effort in Southeast Asia contributed to this progress, but whatever the case, it involved substantial costs incurred by a generation in America and to several generations in Vietnam. And the costs linger.

In May 1972, 137 Americans died in Vietnam, 22 of them in the first six days of that month, as the White House and MACV were exchanging notes. The South Vietnam part of the "game" was not over. But it had changed: It was now an air war. Eleven of the dead in those first days of May were in the air force, and 3 were navy or marine aviators. Five of the 8 soldiers were killed in a helicopter that was struck by a rocket. Of the remaining 3, one was killed by "accidental self destruction" due to a detonated explosive, one died in a hospital due to illness, and the third was killed by enemy fire when he was moving to a night defensive position. There were no combat fatalities as a result of American-initiated ground actions.

President Nixon's "plan" for ending the war turned out to be a set of steps and half steps that evolved over the first year or so of his presidency. He began with objectives that had an intrinsic tension: to reduce the American engagement in the war in a way that would ease the domestic political pressure while also obtaining North Vietnamese agreement on a mutual withdrawal from South Vietnam. He regularly assured the South Vietnamese that they would be secure. These elements would provide the promised "peace with honor." Frances FitzGerald would later observe that the government had difficulty facing "the consequences of peace." It was "one thing to wish for an end to the war and quite another to confront the issues upon which the war had begun."[6]

President Nixon worked very closely with Henry Kissinger in strategic planning for Vietnam. Secretary of Defense Melvin Laird, a former Republican congressional leader, as wise in the workings of American politics as Dr. Kissinger was in the intellectual machinations of real-politik, had a different approach. He and Kissinger sparred in efforts to influence the president. Kissinger insisted that the goal in Vietnam was framed globally: to persuade the North Vietnamese to negotiate a withdrawal from the South and to allow the people of South Vietnam to determine their own future. This would convince the world of

America's strength — and resolve. Secretary Laird believed the major goal for the Nixon administration was to lessen the political conflict in the United States and to do this by conveying a commitment to reducing significantly American involvement in Vietnam. He believed that by demonstrating that the South Vietnamese could handle the military action themselves, the North Vietnamese would acknowledge that they should negotiate. And in any event, the Americans would have ended their part of the war. While each of these approaches would use military force as a threat and a bargaining chip, a primarily military resolution was not a part of either of their scenarios.

The plan that evolved was a series of approaches that were related in concept far more than they were in operation. Their inherent tensions would become evident. At the top of the list of means and of goals was Vietnamization, which the president had announced in June 1969 and which came to involve several components. First was an accelerating drawdown of U.S. troops, the de-Americanization of the ground war. It was Secretary Laird who suggested that Vietnamization was a more positive description of this process. Reducing the American military force necessarily involved a commitment to turning the war effort over to the South Vietnamese military, which in turn required paying far more attention to preparing them for this expanded role. And the objective of these efforts was to have a secure South Vietnamese government and a supportive, secure population. The latter was summarized as "pacification."

A corollary to the several components of Vietnamization was the determination to negotiate with the North Vietnamese a settlement of the war. This was spotlighted at the Paris meetings initiated by President Johnson. And this process was supplemented by secret meetings between the United States and North Vietnam that Dr. Kissinger commenced in August 1969. A mutual withdrawal of North Vietnamese and U.S. military from South Vietnam was the American objective in these discussions.

Kissinger and Nixon both believed that successful negotiations, either at the public conferences or in the secret conversations, would require some greater leverage. This was essential to encourage the North Vietnamese to negotiate — and to make concessions. They sought this leverage in two ways. Early in the administration, President Nixon had authorized overtures to the People's Republic of China. Dr. Kissinger flew to China for secret meetings, and in the summer of 1971, President Nixon announced he would visit China in February 1972. It was a historic trip that initiated a measurable warming relationship. This clearly advanced American interests and provided benefits that went beyond the war. But an important additional advantage was that these renewed ties would complicate the support of one of Hanoi's major benefactors. A few months following his visit to the PRC, President Nixon had visited the Soviet Union. In meetings in Moscow, he and Secretary Leonid Brezhnev signed off on important agreements, including the Strategic Arms Limitation Treaty. While the Soviet Union's support for North Vietnam had never been unconditional, it had been consequential, and this move to détente seemed further to erode Hanoi's international support.

The twin détente initiatives were necessarily slow to proceed and never certain in outcome. So the United States had one additional tool to press the North Vietnamese to negotiate. It was a military tool, but not one involving American troops on the ground and with far fewer American casualties. Beginning in March 1969, the White House had authorized major bombing campaigns in eastern Cambodia and Laos. Operation Menu, with its sequence euphemistically called "breakfast," "lunch," "snack," "dinner," "supper," and "dessert," masked the major destruction of these raids. There had been American bombing in these countries before, but it had been relatively low-key and carefully controlled. Now it would be more aggressive and would include B-52s. All of this was part of what came to be called the "madman" theory: intimidate North Vietnam into making concessions by convincing them that President Nixon was easily angered, perhaps irrational, and unpredictable. As Secretary Laird would describe it, the president "wanted adversaries to have the feeling that you could never put your finger on what he might do next."[7]

What would happen next was a matter of great debate in the White House during the summer and early fall of 1969. Nixon and Kissinger ordered MACV to organize and plan a major military operation, called Operation Duck Hook (in Saigon it was called Pruning Knife). The elements of this would include a massive bombing campaign in North Vietnam, rescinding the bombing pause that President Johnson had ordered in late 1968. The White House even asked for some assessment of the possible use of nuclear weapons in this assault. The military was instructed to plan more than five hundred sorties a day in the North, as well as to be prepared to mine ports in Cambodia and North Vietnam and to organize, position, and equip troops, largely South Vietnamese, for a possible major ground offensive across the Demilitarized Zone.

The White House made clear that they

wanted a massive and decisive assault. When the military reminded them that it had so far proved difficult to harm North Vietnam with bombing campaigns, Kissinger replied, "I refuse to believe that a little fourth-rate power like North Vietnam does not have a breaking point." He urged the development of "the option of a savage, decisive blow against North Vietnam."[8]

Henry Kissinger was opposed to any significant reduction in the American military presence in South Vietnam. He did not want to lose this implicit threat as a bargaining chip in pressuring the North Vietnamese. He urged Nixon to "go for broke" and to always have a threat to escalate on the table. And he pointed out that in order to maintain this as a realistic threat, it would be necessary to escalate progressively, inflicting greater damage with each step. He and Nixon fed each other's aggressive instincts, with the president saying he would "level" Hanoi before he would hand over South Vietnam to the Communists. The counterforce to these saber-rattling sessions was Secretary Laird.

Throughout 1969, Melvin Laird reminded the president of the domestic political threat that he faced. Antiwar demonstrations had picked up again in the summer with a major mobilization threatened for mid-October. And Congress was now becoming feistier. Richard Nixon was the first president since

Zachary Taylor in 1849 to begin his first term with a Congress in which the opposing political party controlled both houses. And the Democrats on the Hill had fewer partisan constraints now with a Republican in the White House. Laird pressed upon the president the argument that Vietnamization would allow the war to end successfully. The South Vietnamese would be able to defend themselves, American casualties would end, and the North Vietnamese would agree to a negotiated settlement. It was a win-win situation. Kissinger countered that the North would not negotiate without a threat that was real, *"the action must be brutal."* He insisted that troop withdrawal would result in an empty threat — and furthermore would initiate a process that domestic political considerations would not allow to be stopped. A drawdown would "become like salted peanuts to the American public."[9]

By October, President Nixon had decided to back off from Operation Duck Hook, at least for the time being, and to throw in with the Laird plan. He clearly had been influenced by a number of factors, including the senior military leadership's conclusion that the situation was looking good in South Vietnam and their warning that bombing likely would not sway North Vietnam — unless, of course, it was massively destructive. Nixon was always sensitive to the domestic political situation. Laird and Secretary of State William Rogers, who had been largely cut out of the planning but did agree with Secretary Laird, warned that following any significant escalation, the president should expect in Congress and in the streets a massive pushback that could stifle his ability to accomplish any of his goals. The president was already facing a major preview of this with the planning on track for a major protest mobilization in Washington. So he chose the path of deescalation. Once begun, as Dr. Kissinger warned, this would be hard to stop.[10]

If the president was going to step out on the path of de-Americanizing the war, he was not doing it without a fight. Actually, without fights on two fronts. Over the next two and a half years, the Nixon "peace" initiative was a muscular one. In the spring of 1970, he would commence a new military initiative in Cambodia and Vietnam. But first he needed to confront his domestic critics. He went ahead with his planned November 3 speech to the nation. Originally this was going to be the occasion to announce the military campaign provided in Duck Hook, but instead he used it to describe his effort to be a peacemaker. And he initiated a new domestic campaign in the process: to mobilize the "silent majority" of Americans to stand firm against that "vocal minority" who wanted to withdraw from American responsibility. These were represented by a protester the president said he had recently seen in San Francisco with the sign LOSE IN VIETNAM, BRING THE BOYS HOME. This president would not "lose," because the country would just have to face the same problems in the future. And another generation of Americans would have to fight.[11]

The president asked the American people to show their support for his approach to secure an enduring peace. He received it. The silent majority wrote and organized to push back against the vocal minority. It was not as spontaneous as it appeared. White House aide Alex Butterfield and others had organized an operation to generate public support for the president. The president had previewed this effort to organize a counterthrust as early as June when, speaking at the Air Force Academy commencement, he said that it was "open season on the Armed Forces," a time when "patriotism is considered by some to be a backward fetish of the uneducated and the unsophisticated." He was prepared to take on the "skeptics and the isolationists." And of course he would have the considerable assistance of Vice President Spiro Agnew in this encounter. The latter, well armed with alliterative insults, dismissed the war protesters as an "effete corps of impudent snobs," "nattering nabobs of negativism," and "pusillanimous pussyfooters."[12]

President Nixon would later claim that his November 3 speech was "the most effective of my presidency." He insisted that the cause was right and that the country would not follow "the easy way out, but the right way out." He pointed to the calls and letters and polling data as evidence that "the American people showed that they concurred."[13] The speech and the effort to organize support for the Nixon teams were not sufficient to halt another, even more substantial demonstration in Washington. A half million gathered on the Mall on November 15, and Pete Seeger led the crowd in singing "Give Peace a Chance." For the previous two days, some 40,000 demonstrators had marched from Arlington National Cemetery to the White House. Each carried a candle and a sign with the name of an American who had died in Vietnam. They read these names at the White House and then went on to the Capitol, where they deposited the signs in a coffin. Seventy-one more Americans died in Vietnam between November 13 and 15, 1969.[14]

The Nixon team would pursue a path of negotiation to conclude the war — but also would confront the antiwar activists and work to force the North Vietnamese to cooperate. It was a multipronged assault, iron fist and velvet glove. The campaign against the antiwar demonstrators would continue. But so would the campaign in Vietnam and the negotiations in Paris. Even as President Nixon was continuing the drawdown of American troops, he was pressing ahead with a planned attack on the North Vietnamese positions in Cambodia. This would aim to provide greater security to South Vietnam — and would be a pointed signal to the North Vietnamese. The president calculated that it would be the sort of "bold move" that would force Hanoi to reconsider its stubborn refusal to negotiate a mutual withdrawal.

President Nixon addressed the nation from the White House on April 30, 1970, to announce this offensive. Using maps, he pointed out places such as Parrot's Beak and Fishhook as he reminded Americans that just ten days earlier he had announced the withdrawal of an additional 150,000 American troops from Vietnam. But he had warned then that there was an increase in enemy activity in these border areas, and if this seemed to endanger Americans he would take "strong and effective measures" to protect them. He was doing that.[15]

Announcement of this action generated major protests on American campuses and in the streets, including the bloody confrontation between National Guard troops and demonstrators on the campus of Kent State University on May 4. Guardsmen fired 67 shots in 13 seconds; 4 were killed and 9 were wounded (some of the wounded had not been part of the demonstration). This proved to be a powerful incident that seemed to challenge the growing Nixon team's effort to marginalize the protesters. The president would continue to refer to some of the "bums" who were in the antiwar movement, and Kissinger would describe college presidents as a "disgrace," but now the counter-image was the news photograph of Mary Ann Vecchio, screaming as she knelt beside the body of a dead student.[16]

The massive attacks involving U.S. airpower and American army units as well as major ARVN forces successfully took out some of the essential North Vietnamese storage areas. But the North Vietnamese were able to avoid a large-scale military encounter. In addition, the American units were constrained somewhat in this cross-border operation as a result of MACV instructions to minimize losses.[17]

President Nixon would claim that the Cambodian action had been successful. He insisted that it halted North Vietnamese aggression in the South. Surely it had delayed many operations because of significant North Vietnamese Army losses of ammunition, supplies, and infrastructure. But privately, he and his team also knew by the summer that this offensive had failed to convince the North Vietnamese to concede any of their positions. And he knew that any further escalation would have wide political repercussions at home. Moreover, Congress now was acting to limit his ability to send any American troops into action in Laos and Cambodia. With these restrictions in place, public dissent with the war received even greater legitimacy.

Despite these constraints, the president would authorize another major cross-border attack a year later. In February 1971, in Operation Lam Son 719, the allies mounted an offensive across the border from Khe Sanh into Laos. This assault involved major ARVN forces, but the only Americans were those flying helicopters or planes. American helicopter crews flew well over 100,000 sorties during the Lam Son operation — ferrying troops in and out but also providing covering firepower. And after some initial successes, the South Vietnamese fought a major battle with the North Vietnamese at Tchepone. They and President Nixon declared victory and hurried out — in fact so hurriedly that newsreel footage of South Vietnamese soldiers clinging to the skids of U.S. helicopters proved very embarrassing to Saigon. President Thieu was not eager to suffer major losses in a battle. President Nixon said the operation proved that Vietnamization was successful. The North Vietnamese came out of the experience with increased confidence they could defeat the South Vietnamese on the battlefield.[18]

No U.S. ground troops were allowed to cross into Laos for this assault. Congressional restrictions prohibited American ground operations in Laos and Cambodia. In fact, there were very few American ground troops remaining in Vietnam in the spring of 1971. Army units did engage in Operation Dewey Canyon II, which involved clearing Highway 9 west through Khe Sanh to the border with Laos to facilitate the passage of ARVN troops and supplies. There were 253 Americans killed or missing in the Dewey Canyon/Lam Son operations — most of them were on the 107 helicopters and 6 air force fighter bombers that were lost.[19]

Even as he declared the sweep into Laos an ARVN victory, President Nixon privately expressed his impatience with the progress of the South Vietnamese Army and with the judgment and candor of General Abrams and the MACV leadership. This impatience expanded significantly a year later, when the North Vietnamese Army attacked South Vietnam in the spring 1972 Easter Offensive.

By then American advisers were serving with the defending ARVN forces, but the remaining units were assuming only a limited defensive combat role in Vietnam. The last marines had left nearly a year earlier, and the army's 101st Airborne withdrew on March 10. The total number of American forces was down to around 75,000 in the spring of 1972;

too few of them were combat units to be of much support on the ground. However, American advisers were crucial in several operations, and U.S. airpower was decisive. After several months of battle, the North Vietnamese withdrew from most of the positions they had taken in the South during this offensive. But the cost was heavy — for all sides. Civilian casualties were high due to the widespread use of American airpower — the only weapon the U.S. military had available. Nonetheless, the White House claimed the successful turning back of the offensive as a "victory."[20]

The North Vietnamese leadership had debated at length on the timing of the offensive. Finally, they had determined that American troop strength was not sufficient to be consequential and they were confident they could defeat the South Vietnamese forces, proving that Vietnamization had failed and forcing the United States to negotiate a resolution more favorable to the North. They were wrong in this calculation — they suffered some 100,000 casualties during their 1972 spring offensive and provided a rationale for the United States to unleash major air and naval attacks on the North again — including the mining of the harbor at Haiphong. Yet it was hard for the South Vietnamese to conclude that they had really "won" — even if they were elated at having stopped the attack. They had more than 60,000 casualties, and while some of their units fought courageously and well, their military and civilian leadership failed them on many occasions. The scale of the North Vietnamese attack "rippled" across South Vietnam. Officials there recognized that American air and naval firepower had been the most significant factor in halting the North Vietnamese armies.[21]

The thwarted offensive had also been costly for the American military, and not only in terms of the level of casualties which, while substantial, did not reach the scale of previous years. More than 900 Americans died in Vietnam in 1972, the bulk of them in the spring. And most were involved in air support or attack activities. This Easter campaign was costly in political terms as well. It brought the tension between the White House and the Pentagon/MACV axis to the breaking point.

President Nixon sought to respond to the major North Vietnamese initiative by showing them that they could not escape punishment. He wanted to focus the response with a massive bombing assault of the North, whereas General Abrams wanted to direct airpower tactically to support the South Vietnamese forces under attack. This tension was behind the exchange between Dr. Kissinger and Ambassador Bunker reported at the beginning of this chapter. And Kissinger was only echoing the president: On the Monday morning following Easter, Nixon said, "We're playing a much bigger game — we're playing a Russia game, a China game, and an election game and we're not gonna have the ARVN collapse."[22]

Obviously, neither the president nor his national security adviser used "game" to mean a frivolous contest. They understood the seriousness of this engagement. But they also were focused strategically on a bigger picture, and the outcome of military battles along Highway 9 going into Quang Tri or of outposts near Kontum were important only to the extent that they influenced the grander strategic goals. They were convinced that the most influential use of force would be in the Hanoi-Haiphong region rather than on the plateaus of the Central Highlands. They were frustrated by any sense of higher priority on the tactical deployment of B-52s in the South rather than striking the area around the North Vietnamese capital. And they had little patience with military officials pointing out that bad weather conditions prevented their striking Hanoi and Haiphong. President Nixon thought of the tactical air support of the American troops during the Battle of the Bulge — mistakenly believing that had been in the middle of a blizzard. The president exploded to Admiral Thomas Moorer, chair of the Joint Chiefs of Staff: "The goddamned Air Force has to take some goddamned risk, just like they did during the Battle of the Bulge in World War II." Moorer insisted that the air force was not reluctant to "take risks" but was impeded by an inability to see the antiair missiles that the North Vietnamese were moving around.[23]

North Vietnam was heavily bombed, as were the contested areas in the South. But the conflict over strategic bombing and tactical operations was not forgotten. In addition, the White House lost even more confidence in Secretary Laird and his team — and certainly in Creighton Abrams and MACV. Many had blamed Abrams for the failings of the Lam Son Operation a year earlier. The disagreements over the directing of bombing raids during the Easter Offensive increased this criticism. The president privately labeled Abrams "tired, unimaginative." Within a few months, he would be "kicked upstairs" to a position of army chief of staff.[24]

General Abrams was a decorated World War II hero who failed to navigate skillfully the complicated course set for Vietnam under President Nixon (in fairness, it is not clear that anyone could have done this). Abrams had not in any dramatic way changed the Westmoreland approach to the war, but beginning in 1969 he had to juggle an increasingly rapid downsizing in troops, instructions to minimize American casualties, and orders to strengthen the ability of the South Vietnamese military forces. He needed to proceed under these new circumstances while continuing to protect and assist South Vietnam's operations and also being prepared to undertake new initiatives, such as the offensives into Cambodia and Laos. He did not have the resources to attempt seriously to do all of these things. But the burden of doing it fell not simply on the commander but also on the troops in the field. Vietnam deployment was never an uncomplicated assignment, but the last years of the war proved to be a particularly difficult time to serve. The military mission became even less clear, and as had always been the case, it was the troops on the ground who paid the price.[25]

The last American combat troops left Vietnam on August 23, 1972, and the last support units withdrew on November 30. There were some 16,000 army advisers and administrators remaining in Vietnam at the end of the year, coincidentally about the same number that was there when President Kennedy had been assassinated nine years earlier. They were playing the same nominal advisory role, but surely the attitude, the sense of mission and optimism of the early 1960s were gone by the end of 1972. Indeed, these characteristics began to decline shortly after the beginning of ground operations in 1965, and they played out rather quickly when the military goals and the military role changed in the spring of 1969.

There were 11,987 American deaths in Vietnam in 1969 — from the June 8 announcement of Vietnamization to the end of the year, the number was 4,645. The next year the total dead was 6,327; in 1971 it was 2,453; and in 1972 the tally was 906. In the years 1973–1975, 528 died. By late 1971, these increasingly reflected air casualties — or, more and more commonly, a belated finding or acknowledgment of the death of some of the men originally listed as missing. It was a different war and morale slipped — not only in the rear support bases where it had always been lower, but now also out in the field. Because the field was not quite the same. One critic of the army's conduct during this period observed that the few combat actions "were only conducted if designed to 'stimulate a negotiated settlement.' There was no more mention of military victory."[26]

It was a long — and a costly — drawdown, which began in the spring of 1969 and would conclude three and a half years later. Operation Apache Snow, the major offensive in the A Shau Valley that included the assault on Hamburger Hill, officially ended on June 7, 1969. And almost immediately, as Vietnamization evolved from process to goal, the U.S. military stepped back from initiating significant offensive operations. Some ongoing major initiatives, such as Operations Lamar Plain, Herkimer Mountain, and Pipestone Canyon, concluded by August. Some comprehensive actions, such as Operations Frederick Hill, Iron Mountain, and Geneva Park, would continue into 1971.

The patrols and operations could still be substantial — and deadly. And as the Washington leadership grew more cautious, and more sensitive to American casualties, not surprisingly there were signs of change in the field. In August 1969, south of Da Nang in the Song Chang Valley, A Company of the 3rd Battalion of the 196th Infantry Brigade was ordered out on a patrol for a sixth consecutive day. The men balked. James Reston of *The New York Times* described the action as a "Whiff of Mutiny." Reston wondered why there had not been more instances of this and insisted that President Nixon had better pay attention because there was the possibility of "revolt" if he continued to ask men "to risk their lives in a war that he has decided to bring to a close." Veteran *New York Times* war correspondent James Sterba stepped back from the mutiny description when he wrote of the unit and the incident. He said that the men did not explain their initial refusal by complaining about "fighting in lost causes, fighting for no apparent reason, anti-war sentiment, troop withdrawals, or the Paris peace talks." Instead they described intense heat — reaching 118° at midday — pressing through the sharp-edged elephant grass, spending several days in the field with little water, their bodies marked by cuts and scabs and infections, and sapped by several nights with little sleep. They resisted — and then they went out. As one said, "Everybody gripes." Another commented, "A lot of guys don't want to go back in there and they say so. But they do it anyway. They complain all the while, until the shooting starts."[27]

By early 1970, nearly all aggressive patrols, those that for the past several years had sought, even invited, a confrontation, and certainly all major American-led ground operations had pretty much stopped — with the obvious and significant exception of the Cambodian incursion in April. Even here, it was clear that operational control had shifted. The military had long pressed for authorization to go after the sanctuaries in Cambodia, but the decision to do so in 1970 had to do with pressuring the North Vietnamese in Hanoi. Disrupting the supply and control positions in Cambodia was a means of accomplishing that rather than an end in itself. When Washington decided to authorize the attack, American troops had little time for updated planning for the operation. The 1st Cavalry Division, one of the lead units in the assault, had four days' notice and did not have any maps of Cambodia when they crossed the border.[28]

While all of the attention that spring was on the Cambodia invasion, few noticed an operation on familiar ground to the north that perhaps would be even more revealing of the changing war. Back up in the A Shau Valley, nearly a year after the Hamburger Hill battle, the 101st Division was again undertaking an operation to disrupt the North Vietnamese supply lines coming in from Laos. Across from Dong Ap Bia, on the eastern slope of the valley, the 2nd Battalion of the 506th Regiment moved onto a ridge and built Fire Support Base Ripcord. They were joined there by units of the 2nd Battalion of the 501st Regiment. Their goal was to be able to assault and interdict supply bases located throughout that region of South Vietnam and across the Laotian border. The Americans called this the "Warehouse Area" because of all of the weapons and ordnance caches there.

There were enemy forces all around Ripcord, and the North Vietnamese started a series of attacks on the base on July 1, 1970. Back at Camp Evans, the 101st Division commanders were reluctant to be drawn into a major battle that would evoke memories of Hamburger Hill. One soldier who was several miles away said that when Ripcord was attacked, they could see it through the hills, "and watched it light up."[29]

It was a nasty fight with daily rocketing and mortaring of Ripcord. Some feared that it would become another Dien Bien Phu, and on the twenty-second day of the battle, the army withdrew the battalions. The 101st Division had suffered more casualties on Ripcord, including 75 killed, than they had on Hamburger Hill. MACV kept the entire operation low-key — there were few reports during the battle itself. After the withdrawal, American airplanes bombed the base out of existence. And a few months later the army abandoned nearby Firebase O'Reilly, the last of the American bases in the valley.

Some of the men who fought and lost friends at Ripcord were angry. They thought they had been set out as "bait" to invite an attack and then were left "hanging" when the enemy closed in because the army did not want to risk an even larger fight. One of their officers had assumed that their role was to go in to instigate a fight: "It never occurred to me that the will did not exist to engage the enemy and destroy him once the battle was joined."[30]

A few weeks after the withdrawal, the 101st sent in helicopters with a platoon to try to retrieve the bodies that had been left behind. The patrol found 8 bodies and placed them in body bags and flew them out; a few weeks later they went back and retrieved another body. The historian of the Ripcord operation described the impact and the symbolism of this bloody fight: "Ripcord was the last big battle that the American infantry fought in Vietnam. It marked the end of an era. As the withdrawals continued, battalion commanders, acting upon the unspoken wishes of their superiors, crossed known enemy strongholds off their maps, and the troops basically went through the motions on patrol, none wanting to be the last man killed in a war that was not going to be won."[31]

By late 1969, most understood that this war would end through negotiation rather than victory. Perhaps this had always been the case, but now it was explicitly acknowledged. From the White House to the Pentagon to MACV in Saigon, all recognized the reframed objectives and shifting rules of engagement. The men in the field understood this as well. Inevitably, this understanding blunted any remaining feelings of military purpose and intensified the common battlefield instinct of survival. The drive to survive seemed officially validated as word came down that the American military was under orders to reduce casualties. This elevated self-preservation from a personal concern to a military objective. Obviously, the American command had never been indifferent to U.S. casualties, but now it was an even more tightly constrained, cautiously executed war. And those on the ground recognized this quickly. One correspondent quoted a young officer out in the field: "Whenever we can get away with it, we radio the old man that we are moving our platoon forward into the bush to search for the enemy." But, he acknowledged, "If there is any risk of getting shot at, we just stay where we are until the choppers come to pick us up." Quite a change from just six months earlier when the officer on Ripcord expressed his frustration that the army was not looking to fight the enemy.[32]

By the spring of 1971, as troop numbers declined significantly, a series of events sharply influenced the perception of not just the war but also the young men who had been sent to fight it. In this different war, the American military found it harder and harder to maintain its professionalism and discipline. Not surprisingly, this was far truer back at the base camps among noncombat units. Traditionally, these had lacked the organizational edge and close teamwork that was essential out in the bush. In the early '70s, most accounts suggested a general deterioration of military readiness because basically there seemed to be less to be ready for — except for rotation back home. Meanwhile, back home, Americans read or heard accounts from Vietnam describing drug use, breakdown of discipline, racial tensions, antiwar protests among soldiers, and the fragging or assassination of officers and NCOs.[33]

On March 29, 1971, a U.S. Army court-martial board convened at Fort Benning, Georgia, found Lieutenant William Calley guilty of the premeditated murder of at least 29 civilians at My Lai. Two days later, the same panel sentenced him to life imprisonment. It had been a lengthy and emotional trial, with soldiers' photographs and chilling accounts of the murder of civilians in the village. Men told stories of soldiers shooting children, of automatic weapon fire aimed close up at groups of scared and weeping families. It had taken three years for the army's discovery, investigative, and legal processes to conclude the case of Lieutenant Calley.[34]

By then, the outlines of the story were well known. On March 16, 1968, Charlie Company of the 1st Battalion of the 20th Infantry Regiment, part of the 23rd Infantry Division, the Americal Division, attacked the village of Son My, known on the army maps as part of "Pinkville" and remembered as My Lai. The first platoon, headed by Lieutenant Calley, led the assault on the village, where allegedly there were NLF soldiers. But in fact there were not. Before the first platoon left, they had killed between 347 (U.S. Army estimates) and 504 (Vietnamese counts) Vietnamese civilians. These included old men, women, children, and even infants. This was far more than hapless cross fire with "collateral damage." There were mass executions of groups, gang raping and then the killing of women and girls, and mutilation of bodies. There was no evidence of anyone in the village attacking the soldiers. Some would insist there were "Viet Cong sympathizers" there, and perhaps there were. But that was irrelevant to — and most certainly not an excuse for — what happened that day.[35]

Many were convinced that the military had covered up the event and was unwilling to fault anyone in senior command positions. Calley would be the only one found guilty of the incident. His senior officers were not charged in most cases, and when they were, they were acquitted. The men who joined Calley in the killing were either not charged or were acquitted.

March 16, 1968, was the U.S. Army's darkest day of the war. It was also the nation's darkest day of the war. The shame is heaviest obviously as a result of what actually happened. But the shameful tragedy was attenuated greatly by the military culture that allowed it to happen — and without any real consequences. The World War II Nuremberg precedent held that following orders was not a defense for crimes. The Yamashita Precedent from that war held that senior officers could be held accountable for crimes committed under their command even if it was not demonstrated that they knew about these actions, if it was clear that they *should have* known about them. These rulings had resulted in the execution of senior German and Japanese officers after the war. In 1971, they were deemed not relevant in the My Lai murders and the subsequent failure of the command to follow up on them. "I was following orders" and "I was not aware of what happened there" became acceptable defenses.[36]

The crimes that day would be followed by a series of actions and inactions that resulted in trying and then, finally, essentially exonerating Calley, an exoneration all the more troubling because it was facilitated by an attitude that spread the blame and the shame to all who served in Vietnam. The suffering of those villagers and the grief of their families is a tragedy for which there must be guilt and can be no excuses. Yet the blaming of everyone — in essence meaning that no one was held accountable — is equally inexcusable. Such a defense has no standing in military culture, which stresses individual responsibility. And it surely has no place in American military justice or in the civilian criminal code. The official and the dominant public response to the Calley conviction first exonerated and then celebrated criminal behavior.[37]

The men of Charlie Company were tired

and angry and scared on that March morning. They did not know what to expect. They had been told there would be enemy combatants in the village. They were grieving the loss of some buddies and were eager to take revenge on the enemy. All of these tensions and emotions are natural in combat. They are contained by unambiguous command values and discipline and by officers and NCOs who make certain that professional instincts control human emotions. And by having a chain of command that follows up aggressively on accusations and suspicious after-action reports. None of these controls were in place at My Lai. In fact, the leadership largely vented their own emotions and directed others to do the same.

On April 8, 1971, President Nixon in a private conversation with Henry Kissinger said that "most people don't give a shit" whether Calley killed the Vietnamese in that village. Despite the overwhelming evidence, the great majority thought that Calley had been unfairly prosecuted. His defense lawyer described him as "a good boy" who had been taught to "kill, kill, kill." Country music stations played "Battle Hymn of Lt. Calley," who was "a soldier of this land." Political leaders defended him as either a scapegoat or even a hero. Officials from the American Legion, the Veterans of Foreign Wars, and the Disabled American Veterans described very angry memberships. Polls showed that nearly 80 percent of Americans disagreed with the verdict. President Nixon, sensitive to this, one day after the sentencing, ordered him moved from the stockade at Fort Benning to house arrest in his bachelor officer quarters. Following a series of appeals, he would serve only three and a half years under house arrest.[38]

Accepting My Lai as a normal part of the Vietnam War meant a lowering of expectations for all who served there. Other reported incidents in the spring of 1971 resulted in the continued decline of their image. On March 29, the very day that the court-martial panel found Lieutenant Calley guilty, his old Americal Division was struck by a night enemy attack on its Fire Support Base Mary Ann west of Chu Lai. Thirty-three Americans were killed and 76 wounded, the heaviest American losses in a single battle in more than a year. The army was embarrassed that the enemy managed to infiltrate the base while the men slept. Published reports passed along rumors of drug use and general carelessness on the base. Even though these later proved to be exaggerated and even false, they nonetheless were part of a record that suggested the military was losing its grip.[39]

There were other incidents that seemed to indicate army units refusing orders to advance into hostile territory. The incidents were real, but the suggestions of mutiny would not stand up to investigation and scrutiny. The assault on FSB Mary Ann had followed by fewer than ten days the account of an Americal Division up on Highway 9, working to clear the border to Laos for Operation Lam Son 719. The men there had refused to proceed down a road to recover a downed helicopter before it fell into enemy hands. The men were replaced by another unit, which did go in to secure the helicopter. One analysis indicates that this came closest to a breakdown. Reporters covered this story, as they had an incident a year earlier when a platoon in the 1st Cavalry Division had ignored an order to move into an area near the Cambodian border. The exchange of the men and their officer was captured by a CBS-TV crew. Correspondent John Laurence would later regret using the word "rebellion" in describing this incident. And the company that had been involved was acknowledged to have had a good combat record both before and following this incident.[40]

Although later all of these reports and incidents were qualified or explained, the image set by these accounts of the conduct of the men serving in Vietnam and an army in revolt would remain. It was exaggerated, but there was no doubt that some of the earlier sense of discipline had faded as the military objectives became less clear.

The most widely covered incident involving soldiers balking at orders took place a few months later out at Fire Support Base Pace, near the Cambodian border, in the fall of 1971. Pace was a well-armed defensive position that aimed at blocking enemy activity and often found itself under heavy siege, including artillery fire from across the border. On the night of October 9, 6 men from Bravo Company of the 1st Battalion, 12th Cavalry refused to go out on a night ambush patrol; they insisted that their role was to defend the base and not to engage in offensive patrols. In addition, engineers serving there had warned them that the area where they would go was filled with Claymore mines and regular NVA night probes. Following a confrontation, the command reviewed the situation and canceled the order to go out. As a result, the incident was no longer technically a case of refusing orders. This ended the matter for the military justice system, but it didn't remain at this isolated jungle base. The confrontation at FSB Pace came to represent to many Americans a prime example of soldier resistance.

A number of men in the unit decided to call attention to their situation, and they wrote a letter to Senator Edward Kennedy, believing that he would be sympathetic to their concerns. They wrote as "the last remaining ground troops that the U.S. has in a combat role" and questioned this role. They said their border outpost was surrounded, and every day they had to deal with orders that could put them in a dangerous situation even though there seemed to be no reason for it. They acknowledged that six of their men refused to go on a night ambush. They wanted the American citizens to know that there were still ground troops at risk and that they could face "mass prosecution" due to their challenges. One later commented, "We're not supposed to be fighting this war anyway. We're supposed to be turning it over" to the ARVN forces. Sixty-six soldiers signed the letter, about two-thirds of the men in the company. The signatories included 12 sergeants.[41]

The incident and the letter received a great deal of publicity due to the efforts of Richard Boyle, an unaccredited journalist and antiwar activist. The South Vietnamese government had earlier asked him to leave the country due to his antiwar activities. But he came back in via Cambodia and crossed the border to Fire Support Base Pace. He met some of the men on October 9 and decided that their actions needed to be shared with the people back in the United States. He left the country with tape recordings of their comments and with the letter to Senator Kennedy. He wrote a description of the events in the French newspaper *Le Monde,* describing it as a "mutiny." American publications picked it up, but most avoided that description. Boyle went to Washington, where he insisted on personally presenting the letter to Senator Kennedy. Kennedy was very cautious — there is some indication that after all of the attacks directed at him following his Hamburger Hill criticism, he was not looking to appear to approve of an alleged mutiny. Boyle later wrote a book about the experience, and he continued to exaggerate it. What happened at Pace was a consequential matter, which revealed much about the nature of the war by late 1971 and about the mood of the men who remained in combat outposts. But it was not a mutiny. *Newsweek* reporter Nicholas Proffitt, a very good Vietnam correspondent, described it as a "minor example" of the situation in Vietnam where the men feel "forgotten" and worry about an anonymous death in a forgotten war. No one, he observed, wants to be "the last to die in a war everybody else considers over."[42]

To many in the United States, the reported resistance at Pace fit into a pattern of young men in Vietnam rebelling against the war: disobeying orders, checking out with drugs, or even assassinating their leaders.[43] There is clear evidence that the incidents of men attacking and killing their NCOs or officers increased in the last years of the war. In 1969, the military first began to recognize this as a problem. In July of that year, the Marine Corps initiated a program to identify, investigate, and pursue these alleged cases. It came to be called fragging because the most common weapons were the fragmentation hand grenades — the M26, M61, or the M67. These are deadly weapons, not traceable in the way a rifle or pistol might be.

A scholar who undertook a comprehensive study of the subject observed that "by the time Vietnamization began, many of the NCOs who had manned the proud military of 1965 were either dead, wounded, or had left the service, and sufficient numbers of replacements were not forthcoming." He concluded that the "high standards of discipline maintained during the buildup years deteriorated" and attributed this partially to growth of "social problems like drug abuse, racial tension," and "the authority crisis" that became more common "within the ranks."[44]

There is no accurate count of fragging incidents or casualties. Deaths by explosions are part of the casualties of war and can be the result of enemy action, battlefield or booby trap, unintended friendly fire, or accidents. Or deliberate homicide. One study found that 15 marines were killed in possible homicide incidents, but over half of these were privates or PFCs, suggesting that not all the homicides were directed against superiors. Army studies later described between

600 and 850 "incidents" and confirmed 42 fatalities, 6 of which were officers. Military tribunals convicted 6 soldiers and 4 marines of homicide in the fragging category.[45]

Clearly, many of these homicides and attempted homicides were personal attacks rather than acts of rebellion. This does not dismiss them. Military units depend upon respect and trust, and these were in shorter supply as the war moved to conclusion. The reasons for the attacks were complicated. A study of 54 soldiers and 17 marines convicted of assaulting fellow servicemen with explosives found that those convicted were disproportionately nonwhite, young, and tended to be enlistees rather than draftees. They were significantly less likely than others in uniform to have completed high school, and more than half of them had civil arrests prior to enlistment. Over two-thirds had earlier military charges against them. Only 15 of the 71 served in the infantry, and of these, their battlefield record was "undistinguished to say the least." One analysis found that 87.5 percent of the assaults were initiated under the influence of drugs or alcohol.[46]

In the summer of 1971, the correspondent Donald Kirk spent an extended period in the old I Corps region. By then all of the marine and most of the army infantry units had been withdrawn. Kirk noted that it was in the rear areas, among those "whom the grunts disdainfully call the REMF's, for Rear Echelon Mother ———, that talk of fragging, of hard drugs, of racial conflict seems bitter, desperate, often dangerous." He wrote of a place called the "head hootch" at Quang Tri, where "potheads" from all over the base gathered. The men he met there were largely white, had ten to twelve years of education, and many admitted to some record of juvenile delinquency or crime. All told him they also smoked scag (heroin). They seemed "hopelessly demoralized by the war and by their immediate surroundings." Their army assignments were minimal, taking a few hours a day. So they spent the rest of the time smoking and complaining, suffering "from the same sense of futility, of pointlessness, that affects thousands of other G.I.s in the midst of withdrawal of American troops." Kirk said that the drug use back at base camps explained the high level of theft there — to get money to buy drugs — and also it was a factor in fraggings. Based on his conversations, he estimated that 20 percent of the men at the base camps used hard drugs.

It was hard to be an officer in this environment. One army major, back for a second tour in Vietnam, was "totally unprepared for the new mood among G.I.s" back at the rear base camp where he was assigned. He challenged the men and found that most officers ignored the problem. He found hand grenade pins on his pillow — a warning. But he continued. Kirk also spent some time out in the bush with the remaining combat units. He said there was little drug use there. One soldier out near Charlie Ridge told him, "We see a guy using it out here, we take care of him, or the C.O. sends him back to the rear."

Kirk observed that racial tension was not much of a factor out in the field, but in some of the base camps it was explosive. Some black soldiers formed their own "Panther" groups that challenged the normal authority. A black NCO serving his second tour at the base at Chu Lai said that earlier "we were all together. We worked as a team." But this time "they don't really care no more." He challenged them and cursed at them but was now thinking that it was a "lost cause." He too found grenade pins on his pillow.[47]

As opposition to the war picked up in America in the 1960s, a small but very active and influential group was the Vietnam Veterans Against the War. Formed in 1967 by six antiwar veterans, the organization earned a great deal of attention. They accepted as members only veterans who had served in Vietnam and they focused on services and support for veterans, but they also believed the war was a mistake, that it supported a corrupt antidemocratic government in Saigon, and was carried out in a cruel manner toward civilians with too many atrocities. The

591

organization joined in protests at the Democratic Convention in 1968 and with the Vietnam Moratorium Committee in 1969. The news of My Lai at the end of that year provided them with public understanding of the atrocities they said they had witnessed and in which they admitted participating.[48]

On Labor Day weekend of 1970, the group organized a march along a Revolutionary War route from Morristown, New Jersey, to Valley Forge, Pennsylvania. The VVAW coordinators named it Operation RAW (Rapid American Withdrawal). They invited veterans in wheelchairs or with missing limbs to join them and told them that they should "publicize and feature that condition" as a means of "attracting attention to our cause." Along the way, working with a Philadelphia guerrilla theater group, they dramatized the taking of villages in Vietnam, racing in with plastic weapons and abusing the citizens. People who watched this were stunned by the brutality of these assaults. And at Valley Forge, among the speakers was Jane Fonda, who argued that "My Lai was not an isolated incident."[49]

In January 1971, the VVAW organized the Winter Soldier Investigation hearings in Detroit. They collaborated with the attorney Mark Lane, an antiwar activist and the author of a book critical of the work of the Warren Commission's finding that Lee Harvey Oswald had worked alone to kill President Kennedy. At these hearings, a series of Vietnam veterans described their observation of and in many cases their participation in atrocities committed against civilians. Their accounts of killing children were particularly gruesome and troubling.[50]

Following up on this, in late April 1971, the Vietnam Veterans Against the War organized a major demonstration in Washington, where they repeated many of the Detroit Winter Soldier Investigation accounts. A young navy veteran, John Kerry, who had earned three Purple Hearts and a Silver Star in Vietnam, told a Senate committee what the war was doing to his generation of Americans — and to the Vietnamese. Kerry summarized the findings of the Winter Soldier Investigations, of men testifying that "at times they had personally raped, cut off ears, cut off heads, taped wires from portable telephones to human genitals and turned up the power, cut off limbs, blown up bodies." The veterans had admitted that they "randomly shot at civilians, razed villages . . . , poisoned food stocks, and generally ravaged the countryside." This was in addition "to the normal ravage of war, and the normal and very particular ravaging which is done by the applied bombing power of this country." Kerry insisted that these "war crimes" were "not isolated incidents but crimes committed on a day-to-day basis with the full awareness of officers at all levels of command."[51]

Lieutenant Kerry spoke critically as well of the treatment of Vietnam veterans — their high unemployment rates, the failure of the VA hospital system to accommodate and treat them. He argued that suicide rates among veterans were high because they came back from Vietnam to "find the indifference of a country that doesn't really care, that doesn't really care."

The day following Kerry's testimony, many veterans, estimated at numbers ranging from 600 to 2,000, threw their Vietnam combat medals on the steps of the Capitol. It was a powerful, even poignant, scene, as a number of them wept and some made statements about the crimes they had committed while serving. The VVAW probably never had more than 20,000 to 25,000 members, but they were vocal and influential. They had an experience, a credential that few other antiwar groups could bring. No one could dismiss them as "draft dodgers."[52]

The veterans' group made the White House nervous. They were far harder to ridicule as "bums" than a group of campus protesters. President Nixon also worried about the potential political impact of the National League of Families of American Prisoners and Missing in Southeast Asia. Founded by the wives of some American prisoners, they became increasingly influential. They made certain that no one forgot about the prisoners and missing — and securing the release of all of the prisoners became a key part of the negotiations in Paris. During the April demonstrations in Washington, President Nixon warned Kissinger that they had to address this issue because of its political potential: "I don't give a damn about the Congress, demonstrators, or anything else, but I've got to keep the POW wives from taking off. They could really hurt us."[53]

The dramatic change in public understanding of the purpose of the war in Vietnam was underlined in June 1971, when *The New York Times* began publishing the Pentagon Papers. These government documents, assembled at the request of Secretary of Defense Robert McNamara, were made available by RAND officer and Pentagon consultant Daniel Ellsberg. They provided an unimpeachable record of the Johnson years and the government's uncertainty and duplicity and its previously undisclosed internal disagreements about the circumstances and the objectives that led the United States into Vietnam and marked that engagement down to 1968. These documents sustained the cynics and enabled the critics, documenting the worst assumptions of everyone. As commentator William Pfaff pointed out, "At no point does there seem to have been a serious, responsible assessment made and generally agreed to within the government on the national interests actually at stake in Vietnam."[54]

The Nixon administration sought and received an injunction to stop publication of the documents, and much early controversy focused on the government's ability to suppress material prior to publication and on the whole idea of secrecy designations. After the Supreme Court ruled that the government could not stop publication, the remaining papers were published and the nation joined in the broader debate over the origins of the war. As *Time* magazine, an aggressive advocate of American engagement in those early years, summarized, these records "revealed a dismaying degree of miscalculation, bureaucratic arrogance and deception."[55]

Leslie Gelb led the team that had prepared these documents for Secretary McNamara at the Pentagon. After the papers were released, he observed that most "leaders" they had studied engaged in "concealment and half truth" and that this was not limited to statements on Vietnam. He insisted that these leaders tried "to protect themselves against public pressures, and in the process they shielded us from the information we needed to make up our own mind." Gelb said this unwillingness to share complexity and nuance and candidly preview possible consequence was common in Washington: "This paternalism has marked the whole history of

U.S. involvement in Vietnam. Our leaders knew the world was full of uncertainties and unknowables, that the choices were all tough ones, but they did not challenge their basic assumptions and would dismiss anyone who did as 'soft-headed.' " Gelb worried that the Nixon administration was following the same approach, "adding another chapter to the Pentagon papers."[56]

It is not clear what effect publication of the Pentagon Papers had on the men in the field. They had already come to understand the American war in Vietnam was no longer, and perhaps had never been, the upbeat cold war assignment that the Kennedy and Johnson teams had described. They were ready to go home. The Pentagon Papers called into question the very assumptions and objectives of the war. Troops deployed there had raised the same questions from the mid-1960s. Now they had to address more direct questions about their conduct of the war. The spring of 1971 had not been kind to them.

Americans increasingly saw photos and television footage and read accounts of soldiers whose disheveled uniforms scarcely covered the fact that they seemed to be long-haired, peace-symbol-wearing hippies. They heard stories of drugged-up embarrassments, killing of officers and NCOs in so-called fragging incidents, psychopaths killing civilians. They were participants in a scary American race war now exported to Vietnam. So even as Americans divided over the war in Vietnam, more of them came to hold an increasingly negative image of the soldiers who fought there. Many in the antiwar movement applauded them as resisters and activists in uniform — and exaggerated their numbers and their activities. Surely many also exaggerated the unprofessional and undisciplined conduct in Vietnam. Nonetheless, all exaggerations aside, the professional edge was gone.

Unfortunately, individuals and groups who did not agree on much else regarding Vietnam came to share this basic view of the troops. And nothing dominated the imagery in the way that My Lai did. A Gallup poll in early April 1971 found that 50 percent of Americans thought that the My Lai killings were a "common" incident while only 24 percent believed the massacre was an isolated incident. And 83 percent of those polled approved of President Nixon's releasing Lieutenant Calley. One observer wrote that the near unanimity in support of Lieutenant Calley resulted in "the coupling of [conservative Alabama governor] George Wallace and [antiwar activist, Doctor] Benjamin Spock on the same side of a major sociopolitical issue." Antiwar senator George McGovern disagreed with the verdict and was "disturbed by any implication that one young junior officer should bear the burden for the tragedy of this war." Columnist William Greider wrote that Calley was "the authentic folk figure of Vietnam. Calley is the only name to emerge from this war with the special status of instant recognition. The name reminds the public imagination of the war's treachery and confusion which obscures the heroism."[57]

The antiwar groups accepted the negative stereotype of the men serving in Vietnam, sometimes with a condescending sympathy and sometimes with contempt and occasionally with applause. My Lai demonstrated that innocent young men were trained and forced to do awful things. The testimony of the Vietnam Veterans Against the War confirmed this. The Calley everyone-did-it defense had a resonance with those who wished the war to end, because they could argue that everybody was still doing it. And the allegations of mutiny were applauded on the left as examples of young Americans resisting foolish orders, challenging authority.

Gary Kulik, a Vietnam veteran and a historian, concluded his analysis of the accounts of those who claimed to have committed criminal acts and insisted that they were truly victims: "No other war in American history produced so many soldiers who lied, not about being heroes, but about being victims. And no other war in American history produced so many apologists for those 'victims' who committed real atrocities."[58]

Even Philip Caputo placed the blame on distant authorities for the murder of two Vietnamese civilians for which he and others were charged and acquitted. He wrote that "the war in general and U.S. military policies in particular were ultimately to blame" for these deaths. The *New York Times* book reviewer of Caputo's *Rumor of War* accepted this assessment: "The ultimate effect of this book is to make the personal and the public responsibility merge into a nightmare of horror and waste." All shared in the guilt. Peter Prescott wrote in *Newsweek* that with Caputo's book and the powerful novel *Close Quarters* by Larry Heinemann, Vietnam finally had its literature. The books implied "that this kind of war, with its peculiar combination of stress and fatigue, of futility and lunatic violence, batters the average American boy loose from his reason — as well as from whatever moral and spiritual resources he has."[59]

Most groups supportive of the war also accepted the negative image of the troops but explained its cause and consequence differently. As with their antiwar opponents, rather than dismissing Calley and his homicidal men as aberrant and holding them individually accountable, many accepted their actions at My Lai as a natural and inevitable part of war. For the prowar group, it was too bad about the civilians, but this is what happened in war zones — or, perhaps, some darkly suggested, the civilians deserved it because they were supporting the Communists. In any event, the war supporters were incensed that a soldier would be punished for doing his duty. More troubling, they worried that soldiers doing their duty had become rare. The prowar groups also largely accepted the image of the soldiers as increasingly undisciplined, unheroic, mutinous peace activists. They pointed to the example of the Vietnam Veterans Against the War. This decline of military pride and discipline, they insisted, was a result of American society being poisoned by the antiwar cultural left, and it was the resulting conduct of the men in Vietnam that illustrated why we were losing the war.

One navy chaplain who had served with the marines in Vietnam explained the apparent incidents of physical violence committed by marines against other marines by pointing to "the dearth of a real inner sense of right and wrong within the perpetrator, a lack of moral development, a moral cripple." And they were in a place where the normal restraints of family and society were missing and where the ready availability of drugs and alcohol eroded all "inner inhibitions."[60]

Donald Kirk spent some time with an army unit out near Charlie Ridge, southwest of Da Nang. He spoke there to a young army captain, a West Point graduate, who had a man in his unit wounded the previous day. The officer said, "Once we've decided to get out, and then keep fighting, it seems kind of worthless." Expressing a sentiment that became more and more common in those last years, the officer continued, "Nobody wants to be the last guy to die in Vietnam." In what might be a summary of the war experience, the next night they were fired upon, apparently by a single enemy soldier with an AK-47. The Americans responded to the assault with their M16s, with machine guns, and finally with helicopter gunships they called in. After the exchange, a soldier said, "They got some nerve opening up against all our firepower like that." But he then reflected on it. "Far as I'm concerned they can have this whole country. There ain't no reason for us bein' here. We were fightin' to win, that'd be one thing, but we're just here wastin' time." Kirk described this as a typical attitude "at the butt end of a bad war."[61]

A year later, on August 5, 1972, American troops ran their last combat patrol. As Delta Company of the 3rd Battalion, 21st Infantry of the 196th set out on a patrol in the Antenna Valley southwest of Da Nang, they did not know this would be their final ground patrol of the war. One of the men on that patrol said, "I've heard this standing down BS before and even if this was our last patrol, everybody knew you could die on the last as quick as you could on the first." Two men were wounded by booby traps.[62] Delta Company was with the final ground troops that left the country on August 23. On November 30, the last U.S. troops left the country — only the 16,000 advisers and administrators remained.

The end of American operations in Vietnam coincided with the end of the selective service system. During the 1968 election campaign, Richard Nixon had promised to end the draft, a politically charged component of the Vietnam War. He established a commission chaired by former secretary of defense Thomas Gates. Libertarian and free-market thinking converged with antiwar sentiments and all were informed by a recognition of the inequities involved in the draft system of the 1960s. The Gates Commission recommended an all-volunteer military. Following a two-year extension of the existing law, with a lottery selection system, in order to complete the Vietnam theater of operations needs, the all-volunteer force was initiated in 1973. This proved to be a marker year for the end of a war and of an era. The lottery would move to a more equitable system, but resistance toward the draft continued until it ended. And the war ended.

On October 22, 1972, the United States and North Vietnam agreed on the terms of a peace agreement. The Americans dropped their demand for a mutual withdrawal of troops and the Hanoi government withdrew their insistence upon a regime change. The United States agreed to withdraw all forces, and the North Vietnamese agreed to release all prisoners. The Thieu government refused to sign because the South Vietnamese president knew that his government could not be sustained under these terms. After President Nixon won an overwhelming reelection over the antiwar Democrat George McGovern, he launched a major bombing campaign in the North in mid-December. Operation Linebacker II involved more than 1,700 sorties, including 700 by B-52s. He insisted that what came to be called the Christmas bombing would show the South Vietnamese that they could count on the Americans. On January 23, 1973, the president announced that all sides now had signed off on the agreement. There would be a cease-fire on January 27, and within sixty days all American troops would be withdrawn and all POWs would be released. In June, Congress approved the Case-Church resolution prohibiting any further U.S. military action in Vietnam, Cambodia, or Laos without congressional approval. President Nixon fought back, but he was by then engaged in defending himself against the Watergate allegations.[63]

On August 9, 1974, President Nixon resigned in the face of an impeachment vote following the Watergate revelations. He was succeeded by Vice President Gerald Ford, who had earlier succeeded Vice President Agnew following the latter's October 1973 resignation with criminal charges pending for actions taken when he was governor of Maryland. President Ford had no troops in Vietnam other than advisers and administrators, and he was bound by significant congressional restrictions on what he could do there. So he was unable to do anything when the North Vietnamese launched a major attack on the South in March 1975. The ARVN troops fell quickly with little resistance. President Thieu resigned, critical of the Americans for pressing his government to sign the peace accords and then abandoning them. The South Vietnamese government officials left the country. On April 30, the last American troops left hurriedly, with South Vietnamese who had worked with the Americans hanging on the skids to try to get on the last helicopter as it left Saigon. Most failed. The North Vietnamese Army occupied the city, soon to be renamed Ho Chi Minh City in honor of the North Vietnamese leader.

Most Americans were stunned by how quickly this happened. They were sorry and perhaps embarrassed. But very few wanted the United States militarily to do anything to try to stop what by then seemed to be inevitable. Those who had served there were perhaps less surprised and were not inclined to want to intervene again. But many were frustrated by this outcome as they recalled the sacrifices. Few expressed those sentiments in 1975. Most didn't want to talk about it, and fewer wanted to listen to it. It was over. One veteran commented, "The fall of Saigon was very disheartening to me and I wish I had someone at the time to talk to about it. I thought about the waste of human life and effort as I watched those tanks roll into the presidential palace." He thought about the four friends he had lost there.[64] But in 1975, most veterans were moving on. Or were attempting to move on. As they had learned in Vietnam, grieving would have to wait. And moving on sometimes involves a long and circular path.

9
ENDURING VIETNAM: A STORY THAT HAS NO END

In the summer of 1969, a veteran reporter covered a group of 8,000 men of the 9th Marine Regiment as they prepared to join the first troops in the drawdown of forces. While they waited at Vandegrift Combat Base for flights to Okinawa, there was "little gaiety." No "frolicking" or joking. In one tent, James Sterba found the the men listening to a tape recorder playing Country Joe and the Fish singing their iconic "I Feel Like I'm Fixin' to Die." In another tent, men looked at the June 27 issue of *Life* magazine to find familiar faces. A young marine said, "The people just don't understand what these guys have been through." He predicted, "No one anywhere from now on will be able to tell them anything about fear and bravery and all that other stuff."[1]

There is an intellectual and even a moral tension in trying to summarize the lives of the Vietnam generation in the decades following the war. Each individual has a different account. One might generalize that despite the searing experience many had in Vietnam and despite the indifferent receptions some encountered when they came home, this generation, by almost every measurement, adapted well. But the tension in this assessment is the danger of a Pollyanna-ish view that ignores the pain that many felt — and that many continue to feel.

Focusing on their successes cannot ignore the problems that many faced. And here I am not referring to the short-term problems of negotiating their transition back into civilian life in "the world." They accomplished this with little understanding and few helping hands from their contemporaries. Coming home was not a trivial process, and some experienced problems that were more than transitional. And for too many these problems would turn out to be their companions for a lifetime. Chronic difficulties included physical disabilities, untreated medical conditions, notably those caused by America's own Agent Orange, the nightmares and personal demons of what came to be called post-traumatic stress disorder (one veteran observed that he had moved beyond nightmares to daymares), alcohol and drug abuse, interpersonal tensions, unfulfilled dreams. One marine, speaking about the 567 marines and corpsmen of the 1st Battalion 1st Marines killed in action, said, "To this day, it is difficult to fully comprehend and reckon with the tragedy of these losses. For every death there were at least four times, or five times or maybe six times that many of us wounded. There is no way to know exactly how many. And these wounds included horrible losses of limbs and bodily functions — not the kind you see in the old time western movies. These were wounds that forever changed your life, and inflicted long term suffering and misery."[2]

Far too many Vietnam veterans carried uncomplainingly the hurt of engaging a country that waited too long to say "Thank you for your service" — and then seemed to think that saying this was a magnanimous gesture that provided an adequate gratuity, a sufficient acknowledgment and apology from which all should then move on. One still angry veteran said of this salutation, "Bullshit!! They're just trying to make themselves feel better for the way they shit on us forty-five years ago. They say it automatically, much the same as people say 'Bless you' when some sneeze." He added, "If those other people had to spend just one night inside my nightmares, they would fall to the floor with tears in their eyes." Another said, "People may be more accepting these days, but they still do not want to hear our stories. More recently I am hearing 'Thank you for your service.' Mostly from store clerks who seem to say it as part of their training, or from the children and grandchildren of those who scorned us when we came home. When I hear those words, they really seem hollow . . . I wish they would just not say anything."[3]

The pain endures. There is a risk of generalizing these lingering hurts into the stereotype of a pathetic, haunted, angry generation. The contrary risk is to ignore the personal agonies of too many. Or, perhaps cruelest of all is to dismiss these as personal shortcomings or individual maladies, character flaws, that separate the condition from the experience from which it stemmed.

For those who came home in the first years of the war, from 1965 to 1968 or 1969, their encounters and transitions were sometimes strained, generally uncomfortable, and often disappointing. But they were rarely hostile. This began to change by 1969, as the image of the men fighting the war was filtered through the more negative view of the war itself. The most common manifestations of this were those embarrassing encounters in which the war that had no name was not mentioned. But these sometimes flared into difficult confrontations. From 1969 into the early 1970s, the rapid drawdown of troops from Vietnam increased the number returning at a time when the domestic economy was in a downturn and the stereotype of the Vietnam veteran was the most negative.

Veterans of American wars who have felt

disappointed or frustrated or angry about their reception are not unusual in American history. The veterans of the American War in Vietnam were no exception — they confronted all of these emotions. But the *mutual* discomfort and even the abrasions of their homecoming had no precedent, and these were compounded because they encountered an American public that too often was disappointed or angry or frustrated about the war itself — its inception, its operations, their perception of its conduct, and its conclusion. In retrospect, it is striking that there was not even any pretense of a welcome home except from families and from some neighborhoods or communities. These veterans were a symbol of something their fellow citizens and even their family and friends were trying to forget.

The distinguished American historian Frank Freidel wrote in 1980 that unlike those who served in previous American wars, few of those returning from Vietnam were ever viewed as heroes. "What has distinguished Vietnam veterans from most of their predecessors is . . . that a considerable part of the articulate abhorrence of the war seemed to spill onto them. They returned not as heroes, but as men suspected of complicity in atrocities or feared to be drug addicts. Not only the underprivileged but even the most prestigious were under a cloud."[4]

By April 1975, those who had served in Vietnam watched on television the last scramble to evacuate Saigon. They were seldom surprised at this outcome, but some nonetheless had an emotional reaction to it. One marine said simply that he was "glad it was over," and another said, in frustration, "It stinks." A soldier who had risked his life once to save his M16 rifle now watched all of this equipment abandoned. He felt guilty about leaving behind all those "we were trying to help." Another watching it on TV with his parents exclaimed, "You got to be kidding me! What a waste." A Hamburger Hill veteran said the fall of Saigon "just cemented the attitude that the whole thing was a terrible loss of life for no purpose." Another soldier, who had seen a lot of death, said, "I was appalled and felt tremendously betrayed. That war cost me two years of my young, married life . . . probably fifty years counting the aftermath. However, for over 58,000 of our KIAs, it is a permanent disgrace." Another observed, "I followed the war after we left and wasn't surprised by the fall and pretty disgusted about the whole thing. Lost a lot of friends there."

One veteran would continue to insist, "We didn't lose." He emphasized his point: "We. Didn't. Lose." Instead, "We were withdrawn." Another described this as coming to terms with the conclusion that "it was like everything we did was for nothing. The year I spent putting my ass on the line over there? It was like it didn't matter."[5]

A reporter spent some time with veterans in Denver following the television footage of the last days before Saigon itself fell. One marine, who had been seriously wounded in a fight in which he watched his best friend die and every other man in his squad killed or wounded, now said that the South Vietnamese just "walked away and gave up those provinces as if nobody had ever died there." These Denver veterans were angry with Washington, with what they considered cynicism and hypocrisy, about the unwillingness of the South Vietnamese to fight, and they felt pain about the friends — and the limbs — they had left behind. Yet none of them talked about going back to save the country.[6]

William Ortiz, a Vietnam veteran and the vice president of the National Congress of Puerto Rican Veterans, admitted that the war "messes me up." He often believed that the United States "should step back in and do something, but then I think we shouldn't because so many lives would be lost." Beallsville, Ohio, a blue-collar mining and manufacturing community of 450, lost 7 young men in Vietnam. In April 1975, it was struggling more with jobs and its economy than with the impending fall of Saigon. One father, looking at a high school graduation photo of his son who had died there, teared up as he said, "This little boy lost his life for nothing," and his wife added, "He was our only child." Three young men in Beallsville, one who had served there and two who had lost brothers there, talked about the end of the war and whether the United States should return to support the South Vietnamese. "I think we ought to stay out," one said. The other two agreed.[7]

By a significant margin, most Americans did as well. In the spring of 1975, only 12 percent of Americans thought the United States should send military aid to Vietnam; 78 percent opposed. The veterans of the war did not disagree. The veterans lost again, though, because Americans, in their haste to forget the war, worked to forget those who had served there. *Washington Post* columnist Mary McGrory had long criticized the war. But she also believed the country had an obligation to those who had fought. She caustically asked the nation at the end of 1975, "You remember the Vietnam veteran? There is no particular reason why you should. Hardly anybody does. He had the poor taste to fight in an unpopular war, which made little sense while it was going on and none at all when it was lost." She said that the regular Vietnam veterans lacked "the cachet of the prisoners of war, who were lionized by Richard Nixon for his own purposes." The POWs received parades and gifts. "The grunt just came home."

McGrory pointed out that the old veteran groups did not like this new veteran because he was "unclubbable." She observed that his "contemporaries who had the wit or the money to go to college or Canada look down on the Vietnam vet. Defeat has vindicated them and deepened his sense of being had." And, finally, these new veterans could not escape the stereotype: "When he sees a Vietnam veteran on a television drama, it's likely to be a drug-crazed time bomb or a clean-cut baby killer, and that doesn't add to his self-esteem." She concluded that on top of all of this, the veteran confronted unemployment double the rate of nonveterans of his age, and the GI Bill was inadequate to meet his needs.[8]

This assessment was a pretty comprehensive summary of the world of many Vietnam veterans in the early 1970s. Most Americans did ignore them — many disliked them for what they represented, and some feared them for the dark anger it was believed they harbored. One reporter wrote of the returning veteran, "Silently he is slipping thru the back door of the nation which sent him to war." There were no parades, "no frenzied homecoming celebrations." Instead, the veteran has been "vilified, condemned, ostracized. He has been branded a murderer, a junkie, an undisciplined disgrace." Perhaps

615

most cutting, "for the first time in American military history, he has been labeled a loser." The stories of "heroism and dedication" had "been lost under a sea of public disgust."[9]

Following the Paris accords, the prisoners of war returned home in the early spring of 1973. This was a powerfully emotional moment. One reporter sat in a San Diego bar with a group of veterans, including a marine missing his legs who sat in a wheelchair. They joined an elated nation watching the return celebrated on television. They saw the emaciated POWs coming down the ramp from an airplane, with military and civilian officials waiting to welcome them and their emotional families watching for them, with military bands playing in the background. One of the men watching in the bar wept. This contrasted so sharply with his own homecoming: "Instead of saying, 'welcome home' they gave me the finger." Another veteran told the reporter, "When I got out, all I got from people around me was that Vietnam veterans were drug addicts, murderers, freaked out criminals."[10]

One veteran in Chicago spoke of returning home from Vietnam: "When you're over there, it's supposed to mean something to come home — but it don't mean nothing. You feel excluded." Another, who had left a factory job in Yonkers, New York, came home to find his job had been eliminated. "People don't want to be reminded of you. They don't want to know you've been in Nam."[11]

Certainly most received a warm welcome from family and neighbors — but even among those who cared for them deeply, they frequently confronted a cold silence or at least an absence of curiosity about their war experiences.[12] One came home just before Thanksgiving, and at a large family celebration he expected to "be bombarded by questions and stuff," but no one mentioned Vietnam to him. So he never talked about it to them — for the next forty years. One soldier returned home right before Easter in 1970, and his parents had a big family gathering for him. "It didn't dawn on me till a couple of days later, but not one person said one word to me about anything. They would have asked somebody that went to Florida more questions about their tan . . . And that's how it continued. Nobody — when I think back on it — nobody said a word to me about anything." But another recalled, "First thing Mom asked was to show her my wounds."

Another soldier said that his dad, who had served with the marines on Iwo Jima in World War II, never once asked his son about Vietnam. One said that his parents never understood or wanted to know about his experiences or asked him why he was having flashbacks. He admitted that he was "pissed that too many people could care less about

Vietnam." An injured marine "never talked to nonveterans." He knew that they "wouldn't understand and didn't care anyway." Another found that "there were two kinds of people . . . those who were dead-set against the war and all of us who were there, and those who were not the least bit interested in my problems." He admitted that he was troubled by those who "had successfully dodged the draft, how they did it, and what they had accomplished in the last two years." When Karl Marlantes returned, he was surprised that there were not more people waiting at the airport to welcome him home. "To me, and to my parents, I'd been gone an eternity; to everyone else a flash."[13]

The veterans had been coming home quietly for years, and they remained quiet as they moved on with their lives — or attempted to move on. It was not that they were eager to talk about Vietnam back home, but they were struck by how few even acknowledged that they had been there. One recalled, "It was a big adjustment to come out of war . . . people are going to McDonalds, people are going to the movies. I was like, 'What's going on here? We need to round up some of these people and send them over to help my pals.' "[14]

One returning marine went to Sunday Mass in his New Mexico parish. A parishioner asked him, "Hey, where you been? Haven't seen you in about six weeks." The veteran was angered by this but said nothing, deciding, "So what?" Few encountered hostility in their hometowns, but most confronted indifference. And that seemed okay at first, since these veterans were not eager to talk about what they had been doing. A generation that had learned as youngsters to duck and cover and had spent a year in Vietnam keeping their head down was well prepared to hunker down now. In truth, most veterans preferred not to talk about — or recall — their experiences. "I soon buried Viet Nam so deeply that I could barely remember what I had done on a day-to-day basis." One soldier was back home in Arlington, Virginia, and pumping gas again at the Esso station three weeks after leaving Vietnam. People didn't ask where he had been. He and other veterans were reflecting on what to do next. This was not an easy question to confront for this group of baby boomers. They had lost two or three critical years of their lives. By the early 1970s, the job market was tighter and there were few programs and basically no effective programs that aimed at encouraging people to hire Vietnam veterans. An unemployed black veteran said, "I went to this dumb war and I did my share for my country. But I came home to hard times and no appreciation."[15]

The Veterans Administration in the early 1970s often proved incapable of assisting these newest veterans and their casualties.

When the injured veterans started to seek help in significant numbers, they were competing with the World War II and Korea veterans, who had begun to confront the medical challenges of middle age. There wasn't room for everyone, and the federal budget support was inadequate. Conditions in many hospitals became scandalous.

A *Life* magazine reporter in 1970 studied the "bleak backwaters of our Veterans Administration hospitals." He discovered that the VA then was treating 800,000 patients a year, many from earlier wars, and the hospitals were "disgracefully understaffed with standards far below those of an average community hospital." Doctors at Wadsworth VA Hospital in Los Angeles acknowledged that conditions there were "medieval" and "filthy." Congress then was spending about $1.6 billion a year on the VA medical system — a little less than what the war in Vietnam was costing every month. The report profiled a young marine, a veteran of Khe Sanh, who was paralyzed from the neck down when his vehicle was struck by a rocket. After good medical treatment and physical therapy at the Philadelphia Naval Hospital, he was released from military service and transferred to the Bronx VA Hospital. There he found filth and neglect. The magazine reported, "He is so helpless that he needs almost constant care. But the hospital cannot give it." The facility was greatly understaffed — one night nurse looked after three wards with 140 patients. Patients lay in filthy beds and had to contend with mice and rats, which sometimes crawled on the paralyzed patients. The others put out traps and set up a system to look after them — just as they had in Vietnam. They looked after each other. Killing rats.[16]

Disabled veterans especially found the VA frustrating. They wanted the VA to help prepare them to live good and productive lives. One veteran who left his legs in Vietnam observed that businesses had little interest in disabled vets: "Employers don't make an effort to understand them." So they needed help. But there was not much of a vocational-training program at the VA, and "there's no post-hospital follow-up program." He said that veterans wanted jobs, but "what they most want is meaningful work. They don't want to weave baskets."[17]

Ron Kovic had eagerly joined the marines in 1964 and volunteered for a second tour in Vietnam, where he was permanently paralyzed from the waist down. When he was at St. Albans Naval Hospital in Queens, he remembered what a priest had told him in the hospital in Da Nang: "Your fight is just beginning. Sometimes no one will want to hear what you're going through. You are going to have to learn to carry a great burden and most of your learning will be done

621

alone."[18]

A veteran who suffered from war wounds went to the VA shortly after he returned. "We were treated like dogs," he said. "They wanted nothing to do with Vietnam Vets." He didn't go back for twenty-six years and then found that the VA medical "people were nice, doctors seemed to care. Complete turn-around." This was not an uncommon story among the veterans I interviewed: a negative experience in the first year or two after discharge from the military, then, more often than not decades later, they returned to the VA and had a very good experience. The VA adjusted — American society adjusted. But of course the veterans made the greater adjustments. They had learned to do that in Vietnam. In the first five years following their discharge, Vietnam veterans had higher rates of suicide, accidental death, and homicide than did veterans of their era who had served somewhere other than Vietnam. After five years, the two groups had a similar mortality pattern — with the Vietnam veteran rates having decreased.[19]

One of the disappointments of the Vietnam veterans was how coldly — dismissively even — some veterans of World War II and Korea treated them. This was their fathers' generation, the ones who had supported the general principles that led the United States to Vietnam. The older generation of veterans of course cared about this new generation — but did so warily. Part of this stemmed from a concern about the pressure on finite veterans' benefits. And part of it was a general unease with the values and cultural conduct of the baby boomer generation asserting themselves in the 1960s and '70s. These newest veterans were part of this group.

A Dayton, Ohio, World War II veteran expressed his disappointment with the Vietnam veterans: "Now don't think I hold anything against these young fellas, but you know, my buddies and me, we won our war, and my old man won his war. I know these boys have done all they could and they've been brave — but still they broke that old winning mold." A VFW official described the newest generation of veterans as "smarter, tougher, more dependent on themselves. They don't express any feelings of patriotism, either. Before, veterans were proud to wear their uniforms and say they were veterans. These men can't disappear into civilian life quickly enough."[20]

Veterans described their experiences with the older veterans, many of them family members or neighbors. One said that his uncles, World War II veterans, told him to shut up and go back to work: "It's you guy's fault. We didn't have this trouble in World War II." Another said that some of the older veterans reached out, but others "disrespect us." A veteran with a prosthetic limb tried to join local veterans' organizations, but even with his obvious war injury, they "did not treat me as a fellow veteran." One went to the local American Legion with another veteran and discovered "they were not at all welcoming when they learned we had been in Vietnam." One man who got involved with the American Legion said that most of the men there were World War II veterans and they "didn't even want to really recognize you a whole lot." Another said when he returned to his small Midwestern hometown, "I made friends with two other Vietnam combat veterans," and they "went drinking almost every night, usually at the American Legion. The members never said hello to us or asked us to join the Legion, and this is a very small town, they knew who we were."

As one put it, these older veterans "thought they had the world cornered with their wars, especially the big war." He soon discovered that "many of them thought our war was nothing but a little scrap. I also think that some of them think of us as druggies and had us crossed with the ones on TV in the streets or at Woodstock." This tension persisted. All these years later, a veteran said that "the Greatest Generation never came to grips with" the Vietnam generation. And based on his own experiences, he believed they would "take their thoughts to the grave without so much as a whisper of repentance."

On the other hand, when Chuck Hagel returned to his small Nebraska home town, he found the veterans at the local American Legion and VFW were "completely accepting and proud and . . . encouraging." They were very gracious and made him feel welcome. He wasn't certain if he would have had the same experience in other places.[21]

By the early 1970s, World War II veterans were in leadership positions in the various organizations and at the Veterans Administration. And some of them did reach out. The Veterans of Foreign Wars told their local posts to just ignore "the floppy clothes and long hair" of the Vietnam veterans. But even when they reached out, many Vietnam veterans were not interested in joining these groups at that time. They recognized the differences: "They fought their wars to win, but there's no way we're going to win this war" observed a Vietnam veteran late in 1971.[22]

One reporter spent time with some of the 350 Vietnam veterans who returned to Roswell, New Mexico. He learned that "for the most part they do not want to talk about Vietnam, even to the point of refusing to associate with veterans' organizations. And their feelings about American involvement in Indochina are often ambivalent." Mainly, they wanted to get on with their lives and wipe Vietnam "out of their minds, including for some an occasional nightmare." They wanted to go to school, get a job, get married, get a car, "plant grass in their own yards, watch it grow, then cut it." They did have some adjustment problems. One wife said that she and her husband didn't have much to talk about: "He didn't want to talk about Vietnam and he wasn't interested in my job at the bank." Another veteran had nightmares and told of "screaming in terror when his wife brushes against him at night in bed."[23]

Fitting in and getting on with their lives was difficult when the memories intruded and cried out for attention. It was more than difficult in the early years, when the veterans had to contend with a system that ranged from indifferent to incapable to antagonistic when dealing with psychological stress. One veteran told the Veterans Administration in 1972, I "couldn't sleep and I had a roll call of the dead I processed and many vivid flashbacks of the bodies, smells, and what was there." But "those World War II Veterans that were running the show at the time" told him "to get out of here as we don't deal with this nonsense." The sleepless nights and the memories continued, but he didn't seek help from the VA again for thirty years. In the early 1970s, the head of the House Committee on Veterans Affairs was Texas congressman Olin "Tiger" Teague, a World War II veteran with two Purple Hearts and the Silver Star. He looked out for veterans — at least for his generation of veterans. He called the Vietnam veterans "crybabies." This sentiment was shared by some of the senior leadership at the VA.[24]

These newest veterans sought informal gatherings rather than organizations. A group enrolled at the Chicago Circle Campus of the University of Illinois got together to talk at their veterans' club. "Guys sit around and tell war stories, but we don't talk about gruesome experiences." If anyone boasted about killing enemy soldiers, "there's usually a very bad response." And even though most came to oppose the war, they had no interest in joining groups such as Vietnam Veterans Against the War. One veteran who was trying to recruit members for that group said that "probably 80 percent of the Viet Nam veterans don't want to join any kind of protest." They "just want to forget about the war and go back to whatever they were doing."[25]

Many veterans wanted to continue with their education, but they discovered that by the early 1970s, the GI Bill program in support of veteran education was inadequate. The support was in the form of a monthly payment to the individual veteran that was not always sufficient to cover tuition, especially at private schools. And even when it did, the remaining funding seldom covered living costs, especially for married veterans.

In 1977, 30 percent of the veterans eligible for benefits were enrolled. Veterans were 12 percent of college students that year. For those considering college, there were issues in addition to financial ones. One veteran described his decision not to enroll in the University of Minnesota but instead in a nearby private school because he thought he would encounter fewer protesters there: "Being a Vietnam veteran was a scourge for many years." He found himself with students who hadn't served, and "it was like a black mark to be a Vietnam veteran" in the early 1970s. Another, at the "peak of the antiwar movement," just "hid" his service.[26]

One day Fred Downs, who had lost part of an arm and wore a prosthesis with a hook, was walking across the University of Denver campus where he was enrolled. He encountered another student, who stopped and said "Hi," and then pointed at the prosthetic hand and asked, "Get that in Vietnam?" When the veteran said yes and began to continue the conversation, the other student said, "Serves you right," and walked away. The veteran just stood there, "rooted, too confused with hurt, shame, and anger to react."[27]

They persevered, knowing that if they could complete their education they would be more competitive in the job market. In 1971, the Bureau of Labor Statistics did a survey of Vietnam veteran employment. They learned that for veterans under age twenty-four, the most recent group, the unemployment rate was 14.6 percent, while for nonveterans of the same age it was 10.8 percent. African American veterans were suffering the most — as were all young black Americans. For those under twenty-four, unemployment was 20.9 percent, while for black nonveterans of the same age it was 17.4 percent. Many employers were not persuaded that military service — in Vietnam, at least — was a positive factor. As one unemployed marine officer with a Purple Heart said, "Most employers just don't give a damn how many Purple Hearts you've won or how well you can lead men."[28]

When one veteran went for a job interview in 1971, the employer looked him right in the eye and told him, "We don't hire Vietnam veterans." He was very angry, wondering, "What do you gotta do to get a break here?" He was neither a killer nor a heroin junkie, he said, "not somebody who's going to suddenly go berserk and, you know, start killing everybody at the workplace." He stopped listing his military service on his job applications and finally wrote to his congressman about his difficulty getting a job. The congressman managed to get him and two other unemployed veterans a temporary job at the local VA center, as plasterers.

One expressed his frustration with the

catch-22 they faced. Before he went into the army, he had trouble getting a job because employers did not want to hire and train people who were still facing military service. So after he got out, having completed this service, "Employers would not hire Vietnam vets as we were purported to be psychotic and they were afraid we would go postal." So he stopped telling people he was a Vietnam veteran because he needed to support his family.

In the popular early 1970s television detective series *Kojak,* the lead character, played by Telly Savalas, suggested to his detectives that when they were looking for leads to find a murderer they should check to see if there were any recently discharged Vietnam veterans living nearby. The hit show *Hawaii Five-0* had several episodes involving psychotic and criminal Vietnam veterans. One veteran wrote an essay in *TV Guide* protesting the coverage of veterans in television drama shows. "If I acted according to what I have seen on television, I should probably be harboring extreme psychopathic tendencies that prompt me to shoot up heroin with one hand while fashioning plastique with the other, as my war-and-drug-crazed mind flashes back to the rice paddy where I fragged my lieutenant." An official with the New York City Office for Veterans Action believed that the television portrayal of Vietnam veterans "completely turned off employers."[29]

The employment problem was complicated by more than the stereotypes and the hostility. The downturn in the economy did not help. Neither did the time lost in service. Nor the fact that infantry and other military skills were not considered very transferable. But the stereotype, the scary image and the negative view of conduct of the war, made it still more difficult. Vietnam veteran James Webb wrote of a young radio operator in his platoon who had lost an arm to shrapnel. He could not get a job, a real job. The economy worked against him, as did the assumptions of potential employers: *Vietnam Veteran, Drugs. My Lai. Walking time bombs.* Another marine, whose legs were paralyzed due to a battlefield spinal cord injury, got the young veteran a good job.[30]

A veteran who was a West Point graduate and had a degree from the University of Michigan Law School interviewed for a job with a large Washington law firm, "the first formal job interview" of his life. "I was asked whether I committed any war crimes in Vietnam. It blew my mind."[31] Another veteran said that "people seemed to be scared of me; thought we all carried a rifle and shot people; some felt ashamed they didn't go to Vietnam." He tried to open a bank account after he returned, but when the teller learned he had recently returned from Vietnam, she was frightened and "just threw the papers at me." At a job interview, when the interviewer asked if the applicant had served in Vietnam, "he was disgusted when he learned I had served."

The job market in the early '70s was a tough one. The Vietnam veterans were younger than their World War II and Korean War predecessors. Many had not held a real job before they went into the service. In addition, they carried the burden of their war. The anecdotal evidence confirms that some employers were not comfortable hiring Vietnam veterans due to the stereotype of drug addiction and hostility. So in 1971, it was the case that veterans, black and white, had higher unemployment rates. But this disadvantage disappeared over a few years as the veterans completed their education and/or obtained more experience in the labor market. Their conduct, their hard work helped to eliminate the negative stereotypes. Unfortunately, racial differences continued. A 1980 study found that white veterans age thirty to thirty-four, essentially the baby boomer Vietnam-era cohort, were more likely to be employed full time and earning more money than their black counterparts. The Hispanic veterans lagged even more.[32]

The confounding thing about those early years was that many Americans accepted at least some elements of the stereotype of the

Vietnam veterans. Yet at the same time they expressed support for them — whether this support was always perceived by the veterans is another matter, as is the unanswerable question as to whether it was more than superficial. But in the summer of 1971, the Senate Committee on Veterans Affairs commissioned a survey and found that 81 percent of the public "agreed strongly" with the statement, "Veterans of the armed forces today deserve the same warm reception given to returning servicemen of earlier wars"; 13 percent "agreed somewhat." This was not hostility. It is interesting, but not really surprising, that in the eighteen-to-twenty-five-year age group, the boomer generation, only 69 percent agreed strongly and 18 percent agreed somewhat — still a strong margin of support even if a little more reluctant to embrace the veterans warmly.[33]

These expressions of support for the veterans continued strong — and grew. A Harris poll in November 1979 asked people if they felt "warm or favorably" toward Vietnam veterans. They emphatically expressed warmth and favor, averaging 9.8 on a 10-point scale. Another Harris survey of that year found that 83 percent "agreed strongly" that the Vietnam veterans deserved respect and 14 percent agreed somewhat. These findings were important, but there were continuing subtleties in the public's attitudes.[34]

The various surveys suggest that sympathy, or perhaps gratitude, and not admiration were the driving variables. For example, a 1980 survey that found 97 percent of respondents supportive of the veterans also revealed that 64 percent of this same sample believed that those who served during the war "were made suckers" and only 27 percent disagreed with this observation. Vietnam veterans too agreed that they had been "suckers," but by a narrower 54 percent to 44 percent margin. More striking were the different perceptions of the veterans themselves. A few examples: 39 percent of the general public believed that they suffered from "mental or emotional problems," while 34 percent of the veterans agreed. Some differences were even sharper: 38 percent of the public thought the Vietnam veterans had employment problems while 48 percent of the veterans thought they did; 24 percent of the public thought the veterans had drug and alcohol problems while 15 percent of the veterans did. Most intriguing, the public believed more than the veterans did that the veterans suffered from discrimination (15 percent compared to 12 percent), had disillusionment with government (9 percent to 6 percent), and had problems with "insufficient benefits" (8 percent to 4 percent). On the other hand, the veterans were more likely than the general public to describe one of their issues as "money problems" (10 percent veterans and 5 percent general public).[35]

President Jimmy Carter defeated Gerald Ford in 1976 and was inaugurated in January 1977. He reached out to the veterans and kept reminding people to separate the war from the warriors. And he, along with Vietnam veteran Max Cleland, the director of the VA, did much to support veterans' programs. But probably even more than Carter, President Ronald Reagan (1981–1989) rhetorically and eloquently endorsed and embraced the veterans. He welcomed them into the American narrative. If he backed off from an early claim that Vietnam was a "noble cause," he continued to salute those who served there as "heroes." And the public attitude continued to shift positively in support of veterans. When the Reagan administration was looking to address a major budget deficit with budget cuts, 81 percent of the public disapproved of any cuts to veterans' benefits. Four years later when given the option, 86 percent said the government should cut defense spending before it cut veterans' benefits.[36]

In the several years following the fall of Saigon, many things combined to facilitate the transition of the veterans and the public's view of them. Perhaps time is the most important variable. People moved on from Vietnam and the nation faced an economic downturn, the Arab oil embargo and greatly increased energy costs, a rapid growth in inflation, confrontations with Iran, and instability in parts of Central America. More directly, there was greater support for the Veterans Administration, especially for its programs that recognized the needs of its youngest veterans, including counseling and physical therapy. Congress increased the VA budget from just under $7.5 billion in 1969 to $19.3 billion in 1976. (Given the higher inflation rates, looking at this in constant 2011 dollars, the budget increased by 68 percent. It was the highest level of support in constant dollars since 1947.) And the VA began hiring more veterans. By 1985, 20 percent of all employees of this major agency had served in Vietnam.[37]

There were several critical developments along with the growth in budget support. For many veterans, there was finally some slow acknowledgment by the Veterans Administration and Congress of the toxic effects of Agent Orange, and in 1980 the American Psychiatric Association recognized a new clinical condition, post-traumatic stress disorder. These changes extended a stronger helping hand to the Vietnam generation. A crucial development, substantive as well as symbolic, was the dedication of the Vietnam Veterans Memorial on the National Mall on November 13, 1982. This was more than a transient gratuity; it was an enduring national monument.

Related to this process of moving on was President Jimmy Carter's 1977 order providing pardons for those charged with or convicted of draft evasion in the 1960s. It was a controversial move at the time, but it had the effect finally of putting behind another major division of the war.[38]

President Carter's appointment of Vietnam veteran Max Cleland, a thirty-four-year-old triple amputee, as head of the Veterans Administration in 1977 was important not only for its symbolism but also for what it actually provided. Cleland became a vivid and moving example of what his generation of veterans could accomplish. He confronted a senior management team that had been there since the 1940s. "They had not dealt with genuine combat casualties fresh from the battlefield since the early 1950s." He learned that the VA was sending out to young veterans Guy Lombardo records as "morale boosters." "Guy Lombardo for kids like me who had been raised on rock and roll? Are you kidding?" In 1980, he dedicated a new VA hospital in the Bronx. Congress had appropriated money to raze the old structure that *Life* magazine had featured, with its rats, in 1970.[39]

In 1979, Cleland assessed the state of his fellow Vietnam veterans. He said that "intangibles" continued to hurt this group the most.

Each veteran who served in an American war wanted to believe that "what he did was fine and noble and that his sacrifices made a difference and counted for something." Vietnam veterans had been denied that satisfaction, so he and the others now "have to come to terms with that and pick up our lives and move on." He said that most had done just that. About 65 percent had used the GI Bill, nearly 60 percent of them to attend college. And he pointed out that the unemployment rate for veterans was now lower than that of nonveterans of the same age. The median income of veterans was higher than that of their counterparts. He acknowledged, however, that unemployment for minority veterans continued to lag. Cleland expressed his concern about the persistence of drug and alcohol problems among veterans and assured them that he was asking Congress for a "psychological readjustment counseling program" to support those veterans "who need it."[40]

The returning veterans brought back two significant medical conditions that were considered unique to their war, one of which was unique. This involved a whole range of serious medical problems that resulted from exposure to the herbicides that came to be categorized under the most common and most toxic of them: Agent Orange. This was an infectious time bomb that veterans carried with them — and that of course the Vietnamese — perhaps one million or more — carried with them as well.

By the late 1970s, a number of veterans who had been exposed to the herbicides raised questions with the VA, health officials, and Congress about the significant health problems they were experiencing, and they insisted these had to do with Agent Orange. The Veterans Administration resisted making this linkage. Even as they were selectively determining some conditions to be "service-related," they insisted there was no scientific evidence that exposure to Agent Orange led to conditions that many veterans developed following deployment. Some VA caseworkers were suspicious, though, and along with some veterans and their advocates began pushing hard for a major investigation into this defoliant. In 1978, the CBS affiliate in Chicago, WBBM, aired the powerful documentary *Agent Orange: Vietnam's Deadly Fog,* which persuasively made the case that this herbicide had significant human health dangers. Then Congress got involved. The major companies that had manufactured the several herbicides resisted any connection with medical problems; nevertheless, in 1984, they settled a class-action suit with a group of plaintiffs. Most considered the settlement inadequate, but it increased the pressure on the VA and on Congress. The VA incrementally accepted responsibility for some conditions relating to Agent Orange, even if not accepting the causal relationships.

By 1991, it was impossible to ignore this situation. Congress — and thus the VA — defined a number of cancers and nervous system conditions as being presumptively related to Agent Orange exposure and thus eligible for medical and disability coverage. In 2015, a half million Vietnam veterans were on the Agent Orange Registry, which provided for monitoring and medical support. By 2016, there were fourteen diseases on the list that were presumed to result from Agent Orange. There has been far less willingness to extend the same scientific findings and medical assumptions — and financial compensation — to the Vietnamese.[41]

Early on in the war, doctors and counselors observed symptoms of emotional trauma among some of the veterans. A psychiatrist at New York University who had treated veterans of three wars said, "We have identified an entire post–Viet Nam syndrome." He described it as a condition in which "most of these guys have a profound distrust of other people. In Viet Nam they learned you couldn't trust anybody. After they get back they have nightmares. They can't sleep." Within a few years, other counselors and psychiatrists observed this and talked about "alienation from society and from themselves, an inability to express grief for dead buddies, apathy, distrust, frustration." They were increasingly describing this as a distinct syndrome, a "traumatic neurosis" or, commonly, "Post–Vietnam Syndrome," which some were abbreviating and thus informally certifying as PVS.[42]

Ironically, a customized, unique label for those Vietnam veterans with identifiable psychiatric reactions ended up stigmatizing this generation. They were the whining baby boomer generation, and they just needed to grow up and get over it. This observed condition was not singular, of course, for it was as old as warfare. Whether Soldier's Heart or shell shock or combat fatigue — it had afflicted Homer's Odysseus and Shakespeare's King Henry IV. It took awhile for professionals — and for the public — to recognize that this generation of veterans was stricken by a clear medical condition.[43]

Veterans spoke about alcohol problems and continuing apprehension — and persistent images and memories. One described combat as "a very traumatic experience that you do not forget — seeing your friend wounded or killed; then the dreams continue over and over." Another "considered suicide and had the gun to my head many times. I couldn't find the courage to do it. A couple times I put one bullet in the chamber and would spin it and pull the trigger. That's the way I felt back then; that I was a coward for not doing it as I had no peace of mind and guilty as heck and friends I knew and didn't know died. It was all such a waste." One found that as he drank more, he was "not the happy drunk I used to be." He had marital and employment problems, and when he went to a Veterans Outreach Center and the secretary asked his name, "I immediately broke down, cried and couldn't even tell her my name." His "thoughts of Vietnam and the numerous bodies kept coming back, during any quiet time." A man who had been in very difficult combat situations said, "There is no possible way for me to describe it to anyone. The depression, the fear, the anger, the nightmares are beyond my words."

For one veteran, the "ghosts and bad dreams" started soon after he came home. He continues to have to watch his temper; it "has cost me things in life, but I have never even raised my voice. The look I give them is enough." He admits he "has a hard time letting people into my life. I am afraid of losing them, and that is sad." He continues to "have a problem with Orientals" but is "working on it." This man acknowledges "survivor's guilt." He saw a number of men killed, and he was wounded twice. So he asks, "Why me?" When he does have contact with the men with whom he served, they never "tell stories of death," but instead recall one occasion when they stood under a 150-foot waterfall to cool off and to wash away the dirt. A few years ago, a "buddy" looked him up and thanked him for saving his life. The veteran had forgotten the incident until his visitor reminded him. The visiting veteran had his jaw shot away and was choking on his own blood when his buddy cleared his throat and turned him over to drain his throat and windpipe. The grateful survivor showed him pictures of his five children, children he never would have had if he hadn't survived that day.

One veteran spent years wondering why he was spared and his friends were not. He was particularly troubled that one of his buddies had died in a foxhole this survivor had dug — but not deep enough. He thought that if he had done a better job, this friend would be alive. Finally, he shared his regrets with the dead soldier's son, who told his father's friend, "Stop digging that hole any deeper after thirty-nine years." That helped. A pilot recalled his last flight with his back seater and friend who was about to meet his wife in Hawaii on R&R. The pilot tried to convince his friend not to fly more missions before the R&R but they went on one more mission together. They were shot down and this pilot was able to eject, but his friend was not. Years later he still wondered if he could have done something to save his friend and whether he was responsible for his death.

The VA increased support for drug and alcohol problems as well as psychiatric counseling throughout the '70s, but it was still with an understanding that this was a special need of this generation of veterans. Meanwhile, the American Psychiatric Association was working on a new edition of *Diagnostic and Statistical Manual of Mental Disorders (DSM)*, the main authority for clinical conditions. The committee assigned to this task found the evidence overwhelming that there was a medical condition that they called post-traumatic stress disorder (PTSD). This was an important landmark recognition — one that would expand the support for this disorder and would remove the singularity, the idiosyncrasy, of the Vietnam Syndrome. The *DSM-III* was published in 1980 and had a major impact on several significant medical and behavioral areas, most certainly PTSD. Having this as an officially recognized condition did not always make it easy for a Vietnam veteran to acknowledge that he might be suffering from it, but for any who did take this step, the new identification meant that he suffered from a medical condition rather than some sort of personal weakness or flaw. And this was important.

Karl Marlantes, who acknowledged his own problems, reminded everyone of the toxic nature of the disease. Wives endured "the deeply disturbing experience of living with a man with post-traumatic stress disorder without knowing where all the craziness was coming from." He underlined this: "For every veteran who goes through a divorce, a wife goes through one too. For every veteran alone in the basement, there is a wife upstairs, bewildered, isolated, and in despair from the dark cloud of war that hangs over daily family life."[44]

One veteran described his delayed and difficult trials, through which "somehow my wife stayed with me through it all." He had been involved in the advance into Cambodia in 1970. "When I got home from Vietnam I felt numb. I didn't want to talk about the war. I'd lost a friend in combat, seen things and done things that would shock the people who knew me before I got drafted. I also felt alienated by the social chaos. I bottled up two years of my life and did my best to slip back into civilian life . . . Like a lot of us, I kept it all to myself until I couldn't." He dealt with some "mild" depression that he didn't relate to his war experiences and was successful in business but worked harder than was healthy. He thought this pattern helped him to "keep the lid on." But when the Twin Towers crumbled on 9/11 and he and his wife worried about their son who was nearby, his memories flared up. He was obsessed by the war in Afghanistan and had frequent nightmares about Vietnam. Within a short time, his was "a family in trouble." He joined some therapy groups at the VA and over the years he has come "back on my feet, but not back to the life" he knew before. He still meets with a VA Vietnam veterans group but now "only occasionally do we talk about Vietnam."

By the late '70s, things were improving, but the stereotypes persisted. Hollywood played on them and extended them. The 1978 movie *Coming Home* secured Academy Awards for Jane Fonda and Jon Voight. It was a movie about Vietnam veterans that featured the physical and emotional trauma of the war. These veterans were less threatening than the haunted Robert De Niro in Martin Scorsese's 1976 *Taxi Driver.* At the 1979 Academy Awards, *Coming Home* competed with *The Deer Hunter* for honors, and each won several Oscars. *The Deer Hunter* won the best picture award for its portrayal of three young Pennsylvania steelworkers who went to Vietnam together. They were captured and tortured by sadistic guards and finally managed to escape, but they suffered the physical and the emotional wounds of war that played out in a gruesome Russian roulette scene in Saigon as the city was falling to the Communists. Many protested that *The Deer Hunter* was racist for its portrayal of the Vietnamese. Jane Fonda agreed, describing it as the Pentagon's view of the war, although she acknowledged that she had not seen it. An army veteran who had extended tours in Vietnam and then went to Harvard and Oxford said, "What I find offensive is the feeling that all Viet-Nam vets are latent psychos or, like Jon Voight in *Coming Home,* sensitive and guilt-ridden. These are comic-book caricatures."[45]

As *The Deer Hunter* and *Coming Home* competed for best picture in the spring of 1979, a new epic was released, Francis Ford Coppola's *Apocalypse Now,* starring Marlon Brando, Martin Sheen, and Robert Duvall. It was an expensive, powerful movie that built loosely upon Joseph Conrad's *Heart of Darkness* and presented most of the stereotypes of the Vietnam experience.

There were no heroes here. *Apocalypse Now* was Woodstock with blood and guns and a near total absence of men with moral principle. The movie had drugs and music and surfing. This juxtaposed easily with a happy "I love the smell of napalm in the morning" mood. The soldiers had a casual indifference toward the Vietnamese. When the patrol boat pressing upriver came across Vietnamese civilians carrying food and supplies, their crew started shooting. One said, "Let's kill them all . . . why not?" They did.

The enigmatic Colonel Kurtz (Marlon Brando) says at the end that the war required a special type: "You have to have men who are moral . . . and at the same time who are able to utilize their primordial instincts to kill without feeling . . . without passion . . . without judgment . . . without judgment! Because it's judgment that defeats us."

Many consider *Apocalypse Now* one of the great films of all time. Film critic Roger Ebert wrote that the film "achieves greatness not by analyzing our 'experience in Vietnam,' but by re-creating, in characters and images, something of that experience."[46] A veteran, on the other hand, expressed his frustration with the images in the movie, "druggies and baby killers." He was brought up in a strict family and was an altar boy, but he wondered why the movies of his childhood about World War II were "good plots with lots of duty, honor, and country" but his war was reduced to drugs and violence, "like we were of a weird generation or something. Seemed they couldn't find any heroes among us."

It was hard to escape the stereotypes when they were presented in well-done, award-winning films. Interestingly, even as Americans by the late '70s were embracing and supporting the Vietnam veterans, it was still the case that of the 5 percent of respondents to a poll who had seen *Apocalypse Now,* 61 percent thought the movie provided "a fairly accurate picture of what the war in Vietnam was like." Thirty percent had seen *Coming Home,* and 63 percent found it a "realistic picture of war."[47]

A number of veterans disagreed, saying that movies like *Apocalypse Now* and *Taxi Driver* were "depressing, as they projected the Vietnam veteran as a loser" and all those who served there as "a mentally deranged group." One said the films "made me sad and I didn't relate to them." Another realized they were meant to entertain, but when someone said they were so "realistic," he had to walk away. One veteran commented that in these movies, "the leaders were incompetent, the soldiers were heavy drug users, and they routinely killed innocent civilians." These images increased what he called "the negative perspective that all members of the military were like that."

In the spring of 1979, as *Apocalypse Now* was showing in the theaters, President Carter proclaimed a week to honor Vietnam veterans. Mayor Ed Koch kicked this off with a program in New York City. Marine veteran Bobby Muller spoke at City Hall Plaza to a group of about one hundred people who turned out for the event. In an interview before the program, he said that "going to war is a landmark experience in the life of an individual," but those who fought in Vietnam learned "very quickly to repress it, keep it secret, shut up about it, because people either considered you a sucker or some kind of psychopath who killed women and children."[48]

Muller was a paraplegic and activist who had spent time in the VA hospital in the Bronx. He told the small crowd at City Hall Plaza that the veterans at the hospital had to cope with the physical deterioration of the facility, the lack of attention from staff, and a view that Americans considered them "Lieutenant Calley types, junkies, crazed psychos or dummies that couldn't find their way to Canada." He said this was especially hurtful "when you remember the pride we had. We fought hard and we fought well." A few days later, Muller was at the White House with a group of 400, mainly Vietnam veterans. President Carter pledged to support a study of the impact of Agent Orange and assured them that the country was ready to "change its heart, its mind, and its attitude" toward them: "Our nation has not done enough to respect, honor, recognize and reward the special heroism" of the Vietnam veterans.[49]

Jan Scruggs was one of the veterans at the White House gathering that President Carter convened on Memorial Day 1979. A young army veteran with a Purple Heart, Jan Scruggs recalled "how bad it was coming back from Vietnam" in the early 1970s. "We were so vilified, and it was so hurtful. In one sense it wasn't personal. People could not separate the war from the warrior." He would end up devoting his life to assisting the nation in accomplishing this separation.[50]

Following his discharge from the army, Scruggs used the GI Bill to attend American University, where he studied what was described as combat fatigue — and then Post-Vietnam Syndrome — in the early 1970s. This study gave him a greater understanding of and concern about the status of veterans and of their support.[51]

When the president talked about finding ways to remember the service of the Vietnam veterans, Scruggs already had a plan for doing that. After seeing *The Deer Hunter,* he had resolved that those who had died in Vietnam needed a memorial, as did those who served there — and he would work to make it happen. Admitting that he was sometimes naïve and always stubborn, Jan Scruggs, along with other veterans who joined his team, notably Robert Doubek and Jack Wheeler, and then men like the formidable Jim Webb and Thomas Carhart, took on the task of securing congressional approval for a memorial on the National Mall, raising money to construct this, and developing a design for it. This turned out to be intimidating and remarkably complicated, marked by political, cultural, and aesthetic obstacles and burdened with the still fresh emotions of the American War in Vietnam. It was a task for which characteristics such as naïveté and stubbornness were essential, along with indefatigable energy, laser focus, and contagious enthusiasm — and confidence.

On November 13, 1982, the Vietnam Veterans Memorial was dedicated near the Lincoln Memorial on the National Mall. The trail from Memorial Day 1979 had been rocky and contentious, marred by disputes along the way. Perhaps not unlike many trails that these participants had walked in Vietnam. The greatest controversy was over the design proposed by the young Yale University architecture student Maya Lin. It provided for a simple polished black granite wall that would include the names of all the men and women who died in Vietnam or died later as a direct result of injuries suffered in Vietnam. In 1979, there were nearly 58,000 American servicemen and -women who qualified to be included on the proposed memorial. Some veterans and their supporters were horrified at Lin's design — calling it a "black gash of shame." The black was symbolic of this perceived insult — critics pointed out that all the other memorials in Washington were white marble. And they all had statuary or inspiring, uplifting salutes, such as the nearby Washington Monument. Early supporters such as Webb and Carhart moved into opposition, as did an early benefactor, Texas businessman Ross Perot. They wanted something heroic rather than funereal. Perot called

Lin's design "a cemetery" and a "slap in the face" of veterans. The novelist Tom Wolfe described it as a "tribute to Jane Fonda" and the antiwar movement. And for some other critics, racism was right below, if not on, the surface, and they expressed shock at the idea of a Vietnam memorial designed by "an Oriental."[52]

The politics of the war, the political divisions in the United States in the election of 1980, the genuinely different views of how to remember Vietnam, the critical oversight of various arts commissions and U.S. Capitol overseers — all these made for a very difficult situation. In the fall of 1982, the various parties and the Reagan administration agreed on a compromise that fully satisfied no one but allowed the dedication of the Wall to proceed. President Reagan had been very supportive of the veterans but found himself in the middle of this controversy. His representative in the conversations, Secretary of Interior James Watt, was not always the most nimble in these matters. But when the Vietnam Veterans Memorial Fund commissioned the sculptor Frederick Hart to complete a statue of three soldiers and to place a conspicuous American flag at the center of the wall, the secretary issued the final authorization.

Even though the statue was not yet completed, the dedication of the Wall took place over Veterans Day in November 1982. There was a five-day National Salute to Vietnam Veterans. At the National Cathedral on November 10, people began reading the names of the 57,939 men and women whose names were on the Wall. Reading about 1,000 names an hour, the remembrance concluded on November 12. President Reagan had decided at the last moment not to attend the ceremony at the Wall. There was fear that the antiwar protesters there would focus on him, and his advisers were not comfortable linking him with a memorial that was still controversial. But when there was some criticism of him for this decision, he and Mrs. Reagan came to the cathedral unannounced and remained there for a time while the names were being read. The parade preceding the November 13 dedication was a collage of the Vietnam War. It was led by General William Westmoreland, who left the reviewing stand to join the march, and included state units and representatives of the Vietnam Veterans Against the War. It brought in veterans in jungle fatigues, in dress uniforms, and in wheelchairs, Sioux veterans in headdress, men trying to call cadence and march seriously, others loping casually along, and some carrying signs with the names of friends who were lost. About 150,000 people stood along Constitution Avenue to watch some 15,000 marchers.[53]

Mary McGrory described the celebration, especially the parade, as helping with reconciliation. But she pointed out that veterans had taken this on. "Naturally they had to organize it themselves, just as they had to raise the money for their wall, just as they had to counsel each other in their rap centers, just as they had to raise the cry about Agent Orange." She was delighted by the "general raffishness" of the parade, with men out of step marching together and enjoying each other. "With their beards, their ponytails, they looked like their demonstrating contemporaries of 15 years ago." Here prowar and antiwar veterans embraced each other for what they shared.[54]

The controversy over the design did not end at this celebration, but by the time Frederick Hart's statue was dedicated two years later, it was pretty much concluded. President Reagan spoke positively about the Wall and the names embossed on a granite surface that reflected the Washington Monument and the Lincoln Memorial. And he spoke to the veterans: "Those who fought in Vietnam are part of us, part of our history. They reflected the best in us. No number of wreaths, no amount of music and memorializing will ever do them justice but it is good for us that we honor them and their sacrifice. And it's good that we do it in the reflected glow of the enduring symbols of our Republic."[55]

Individual antagonisms remained, but most acknowledged that Maya Lin's Wall, supplemented by the statue, provided a place for healing. In 1993, the Vietnam Women's Memorial was dedicated at the site — a moving statue showing four figures: a nurse holding a wounded soldier, another nurse looking up as if for a helicopter, and a third nurse holding the wounded man's helmet and looking sadly at the ground. It recognized the women who served in the military in Vietnam, almost all as medical personnel where daily they handled and confronted and comforted those bearing the terrible wounds of the war.[56]

Richard Harwood and Haynes Johnson, two reporters who had covered the war, reflected in 1982 on the war over the Wall. They wrote of the hurt and the rage of the "members of the generation who were not given the political luxury of changing their minds and who came home to find themselves, in many cases, ignored at best, and at worst, regarded and treated as war criminals." Out of that rage, out of their "desire for recognition and respect, for what they had gone through, and out of their pride as soldiers, the Vietnam memorial was born. Not surprisingly, even that simple longing for national understanding brought with it controversies and anger over what the memorial should be and what the war had meant."[57]

One veteran had been troubled by the reports about the design of the Wall and was not sure about Maya Lin, but when he finally went to visit, he said, "Seeing it has become the Holy Grail for Vietnam Veterans." Another described it as "a place of healing like being in a church all by yourself." And on the same theme, one said that "the Wall is my holy ground." When he first visited it and approached the wall with his wife and children, "I cried and went off by myself and cried some more." Of the men remembered there, "I will never forget them." One found it "overwhelming," a "moving experience beyond what I could of imagined." And one who looked up the names of several friends said of going to the Wall, "The setting and the site are beautiful. The grounds were immaculate and the respect and reverence was everywhere. It was like going into a great cathedral." As far as he was concerned, Maya Lin "did a remarkable job."

An army medic who had been in major battles and was on 100 percent disability due to PTSD, waited for more than twenty years before he went to the Wall. "I went at night and walked up and down twice. I sat on the grass and tried to remember names and dates and all I got was a blank. I cried when I thought about those who died in my arms or as I worked on them. I could see their faces, see their wounds, hear their cries. I was the last thing some of these men saw, and I couldn't even remember their goddamned names." A veteran who worked with Graves Registration left a note behind: "You were young, some of you not so young, you were kids, you were men. Some of you I never saw. Some of you were just reports, coordinates, and places listed on maps, you were missing. Some of you were listed in places where our Government said we weren't. So I just gave you 'coordinates unknown.' "[58]

One veteran wrote of how America "had done its best to forget" the Vietnam War. But now, seeing the names "stretching down long expanses of black granite at the new Vietnam Veterans Memorial, is to remember. The war was about names, each name a special human being who never came home." He encountered other veterans who were crying, and he was crying himself. "I cried for the men who had been there, for their families, for the country, for myself. I cried because I couldn't help it. It was beyond knowing." When he mentioned crying to another veteran he encountered, who owned a Cleveland bar, this man said, "We all did. We all did."[59]

One marine, after visiting the Wall and seeing the names of seven men in his platoon who had been killed by friendly fire, wrote:

I cried, but not enough, nowhere near
   enough.

I carried on.
We moved out an hour later, First Platoon
    on point.
I passed the night dug in next to a 4-deuce
    mortar,
My insides jerking each time it blasted out
    another load of what blew you to bits.
Now I live here and you live on this wall.
You live in my life, too.[60]

Over the years, most veterans have visited
the Wall, a tangible and a symbolic place
where they can return to remember and to
grieve. In November 1984, a young Port Arthur, Texas, veteran came to the Wall. Now
living outside Washington, he had been to the
memorial a number of times. He had served
in Vietnam with the 101st and had watched a
number of his friends die. He was haunted
by a memory of someone who ran toward
him when they were on patrol in a village.
He shot at the approaching figure — and
killed a young boy. He thought of him often.
Jeffrey Davis drank a lot and argued with
loved ones. His mother said, "He became
obsessed with his Vietnam experience." That
November night, Davis sat near the Wall with
some other veterans. They talked and he
cried. They tried to comfort him, but he only
wept and did not want to talk. Finally, he
walked off into the darkness, and leaning
against an oak tree, he shot himself in the

head. Jeffrey Davis's name is not on the Wall.[61]

In the 1980s, there were alarming claims that suicide was epidemic among Vietnam veterans — with some insisting that the figures were as high as 50,000, nearly as many as had died in Vietnam. A major study in 1990 determined that these stories were greatly exaggerated — in fact, the suicide rate among Vietnam veterans was a fraction of this number, but even an estimated 9,000 is a tragic number. This was nearly 25 percent higher than other veterans or nonveterans of similar ages. A subsequent study concluded that among Vietnam veterans, the highest risk of suicide was among those who had been wounded more than once and hospitalized as a result. Combat trauma was a factor. A major study completed by the VA in 2012 determined that veterans of the Vietnam age group, fifty to sixty-nine, had suicide rates higher than those of nonveterans. And older veterans had far higher rates than younger ones. Troublingly, those who had been treated by the VA had even higher rates than other veterans. Of course, some of those with more serious forms of depression or PTSD were under VA care.[62]

The veterans have gotten together more often as they have aged. For friendship, for remembering, for support. Whereas in the first years after the war most had little interest in gathering with veterans' groups or even reuniting with those with whom they had served, this changed for many in the 1990s and after. Unit reunions are more common, although they still are not for everyone. "I guess you try to forget about it as much as possible and move on," one said. Even though some of the men in his unit encourage him to join them, "I have a hard time with it. You know, it's like, do I want to bring this back up to the surface again?"

And while some have returned to Vietnam, others have avoided going back. One said, "I have never gone back to Vietnam and I didn't want to go in the first place." Another had gone back to Vietnam many times — "in my dreams and flashbacks." That was enough. Besides, "I couldn't stand the heat anymore." A veteran said that when people ask him when he was in Vietnam, he replies "last night." Those who have returned wanted to see places again, to show and to share with family members, to meet and reach out to Vietnamese people, to remember or to grieve, and hopefully to conclude the chapter of their lives. Some have done this by volunteering in Vietnamese clinics or schools, or by joining efforts to locate and disarm unexploded ordnance.

One marine who returned to Vietnam to find the place where one of his best friends died said when visiting that rice paddy, he thought of the "music and the lyrics of that Nam song by the Animals, 'We Gotta Get Out of This Place.' " Another who returned remembered how innocent and then scared he was when he arrived there in 1968. But he also was surprised by other memories: "When I look back on Vietnam, it is our resilience that stands out as the most remarkable quality we both felt and witnessed. Without it, we would have melted away. It not only brought us through, it enabled us to find a strange but true-to-the bone joy in being together in such a hellish place on such a hellish mission that gave us no opportunity to believe in it. Whatever happened, we kept on being a fire team, a squad, a platoon. And we soon found ourselves laughing again, swapping c-rats, sharing pictures of girlfriends, playing back alley bridge. In this way, resilience let the innocence and mystery live on."

Bob Kerrey returned from Vietnam seriously wounded and was awarded the Medal of Honor for his heroism in a fierce fight on an island in Nha Trang Bay. He served as governor of Nebraska, as a U.S. senator, as a candidate for the Democratic presidential nomination in 1992, and as president of the New School in New York. In 2002, the story broke of his patrol killing civilians in Thanh Phong in 1969. Kerrey admitted to this and expressed regret.

In 2016 when Kerrey was nominated to

head a new Fulbright University in Hanoi, many Vietnamese protested having someone with his record assume this position. Others thought it was an important step in the process of reconciliation, noting Kerrey's deep regret for this incident. Pulitzer Prize–winning novelist Viet Thanh Nguyen, who left Vietnam as a child with his parents in 1975, disagreed with those who saw this as a step toward reconciliation. Despite Kerrey's acceptance of responsibility and contrition, Nguyen said the appointment was a "failure of moral imagination." He insisted that thinking of the war as an American tragedy avoided confronting the major tragedy suffered by many Vietnamese.[63]

The sons and daughters of those who were lost in Vietnam have also returned. One man came to the riverbank near where his father drowned and left behind a picture of the Camaro that his dad had owned, along with some cigars. Another dropped to his knees at the battleground at Khe Sanh where his father died and said, "I've come back." Some met with Vietnamese who had lost family members. One Vietnamese man admitted that for most of his life he had wanted revenge for the bombs that had killed his father as well as classmates in his school. Now, he told the Americans, "Revenge cannot help us," but "we can do something more useful for our countries and our people."

Some have returned looking for the remains of their fathers. Air Force captain John Carlson died near Long Nguyen village in December 1966. His remains were never found. Nearly fifty years later, his daughter used DoD records and modern GPS systems to find a site near some rubber trees where there was an unnatural large crater. She dropped to her knees and sobbed and then dug a small hole and buried the missing-in-action bracelet she had worn. Looking at the peaceful landscape around her, she said, "I don't understand how someone who was so loving — and kind, and handsome and great — could be at war with this place."[64]

Sometimes the remains were nearby but unidentified. On Memorial Day weekend 1984, President Reagan spoke at a ceremony at Arlington National Cemetery, interring an unidentified Vietnam casualty at the Tomb of the Unknowns. Here the remains joined those from Korea, World War I, and World War II. President Reagan said all Americans could wonder who this Unknown Soldier was: "As a child, did he play on some street in a great American city? Or did he work beside his father on a farm out in America's heartland?" The president observed that most of the country's wounds from the Vietnam War had been healed and that everyone now could celebrate those who served there. But he reminded his audience that those whose sons remained missing could not yet heal. "They live day and night with uncertainty, with an emptiness, with a void that we cannot fathom."[65]

Remarkably, in this instance the uncertainly was removed. Using modern DNA analyses, Michael Blassie's family was able to identify their missing son. In the spring of 1972, American air operations were continuing at a heavy pace in response to the Easter Offensive. Michael, an air force pilot who had been in Vietnam for less than four months, had already flown 130 combat missions in his A-37 Dragonfly, a light attack plane. On May 11, his plane was shot down by antiaircraft fire when he was on a close air support run in support of the defenders at An Loc. On July 11, 1998, his remains, having been exhumed from the Tomb of the Unknowns, were reburied at Jefferson Barracks National Cemetery near St. Louis. Blassie's father, a World War II veteran, was buried nearby. His mother had said, "I want to bring my son home."[66]

The crypt at Arlington that had contained the remains of Lieutenant Blassie remains empty. Modern science enables the identification, or at least the likelihood of identification, of remains. The cover on the crypt now is inscribed, "Honoring and Keeping Faith with America's Missing Servicemen, 1958–1975." When the last American troops withdrew and the prisoners of war were repatriated in the winter of 1973, there were still 2,646 American servicemen listed as "missing" in Southeast Asia. In 2016, 1,590 remain missing. The others have been officially "accounted for" — either through the location and identification of remains or by establishing that the missing was clearly lost in a crash at sea or in a fire or explosion that left no remains. Search teams continue to work in Vietnam — not always at a pace or on a scale that families of the missing seek. The black-and-white POW/MIA flag, created in 1972 by the National League of Families and recognized by Congress in 1990, still flies at many facilities as a reminder of them.[67]

One veteran who thinks of Vietnam often and confronts his own war-related disability, said, "People ask me, Would you do it again? My response is, 'Would you agree to getting into the worst car accident of your life again?' I think, 'What a dumb fucking question that is.' " He admitted that he hated the question even more than "Did you kill anyone?" He still suffers a lot from all he saw in Vietnam. It clearly haunts him. But "then I lay in bed at night and ask myself, '*Would* I do it again?' Yes, I think I would." Whether or not other veterans would say this, probably most would understand it. Many in this Vietnam generation would recognize the complicated emotions and very personal sense of pride that persists despite the bad memories and the grieving and the regrets.

As happened after past wars, the years eased some emotions, not so easily things like grief and regret and guilt, but at least most veterans have moved beyond hatred. One veteran spent many days and nights on a Swift Boat in the Delta. They had regular encounters with enemy forces. Most of their firefights had been at night. But in April 1969, they were attacked in the daytime at close range. They returned fire from their boat, using .50 caliber machine guns and 81mm mortars. They literally blew the attackers away — they saw the two enemy soldiers blown into the air. They cheered this victory, "celebrated our 'kills.' " For years he remembered and described with pride the encounter. But fifteen or so years following this firefight, he and his wife were on a church retreat in the Shenandoah Valley. He was walking on the retreat labyrinth when "I suddenly and unexpectedly began thinking of those two Viet Cong soldiers. A sharp sense of sadness and remorse swept over me. I ran into the woods and wept. It mattered not then that those were the enemy and were intent on killing us." He has never since thought of the moment with pride but only with sadness. "I had taken human life."

Although most veterans in this generation have done well in the years after Vietnam, it has, not surprisingly, been complicated. There have been two comprehensive studies of the Vietnam generation and PTSD. The National Veterans Readjustment Study, completed between 1984 and 1988, found that 15.2 percent of the men and 8.5 percent of the women who served were suffering with PTSD. One of the investigators in the study, Dr. Charles Marmar, reflected on it twenty-five years later in a congressional hearing and observed that by the 1980s, the "majority of Vietnam veterans had made a successful re-entry into civilian life and were experiencing few symptoms of PTSD or other readjustment problems." But he noted that Hispanic veterans had far higher patterns of PTSD, and that African American veterans, while not as high, had a disproportionate incidence of it.

Dr. Marmar pointed out that PTSD is a cruel condition, one that has a "substantial negative impact not only on the veterans' own lives, but also on the lives of spouses, children, and others living with Vietnam veterans with PTSD." He shared the finding that although veterans with different assignments in Vietnam suffered from PTSD, combat stress was an important factor. He said that they had done a subsequent analysis of actual records of service to test whether veterans who claimed combat experience actually had it. The researchers learned that there was "little evidence of falsification" of these claims and there was a "very strong" relationship between verified "war-zone stress or exposure and risk for PTSD."[68]

A follow-up study, the National Vietnam Veterans Longitudinal Study, carried out from 2012 to 2013, found some important patterns. Building upon the earlier database, the later study found that those veterans identified as having PTSD in the middle 1980s were twice as likely as those who had not been diagnosed with the condition to have died between the studies. Those with "war-zone stress" had the greater mortality risk. The second study determined that about 30 percent of the Vietnam veterans had suffered from PTSD at some point since the war. Those most likely to have PTSD were minority veterans who had enlisted before finishing high school and combat veterans "who had killed multiple times." The investigators determined that even though PTSD could be treated, for some it would be a chronic condition and that 11 percent of their Vietnam sample "could live with traumatic stress for the remainder of their lives."[69]

The follow-up study looked at veterans who by then were largely in their sixties. More than a third of them reported annual family income greater than $75,999. Approximately 12.1 percent had incomes of less than $25,000. For comparison, the median family income in 2013 was $52,250 and the poverty level for a family of two was $15,510. Importantly, despite their description of the continuing trauma some veterans endured, both studies concluded that in the 1980s and again thirty years later, the great majority of Vietnam veterans were "mentally and physically healthy."[70]

Another systematic look at the economic status of veterans found that the older group of Vietnam veterans, born right before World War II, were better educated, healthier, wealthier, and more likely to be working than nonveterans when they reached the age of fifty-one to fifty-six in the early 1990s. Ten years later, the veterans of this age group, now the boomers, were more likely to have had some college than were the nonveterans of their cohort. The older boomers were more likely than the younger ones to be married and have good health than the nonveterans their age. The decline in these advantages had some association with race — the younger Vietnam veteran group, born between 1948 and 1953, was more racially diverse than those in the earlier group born between 1942 and 1947. Nonwhite veterans had higher military disability rates.[71]

Beginning in the 1980s, the Vietnam generation assumed positions of responsibility and leadership in the public and private sectors. They have not always stressed their service, but they have not hidden it either. And they adapted. As one described the process, even though coming home was very hard and trying to reconcile Vietnam and their lives has taken much time, what they learned in Vietnam "has continued to see us through. We brought all the rest of it home too, and as we figured out, bit by bit, how it fit, all we had learned and could not deny into peacetime life, we could let ourselves become more and more alive, and let what we now knew serve us instead of sink us."

After those difficult years in the early '70s, service in Vietnam for most veterans has been a source of pride and a valuable, if difficult experience. Intriguingly, in three presidential elections in a row, 2000, 2004, and 2008, Vietnam veterans lost to men who had not served there (George W. Bush had served in the Texas Air National Guard). Al Gore was an army journalist at Bien Hoa, but John Kerry and John McCain were decorated combat veterans, McCain an honored prisoner of war. There certainly was no indication that their Vietnam service caused them to lose — no one used it against them except one group of veterans who vilified Kerry for his VVAW activity as well as questioned his military service. But if serving in Vietnam didn't hurt them, it was not clearly positive. Perhaps more intriguing, in the two elections before those, in 1992 and 1996, two genuine

World War II heroes, President George H. W. Bush and Senator Bob Dole, were defeated — by Bill Clinton, a baby boomer who had opposed the war in Vietnam, protested against it, and successfully and explicitly used the system to evade the draft.

For those of this generation who served in Vietnam in different ways, the memories live on in different ways. They are reminded regularly of this, because "Vietnam" still hangs there as a negative chapter of the national narrative. In American political and intellectual debates, people refer to Vietnam almost always as a bad precedent or a negative analogy. When Americans consider any aspect of foreign or military policy, "Vietnam" is posed as something to be avoided. And the referencing is pretty comprehensive — avoid Vietnam's origins and assumptions, avoid Vietnam's war-fighting methods and procedures, avoid the nature of the withdrawal from Vietnam, and avoid the outcome. There is not much room there for a positive memory, for a sense of pride of service that would be understood. At least understood by anyone who had not been there.[72]

One veteran's therapist asked him if he enjoyed the feeling when he did not think about the war. "Of course I answered yes." So then she said, "Well, then just stop thinking about it." He stopped going to therapy. A friend had given him a pin with a soldier riding on the back of a tiger, and told him that according to the Vietnamese, once you get onto a tiger, do not get off or it will kill you. "We are still riding that tiger."

One marine described the legacy of grief in remembering a close friend killed in an ambush, leaving "behind a powerful sadness at his demise. We who have the solemn duty to remember, carry the burden of this sadness from many, many similar losses to this day. It is that load, willingly carried, that has changed us forever. How to describe that to others has eluded me."

The public gratitude for the Vietnam veterans has seldom meant a warm embrace. One marine veteran who had gone to Washington in 1992 for the celebration of the tenth anniversary of the dedication of the Wall was pleased to join a parade that organizers had planned. American views had changed, and he and others had recently watched the national celebration of parading veterans of Operation Desert Storm. This veteran joined with the state contingents to parade through central Washington. He "kept expecting to see people on the sidewalks. There'd been a lot of press about the anniversary. There'd been the big turnaround about veterans after the Gulf War. And there were lots of veterans there." But it turned out "there wasn't anybody there" watching the parade. The marching Vietnam veterans kept expecting crowds to cheer. Finally, at the end of the parade route, as they neared the memorial, they heard cheering up ahead. They tightened up their ranks to parade in. They discovered that the applause "was the veterans at the front of the parade welcoming the ones at the back." They still looked after each other, even if few others did.[73]

Max Cleland described his reaction when he heard Maine senator Edmund Muskie in the early '70s insist, "We must come to the conclusion that Vietnam was a mistake." Cleland wrote, "What do you mean, a mistake? Where's the meaning? Where's the purpose? What does that do to a guy like me, who lost so much? What does it do to all those who lost so much in Vietnam? Those are questions I'll be trying to answer for the rest of my life."[74]

If the public now looks more positively on the Vietnam veterans and even thanks them for their service, it is an acknowledgment of their serving, seldom intended as a salute to heroes and surely not to the war itself. It recognizes their bad timing and thanks them for being good sports in enduring their bad fortune. Those members of this generation who served there may well think of their bad timing. But they have additional, often complicating, dimensions and emotions to recall.

One sailor who rode on the waters of the

Delta on a Swift Boat kept a diary while he was in Vietnam, and it was filled with workaday accounts and occasional poetic reflections. On May 12, 1969, as the 187th was confronting Dong Ap Bia, a tragic day when 174 Americans died in Vietnam, this young veteran was in Saigon watching a fierce storm come in at nightfall. This was just before Secretary of State William Rogers and Mrs. Rogers, along with their delegation, arrived. And it was the sort of storm about which they had been warned.

For this sailor on R&R, it was exactly a month since he had seen his best friend and two others killed in a river ambush. He recorded in his diary the storm moving into the city:

The sky is black now,
Illuminated now and then
By silent strobes of lightning
People hustling about before the storm
. . . and before the curfew.
But soon the rains will come and cool us
    all and slow the motion.
And the city will become quiet under the
    soothing rhythm of the rain.
People will move inside and watch the
    monsoon downpour
from a darkened window.
And some, perhaps, will reflect on the day
    just ended.[75]

ACKNOWLEDGMENTS

This is that stage in the writing and publication of a book when even a limited sense of modesty requires and candor demands a full acknowledgment of all of the individuals and groups that enabled the author. As I review the list of those to whom credit and thanks are due, I am humbled and even overwhelmed by the large number of people who stepped up and supported my work. I am deeply grateful to them for the extent of their contributions. Quite simply, I would not have completed this book at this time and never would have finished a book with this range without the generous involvement and support of many people. Beyond their substantive assistance, I have been encouraged by so many who supported my interest in writing a book that would capture the experience of the generation who served in Vietnam.

At Dartmouth, President Philip Hanlon, as well as his predecessors Carol Folt and Jim Yong Kim, have been supportive, generous, and encouraging. They and the Dartmouth Board of Trustees, along with other colleagues on the faculty and in the administration, have reached out to help me return to my work as a historian and to support my involvement with veterans issues and activities. I am grateful to a number of Dartmouth friends who have provided financial support for these projects. I especially want to acknowledge and to thank Nancy and Wade Judge, Kathy and Richard Kimball, Pat and John Rosenwald, Daryl and Steve Roth, Karen and Samuel Seymour, and Kimberly and Macauley Taylor. Steve Roth has been a special friend who has encouraged and supported me through several iterations of my work.

A book such as this one is always dependent upon the scholarly lifeline of a library. The Dartmouth College library has stepped up for me as they have been doing since 1969. A special acknowledgment to Jeff Horrell, who served until 2016 as Dean of Libraries and College Librarian, for his leadership and all of his support of my work. His colleagues came through always. From the Circulation Desk — where a librarian informed me at one time that I had checked out more books than any other user of the library — to the Resource Sharing staff to the librarians working in the Jones Media Center and the Rauner Special Collections Library, so many have promptly and professionally supported my research. I am deeply in their debt — yet again.

A special thanks to Lucinda Hall for her good work in preparing the maps included here. A Reference Librarian in the Evans Map Room of the Dartmouth Library, Ms. Hall worked patiently and professionally to respond to my evolving requests. Dartmouth colleagues Randy Baker and Warren Belding, with their impressive understanding of information technology and systems and their assistance in our development and presentation of data, were critical to so many parts of this study. Hillary Beach was indefatigable in transcribing interview tapes. She worked on nearly all of the more than 160 interviews that I completed and she finished them quickly and well.

Megan Harris at the Veterans History Project of the Library of Congress was very helpful in providing interviews from their very rich collection. My thanks to her. I am also grateful to the responsive staff at the National Archives and, once again, I want to thank Dr. Charles Neimeyer at the Marine Corps History Division. He along with Annette Amerman followed up on my inquiries promptly and generously.

It is not possible to acknowledge sufficiently the support of Ken Davis and his team at the Coffelt Database of Vietnam Casualties. This comprehensive database of all of the men who died in Vietnam was initiated through a tremendous personal commitment from Korean War–era veteran Richard Coffelt from Hays, Kansas. He and his wife, Jo Ann, and a few volunteers compiled a major database, and Ken Davis and a group of other Vietnam veterans have maintained and enhanced it. I am especially grateful to Mr. Davis for his prompt and generous responses to many of my inquiries. His knowledge of this huge data set and his expertise in handling it are truly impressive.

Bernie Edelman of the Vietnam Veterans of America assisted me in reaching out to Vietnam veterans for possible interviews. Richard Kolb, editor in chief of *VFW,* the Veterans of Foreign Wars magazine, encouraged me and was an important resource in helping me with these connections. I also thank Jan Scruggs and his team at the Vietnam Veterans Memorial Fund for their help.

Colonel Warren Wiedhahn, USMC retired, a veteran of the Chosin Reservoir in the Korean War and of the Vietnam War, founded Military Historical Tours in 1987. This organization provides opportunities for veterans and their families as well as other interested individuals to visit some historic battlefields. Warren was very responsive to my inquiry about a customized trip to Vietnam so I could visit some of the places about which I was writing. He and John Powell aided in the general planning for my tour and a remarkable old marine veteran, Captain Ed Garr, organized it and led the first part of it.

The late Captain Garr had served two tours in the Vietnam War and he subsequently took over 100 tour groups back to the country. He was a great resource, a remarkable travel leader, and delightful companion for part of my trip. He died a year later from a stroke that he suffered while leading another group to Vietnam. Bruce Jones, an army veteran of the Vietnam War, was a resourceful guide and interpreter. Working with Captain Garr, Bruce and Vietnamese guide and interpreter Tran Thanh arranged for my custom tour of several places in I Corps and II Corps. They were wonderful travel companions who climbed Hamburger Hill with me. Bruce Jones also read an early draft of my chapter on Dong Ap Bia.

This book has been enriched significantly by careful and generous readings by a number of people. James Patterson, history professor emeritus at Brown University, Greg Daddis, retired army colonel and former history professor at West Point and now on the faculty at Chapman University, have each published significant scholarly books related to the 1960s and to the Vietnam War. I am indebted to them for reading this manuscript and offering advice to me. Peter Prichard, the retired editor of *USA Today* and a veteran of the Vietnam War was a thoughtful resource and critic for this book. Jeff Hinman, also a Vietnam veteran, connected me with a significant number of individuals and helped locate resources for this study. Each of them read the entire draft manuscript. And my Dartmouth history department colleague, Professor Ed Miller, an excellent Vietnam historian, read parts of the book and offered me advice and criticism on many aspects of this study and on resources that I might consult. Despite the substantial effort of this group, obviously any errors that remain are mine alone.

Those students who enrolled in my Dartmouth history department seminars on America's wars asked good questions and provided thoughtful insights. I thank them. Their papers provided opportunities for me to think again about any of a number of subjects. I especially learned from their research on the subject of one of the fifteen Dartmouth students whose names are memorialized on the Vietnam Veterans Memorial Wall.

I met Scott Manning at the William E. Colby Symposium at Norwich University a few years ago. He is an experienced publicist who has represented authors, organizations, and institutions through his firm, Scott Manning & Associates. Scott was interested in this project and he and his colleague Abigail

Welhouse have been very supportive of this study and have agreed to work with Thomas Dunne Books in promoting this book. I am grateful to him for all of his skilled assistance, from the proposal drafts through publication.

It was Scott who introduced me to Michael Carlisle of Inkwell Management and Michael agreed to represent me as an agent. Michael Carlisle is a wonderful advocate, adviser, and friend. His professional support and guidance have been essential to me. Michael connected me with Thomas Dunne, who has his own imprint within St. Martin's Press. We hit it off from the start. I have enjoyed greatly my affiliation with Mr. Dunne and have found his encouragement and judgment indispensable. He liked the idea of this book and I am honored to be part of his list.

Peter Joseph has served as my editor at Thomas Dunne books and he has been a rich resource, a fine guide, and a very helpful editor. He and his associate, Melanie Fried, have really added much to this book and have been expert navigators through the publishing process. Their entire team has moved my manuscript to a book with sensitivity, intelligence, and professionalism. I am grateful to them.

Having a manuscript copy edited by a professional is a humbling experience. I had the good fortune to have my production team arrange for Cynthia Merman to copyedit this manuscript. She had quite an assignment and she handled it remarkably well. She worked very hard to seek consistency in style and clarity of language. She made this book better and I thank her for that.

Mary Donin has been a friend and colleague for many years. When Mary retired a few years ago as a librarian at the Dartmouth College Rauner Special Collections Library, she was interested in helping out on this project. She surely has. Mary has time and again followed up on my inquiries and tracked down in the library or on the Internet newspaper and magazine articles and government and other reports that informed and enriched my understanding. She helped to organize the transcripts of my interviews, including some follow-up work with interviewees. As the various drafts of the book took shape, Mary Donin proved to be an able reader and a good critic and editor. She has done more than help out — she has made this a richer and a better book.

Louise Moon has now worked with me on two books and she has contributed to every part of *Enduring Vietnam,* from design, to interviews, to data analyses, to research in secondary and primary sources. She has come to know this material and this subject well, and even more than that, to feel a personal commitment to seeing it through. She often was the primary contact with potential interviewees and she has an impressive knowledge of each of them and has been critical in suggesting to me places in the narrative where their accounts could enrich and expand my coverage. She developed creative ways to help analyze and understand casualty lists and other data sets. And Louise is an excellent editor who has influenced this presentation in many ways. I truly would not be at this place at this time without her tireless work, her dedication to the project, and her professional standards and expectations. It is simply not possible to recognize her sufficiently or to thank her adequately.

The acknowledgment that should be simplest is the hardest. I can't describe easily my gratitude and my debt to Susan Wright. I have said on other occasions that writing a book is finally a very selfish process. At least it has not been my style to come home at the end of a day and share what I had done that day in more than a brief summary. In fact many of the things in this book do not summarize easily and they often do not replay very well — they linger troublingly in the mind but are not good topics for conversation. But Susan daily asked how things were going and always accepted warmly my not-very-informative answers. Beyond this role of encouraging and supporting, and despite her own substantial obligations, she made important suggestions on the design of the book and has read several parts of this with a very critical eye. She is a careful reader and a good editor — as one might expect from a Vassar history major, a Carl Degler student at that! She has sustained me at every step of this process — as she has in all things. I may have given up on this book a number of times if it were not for her unqualified support and encouragement. Having the name of a dear friend on the Vietnam Veterans Memorial Wall, she believed that this book could be important to a number of readers — and she knew that it was important to me. *Enduring Vietnam* owes much to her and here I shout out my gratitude — and my love for her and her wisdom and generosity.

Finally, words are totally inadequate to acknowledge properly and to thank fully all of the veterans and the family members of veterans who agreed to be interviewed and/or shared correspondence and other materials with me. I list them at the end of this section. A book aiming to describe the human face of the American War in Vietnam would not have been possible without their stories. While their names on this list may record my gratitude it can never describe my debt. Some of those who agreed to be interviewed said they had never talked to anyone about their experiences in Vietnam. But they were willing — some even eager — to help me to tell the story of their war, especially the story of friends or family that they lost in battle. We had some very moving conversations. Only a few finally declined to be identified. Their stories are here but their names are not.

Whenever I return to their interviews I am touched again by their accounts. I wish I could have shared far more of the very rich and very human recollections of those whom I interviewed. These men and women have invested part of themselves in this project, and I only hope they approve of the book that resulted from their generosity and commitment.

LIST OF INTERVIEWEES AND OTHER CONTRIBUTORS

William D. Adams
Bobby W. Alexander
Damaris Anderson
Drummond B. Ayres Jr.
Gary Bain
Joseph Bakos
Frank D. Balazs
Peter D. Barber
Don L. Bartley Jr.
Richard Batche
Sharon Blackman Battles
Mary E. Benton
Elvira R. Blackman
Frank Boccia
Sandy Boyer
Gwen L. Brainard
Harry L. Breski
Daniel P. Bresnahan
Donald K. Brief
Adam Brochetti
Jim Brown
Kathleen Brown

Gregory L. Burnetta
Christopher Burns
Alexander Butterfield
Talmadge M. Cain
Mac M. Campbell
Edward W. Campion
Jose G. Cantu
Brenda Miller Carpenter
Alexander H. Carver III
Allen M. Collins
Dawn Collins
Jerald Collman
Warren C. Cook
Lawrence Cox Jr.
Thomas Crawford
Jack Croall
Dale Dailey
Richard DeLotto
Reverend Grover G. DeVault
Lucy Doffee
General Joseph F. Dunford
Donald C. Dyer
Charles A. Edwards
Kenneth Eichholz
Diane Carlson Evans
David S. Ferriero
Warren Finkler
Michael A. Fredrickson
Richard Freidhoff
Jay L. Gearhart
Jim Goss
General Alfred M. Gray

Charles Grebinger
Lonnie F. Greckel
Frank Grieco Jr.
Gladys A. Grubb
Robert M. Hager
Gregg Hanke
Gerald R. Harkins
Richard J. Harris
Stephen Hayes
Larry A. Henry
John J. Hickey
Jeff Hinman
David W. Hogan
Robert Holmen
General Weldon Honeycutt
Rich Hosier
Russell Howard
Kent S. Hughes
William Jefferson
William R. Jevne
Kenley Jones
James F. Jordan
Faith Kaiser
G. Randall Kehler
Frank Kelly
Joseph A. Kenny
Bruce H. King
Richard A. Kirshen
Robert C. Koury Jr.
George Kovach
Stephen Kraus
Kenneth R. Kruse

Michael J. Kuklenski
Stephen R. Landa
John P. Lavelle
John M. Littleton
James W. Long
David Loring
Stephen F. Lotterhand
Dwight Lovejoy
David H. Lovelace
F. Beirne Lovely Jr.
William Lucier
James M. MacLaughlan
Thomas P. Martin
Ronald S. McCarthy
Thomas W. McGall
Frank McGreevy
Michael J. McGuire
John McMackin
Kenneth J. Medeiros
Ronald L. Menhorn
Daryl and Leona Miller
Maria Miller
James W. Milliken
James Mills
Deborah A. Moore
Douglas E. Moore
Arthur L. Mosher
Nan Nall
Antoinette Newcomb
John E. Noble
James M. Ottman
Robert Paladino

Richard Pils
Steven R. Piscitelli
Gary Radford
Eric M. Rairdon
Richard A. Rajner
Gary T. Redlinski
Thomas J. Reilly
David E. Rogers
Jeffrey L. Rogers
Pat Sajak
William Scandrett
Kyle Schroeder
Jan C. Scruggs
Dave Shearer
James H. Sheppard
Matthew D. Shorten
Carol C. Silcox
Terence F. Smith
Wayne Smith
Nancy Smoyer
John F. Snyder
Brad Sommer
Kenneth A. Stearns
Donald L. Sullivan
Robert Tortolani
Helen L. Trammell
Joel R. Trautmann
Josephine Cyran Vetanovetz
Gary G. Weaver
Mark Weston
Michael C. Wholley
Robert A. Williams

David L. Willse
Rickey L. Winters
Michael J. Wright
Ed Yasuna
Joe L. Ybarra
Carl J. Zarzyski
Micheal Zimmer

NOTES

Preface. Visiting Vietnam

1. The National Liberation Front was commonly described as the Viet Cong by Americans. The term was a contraction of the Saigon government's description of these forces as "Viet Gian Cong San" or Vietnamese Communist Traitor. "Viet Cong" was the widespread description by most Americans, and probably with little sense of it being a pejorative term. I use NLF except when quoting from participants and observers. I use NVA to describe the North Vietnamese Army (this force also was called the People's Army of North Vietnam, or PAVN). I use ARVN, the common contemporary name, for the Army of the Republic of Vietnam, the South Vietnamese regular army.

Introduction. A Generation Goes to War

1. Baskir and Strauss, *Chance and Circumstance,* 3–5.
2. Warren Cook, "My Vietnam Reprise," shared with author; e-mail exchange with Edward Yasuna, April 26, 2016.
3. There are many powerful accounts of the experiences of the Vietnamese. A recent compelling book is Viet Thanh Nguyen's prize-winning novel, *The Sympathizer:* "The majority of Americans regarded us with ambivalence if not outright distaste, we being living reminders of their stinging defeat," 113. Also compelling is his subsequent nonfiction book, *Nothing Ever Dies,* which I encountered only as this book was going to press. This is a thoughtful and provocative reflection of a Vietnamese American whose family left Vietnam in 1975 when Viet was only four years old: "This is a book on war, memory, and identity. It proceeds from the idea that all wars are fought twice, the first time on the battlefield, the second time in memory." He observes that for him the "metonym for the problem of war and memory is what some call the Vietnam War and others call the American War. These conflicting names indicate how this war suffers from an identity crisis, by the question of how it shall be known and remembered," 4.

Chapter 1. Memorial Days

1. A good summary is David W. Blight, "Decoration Days: The Origins of Memorial Day in North and South," in *The Memory of the Civil War in American Culture*, ed. Alice Fahs and Joan Waugh (Chapel Hill: University of North Carolina Press, 2004), 94–129.

2. "Many Activities Scheduled for Junior Fair and Dairy Festival," *Los Angeles Times*, May 29, 1969; *Del Rio (TX) News-Herald*, May 30, 1969; "News Summary and Index," *New York Times*, May 31, 1969; William Currie, "Nation's War Heroes Honored by Parades, Memorial Services," *Chicago Tribune*, May 31, 1969; Martin Weil, "Memorial Day Here Marked by Services, Traffic Jams," *Washington Post*, May 31, 1969.

3. "Spacemen Work Holiday for Big Job of Debriefing," *El Paso Herald-Post*, May 30, 1969; Gunda K. Christiansen, "Memorial Day in Rural Areas," *Chicago Tribune*, May 30, 1969.

4. "Memorial Unit Honoring Five Vietnam Deaths," *Winona (MN) Daily News*, May 29, 1969; "Memorial Day Services at Zuni Pueblo," *Gallup (NM) Independent*, May 31, 1969; "Solemn Ceremonies to Mark Memorial Day in County," *Canandaigua (NY)*

Daily Messenger, May 29, 1969; "We Shall Remember . . . ," *Lowell Sun,* May 25, 1969; "A Time to Pause . . . A Time to Remember," *Columbus (NE) Daily Telegram,* May 28, 1969.

5. Paul Dean, "Pima Parents Still Mourn for Marine of Iwo Fame," *Arizona Republic,* May 25, 1969; Peggy Simpson, "Indian Family Visits Grave of War Hero," *Hamilton (OH) Daily News Journal,* May 31, 1969.

6. Richard Nixon, "D-Day Twenty-Fifth Anniversary Day," Proclamation 3915, May 31, 1969, Woolley and Peters, American Presidency Project, www.presidency.ucsb.edu/ws/?pid=105930.

7. "Nixon Hails Armed Forces in Memorial Day Message," *New York Times,* May 24, 1969.

8. Weil, "Memorial Day Here Marked by Services, Traffic Jams."

9. "Residents Listen to Stirring Presentation at End of Ceremonies for Memorial Day," *Hartford Courant,* May 31, 1969; Linda Mathews, "Southland Honors War Dead in Memorial Rites," *Los Angeles Times,* May 31, 1969; "Memorial Day Recalls Deeds of War Dead," *Lovington (NM) Daily Leader,* June 1, 1969.

10. "Memorial Day Talks Focus on Drug War," *Boston Globe,* May 26, 1969; James Strong, "5,000 at Lane Honor Their 24 War Dead," *Chicago Tribune,* May 30, 1969;

Coffelt Database of Vietnam Casualties, www.coffeltdatabase.org/. This is an incredibly rich source of data on the Vietnam War dead, and most of my profiles, statistical descriptions, and individual cases use this resource.

11. "Parades and War Protests Mark Observance of Memorial Day," *Los Angeles Times,* May 31, 1969; "Memorial Day II: It's a Little Late, Folks," *Boston Globe,* May 31, 1969; "Mayor Protests War," *New York Times,* May 31, 1969; "Roll of War Dead Read in Protest," *Los Angeles Times,* May 31, 1969.

12. Gallup polls, January 7–12, 1965; January 22–28, 1969.

13. Morris Kaplan, "Campus Arrests Made Since Last Year's Columbia Disorders Are Crowding Court Calendars Here," *New York Times,* May 18, 1969; John Kifner, "University in Missouri Imposes Curfew After 5 Fires Are Set," *New York Times,* May 21, 1969.

14. James Stack, "New Harvard Study Asks End to All ROTC Ties in '71," and Martin F. Nolan, "McCarthy Wants Nixon to Call up Calif. Guard," *Boston Globe,* May 30, 1969; "600 Troops Attack, Rout Campus Snipers," *Chicago Tribune,* May 24, 1969; *Stars and Stripes* published an article and a photo covering the Berkeley dem-

onstration, titled "Posies Sprout amid the Bayonets," June 2, 1969. Martin Weil, "War Protesters Arrested at Capitol," *Washington Post,* May 24, 1969; Derek Norcross, "Youth Notes: Drop in Campus Recruits," *Boston Globe,* May 25, 1969.

15. "Campus Unrest Cuts Contributions of Alumni at Some Top Colleges," *Washington Post,* May 15, 1969; Guy Halverson, "Backlash Buffets U.S. Campuses," *Christian Science Monitor,* May 21, 1969.
16. Mary McGrory, "University Officials, Students Close Ranks," *Boston Globe,* May 11, 1969.
17. "Radical Students Urged to Use Political Means," *Los Angeles Times,* May 31, 1969.
18. "Gallup Special: Campus Violence," *Middletown (NY) Times Herald-Record,* May 26, 1969.
19. "These Honored Dead," *New York Times,* May 30, 1969.
20. "Memorial Day, 1969," *Washington Post,* May 30, 1969.
21. Michael Lang, a primary organizer of the event, recounts the planning in *The Road to Woodstock.*
22. The Pacific edition of *Stars and Stripes* had a photo of Lennon, Yoko Ono, and Ono's stepdaughter, Kyoko, on the bed, with the caption "3 Doves on a Mattress," May 31, 1969. See Deiter, Athey, and

McGrath, *Give Peace a Chance.*

23. James Stack, "Sen. Brooke Upstaged at Wellesley Commencement: Senior Challenges His Views on Protest," *Boston Globe,* June 1, 1969.
24. Edward Ranzal, "18 Indicted Here as Draft Evaders," *New York Times,* May 30, 1969.
25. "News Summary and Index," *New York Times,* May 31, 1969; *Stars and Stripes* (Pacific edition), May 28 and 31, 1969.
26. "Rifles in Hands, Yanks Pray — in Remembrance of Buddies," *Chicago Tribune,* May 31, 1969. Also "Battlefield Tribute," *Stars and Stripes* (Pacific edition), June 2, 1969.
27. Horace Mann Bond, "Two Racial Islands in Alabama," *American Journal of Sociology* 36 (January 1931): 552–67.
28. Faith Kaiser interview, July 2, 2014; Helen Trammel interview, March 17, 2014; Allen Collins interview, September 23, 2014; conversations with Lucy Collins Doffee and Dawn Collins; correspondence with Damaris Anderson.
29. Faith Kaiser interview, Helen Trammel interview, Allen Collins interview; conversations with Lucy Collins Doffee and Dawn Collins, correspondence with Talmadge Cain and Damaris Anderson. Also Coffelt Database.
30. Gwen Brainard interview, July 1, 2014.

31. Carl Zarzyski interview, July 1, 2014, and correspondence; Coffelt Database.
32. Gwen Brainard interview.
33. Interviews with Jack Croall, February 19, 2014; John Hickey and Carol Hickey Silcox, April 1, 2014; Bill Lucier, June 9, 2014; Arthur Mosher, July 30, 2014. Letter to Carol Hickey Silcox, copy shared with author. Joseph Dunford interview, March 31, 2015, about the marine culture in Quincy and South Boston in the 1960s.
34. Letter to Jack Croall, February 7, 1969.
35. Interviews with Jack Croall and John Hickey and Carol Hickey Silcox.
36. Interviews with John Hickey and Carol Hickey Silcox. Poem, "The Magic Horse," by Philip Byrnes, reproduced by permission of the Hickey family.
37. Graves, *The Life I Led,* 107–08.
38. Ibid., 109.
39. *Life,* June 27, 1969, 32.
40. William Wilson, "I Had Prayed to God That This Thing was Fiction," *American Heritage* 41, no. 1 (February 1990): 44–53.

Chapter 2. Dong Ap Bia: Becoming Hamburger Hill

1. Bud Collins, "Move War to A Shau," *Boston Globe,* May 28, 1969.
2. Release from office of Senator Edward Kennedy, May 20, 1969, tedkennedy.org/

ownwords/event/vietnam. See also William Chapman, "Kennedy Assails Vietnam Hill Foray," *Washington Post,* May 21, 1969, A20, and Hedrick Smith, "Kennedy Assails Vietnam Tactics," *New York Times,* May 21, 1969.

3. "Paratroopers Hit This Beach with Pleasure," *Stars and Stripes* (Pacific edition), May 21, 1969.

4. "General Hails Fight for Hamburger Hill," *Chicago Tribune,* May 23, 1969, B15; Iver Peterson, "Paratrooper Commander Replies to Kennedy's Criticism of Battle for Ap Bia," *New York Times,* May 23, 1969, 3; David Hoffman, "Hamburger Hill: The Army's Rationale," *Washington Post,* May 23, 1969, 1.

5. Donald Sullivan interview, May 9, 2014.

6. Ibid.

7. Quoted by Don Sullivan in e-mail to author, July 7, 2014.

8. Ken Eichholz interview, December 2, 2014; Donald Sullivan interview; Joe Ybarra interview, July 2, 2014; telephone conversations with Antoinette Newcomb, September 26, 2014 and James Mills (former teacher and coach), September 12, 2014.

9. Jay Sharbutt, "US Assault on Viet Mountain Continues, Despite Heavy Toll," *Washington Post,* May 20, 1969, A15.

10. "Hawks Would Get Out with Victory;

Doves Would Get Out in Phases: The Alternatives in Vietnam," *Boston Globe,* June 8, 1969; "War on Capitol Hill," *New York Times,* June 4, 1969.

11. "Emergence of EMK," *Commonweal,* June 6, 1969, 331–32.
12. James Reston, "Edward Kennedy's Challenge to President Nixon," *New York Times,* May 21, 1969, 46.
13. Iver Peterson, "Paratrooper Commander Replies to Kennedy's Criticism of Battle for Ap Bia," May 23, 1969, and Robert Semple, "U.S. Denies Shift in War's Tactics," May 24, 1969, *New York Times;* "White House: Battle Necessary," *Boston Globe,* May 24, 1969.
14. Philip Warden, "3 Rip Kennedy for Opposing Attack on Hill," *Chicago Tribune,* May 27, 1969, 19.
15. Philip Warden, "Kennedy Viet Speech Stirs Senate Clash," *Chicago Tribune,* June 3, 1969, 29.
16. Cosmas, *MACV,* 244–52; Sorley, *Thunderbolt,* 260–61.
17. Michael A. Mira, "Rakkasans on Hamburger Hill," Army Heritage and Education Center, 1, Project CHECO (Contemporary Historical Examination of Current Operations), Report on A Shau Valley Campaign, 5.
18. Major David Lauthers, Command Histo-

rian, cover memo to "Report of 25 August 1969," online Texas Tech University Library material, Army 1969 101st Airborne Division Op Apache Snow.

19. From Vietnamese book *324th Division* (Su Doan 324), Editorial Supervision: 324th Division Leadership and Party Current Affairs Committee, Senior Colonel Nguyen Van Tao and Senior Colonel Pham Van Long; Authors: Lt. Col. Dao Quang Doi and Captains Nguyen Thong and Vo Viet Hoa (Hanoi: People's Army Publishing House, 1992). Translation kindly provided by Professor Merle L. Pribbenow.

20. CHECO report, 48.

21. Ibid., 41.

22. Quoted in "Hill Battle Rages On," *Stars and Stripes* (Pacific edition), May 21, 1969, 1.

23. Combat After Action Report (Apache Snow) of Commanding General, 3rd Marine Amphibious Force to CG, MACV.

24. Donald Sullivan interview.

25. Gerald "Bob" Harkins interview, February 4, 2014.

26. Boccia, *Crouching Beast,* 278, 279.

27. Alton Mattioli interview, Veterans History Project, Library of Congress; Frank McGreevy interview, April 28, 2014.

28. John Snyder interview, January 14, 2015.

29. Alton Mattioli interview. The nickname "Rakkasan" dates back to the period after

World War II when the 187th Infantry was deployed with the 101st Airborne Division in occupied Japan. The 187th was a paratroop regiment and the Japanese called them "Rakkasans," their word for umbrellas, the umbrella men. The soldiers adopted the name.

30. Boccia, *Crouching Beast,* 284, 285.
31. Ken Eichholz interview; interview, name withheld.
32. Weldon Honeycutt interview, December 16, 2014; Frank Boccia interview, December 11, 2014.
33. Frank Boccia interview; Frank Kelly interview, February 7, 2014.
34. Donald Sullivan interview.
35. Boccia, *Crouching Beast,* 287, 294.
36. Zaffiri, *Hamburger Hill,* 80–81.
37. Ibid.
38. Boccia, *Crouching Beast,* 301.
39. Greg Burnetta interview, October 27, 2014. Larsen's parents were notified of his death on May 15. Coffelt report.
40. Tom Martin interview, October 29, 2014.
41. Interview, name withheld.
42. Lee Sanders interview in *Oliver North's War Stories: The Real Story of Hamburger Hill,* video, Fox News.
43. Greg Burnetta interview.
44. Mac Campbell interview, May 21, 2015.
45. Zaffiri, *Hamburger Hill,* 107–24.
46. Boccia, *Crouching Beast,* 341.

47. Frank Boccia interview.

48. Frank McGreevy interview.

49. Boccia, *Crouching Beast,* 401.

50. Joe Galloway, "The Mountain of the Crouching Beast," *VFW Magazine,* June/July 2008, 40; Iver Peterson, "Many Casualties on Apbia Peak Are Attributed to U.S. Mistakes," *New York Times,* June 15, 1969.

51. Dan Bresnahan interview, September 17, 2014.

52. Interviews, names withheld.

53. John Snyder interview.

54. Ken Eichholz interview.

55. Boccia, *Crouching Beast,* 387.

56. Interview, name withheld.

57. Tom McGall interview, February 14, 2014.

58. Tom Martin interview; Eric Rairdon interview, November 7, 2014; "Helo Hero Wears Halo for Viet GIs," *Stars and Stripes,* August 25, 1969.

59. Eric Rairdon interview.

60. Interview, name withheld.

61. Mark Weston interview, March 8, 2014.

62. Zaffiri, *Hamburger Hill,* 89.

63. Boccia, *Crouching Beast,* 378–79.

64. Dan Bresnahan interview.

65. Joel Trautmann interview, May 12, 2014, and Trautmann's "Memory Impressions," document written on November 21, 1996 and provided by Mr. Trautmann, 12.

66. Donald Sullivan interview.

67. Charles Grebinger interview, September 19, 2014; Tom McGall interview.

68. Zaffiri, *Hamburger Hill,* 241–42.

69. Boccia, *Crouching Beast,* 448; Zaffiri, *Hamburger Hill,* 261–63. More than forty-five years later, Frank Boccia remained convinced that if Jackson had been white he would have received the Medal of Honor for his action that morning (Boccia interview).

70. Donald Sullivan interview.

71. David Hoffman, "Hamburger Hill: The Army's Rationale," *Washington Post,* May 23, 1969; "General Hails Fight for Hamburger Hill," *Chicago Tribune,* May 23, 1969.

72. Terence Smith, "U.S. Command Defends Apbia Battle as 'Maximum Pressure' on the Foe," *New York Times,* May 23, 1969.

73. Dave Warsh, "Hamburger Hill CO Refutes Ted's Attack," *Stars and Stripes* (Pacific edition), May 24, 1969.

74. Ken O. Botwright, "Army General Again Defends Hamburger Hill," *Boston Globe,* June 7, 1969.

75. Larry Cox interview, March 5, 2014.

76. John Snyder interview.

77. Neil Sheehan, "Letters from Hamburger Hill," *Harper's Magazine,* November 1, 1969, 40.

78. Several letters reprinted ibid., 40–52. On the other hand, several people interviewed

for this book, including Weldon Honeycutt, were very critical of Senator Kennedy's comment. Don Sullivan is certain that attitudes toward the war changed markedly after Kennedy's speech.

79. Ward Just, "The Reality of War on Hamburger Hill," *Washington Post,* May 21, 1969, A34.
80. Tom McGall interview.
81. Charles Grebinger interview.
82. December 2014 inquiries to and replies from Colonel Gregory Daddis, then at the United States Military Academy, and Lieutenant Colonel James Di Crocco at the Army War College.
83. Conversation with North Vietnamese Army veterans Ho Manh Khoa, Ho Viet Loi, and Nguyen Thanh Doi in A Luoi and on Ap Bia, September 4, 2014.

Chapter 3. Passing the Torch to a New Generation

1. "The 44th Inaugural," *Newsweek,* January 30, 1961, 8; Robert T. Hartmann, "Kennedy Urges New Quest for Peace," *Los Angeles Times,* January 21, 1961; www.inaugural.senate.gov/swearing-in/weather.
2. "For John F. Kennedy's Inauguration" by Robert Frost, undelivered inaugural poem, John F. Kennedy Presidential Library and Museum, www.jfklibrary.org/Research/

Research-Aids/Ready-Reference/JFK-Fast
-Facts/Frost-For-His-Inauguration.aspx.
James Reston, "Poetry and Power Is the
Formula," *New York Times, January 25,
1961.*

3. James Reston, "President Kennedy's
Inaugural — Speech or Policy?" *New York
Times,* January 22, 1961.

4. Inaugural Prayers Through History, www
.beliefnet.com/columnists /stevenwaldman/
2009/01/inaugural-invocations-and-pray
.html.

5. Summarized in "Editorial Comment
Across the Nation on President Kennedy's
Inauguration," *New York Times,* January 21,
1961.

6. William Moore, "Inauguration Speech
Hailed as Inspiration," *Chicago Tribune,*
January 21, 1961; "President Kennedy,"
Wall Street Journal, January 23, 1961.

7. John F. Kennedy, speech at American
Legion Convention, Miami Beach, FL,
October 18,1960, Woolley and Peters,
American Presidency Project, www
.presidency.ucsb.edu/ws/?pid=74096.

8. For a thoughtful analysis of the American
engagement with Vietnam in this period,
see Bradley, *Imagining Vietnam and America.*

9. A rich scholarly study of Ngo Dinh Diem
is Miller, *Misalliance.* Miller's Diem was
neither an American dupe nor a Vietnamese

despot; he was a complicated leader deeply committed to nation building.

10. For the Diem visit and reaction, see Logevall, *Embers of War,* 674–75, 677; Anderson, *Trapped by Success,* 161–64.
11. Anderson, *Trapped by Success,* 203.
12. Freedman, *Kennedy's Wars,* 7.
13. Dallek, *Camelot's Court,* 161.
14. Anderson, *Trapped by Success,* 199, 200, 161– 64.
15. Goldstein, *Lessons in Disaster,* 235.
16. Sabato, *The Kennedy Half-Century,* 123.
17. Burner, *John F. Kennedy and a New Generation,* 65.
18. Peace Corps, history, www.peacecorps.gov/about/history/speech/.
19. Rice, *Bold Experiment,* 67–68, 87.
20. John F. Kennedy, Special Message to Congress, May 25, 1961, www.space.com/11772-president-kennedy-historic-speech-moon-space.html; see also W. H. Lawrence, "Kennedy Asks 1.8 Billion This Year to Accelerate Space Exploration," *New York Times,* May 26, 1961.
21. Logsdon, *John F. Kennedy and the Race to the Moon,* 1, 4, 83, 105.
22. Rice, *Bold Experiment,* 59; Freedman, *Kennedy's Wars,* 7.
23. Roberts and Olson, *A Line in the Sand,* 275; chap. 9 discusses the politics of John Wayne and this movie.

24. Dallek, *Camelot's Court,* 269.
25. Ibid., 262, 263.
26. Ibid., 233, 247.
27. John F. Kennedy, commencement address at American University, June 10, 1963, www.jfklibrary.org/Asset-Viewer/BWC 7I4C9QUmLG9J6I8oy8w.aspx.
28. John F. Kennedy, presidential news conference, Bonn, Germany, June 24, 1963, Woolley and Peters, American Presidency Project, www.presidency.ucsb.edu/ws/index.php?pid=9297&st=&st1=-ixzz1pahpd NB4.
29. Edward Miller, "Religious Revival and the Politics of Nation Building: Reinterpreting the 1963 'Buddhist Crisis' in South Vietnam," *Modern Asian Studies* 49, no. 6 (November 2015): 1903–62, journals.cambridge.org/abstract_S0026749X12000 935.
30. Dallek, *An Unfinished Life,* 669.
31. Karnow, *Vietnam,* 293–327; Miller, *Misalliance,* 311–26.
32. Eisenhower quoted in Sloyan, *The Politics of Deception,* 249; David W. F. Elliott, "Official History, Revisionist History, and Wild History," in Bradley and Young, *Making Sense of the Vietnam Wars,* 292; Freedman, *Kennedy's Wars,* 416.
33. Jones, *Death of a Generation,* 442.

34. Jones, ibid., 238. Dallek, *Camelot's Court,* 351.
35. Jones, *Death of a Generation,* 456, www .pbs.org/wgbh/americanexperience/features /primary-resources/jfk-trademart/.
36. Freedman, *Kennedy's Wars,* 312; Dallek, *Camelot's Court,* 158–72.
37. Jones, *Death of a Generation,* 444.
38. Dallek, *Lyndon B. Johnson,* 221–22.
39. Logevall, *Embers of War,* 709.
40. Zelizer, *The Fierce Urgency of Now,* 147; Jones, *Death of a Generation,* 444.
41. Dallek, *Lyndon B. Johnson,* 220.
42. A fascinating study of Hanoi's politics and planning is Asselin, *Hanoi's Road to the Vietnam War, 1954–1965;* for the Ninth Plenum, see esp. chap. 6. Also David W. F. Elliott, "Official History, Revisionist History, and Wild History," in Bradley and Young, *Making Sense of the Vietnam Wars,* 277–304.
43. Transcript of Errol Morris documentary *The Fog of War,* 2003, www.errolmorris .com/film/fow_transcript.html.
44. See Patterson, *The Eve of Destruction,* 20, 21. Also www.youtube.com/watch?v=dDT BnsqxZ3k.
45. "American President: A Reference Resource," Miller Center, University of Virginia, millercenter.org/president/lbjohnson/ essays/biography/5.
46. Lyndon Johnson Conversation with Rob-

ert McNamara, April 30, 1964, Tape WH6404.16, Lyndon B. Johnson Presidential Library, Austin, TX. Transcript provided by Edward Miller.

47. General Al Gray interview, June 3, 2015.

48. See Lieutenant Commander Pat Paterson, "The Truth about Tonkin," *Naval History* 22, no. 1 (February 2008), www.usni.org/magazines/navalhistory/2008-02/truth-about-tonkin.

49. Moïse, *The Tonkin Gulf and the Escalation of the Vietnam War,* chap. 9, esp. 225–26, 234, 241.

50. "Attack on the USS Maddox," *Los Angeles Times,* August 4, 1964; Roscoe Drummond, "Why the Attacks? . . . ," *Washington Post,* August 8, 1964.

51. Dallek, *Flawed Giant,* 143–56; Zelizer, *Fierce Urgency of Now,* 150; Patterson, *Eve of Destruction,* 24.

52. Karnow, *Vietnam,* 423–25; Patterson, *Eve of Destruction,* xi, 34–35.

53. Patterson, *Eve of Destruction,* 94; Herring, *America's Longest War,* 152–55.

54. "The Asia War," *Washington Post,* February 8, 1965, A16; "Reprisal in Vietnam," *New York Times,* February 8, 1965, 24; Walter Lippmann, "Vietnam," *Hartford Courant,* February 9, 1965, 16.

55. Roscoe Drummond, "It's Time for U.S. to Show Muscle," *Los Angeles Times,* Feb-

ruary 11, 1965, A6; "A Look Down That Long Road," *Time,* February 19, 1965, 19; "Pleiku and Qui Nhon: Decision Points," *Newsweek,* February 22, 1965, 32.

56. Hanson Baldwin, "Value of U.S. Raids," *New York Times,* February 10, 1965, 8.

57. "If We Fail to Meet It Here and Now," *Time,* February 26, 1965, 20; Herring, *America's Longest War,* 155–57.

58. Patterson, *Eve of Destruction,* 74–75.

59. *Stars and Stripes* (Korea edition), March 9, 1965; Patterson, *Eve of Destruction,* 79.

60. Patterson, *Eve of Destruction,* 169. Many understood then — and more later would understand — the softness of this support. Americans were not enthusiastic about the idea of war, but they instinctively supported a flexing of strength. See Logevall, *Choosing War,* chap. 12, for a good discussion of the soft nature of this "support."

61. Dallek, *Flawed Giant,* 273, 274–75. Ball's was not a solitary voice, not inside the administration where disagreement was subdued, nor outside where it was not. See Logevall, *Choosing War,* 376–82.

62. Herring, *LBJ and Vietnam,* 1–2.

63. Lyndon Johnson, press conference, July 28, 1965, transcript, Miller Center, University of Virginia, millercenter.org/president/lbjohnson/speeches/speech-5910.

64. "The Presidency," *Time,* August 6, 1965, 19, 21–22.

65. Anderson, *Trapped by Success,* 205.

66. Logevall, *Choosing War,* xxii; see also his *Origins of the Vietnam War,* 85–92. Record, *The Wrong War* is another essential look at the process and the assumptions that led the United States to Vietnam. Also Young, *The Vietnam Wars, 1945–1990,* chap. 7.

67. White House meeting, June 21, 1965, in Beschloss, *Reaching for Glory,* 365.

68. Kearns, *Lyndon Johnson and the American Dream,* 251–52.

69. Lyndon Johnson, July 28, 1965, press conference, millercenter.org/president/ lbjohnson/speeches/speech-5910.

70. "The War No One Wants — Or Can End," *Newsweek,* August 9, 1965, 17.

71. Dallek, *Lyndon B. Johnson,* 224–25.

72. Caputo, *A Rumor of War,* xiv.

Chapter 4. Receiving the Torch

1. Multiple articles in *Stars and Stripes* (Pacific edition), December 26, 1965. Casualty data from Coffelt Database, which includes a Defense Prisoner of War/Missing Personnel Office release of July 5, 2012, on the missing airmen.

2. *Stars and Stripes* (Pacific edition), December 26, 1965.

3. Ibid.; "Bob Hope offers 10,000 GIs Christmas Present of Laughter," *New York Times,* December 25, 1965.

4. "Spellman Arrives for Five-Day Visit with Vietnam G.I.s," *New York Times,* December 24, 1965; *Stars and Stripes* (Pacific edition), December 26, 1965; "Vietnam: A Glorious Quiet for Christmas," *Los Angeles Times,* December 26, 1965; Cooney, *The American Pope,* 288–95.
5. Lyndon B. Johnson, "Remarks at the Lighting of the Nation's Christmas Tree," December 17, 1965, Woolley and Peters, American Presidency Project, www.presidency.ucsb.edu/ws/?pid=27411.
6. Neil Sheehan, "Vietnam Is Calm in Holiday Truce; Incidents Minor," *New York Times,* December 25, 1965; "30 Tons of Gifts Arriving Each Day," *Stars and Stripes* (Pacific edition), December 22, 1965.
7. "Hope Plays to 8000 in the Rain," *Stars and Stripes* (Pacific edition), December 30, 1965.
8. William Anderson, "U.S. Victory Seen in Viet Fight," *Chicago Tribune,* November 20, 1965; "US Battalions Pull Back in Vietnam Battle," *Los Angeles Times,* November 17, 1965; Robert R. Brunn, "US and Viet Cong Test Power," *Christian Science Monitor,* November 18, 1965.
9. "In Vietnam: Suddenly It's a Stepped-Up War," *U.S. News & World Report,* November 22, 1965, 50–51.
10. *Time,* January 7, 1966, 15–21.

11. Holt, *Cold War Kids,* 49–55; Gillon, *Boomer Nation,* 19, 35; Neiberg, *Making Citizen-Soldiers,* 86. United States Census, Population Estimates by Age, Sex, Race, 1970–1979, www.census.gov/popest/data/national/asrh/pre-1980/PE-11.html.

12. Holt, *Cold War Kids,* 20, 21.

13. Ibid., 147.

14. Bankston and Caldas, *Public Education,* 79.

15. Holt, *Cold War Kids,* 48.

16. Whitfield, *The Culture of the Cold War,* 65.

17. "Preview of the War We Do Not Want," *Collier's Weekly,* October 27, 1951, www.unz.org/Pub/Colliers-1951oct27.

18. Holt, *Cold War Kids,* 24–27.

19. Jo Ann Brown, "A Is for Atom, B Is for Bomb: Civil Defense in American Public Education, 1948–1963," *Journal of American History* 75, no. 1 (June, 1988): 78, 84.

20. Jacobs, *The Dragon's Tail,* 102; Brown, "A Is for Atom," 84; see the film at www.youtube.com/watch?v=IKqXu-5jw60.

21. Jacobs, *The Dragon's Tail,* 107, 113.

22. *Life,* March 24, 1958; Holt, *Cold War Kids,* 75–77.

23. Preston, *Sword of the Spirit, Shield of Faith,* 420, 421, 447; Whitfield, *Culture of the Cold War,* 97.

24. Whitfield, *Culture of the Cold War,* 97, 89.

25. *The American Experience,* "God in

America," PBS, www.pbs.org/godinamerica/transcripts/hour-five.html; Preston, *Sword of the Spirit,* 468–70.

26. Whitfield, *Culture of the Cold War,* 95–96; Preston, *Sword of the Spirit,* 412, 433–34, 440.

27. Jacobs, *America's Miracle Man in Vietnam,* 134.

28. William Lederer, "They'll Remember the *Bayfield,*" *Reader's Digest,* March 1955, 1–8.

29. Jacobs, *America's Miracle Man,* 129, 131.

30. Ibid., 152.

31. Dooley, *Deliver Us from Evil,* 205; Jacobs, *America's Miracle Man,* 153–54; Appy, *American Reckoning,* 8–9.

32. See Logevall, *Embers of War,* 666–68; Jacobs, *America's Miracle Man,* 161. Fisher, *Dr. America,* is the fullest biography of Dooley, see esp. 53–55.

33. "Thomas Dooley, M.D.," January 20, 1961, and "Kennedy to Serve on Tom Dooley Fund," February 3, 1961, *New York Times;* "Thomas Dooley's Lasting Memorial," *Los Angeles Times,* January 20, 1961; Patricia Sugrue, "Dr. Dooley's Death at 34 Ends Task of a Life Span," *Washington Post,* January 20, 1961.

34. Robert Cahn, "A Is for Atom," *Collier's Weekly,* June 21, 1952, 16.

35. *What You Should Know About COMMU-*

719

NISM and Why, 5–6. Christian Appy points out that the phrase "communist aggression" appeared in *The New York Times* only 8 times prior to 1946 and in 2,714 articles from 1946 to 1960 (*American Reckoning,* 41).

36. Department of Defense, *Why Vietnam?* archive.org/details/gov.ntis.ava 08194vnb1.

37. Flynn, *The Draft,* 166–67, 170.

38. Ibid., 166–70.

39. Taped conversation, November 14, 1964, in Beschloss, *Reaching for Glory,* 140–41.

40. RAND Report, "Project 100,000 New Standards Program, 1972," 5–7.

41. Baskir and Strauss, *Chance and Circumstance,* 5.

42. Davis and Dolbeare, *Little Groups of Neighbors,* 15–16; Dave Willse interview, August 10, 2015. Willse was called up with his National Guard unit.

43. Bradley, *DEROS Vietnam,* vii.

44. Baskir and Stauss, *Chance and Circumstance,* 9. For equity and fairness in the draft, Christian Appy in *Working-Class War* did the most comprehensive review and found that young men of a working-class background were far more likely to serve. For a different conclusion, see Neil D. Fligstein, "Who Served in the Military, 1940–1973?" *Armed Forces and Society* 6, no. 2 (Winter 1980); and for a study confirming

Appy, see Patricia Shields, "The Burden of the Draft: The Vietnam Years," *Journal of Political and Military Sociology* 9 (Fall 1981). I agree with Appy's conclusion.

45. National Advisory Commission on Selective Service, "In Pursuit of Equity: Who Serves When Not All Serve," February 1967.
46. Russell quoted in Willard Edwards, "Senators Rip Plan to Federalize Draft Boards," *Chicago Tribune,* April 14, 1967; see Davis and Dolbeare, *Little Groups of Neighbors,* 25–28; Flynn, *Lewis B. Hershey,* 246; Chambers, *To Raise an Army,* 257. John D. Morris, "Senate Moves to Extend Draft Law Almost Intact," May 12, 1967, and Neil Sheehan, "House Group Backs Curb on Johnson Draft Lottery," May 19, 1967, *New York Times.*
47. Appy, *Working-Class War,* 84.
48. O'Brien, *If I Die in a Combat Zone,* 26, 27.
49. Longley, *Morenci Marines,* 23, 33, 48–49.
50. Ibid., 51, 55.
51. Shaw in Appy, *Working-Class War,* 58; Muller in Gillon, *Boomer Nation,* 51–52; Sweat in Napoli, *Bringing It All Back Home,* 172.
52. Bray, *After My Lai,* 13–14.
53. Nesser, *The Ghosts of Thua Thien,* 3, 4–6.
54. Jose Cantu interview, January 24, 2014.

55. Steve Landa interview, January 21, 2015.

56. Rick Rajner e-mail, February 11, 2015.

57. Kovic, *Born on the Fourth of July,* 46–75, quote on 75.

58. Appy, *Working-Class War,* 63–64, 67.

59. Appy, *Patriots,* 209, 211, 366–70.

60. Ibid., 362.

61. Berens, *Chuck Hagel,* 24, 28–29, 33–35. See also Myra MacPherson, "Brothers in Arms," *Washington Post,* January 13, 1997, D1; Frank Bruni, "Horrors of Vietnam Spur Senator's Foreign Policy Battles," *New York Times,* August 9, 1999, A10; Charles Timothy Hagel interview, Veterans History Project, Library of Congress.

62. Ehrhart, *Vietnam-Perkasie,* 7–10.

63. William "Bro" Adams interview, February 17, 2015.

64. David Lovelace interview, May 1, 2014.

65. Bill Jevne interview, October 22, 2014.

66. McLean, *Loon,* 23.

67. Dick Harris interview, October 15, 2014.

68. Jim Sheppard e-mail, February 11, 2015.

69. Frank Grieco interview, September 23, 2014.

70. O'Brien, *Going After Cacciato,* 264.

71. Donald Sullivan e-mail, February 10, 2015.

72. David Ferriero interview, February 5, 2015.

73. Michael Wholley interview, February 16, 2015.

74. Jack Croall interview.

75. Appy, *American Reckoning,* 123–25.

76. Of course as with any oral history, particularly gathered years after the events, some of these recollections may have evolved over the years. On the other hand, most contemporary accounts describe similar attitudes on the part of those who served.

77. Dave Balazs interview, January 29, 2014.

78. Napoli, *Bringing It All Back Home,* 125.

79. Chris Burns interview, March 3, 2015.

80. Lonnie Greckel interview, January 13, 2014.

81. Steve Hayes interview, July 15, 2014.

82. Pat Sajak interview, January 26, 2015.

83. Mike Zimmer interview, March 6, 2014.

84. Larry Cox interview.

85. Robert "Obie" Holmen interview, February 27, 2015.

86. Mark Weston interview.

87. Alexander Carver interview, December 12, 2014.

88. Tom Martin interview.

89. Baker, *Nam,* 33–34.

90. Mac Campbell interview; Gary Bain interview, May 26, 2015.

91. Kent Hughes interview, October 17, 2014; Jack Wells poignantly describes the 43 men of his 1967 Basic School class who died in Vietnam, in Wells, *Class of '67.*

92. Napoli, *Bringing It All Back Home,* 12, 13.

93. Peter Barber interview, October 29, 2015.

94. Napoli, *Bringing It All Back Home,* 164.

95. Rod Paladino interview, July 7, 2015; Russ Howard interview, June 3, 2015.

96. Kurson, *Shadow Divers,* 72–73.

97. Debby Maynard Moore interview, September 25, 2014.

98. Baskir and Strauss, *Chance and Circumstance,* 30–31.

99. Ibid., 32.

100. Appy, *Working-Class War,* 44. Appy pointed out that middle-class young men who received the draft summons could wrestle with the moral issues whereas working-class recipients of the summons more likely treated it as an order, a nondiscretionary summons, 51.

101. Remnick, *King of the World,* 285–91.

102. Randy Kehler interview, June 9, 2015. See also his interview in Appy, *Patriots,* 231–37, and Daniel Ellsberg's account on 433–34. See also Ellsberg, *Secrets,* 270–73.

103. Matt Shorten interview, June 8, 2015.

104. Marlantes, *What It Is Like to Go to War,* 134–39.

105. Mike Fredrickson interview, April 1, 2015.

106. Tad Campion interview, October 27, 2014.

107. A very good summary of the literature and a persuasive voice for the idea of

working-class antiwar activity is Lewis, *Hardhats, Hippies, and Hawks,* esp. chap. 3.

108. Fred P. Graham, "Court Backs Curb on Draft Appeals," *New York Times,* December 17, 1968; "A Real Important Break" and John P. MacKenzie, "High Court Cuts Punitive Use of Draft," *Boston Globe,* December 17, 1968; Flynn, *Lewis B. Hershey,* 266–68.

109. "The Inheritor," *Time,* January 6, 1967, 18– 23.

Chapter 5. Not Their Fathers' Way of War

1. Caputo, *Rumor of War,* xiv–xv.
2. Daddis, *Westmoreland's War,* 42.
3. Summers, *On Strategy,* 1; Walter Ulmer, conversation with author, May 17, 2011. Obviously the argument that the United States never "lost a battle" was dependent on how battles were defined and how "loss" was measured.
4. Broyles, *Brothers in Arms,* 12.
5. A good study of the geography and topography of South Vietnam is T. T. Connors, Milton G. Weiner, and J. A. Wilson, *The Land Border of South Vietnam: Some Physical and Cultural Characteristics* (Santa Monica, CA: RAND Corp., 1970).
6. Michael Herr, "Hell Sucks," *Esquire,* August 1968, 66.
7. For a history of this structure and its

rivalries, see Cosmas, *MACV,* 35–62.

8. The most sharply critical study of General Westmoreland is Sorley, *Westmoreland.* He argues that General Creighton Abrams, who replaced Westmoreland in 1968, turned around the war and dealt with it far more comprehensively. See also Sorley's *A Better War* and *Thunderbolt.*

9. Daddis, *Westmoreland's War,* 28.

10. Daddis, *No Sure Victory,* 72.

11. Two recent scholarly books provide a rich and comprehensive history of this entire episode. Martini's *Agent Orange* is a compelling and sobering look. Sills's *Toxic War* provides a particularly strong account of the chemical consequences of the use of these agents.

12. Jeff Hinman conversation, December 2015.

13. Daddis, *Westmoreland's War,* xxi.

14. The best account of this battle, and one of the best of any battle during the war, remains Moore and Galloway, *We Were Soldiers Once.*

15. Van Creveld, *Age of Airpower,* 385–87; Stanton, *Rise and Fall of an American Army,* 60–61; Daddis, *No Sure Victory,* 77.

16. Stanton, *Rise and Fall of an American Army,* 60–61.

17. Van Creveld, *Age of Airpower,* 386; Daddis, *No Sure Victory,* 81.

18. Van Creveld, *Age of Airpower,* 397.
19. A good recent summary is ibid., 387–93. Statistics are from Clodfelter, *Vietnam in Military Statistics,* 216–29.
20. Thayer, *War Without Fronts,* 83–85. The South Vietnamese Air Force flew about 400,000 sorties.
21. Lair, *Armed with Abundance,* 70–72.
22. Ibid., 69–70; Tregaskis, *Southeast Asia,* 2.
23. Steve Lotterhand interview, June 17, 2015.
24. Daddis, *No Sure Victory,* 65, 84; Herring, *LBJ and Vietnam,* 31.
25. McNamara and VanDeMark, *In Retrospect,* 222.
26. Wilkins, *Grab Their Belts,* 22.
27. Just, *To What End,* 167; Wilkins, *Grab Their Belts,* 16–17.
28. Daddis, *Westmoreland's War,* 82.
29. Caputo, *Rumor of War,* 192.
30. Daddis, *No Sure Victory,* 7; Stanton, *Rise and Fall of an American Army,* 85, 107–09, 133.
31. Daddis, *No Sure Victory,* 95.
32. Powell, *My American Journey,* 81–82.
33. Caputo, *Rumor of War,* xiv–xv; Daddis, *Westmoreland's War,* 100; also Daddis, *No Sure Victory,* 95, 123.
34. The best study of this program is Southard, *Defend and Befriend;* see also Krulak, *First to Fight,* 194–200. Daddis, *Westmore-*

land's War, 79–81. General Al Gray interview.

35. Southard, *Defend and Befriend,* 10. For a study of a CAP, see Francis J. [Bing] West's account of his time serving as a marine in the village of Binh Nghia, *The Village.* See also Don Moser, "Their Mission: Defend, Befriend," *Life,* August 25, 1967, 25. A critique and criticism of the program is Gregory Daddis, "The Fallacy of the False Alternative: Reconsidering the U.S. Marine Corps and American Strategy in Vietnam," unpublished paper shared by Daddis.

36. Lee Chilcote speaking at a panel of Vietnam veterans at Dartmouth College, May 11, 2015.

37. Don Moser, "Eight Dedicated Men Marked for Death," *Life,* September 3, 1965, 30.

38. Daddis, *Westmoreland's War,* 96–97.

39. See the powerful account in Schell, *The Village of Ben Suc.* See also Schell, "The Village of Ben Suc," *New Yorker,* July 15, 1967.

40. Terence Smith, "Anti-Vietcong Cordon Disrupts Life of a Village," *New York Times,* September 24, 1969, 6.

41. See, for example, Moser, "Eight Dedicated Men Marked for Death," narrating the story in 1965 of Loc Dien up near Hué in *Life* magazine, September 3, 1965, 30. This is an account of eight influential vil-

lagers the NLF promised to execute. See account of Huu Thanh in "Vietcong Laid a Heavy Hand on Village," *Washington Post,* October 31, 1969, A19.

42. Trullinger, *Village at War,* 97, 100–102.
43. A classic study that remains very important is Race, *War Comes to Long An.*
44. Neil Sheehan, "Vietnam Peasants Are Victims of War," *New York Times,* February 15, 1966.
45. Powell, *My American Journey,* 86–87.
46. Kevin Buckley, "Pacification's Deadly Price," *Newsweek,* June 19, 1972, 42–43; see also Turse, *Kill Anything That Moves,* chap. 6 and 248–57.
47. Gloria Emerson, "In Vietnam a Weary Look Back at a Harsh Decade," *New York Times,* January 1, 1971, 3.
48. Linda Grant Martin, "The 37-Year War of the Village of Tananhoi," *New York Times Magazine,* October 29, 1967, SM30.
49. Daddis, *Westmoreland's War,* 99, 158.
50. Soldier quoted ibid., 104.
51. Caputo, *Rumor of War,* 110, 312–36.
52. "Guilty Minority," *Time,* January 5, 1968, 33.
53. Trullinger, *Village at War,* 117.
54. Kerrey, *When I Was a Young Man,* 180–85. Gregory Vistica, "What Happened in Thanh Phong," *New York Times Magazine,* April 25, 2001; Amy Waldman, "Ex-Senator

Kerrey Says Raid He Led in '69 Killed Civilians," *New York Times*, April 26, 2001.

55. See Daniel Lang, "Casualties of War," *New Yorker*, October 18, 1969, and his book *Casualties of War*.

56. Michael Sallah and Mitch Weiss won the Pulitzer Prize for their reporting and described this in *Tiger Force*. Turse, in his comprehensive book *Kill Anything That Moves*, documents a number of cases and allegations of atrocity and criminal conduct. They are chilling. He concludes that such things are "the essence of what we should think of when we say 'the Vietnam War.' " He insists that he has enough accounts to conclude that this behavior was "unbearably commonplace throughout the conflict." Based on my own reading of this war, I would argue that if this conduct was not uncommon, it surely was not commonplace. For a fuller review and refutation of Turse, see Peter Zinoman and Gary Kulik, "Misrepresenting Atrocities: 'Kill Anything That Moves' and the Continuing Distortions of the War in Vietnam," *Cross-Currents: East Asian History and Culture Review*, E-Journal, no. 12 (September 2014). But see also Nelson, *The War Behind Me*, for a full and disturbing discussion of the filings and hearings on war crimes cases. A very good review of Turse is Gregory

Daddis in the *Journal of Military History* 77, no. 3 (July 2013): 1174–76.

57. Moskos, *The American Enlisted Man,* 151–52.

58. General Cao Van Vien, quoted in Stanton, *Rise and Fall of an American Army,* 26–27; Gregory Daddis's account of attitudes in chapter 65 of *The West Point History of Warfare,* electronic textbook. See also Daddis, *Westmoreland's War,* 159. For an excellent study of the ARVN experience, see Brigham, *ARVN.*

59. The main source of data analyzed for this discussion came from the Coffelt Database, the largest private database of the men and women killed in Vietnam. It is rich in its detail, based on careful use of government reports, and it is meticulous in its accuracy. The trustees responsible for this remarkable resource have kindly and generously provided me with subsets of these data for the month of May throughout the war.

60. E-mail from Tomás Summers Sandoval Jr., chair of History Department at Pomona College, to author, May 11, 2015. Sandoval is engaged in a study of Hispanics in Vietnam.

61. Broyles, *Brothers in Arms,* 135.

62. Appy, *Working-Class War.*

63. Longley, *Morenci Marines.*

64. A good compendium is the Department of Defense report, "U.S. Casualties in

Southeast Asia, Statistics as of April 30, 1985."

65. Charles Edwards interview, May 27, 2015.

66. Webb, *I Heard My Country Calling,* 272, 273.

67. Neil Sheehan, "Officials in U.S. Irked by Report of Low Ratio of Combat Troops," *New York Times,* July 13, 1967. See also Lair, *Armed with Abundance,* 25. Edelman, *Dear America,* chap. 4 for letters from rear echelon.

68. Lair, *Armed with Abundance,* 32–39.

69. Ibid., 74–75, 77–78, 136–37.

70. Ibid., 119–23.

71. Debby Maynard Moore interview.

72. Tom McGall interview.

73. Broyles, *Brothers in Arms,* 138–39.

74. Lair, *Armed with Abundance,* 95.

75. Charles Hagel interview, Veterans History Project, Library of Congress.

76. The fullest study of the operation of the rotation system is Helton, "Revolving Door War." See also Daddis, *Westmoreland's War,* 110, 113.

77. A first-rate study of Komer and the initiation of CORDS is Jones, *Blowtorch,* esp. chaps. 8 and 9. Woods, *Shadow Warrior,* chap. 13.

78. Woods, *Shadow Warrior,* chap. 14. A comprehensive overview and defense of the Phoenix Program based upon substantial

research is Moyar, *Phoenix and the Birds of Prey.* But see also Valentine, *The Phoenix Program.*

79. Gentile, *Wrong Turn,* 75–76.

80. Murphy, *Dak To,* is a comprehensive and rich study of this engagement.

81. General Westmoreland speech, *New York Times,* November 22, 1967, 2; Ted Sell, "U.S. Entering New War Phase — Westmoreland," *Los Angeles Times,* November 22, 1967, 8; Daddis, *No Sure Victory,* 127–29; Willbanks, *Tet Offensive,* 6–7.

82. Chalmers Roberts, "General's Timetable Calls for Victory after '68 Voting," *Washington Post,* November 22, 1967.

83. A good summary of the various plans is in Willbanks, *Tet Offensive,* 8–9.

84. Daddis, *Westmoreland's War,* 140; Murphy, *The Hill Fights,* 6–15; Krulak, *First to Fight,* 205–09. General Al Gray interview.

85. Joseph Alsop, "Climactic Battle Is Under Way," *Los Angeles Times,* January 30, 1968, A5.

86. Westmoreland warning in Peter Braestrup, "Biggest Attack Still to Come," *Boston Globe,* February 2, 1968. See Hanson W. Baldwin, "Public Opinion in U.S. and South Vietnam Is Viewed as Main Target of New Offensive by Vietcong," *New York Times,* February 1, 1968; also "Did Viet Cong Achieve Its Goal?" *Christian Science*

Monitor, February 1, 1968.

87. *New York Times,* January 31, 1968. Also "Vietcong Seize Part of U.S. Embassy," *Washington Post,* January 31, 1968.

88. "Outlook Assessed by Westmoreland," *New York Times,* February 26, 1968.

89. A well-researched and full account of the battle is Jones, *Last Stand at Khe Sanh.* Jones is not convinced that Khe Sanh was simply a North Vietnamese feint, but he acknowledges that it is extremely hard to know their intent — except that they were eager to take the base and they gave up many men in the effort (278–81).

90. James Reston, "Washington: A Strange and Troubled Silence," *New York Times,* February 4, 1968; *Washington Post,* February 26, 1968.

91. Willbanks, *Tet Offensive,* 68–69, transcript of Cronkite remarks, 205–206.

92. Nixon in Hammond, *Reporting Vietnam,* 293; 1972 speech by General Westmoreland quoted in William Hammond, "Who Were the Saigon Correspondents and Does It Matter?" Joan Shorenstein Center Paper, Spring 1999, 1. For a recent summary of this argument, see Hess, *Vietnam,* chap. 6. "Viet Reds Beaten Militarily, Ciccolella Says," *Stars and Stripes* (Pacific edition), February 28, 1969.

93. Hammond, *Reporting Vietnam* and "Who Were the Saigon Correspondents and Does

It Matter?"

94. William Hammond and Clarence Wyatt are important scholars on this subject. A good recent summary is Wyatt's "Wartime Journalists," in Hall, *Vietnam War Era,* chap. 8. Wyatt's *Paper Soldiers* remains essential to any look at the media and the war, as does Landers's *The Weekly War.*

95. A contemporary account is "TV's First War," *Newsweek,* August 30, 1965, 32.

96. Chris Burns interview. Burns was with the 25th Infantry Division Information Office at Cu Chi. On journalism in Vietnam, Bob Hager interview, January 29, 2015; Kenley Jones interview, April 9, 2015; Terence Smith interview, February 6, 2015.

97. Wyatt, *"Wartime Journalists,"* 143–45.

98. Huebner, *The Warrior Image,* 176; "The Press: Room for Improvement," *Newsweek,* July 10, 1967, 76.

99. "Whose Benefit? Whose Doubt?" *Newsweek,* November 13, 1967, 68.

100. "Vietnam on Television," Museum of Broadcast Communications, www.museum.tv/eotv/vietnamonte.htm.

101. "Escalating Opinion," *Newsweek,* March 25, 1968, 97.

102. Louis Harris report in "War Support Spurts After Tet Attacks," *Washington Post,* February 12, 1968; see also Willbanks, *Tet Offensive,* 73.

103. LaFeber, *The Deadly Bet*, 59–61. Dallek, *Lyndon B. Johnson*, 327–32; Herring, *LBJ and Vietnam*, 163.

Chapter 6. The American War in Vietnam

1. Bleier and O'Neil, *Fighting Back*, 79.
2. Department of State Briefing Book for Mrs. William Pierce Rogers. Original binder in possession of Mrs. Rogers's granddaughter, Army Major Cynthia Marshall, and generously loaned to author.
3. Tom Wicker, "Returning to Saigon," *New York Times*, May 15, 1969.
4. Richard Nixon, "Address to the Nation on Vietnam," May 14, 1969, Woolley and Peters, American Presidency Project, www.presidency.ucsb.edu/ws/?pid=2047.
5. Flynn, *The Draft*, 238–39. Robert B. Semple Jr., "Nixon Asks Draft Lottery with 19-Year-Olds First; Orders Deferment Study," *New York Times*, May 14, 1969.
6. Fred S. Hoffman, " 'Vietnamization' Is Now the Word," *Stars and Stripes* (Pacific edition), July 30, 1969.
7. Cosmas, *MACV*, 153–54.
8. Larry Burrows, "A Case of Cowardice Under Fire," *Life*, September 19, 1969, 74–75. Interviews with Jay Gearhart, James Long, and Mike Zimmer.
9. Arthur J. Dommen, "Toll Doubles to 430 U.S. Dead in Week," *Los Angeles Times*,

May 23, 1969; Cosmas, *MACV,* 134.

10. "Assaults by 1,500 of Foe Repulsed at 2 Allied Posts," *New York Times,* May 19, 1969, 1; "1,000 N. Vietnamese Storm Allied Posts North of Saigon," *Washington Post,* May 19, 1969, A1.

11. Thayer, *War Without Fronts,* 116. Over 30 percent of the deaths occurred in the I Corps provinces of Quang Tri and Quang Nam.

12. William Carroll interview, February 4, 2010, Veterans History Project, Library of Congress.

13. Rick Rajner interview, January 13, 2014.

14. Descriptions from a wide range of interviews and accounts. But for a fine summary, see Spector, *After Tet,* chap. 3. Webb, *I Heard My Country Calling,* 286.

15. Bruce King interview, February 26, 2015.

16. See observations in Longley, *Grunts,* 115–16.

17. Tom Reilly interview, February 21, 2014.

18. Rod Paladino interview.

19. Jim Milliken interview, February 3, 2014; Peter Prichard comments to author; Michael McGuire e-mail, February 17, 2014.

20. Appy, *Working-Class War,* 127–29.

21. Dave Shearer interview, April 10, 2014.

22. Milliken, *Enter and Die!* 18–19.

23. Edelman, *Dear America,* 127.

24. Ybarra, *Vietnam Veteranos,* 172.

25. Maraniss, *They Marched into Sunlight,* 17.

26. Pat Sajak interview.

27. Chris Burns interview; Larry Cox interview; William Jefferson interviews, July 16 and August 14, 2014; Chaplain Grover DeVault interview, March 3, 2014.

28. Robert "Obie" Holmen interview.

29. Bill Franklin interview, March 22, 2011, Veterans History Project, Library of Congress.

30. Dale Dailey interview, February 24, 2015; Rick Winters interview, December 2, 2013.

31. Joe Ybarra e-mail, July 4, 2014.

32. Quoted in Longley, *Grunts,* 104.

33. Milliken, *Enter and Die!* 82.

34. Appy, *Working-Class War,* 233–37.

35. Peter Prichard, comments to author.

36. B. Drummond Ayres interview, April 16, 2015.

37. Jerald Collman interview, August 12, 2015.

38. Gerald "Bob" Harkins interview; Bill Jevne interview; Beirne Lovely interview, November 20, 2014.

39. Marlantes, *What It Is Like to Go to War,* 96.

40. Michael Kuklenski interview, December 2, 2013; Ken Stearns e-mail, February 2, 2016.

41. Joe Ybarra interview.

42. Jim Ottman interview, January 10, 2014.

43. Ken Eichholz interview.

44. Interview on January 20, 2014, name withheld.

45. Mark Weston interview.

46. Bobby Alexander interview, January 10, 2014; Ken Kruse interview, April 7, 2014.

47. Dan Bresnahan interview.

48. Appy, *Working-Class War,* 242.

49. Robert Tortolani interview, February 25, 2015.

50. Jim MacLaughlan interview, March 10, 2014; Eric Rairdon interviews, November 7 and 19, 2014.

51. Richard Kirshen, interview, February 26, 2014; Dwight Lovejoy interview, February 3, 2014.

52. Mark Weston interview.

53. Carl Zarzyski interview.

54. Tom Reilly interview.

55. Sherman, *Medic,* 154–56.

56. Bobby Alexander interview.

57. Joseph Kenny interview, April 17, 2014.

58. Bill Jevne interview.

59. Johnson, *Combat Chaplain,* 71–72.

60. Larry Cox interview; Don Dyer interview, May, 8, 2014.

61. Dan Bresnahan interview; Frank Kelly interview; Bill Lucier interview.

62. Interview on Fox Sports, April 30, 2015.

63. Downs, *The Killing Zone,* 27.

64. Frank Grieco interview.

65. Alexander Carver interview; Jerald Collman interview; Jeff Hinman interview, May

13, 2014.

66. Robert "Obie" Holmen interview.
67. Interview, name withheld.
68. Rich Hosier interview, March 10, 2014.
69. Charles Hagel interview, Veterans History Project, Library of Congress.
70. Interview, January 20, 2014, with an individual who requested anonymity.
71. Bill Jevne interview.
72. Mike Zimmer interview.
73. Quoted in Keegan, *The Face of Battle,* 71.
74. Carl Zarzyski interview.
75. Bobby Alexander interview.
76. Puller, *Fortunate Son,* 156–57.
77. Rod Paladino interview.
78. Dick Pils interview, February 17, 2014; Rick Winters interview.
79. Dave Shearer interview.
80. Joseph Kenny interview; Jan Scruggs interview, May 28, 2015.
81. James F. Jordan, YouTube interview, July 18, 2014, www.youtube.com/watch?v=qW7lJOfG0X0, and in his book *Over and Out.*
82. Ken Stearns e-mail.
83. Frank Grieco interview.
84. Peter Barber interview; see also his "Life Support," *Dartmouth Alumni Magazine,* July/ August 2015, 24–25.
85. Larry Henry interview, April 15, 2014.
86. Talmadge Cain e-mail, January 18, 2014.

87. Ken Stearns e-mail.

88. Douglas Moore interview, September 24, 2014.

89. Larry Adams, Lieutenant Colonel United States Marine Corp Aviation, 1964–1982, interview, February 18, 2014, Veterans History Project, Library of Congress.

90. Harry Breski interview, February 7, 2014, regarding his brother Joseph, who was flying this helicopter when it was shot down on June 6, 1969.

91. Dale Dailey interview.

92. Charles Edwards interview. Coffelt Database information on Arnold and Bryant.

93. Frank Kelly interview.

94. David Lovelace interview.

95. Jim Milliken interview; Frank McGreevy interview.

96. Donald Sullivan e-mail, June 22, 2015. Sullivan believes that Colonel Weldon Honeycutt deserved the Medal of Honor for his conduct. Honeycutt did receive the Distinguished Service Cross, a prestigious recognition. There is no indication that Senator Kennedy ever tried to veto a medal award, which of course is not to ignore the possibility that the politically sensitive Pentagon may not have wanted to valorize Hamburger Hill.

97. Richard Davis interview, February 12, 2004, Veterans History Project, Library of Congress.

98. Bleier and O'Neil, *Fighting Back,* 87.

99. Ibid., 98.

100. Downs, *Killing Zone,* 31–32.

101. Don Dyer interview; Larry Henry interview.

102. Jack Noble interview, January 15, 2014.

103. Robert Hager interview.

104. Lonnie Greckel interview.

105. William "Bro" Adams interview.

106. Larry Adams interview.

107. Dan Bresnahan interview.

108. Don Brief interview, February 26, 2015. Dr. Brief met this baby some twenty-five years later, then a successful young woman living in Washington.

109. Jeffrey Rogers interview, April 18, 2014.

110. Jay Gearhart interview, April 9, 2014; Robert Hager interview; Dave Shearer interview.

111. Ken Kruse interview.

112. Letter from Phillip Dennis Barger to his sister, Erin Barger Orgeron and her family, October 20, 1968. Copy shared by Mrs. Orgeron. Description of his fatal crash from Coffelt report.

113. Richard Davis interview.

114. Ken Eichholz interview.

115. Greg Burnetta interview; Bruce Jones interview, June 1, 2015; Jack Noble interview.

116. Terence Smith interview.

117. Charles Edwards interview. For strong

and thoughtful looks at the South Vietnam military, see Wiest, *Vietnam's Forgotten Army,* and Brigham, *ARVN.*

118. Flynn, *The Draft,* 234. See also calculations in Longley, *Grunts,* 5, and D. Michael Shafer, "The Vietnam Era Draft," in Shafer, *Legacy,* 67–68.

119. Appy, *Working-Class War;* Shafer, *Legacy,* 69. James Fallows, "What Did You Do in the Class War, Daddy?" *Washington Monthly,* October 1975. He later wrote a critical analysis of a study that argued that Vietnam was not a class war, "Low-Class Conclusions," *The Atlantic,* April 1993, 38–44.

120. Caputo, *Rumor of War,* xiv.

121. Powell, *My American Journey,* 72.

122. Frank Boccia interview.

123. "Armed Forces: Democracy in the Foxhole," *Time,* May 26, 1967, 15–19.

124. Terry, *Bloods.* See introduction for an overview of this evolution.

125. A good — and chilling — summary of the racial and racist tensions and battles is Westheider, *The African American Experience in Vietnam,* esp. chap. 5. See also Graham, *The Brothers' Vietnam War,* esp. chap. 6.

126. Jack McMackin interview, December 15, 2014.

127. Rod Paladino interview; Jose Cantu

interview, April 29, 2014; Bruce Jones interview; Gary Radford interview, January 20, 2014; Jan Scruggs interview.

128. Powell, *My American Journey*, 133; Appy, *Patriots*, 367; Joe Ybarra interview.

129. Frank Grieco interview; Gary Radford interview; Jan Scruggs interview.

130. Goff, *Brothers*, 23, 121, 123.

131. For a comprehensive and persuasive look at this question, see Kuzmarov, *The Myth of the Addicted Army*.

132. Larry Cox interview; Don Dyer interview; Jay Gearhart interview; Lonnie Greckel interview; Tom McGall interview.

133. Bruce Jones interview; Frank Grieco interview; Dwight Lovejoy interview.

134. Jim Milliken interview.

135. Robert Williams interview, December 16, 2014.

136. Rod Paladino interview.

137. Jim Milliken interview; Joseph Kenny interview.

138. Jim Ottman interview; Mac Campbell interview.

139. The John Laurence CBS broadcast is described in Bradley and Werner, *We Gotta Get Out of This Place*, 1. See www.youtube .com/watch?v=S5T4pcALoog. For a discussion of the music, see Beidler, *Late Thoughts on an Old War*, 111–16.

140. Pat Sajak interview.

141. Jeff Hinman conversation, December 2015.

142. Bradley and Werner, *We Gotta Get Out of This Place,* 135–44.

143. Quote from Nolan, *Death Valley,* 10.

Chapter 7. Getting Out of This Place

1. Sandy Boyer, July 17, 2008, posted on the digital Vietnam Veterans Memorial Wall.

2. Sandy Boyer interview, August 14, 2014; Ron McCarthy e-mail, January 9, 2014; David Balazs interview; Skip Freidhoff interview, May 29, 2015; Jim Milliken interview; Mike Wright interview, June 18, 2015.

3. Peter Prichard comments to author.

4. Larry Henry interview; Gary Radford interview; Jan Scruggs interview.

5. Richard Davis interview.

6. McLean, *Loon,* 206, 208.

7. Micki Voisard interview in Walker, *A Piece of My Heart,* 233–34.

8. Johnson, *Combat Chaplain,* 1.

9. Jacqueline Navarra Rhoads in Freedman, *Nurses in Vietnam,* 21; Warren Cook interview, October 16, 2014; Combs, *Mercy Warriors,* 132–33; Larry Adams interview; Peter Prichard comments to author; Gary Weaver interview, April 30, 2014.

10. Richard Hosier interview; Steve Lotterhand interview.

11. James Long interview, March 17, 2014; Bill Jevne interview; Joel Trautmann interview.

12. Deanna McGookin in Freedman, *Nurses in Vietnam,* 98–99; Jeff Hinman interview.

13. Robert Koury's dedication remarks, delivered at a gathering memorializing men of the 1st Battalion, 1st Marines lost in Vietnam, in Quantico on August 29, 2015 and shared with author.

14. Gary Weaver interview; Richard Hosier interview; Larry Henry interview.

15. Richard Davis interview; Sherman, *Medic,* 281–82; Diane Evans interview, October 22, 2014; Richard Kirshen interview; David Loring interview, October 20, 2014. For a good analysis of the "spitting" controversy, see Lembcke, *The Spitting Image.* An earlier view is Greene, *Homecoming.* I discuss this in *Those Who Have Borne the Battle,* 203–204. A persuasive account of this is the impressively researched book by the Vietnam veteran Gary Kulik, *"War Stories."* Kulik finds little evidence of these aggressive incidents, but he does describe the "metaphorical truth" of these stories — the reception for returning Vietnam veterans seldom was a warm one.

16. Michael McGuire e-mail.

17. James Long interview; Grover DeVault interview; Steve Piscitelli interview, April

16, 2015.

18. Mike Zimmer interview.

19. William "Bro" Adams interview.

20. Joseph Kenny interview; interview, name withheld.

21. Chris Burns interview; Richard Davis interview.

22. John Snyder interview.

23. Combs, *Mercy Warriors*, 13; Neel, *Medical Support of the U.S. Army in Vietnam*, 75, 76–78, chap. II.

24. Neel, *Medical Support*, chap. III.

25. Combs, *Mercy Warriors*, 32.

26. Jeff Hinman interview; Dan Jensen in *Rock River Valley Insider*, April 12, 2015.

27. Sherman, *Medic*, 204.

28. Interview, name withheld.

29. James Long interview; Jay Gearhart interview.

30. Gary Weaver interview; Karen Bush interview in Freedman, *Nurses in Vietnam*, 82.

31. Lonnie Greckel interview.

32. Joan Waradzyn Thomas in Freedman, *Nurses in Vietnam*, 153–55.

33. Statements made in confidence and quoted here anonymously.

34. Johnson, *Combat Chaplain*, 55.

35. Richard Batche interview; Ken Kruse interview.

36. Douglas Moore interview.

37. Larry Adams interview.

38. Eric Rairdon interviews.

39. Donald Brief interview.

40. See Stur, *Beyond Combat*, introduction and chapter 3 for a good overview of women and the Vietnam War.

41. A description of Sharon Lane is in Bigler, *Hostile Fire;* also John Littleton interview, February 24, 2014; John Lavelle e-mail, November 3, 2014; Lorraine Boudreau in Freedman, *Nurses in Vietnam,* 31–33. Letter from Sharon Lane in Edelman, *Dear America,* 285–86.

42. Diane Evans interview.

43. Anne Simon Auger in Walker, *Piece of My Heart,* 77, 78.

44. Maureen Walsh, ibid., 208; Diane Evans interview.

45. Combs, *Mercy Warriors,* viii; Sherman, *Medic,* 204.

46. David Rogers interview and e-mail, March 7, 2014.

47. Michael Kuklenski interview; Joseph Bakos e-mail, November 24, 2013; Jim Goss e-mail, December 17, 2013. Dave Shearer interview.

48. Interviews with Kuklenski and Shearer; e-mail from Goss. For Native Americans in Vietnam, see Holm, *Strong Hearts, Wounded Souls.*

49. Jacqueline Navarra Rhoads in Freedman, *Nurses in Vietnam,* 14–15.

50. Maureen Walsh in Walker, *Piece of My Heart,* 209.

51. John Littleton interview.

52. Millilken, *Enter and Die!* 13.

53. Gary Bain interview; Ron Menhorn interview, February 10, 2014.

54. The 74 men killed on the USS *Frank E. Evans* are not included in the tally of Vietnam War dead, nor are their names on the Wall. Congress is considering action to define these men as Vietnam War casualties and to be recognized as such. Information on Frank E. Evans Association Web site, www.ussfee.org; e-mails from Larry Cuzzupe, February 17 and May 24, 2014, and from Stephen Kraus, March 4, 2014.

55. Analysis based on data from Coffelt Database.

56. *Newsweek,* June 23, 1969, 111; Robert Widener, "Making Something of Themselves: Boys in the Vietnam War," *VFW Magazine,* August 2014, 44–45; *Stars and Stripes* (Pacific edition), June 14, 1969; Steve Piscitelli interview.

57. Greene, *The Quiet American,* 242. Jeff Rogers interview.

58. Johnson, *Combat Chaplain,* 74–75.

59. *Navajo Times,* October 16, 1969, copy supplied by Tom Martin; Tom Martin interview; Sharon Blackman Battles (Lenny Hickson's niece) interview, December 4,

2014; Elvira Hickson Blackman (sister) interview, December 11, 2014.

60. David Lovelace interview; Johnson, *Combat Chaplain,* 26.

61. Jose Cantu interview, April 29, 2014. Copy of program from service provided by Mr. Cantu.

62. An excellent study of chaplains in Vietnam is Whitt, *Bringing God to Men.* See also the spring 2014 issue of the *Military Chaplain.*

63. David Lovelace interview; Whitt, *Bringing God to Men,* 120.

64. Accolades for Don Bartley come from men who served with him. Grover DeVault interview; Larry Henry interview; David Lovelace interview; Gary Weaver interview. A fine summary is in a letter from Colonel Gerhart Hyatt, command chaplain, to Bartley's widow, Kathleen Bartley, on June 11, 1969, copy provided by Kathleen.

65. A good overview of the development of the system is "Memorial Affairs Activities — Republic of Vietnam," a report compiled by Mortuary Affairs Center, U.S. Army, Fort Lee, VA, March 2000.

66. *Stars and Stripes* (Pacific edition), November 26, 1967; Rothberg, "Assuming Nothing"; e-mails from Ken Davis, July 18, and Richard Arnold, July 21, 2014, both with the Coffelt Database.

67. Jay Gearhart interview; James Long interview; Mike Zimmer interview.

68. Mortuary Affairs Center report, 7.

69. This and the following discussion of Graves Registration has been informed richly by interviews with some remarkably sensitive and helpful men who served in this operation. They are still pained by it. Jerald Collman interview; Richard Davis interview; Gary Redlinski interview, July 9, 2014; also army chaplain Grover DeVault interview; army medic Gary Weaver interview. See also Matthew M. Burke, "For Those Who Prepared Vietnam's Fallen, a Lasting Dread," *Stars and Stripes,* November 9, 2014, and Rothberg, "Assuming Nothing," for additional accounts and insights.

70. Burke, "For Those Who Prepared."

71. Tom Martin interview; posting by Howard Tateishi on the Wall of Faces, August 1, 2012, www.vvmf.org/wall-of-faces/.

72. Moore and Galloway, *We Were Soldiers Once,* chap. 25.

73. Spiller, *Death Angel,* 212, 228–30.

74. Ibid., 194–98, 200–205, 212–13, 217–18.

75. Ibid., 218–21, 176–77.

76. Ibid., 181–82.

77. Jean Heller, "Tough Job: Tell GI Wife She's a Widow," *Los Angeles Times,* March 10, 1968.

78. Beirne Lovely interview.

79. Laurent, *Grief Denied,* 9–12.
80. Don Bartley Jr. interview, April 9, 2014; Allen Collins interview.
81. Thomas Crawford interview, June 16, 2014.
82. Harry Breski interview; Harry Breski e-mail, February 10, 2014; letters from Bob Barker and from Frederic Nunes to Harry Breski, copies provided by Mr. Breski. Barker and Nunes served with Joe Breski.
83. Brad Sommer interview, March 7, 2014; Ron Menhorn interview.
84. Daryl Miller interview, July 3, 2014 (Daryl and Terry Miller's mother, Leona, sat with him during the interview and discussed this with him, but she did not join in the conversation); Maria Miller interview, June 12, 2014; Brenda Miller Carpenter interview, July 11, 2014.
85. Josephine Cyran Vetanovetz interview, October 9, 2014; telephone conversation with Richard DeLotto, February 17, 2014.
86. Gladys Grubb interview, March 5, 2014. Steve Grubb died on May 28, but his wife did not have final notification until June 9.
87. Daryl Miller interview; also newspaper clippings provided by Brenda Miller Carpenter; Sandy Boyer interview.
88. Jose Cantu interview, January 24, 2014; Russ Howard interview; e-mails from Jim Brown, July 2014, April and May 2015.
89. "He Escorts War Dead: Slow Business

Pleases Sgt. Sam," *Stars and Stripes,* July 17, 1972.

90. Harry Breski interview; Brad Sommer interview; Sandy Boyer interview; Brenda Miller Carpenter interview; Josephine Cyran Vetanovetz interview; Don Bartley Jr. interview; Allen Collins, interview; Gladys Grubb interview.
91. *Stars and Stripes* (Pacific edition), January 29, 1968.
92. Elvira Blackman interview; Sharon Blackman Battles interview.
93. Coffelt Database on Weitz and Williams.
94. Report of the investigation conducted by Second Lieutenant David A. Andriacco for Headquarters, 1st Battalion, 9th Marines, 3rd Marine Division, provided by Ken Davis of the Coffelt Database. Also Coffelt report and enclosures on Benton and the two marines killed, Yvon Girouard and Donny Lawson; see also "Family Conference" document in Library of Congress POW/MIA Databases and Documents, lcweb2.loc.gov/frd/pwmia/497/159558.pdf; and message posted by Benton's sister Mary describing a 2009 investigation into the remains found by Laotian farmers. There is no indication that this has resulted in a positive identification. popasmoke.com/notam/forum/odds-ends/ask-our-members/4622-my-brother-ssgt-gregory-r-benton-mia-vietnam. Mary Benton continues to

challenge the findings that her brother walked off on his own, and she presses the Joint POW/MIA Accounting Command in Hawaii to push on to try to recover and identify her brother's body. She believes it is the remains discovered in Laos. Mary Benton's e-mails and enclosures, October 23, 2015.

95. Ellen Dale in Byrd, *Home Front,* 16. Major Dale was married with two children.

96. A good summary of this is Rochester and Kiley, *Honor Bound,* 479–87. For an overview of the POW experience and the work to free them, see Townley, *Defiant.*

97. *New York Times,* July 13, 15, and 27, 1969; *Stars and Stripes,* July 14, 19, and 28, 1969.

98. *Los Angeles Times,* July 9, 1969; *New York Times,* July 11, 1969. Robert Hickox was one of 6 men killed by gunfire in a fight. He was twenty years old and had been in Vietnam for six months. Coffelt report.

99. Max Frankel, "Nixon Rewrites Script," *New York Times,* July 31, 1969, 17; for coverage of the trip, see *New York Times, Washington Post,* and *Los Angeles Times,* July 31, 1969.

100. From the archives of the Miller Center, University of Virginia, millercenter.org/president/gallery-image/president-nixon-visits-vietnam.

Chapter 8. Duck and Cover

1. "Backchannel Message from the President's Assistant for National Security Affairs to the Ambassador to South Vietnam," May 4, 1972, *Foreign Relations of the United States, 1969–1976,* vol. VIII, Vietnam, January–October 1972, Document 122, history.state.gov/historicaldocuments/frus1969-76v08 /d122-fnref2.
2. McKenna, *Kontum,* 156–57, 178, 219. Hal Drake, "In Saigon, Indifference Is Victor," *Stars and Stripes* (Pacific edition), May 16, 1972.
3. Willbanks, *A Raid Too Far,* 188–91.
4. Brochetti letters and citation provided by Frank Brochetti's nephew, Adam Brochetti. Adam, then a captain in the Marine Corps, did pass that way, when in February 2013, he along with his brother and a small group of cousins and friends, climbed to the peak of Nui Ba Den. He returned with some dirt from the mountaintop to share with his grandparents, Frank's parents. The poem that Frank shared was adapted from lines attributed to Stephen Grellet, a Frenchman who migrated to Pennsylvania as a Quaker missionary in the 1790s. For An Loc, Willbanks, *Battle for An Loc.* Cobra pilot account is "My Wild Day with the Black Virgin," www.thefirearmsforum.com/threads/my-wild-day-with-the-black-virgin

.59094/page-2. Johnnie Ray is in Rochester and Kiley, *Honor Bound,* 576–77.

5. Memo from Gen. Abrams to Chairman of the Joint Chiefs of Staff, Admiral Thomas Moorer and Commander in Chief of the Pacific, Admiral John McCain, Jr., Document 118, history.state.gov/historicaldocuments/frus1969-76v08/d118.

6. FitzGerald, *Fire in the Lake,* 404.

7. From a 2001 interview that William Burr conducted with Secretary Laird, in Kimball, *Vietnam War Files,* 115.

8. Schmitz, *Richard Nixon and the Vietnam War,* 62.

9. David L. Prentice, "Choosing the 'Long Road': Henry Kissinger, Melvin Laird, Vietnamization, and the War over Nixon's Vietnam Strategy," *Diplomatic History* (2015): 25–26, dh.oxfordjournals.org/.

10. Prentice, "Choosing the 'Long Road,' " provides a good summary of this process. See also Kimball, *Vietnam War Files,* 22–23; Burr and Kimball, *Nixon's Nuclear Specter,* 257–64; Johns, *Vietnam's Second Front,* 237–38; Berman, *No Peace, No Honor,* 55; Schmitz, *Richard Nixon and the Vietnam War,* 60–62. President Nixon's own assessment was that in the fall of 1969 any escalation would have been divisive (*RN,* 402).

11. Richard Nixon, "Address to the Nation on the War in Vietnam," November 3, 1969,

Woolley and Peters, American Presidency Project, www.presidency.ucsb.edu/ws/?pid=2303. There clearly was in the fall of 1969 a greater optimism among American officials that the NLF had been seriously harmed by Tet. See Robert Kaiser, "The New Optimists," *Washington Post,* October 29, 30, and 31, 1969.

12. Alex Butterfield interview, September 4, 2015. Butterfield said the president kept all of the supportive letters and notes on his desk for several days. "He was very proud." Richard Nixon, "Address at the Air Force Academy Commencement Exercises in Colorado Springs, Colorado," June 4, 1969, Woolley and Peters, American Presidency Project, www.presidency.ucsb.edu/ws/?pid=2081.

13. Nixon, *No More Vietnams,* 115.

14. For a summary of this, see Schmitz, *Richard Nixon and the Vietnam War.* The president insisted that during the gathering on the Mall, he was in the White House watching a college football game. Casualty data from Coffelt reports.

15. Richard Nixon, "Address to the Nation on the Situation in Southeast Asia," April 30, 1970, Woolley and Peters, American Presidency Project, www.presidency.ucsb.edu/ws/?pid=2490.

16. Schmitz, *Richard Nixon and the Vietnam*

War, 91–95; Kimball, *Vietnam War Files,* 27–28. The Pulitzer Prize–winning photograph was taken by John Filo.

17. Described in Stanton, *Rise and Fall of an American Army,* 335–42.
18. Kimball, *Vietnam War Files,* 28–30; Stanton, *Rise and Fall of an American Army,* 351–55. The best source on this is Willbanks, *A Raid Too Far,* e.g., 1–3, 158–60; Sander, *Invasion of Laos,* 191, 208. Also Kissinger and Luce, *White House Years,* 992, 1002, and Nixon, *RN,* 499.
19. Willbanks, *A Raid Too Far,* 162.
20. Gregory A. Daddis, "Out of Balance: Evaluating American Strategy in Vietnam, 1968–72," *War & Society* 32, no. 3 (October 2013): 252–70; Willbanks, *A Raid Too Far,* 191–201; McKenna, *Kontum,* is a rich account of one key battle. One of the American advisers there was John Paul Vann, retired from the army and working as a civilian. He played a key role in the tactics of the successful defense and was killed in a helicopter crash as he was leaving the city to return to Saigon following the battle. See also Andradé, *America's Last Vietnam Battle,* 484–94; Neil Sheehan, *A Bright Shining Lie,* 767–90.
21. Andradé, *America's Last Vietnam Battle,* 486; Brigham, *ARVN,* 100–102. Nguyen, *Hanoi's War,* chap. 7, is an important assessment of the North Vietnamese strategy

and politics relating to this major offensive.

22. Randolph, *Powerful and Brutal Weapons,* 86.
23. Exchange from White House tapes, ibid., 88.
24. Ibid., 97.
25. For the Abrams experience, see Willbanks, *A Raid Too Far,* 143; see also Daddis, "Out of Balance," 252, 253; Clarke, *Advice and Support,* chap. 19. Lewis Sorley has argued that General Abrams had a different and potentially more successful war strategy from General Westmoreland. See also Nagl, *Learning to Eat Soup with a Knife,* 168–80. I agree that Abrams was an imaginative and strong leader who was dealt a losing hand. But it is not clear that his strategic understanding was really different from Westmoreland's. Both were constrained by and directed from the Pentagon — and the White House. For a different assessment of Abrams, see Daddis, above, and Gentile, *Wrong Turn,* 66–81. A thoughtful assessment of what was understood in the 1980s as the "lessons" of Vietnam for the military is Petraeus, "The American Military and the Lessons of Vietnam."
26. Stanton, *Rise and Fall of an American Army,* 335.
27. Horst Faas and Peter Arnett, "Told to Move Again on 6th Deadly Day, Company

A Refuses," *New York Times*, August 26, 1969; James Reston, "A Whiff of Mutiny in Vietnam," *New York Times*, August 27, 1969; James Sterba, "G.I.s in Battle Area Shrug Off the Story of Balky Company A," *New York Times*, August 29, 1969. See Shkturi, *Soldiering on in a Dying War*, 184–87. This incident was heavily covered on the evening television news: CBS covered it on August 28 and 29, 1969; ABC on August 28, and NBC on August 29. Basically all of them acknowledged that this was a case of a few men resisting yet another assignment, which they finally accepted, and it was about hot, tired, and frustrated rather than mutinous GIs.

28. Daddis, *No Sure Victory*, 210.
29. Robert Williams interview.
30. Major Herbert Koenigsbauer, quoted in Nolan, *Ripcord*, 412.
31. Ibid., 14. A fascinating account is of Gary Radford, a soldier who was wounded there, going back to the battle area in 1996 and again in 2015 to try to find the remains of friends who were apparently killed on a patrol. His recent effort is recounted in *Spring Valley (IN) Herald*, November 11, 2015. Also Gary Radford interview, January 20, 2014.
32. "The Troubled U.S. Army in Vietnam," *Newsweek*, January 11, 1971, 29.
33. For examples of this, see "The New GI:

For Pot and Peace," *Newsweek,* February 2, 1970, 24; "The Troubled U.S. Army in Vietnam," *Newsweek,* January 11, 1971, 29; "Sagging Morale in Vietnam: Eyewitness Report on Drugs, Race Problems and Boredom," *U.S. News & World Report,* January 25, 1971, 30; Edward Sherman, "Army Blues: A Bureaucracy Adrift," *The Nation,* March 1, 1971, 265; "As Fighting Slows in Vietnam, Breakdown in GI Discipline," *U.S. News & World Report,* June 7, 1971, 16; B. Drummond Ayres, "Army Is Shaken by Crisis in Morale and Discipline," *New York Times,* September 5, 1971; Haynes Johnson and George Wilson, "Army in Anguish," *Washington Post,* September 12–18, 1971; Rowland Evans and Robert Novak, "Last GIs in Bitter Mood," *Washington Post,* September 17, 1971; John Saar, "The Outpost Is a Shambles," *Life,* March 31, 1972, 28.

34. In the two weeks prior to the announcement of the verdict, the three national television news programs covered the trial twenty-five times — most nights each of them had reports from Fort Benning, and some nights one of the news shows had multiple reports about the trial. Compiled from Vanderbilt University TV News Archives.

35. Seymour M. Hersh first broke the story

on My Lai. His account is in *My Lai.* The earliest full display of photographs was in *Life,* December 5, 1969, 36.

36. Nuremberg chief counsel Telford Taylor's *Nuremberg and Vietnam,* chap. 6, provides an important historical and legal perspective. For an excellent discussion of the Yamashita Precedent and the way it was ignored in the My Lai adjudication, see Ryan, *Yamashita's Ghost,* chap. 18.

37. I acknowledge that in describing this as "the darkest day," I am not accepting the view of Nicholas Turse and others that similar events were common (Turse, *Kill Anything That Moves*). I remain comfortable with my reflections on this crime in *Those Who Have Borne the Battle,* 194–96. For full accounts of this, see Oliver, *My Lai Massacre.* Hagopian, *The Vietnam War in American Memory,* has very good coverage of the broader questions raised by the My Lai massacre (for example, 50–54). Additional good sources are Belknap, *Vietnam War on Trial,* and Allison, *My Lai.* See Kulik, *"War Stories,"* 157–59, in which he concludes that "the reason to expose false atrocity stories is so we can retain our outrage at true atrocity stories." He insists that "the credulous belief in such stories dishonors the service of those soldiers who acted with honor," 201.

38. Oliver, *My Lai Massacre,* 154–65; Allison, *My Lai,* 111–14; Belknap, *Vietnam War on Trial,* 189–202; Stephen Lesher, "The Calley Case Reexamined," *New York Times Magazine,* July 11, 1971.

39. Iver Peterson, "Foe Kills 33 G.I.'s, Wounds 76 in Raid South of Da Nang," and Robert D. McFadden, "Calley Verdict Brings Home the Anguish of War to Public," *New York Times,* March 29 and April 4, 1971; *Stars and Stripes* (Pacific edition), April 1, 1971; "The Hell at Mary Ann," *Newsweek,* April 12, 1971, 45; Shkurti, *Soldiering On,* 191–92, 233–34. Keith W. Nolan has written extensively and well on the war. In his book *Sappers in the Wire,* he acknowledges that he and others were incorrect when they first wrote that the men in the 1st Battalion, 46th Infantry were "bored and sloppy." He describes their very strong combat record.

40. The fullest discussion of these incidents is in Shkurti, *Soldiering On,* chap. 16 and 187–90. For the 1970 conflict, see Laurence, *The Cat from Hué,* 643–63.

41. Shkurti, *Soldiering On,* 52–60.

42. Nicholas C. Proffitt, "Soldiers Who Refuse to Die," *Newsweek,* October 25, 1971, 67–68. Again, I depend on Shkurti's research and analysis to sort out this complicated story. See *Soldiering On,* chaps. 9

and 20. Also see Boyle, *The Flower of the Dragon.* In Shkurti's chapter 26, "Pace as History," he points out the influence that Boyle had on other writers who used Pace as an example of mutinous soldiers.

43. For a contemporary critique of this by a retired marine officer, one whose account was largely derivative of the accounts in some of the media, see Robert D. Heinl Jr., "The Collapse of the Armed Forces," *Armed Forces Journal,* June 7, 1971, msuweb .montclair.edu/~furrg/Vietnam/heinl.html.

44. Lepre, *Fragging,* 218.

45. Ibid., 220–21, 227–29. Fragging peaked in 1971, ibid., 67.

46. Ibid., 66–83.

47. Donald Kirk, "Who Wants to Be the Last American Killed in Vietnam?" *New York Times Magazine,* September 19, 1971, SM9.

48. See Moser, *New Winter Soldiers,* esp. chap. 5; Nicosia, *Home to War,* chaps. 1–3.

49. Huebner, *Warrior Image,* 217–22.

50. Ibid., 223–28. A good and important critical look at this gathering is Kulik, *"War Stories,"* chap. 5. He points out the exaggeration in some of the accounts and notes the flawed credentials of some of the organizers, notably Mark Lane and VVAW activist Al Hubbard (100–103). Kulik argues that only one war crime spotlighted at the

WSI hearings was confirmed (151). See also Burkett and Whitley, *Stolen Valor*, 131–34.

51. "Complete Testimony of Lt. John Kerry to Senate Foreign Relations Committee on Behalf of Vietnam Veterans Against the War," Cong. Rec., 92nd Cong., 1st Sess., April 22, 1971, 179–210, www.wintersoldier.com/index.php?topic=Testimony. An overview of Kerry's Vietnam service and the politics that followed is Kulik, *"War Stories,"* 95–117. Also Burkett and Whitley, *Stolen Valor*, 135–36.

52. Huebner, *Warrior Image*, 230. Moser argues that perhaps 20 percent of the Vietnam veterans actively resisted the war (*New Winter Soldiers*, 3). But few were prepared openly to join in the protests. Most of them did not like the image of the protesters.

53. Schmitz, *Richard Nixon and the Vietnam War*, 124.

54. "The Vietnam Papers — A Question of Power," *Los Angeles Times*, June 20, 1971.

55. "Pentagon Papers: The Secret War," *Time*, June 28, 1971, 21.

56. Leslie Gelb, "Today's Lessons from the Pentagon Papers," *Life*, September 17, 1971, 34–36. For his reflections on this entire experience, I suggest Ellsberg's *Secrets*, esp. Part III. It was in many ways the Nixon administration's obsession with Ells-

berg that led to the formation of the secret group known as the "plumbers" that ultimately would break into the Democratic National Committee offices at the Watergate complex.

57. William Greider, "Calley Becomes a Symbol," *Washington Post,* January 21, 1971, B1. Gallup poll, April 7, 1971. Lesher, "The Calley Case Reexamined"; Huebner, *Warrior Image,* 215.

58. Kulik, *"War Stories,"* 182.

59. Caputo, *A Rumor of War,* 330; Theodore Solotaroff, "Memoirs for Memorial Day," *New York Times Book Review,* May 29, 1977, 183; Peter Prescott, "Combat Zone," *Newsweek,* June 6, 1977, 86. A critical account of Caputo's conduct and his explanation — blaming "the war" rather than assuming responsibility — is in Kulik, *"War Stories,"* 178–80.

60. Report of Chaplain Captain John Zoller (United Methodist Church) in Bergsma, *Chaplains with Marines in Vietnam,* 193.

61. Kirk, "Who Wants to Be the Last American Killed in Vietnam?"

62. Hugh Stovall, "The Last Patrol," *VFW Magazine,* August 1992, 32–33. Stovall was with that last patrol.

63. A good summary and analysis of the final peace negotiations is Asselin, *A Bitter Peace,* chaps. 5–7.

64. Rich Hosier, document with e-mail, January 13, 2016.

Chapter 9. Enduring Vietnam: A Story That Has No End

1. James Sterba, "Marines Leaving South Vietnam Are Briefed on How to Act in a Peace Zone," *New York Times,* July 14, 1969.
2. Robert Koury's remarks at Quantico on August 29, 2015, shared with author.
3. The comments from veterans and others in this chapter are all based on questions I posed to a number of the men and women I interviewed. I did these separately, focusing on their experiences after they left Vietnam. Because some of these accounts are very personal, I assured all of them I would not identify them on this part of our interview.
4. Frank Freidel, foreword in Figley and Leventman, *Strangers at Home,* vi.
5. "Four Vietnam Vets Reflect on War 40 Years After Saigon's Fall," *Columbus (OH) Dispatch,* April 30, 2015.
6. John Dunning, "They Just Walked Away," *Denver Post,* April 27, 1975.
7. Ortiz quote in Andrew Krieg, "Veterans in State Bitter over Loss," *Hartford Courant,* April 30, 1975; Douglas Kneeland, "Ohio Town That Lost 7 Men in Vietnam Now

Worries More About Economy," *New York Times,* April 4, 1975.

8. Mary McGrory, "Vietnam Veterans Forgotten," *Boston Globe,* December 29, 1975.

9. Ronald Yates, "Veterans Return Thru the Back Door," *Chicago Tribune,* January 28, 1973, A1.

10. Kathy Burke, "War Is Over — but Vietnam Vets Find No Peace," *Los Angeles Times,* May 5, 1975.

11. Jacquin Sanders, "Viet Vets: America's Forgotten — and Angry — Men," *Boston Globe,* December 5, 1971.

12. The comments here as well as any without citations, were shared with me by the group I interviewed for this study. [See note 3 above.]

13. Marlantes, *What It Is Like to Go to War,* 178.

14. Appy, *Working-Class War,* 306–309.

15. B. Drummond Ayres, "The Vietnam Veterans, Silent, Perplexed, Unnoticed," *New York Times,* November 8, 1970; Ayres, "Vietnam Veterans: A Battle for Jobs," *New York Times,* January 10, 1971.

16. Charles Chiles, "From Vietnam to a VA Hospital: Assignment to Neglect," *Life,* May 22, 1970, 24D–33. The military hospitals were not much better in terms of space. Bob Kerrey recalled that at Philadelphia Naval Hospital it was necessary to move

768

patients out in order to make room for new ones — or to add beds. He was an officer, so had better facilities, but he saw as many as ten beds with enlisted men in single rooms. And they were expected to clean their own spaces (*When I Was a Young Man,* 204).

17. Florence Mouckley, "Indifference: Injured Vets' Foe Back Home," *Christian Science Monitor,* April 7, 1972.
18. Kovic, *Born on the Fourth of July,* 31.
19. Other studies then and later revealed that the suicide rates of the Vietnam veterans remained higher. Ben A. Franklin, "Veterans of Vietnam Found to Have a High Death Rate," *New York Times,* February 11, 1987; Allan Parachini, "Viet Veterans' Death Rates Compare with Other Wars," *Los Angeles Times,* February 17, 1987.
20. Sanders, "Viet Vets," *Boston Globe,* December 5, 1971.
21. Charles Hagel interview, Veterans History Project, Library of Congress.
22. Nick Thimmesch, "Most Vietnam Veterans Will Join Ranks of Middle America," *Los Angeles Times,* April 27, 1971; Donald Kirk, "Ex-GI No 'Joe College,' " *Chicago Tribune,* November 3, 1971.
23. Ralph Blumenthal, "Veterans, Once Home, Want to Work and Forget," *New York Times,* June 26, 1971.

24. Cleland and Raines, *Heart of a Patriot,* 133.

25. Kirk, "Ex-GI No 'Joe College.' "

26. A personal note here. In 1972, I had a student in my history seminar at Dartmouth. He was a pleasant young man and a very good student, but a few years older than the others, which was not unusual at the time. I enjoyed having him as a student. But only in talking to him recently did I learn that he had dropped out of school and spent a year in Vietnam with a small Scout group out in the jungle. He never mentioned this to me, and I regret that I never asked him then.

27. Downs, *Killing Zone,* preface.

28. B. Drummond Ayres, "Job Outlook Is Bleak for Vietnam Veterans," *New York Times,* June 5, 1971.

29. *Kojak* reference in Olson, *The Vietnam War,* 370. Robert Brewin, "TV's Newest Villain: The Vietnam Veteran," *TV Guide,* July 19, 1975.

30. James Webb, "When a One-Armed Man Is Not a Loser," *Boston Globe Magazine,* November 21, 1982.

31. Bernard Weintraub, "Now, Vietnam Veterans Demand Their Rights," *New York Times Magazine,* May 27, 1979.

32. A contemporary study of this is Andrew Kohen and Patricia Shields, "Reaping the

Spoils of Defeat: Labor Market Experiences of Vietnam-Era Veterans," in Figley and Leventman, *Strangers at Home,* chap. 9. Dienstfrey and Feitz, *Chart Book on Black and Hispanic Veterans.*

33. Senate Committee on Veterans Affairs, "A Study of the Problems Facing Vietnam Era Veterans on their Readjustment to Civilian Life" (Washington, DC: Government Printing Office, January 31, 1972).

34. Harris Polls compiled at the Roper Center, Roper Center Questions ID 417318 and 417368.

35. Harris Survey, November 10, 1980.

36. ABC News/*Washington Post* poll, January 11, 1985; Harris Poll, August 18, 1989.

37. Congressional Research Service study by Christine Scott, "Veterans Affairs: Historical Budget Authority, FY 1940–FY 2012," RS22897, June 13, 2012. *VA Annual Report 1985.*

38. One of the most important and insightful studies of these questions and of this period is Hagopian, *Vietnam War in American Memory.* For the late 1970s era, see esp. chap. 2.

39. Cleland and Raines, *Heart of a Patriot,* 129.

40. Warren Brown, " 'Range of Intangibles' Said Hurting Viet Vets the Most," *Washington Post,* May 29, 1978.

41. Martini's *Agent Orange* provides a comprehensive scientific and historical look at this herbicide. It is a critical resource. Scott's *Vietnam Veterans Since the War* remains an essential book on the subject. For an overview of the delayed and inadequate American support for Vietnamese victims, see Congressional Research Service's Michael Martin, "Vietnamese Victims of Agent Orange and U.S.-Vietnam Relations," RL34761, August 29, 2012; and Jessica King, "U.S. in First Effort to Clean Up Agent Orange in Vietnam," CNN, August 10, 2012, edition, www.cnn.com/1012/08/10/world/asia/Vietnam-us-agent-orange/.

42. For descriptions and interviews with psychiatrists and counselors, see Donald Kirk, "Find Viet Vets Feel Rejected, Deceived," *Chicago Tribune,* October 31, 1971; Kathy Burke, "War Is Over — but Vietnam Vets Find No Peace," *Los Angeles Times,* May 5, 1975. Scott, *Vietnam Veterans Since the War,* 28–37.

43. Anyone seeking to understand this must start with two remarkable books by VA psychiatrist Jonathan Shay, *Achilles in Vietnam* and *Odysseus in America.* Scott's *Vietnam Veterans Since the War* provides a good overview of the history and politics of this problem.

44. Marlantes, *What It Is Like to Go to War,* 193.

45. Bruns Grayson in "Heroes Without Honor Face the Battle at Home," *Time,* April 23, 1979, 31. In my conversations with Vietnam veterans, it is clear that Jane Fonda continues to be strongly disliked, primarily because of her antiwar activism and especially her trip to Hanoi in 1972. For a wide-ranging analysis of this, see Lembcke, *Hanoi Jane,* who concludes that the demonization of Jane Fonda was part of a broader conservative effort to marginalize the antiwar left.

46. www.rogerebert.com/reviews/apocalypse -now-1979.

47. Harris Survey, "1979/11/17–12/19 iPoll Attitudes to Vietnam Era Veterans Survey."

48. Bernard Weintraub, "Now, Vietnam Veterans Demand Their Rights," *New York Times Magazine,* May 27, 1979.

49. Anna Quindlen, "A Vietnam Veteran Stills Audience with a Rebuke," *New York Times,* May 30, 1979; Martin Tolchin, "Carter Vows to Focus on Vietnam Veterans Rights," *New York Times,* May 31, 1979.

50. "Voices: Jan Scruggs," interview in *Vietnam* magazine, April 2015, 22.

51. Scruggs published a paper with two American University colleagues: Scruggs, Alan Berman, and Carole Hoage, "The

Vietnam Veteran: A Preliminary Analysis of Psychosocial Status," *Military Medicine* 145, no. 4 (April 1980): 267–69.

52. For full discussion of a very full engagement, see Doubek, *Creating the Vietnam Veterans Memorial;* Scruggs and Swerdlow, *To Heal a Nation.* Hagopian's *The Vietnam War in American Memory* is essential to understanding this history, as is Scott's *Vietnam Veterans Since the War.* Insightful contemporary accounts include Ellen Goodman, "A Memorial as Muddied as the Vietnam War," *Los Angeles Times,* September 27, 1982; Paul Gapp, "Sculpture to Be Scuttled? Viet Memorial Fight Flares Up," *Chicago Tribune,* September 29, 1982; Tom Wolfe, "Art Disputes War: The Battle of the Vietnam Memorial — How the Mullahs of Modernism Caused a Stir," *Washington Post,* October 13, 1982. Christopher Buckley, "The Wall," *Esquire,* September 1985, 61–73. Jan Scruggs offered thoughtful reflections on the entire experience, Scruggs interview, January 29, 2016. Elizabeth Bumiller, "The Memorial, Mirror of Vietnam," *Washington Post,* November 9, 1984.

53. Philip Boffey, "Vietnam Veterans Parade a Belated Welcome Home," *New York Times,* November 14, 1982; Hagopian, *The Vietnam War in American Memory,* chap. 5.

54. Mary McGrory, "It May Have Been the

Best Idea Vietnam Veterans Ever Had," *Washington Post,* November 16, 1982.

55. Ronald Reagan, "Remarks at Dedication Ceremonies for the Vietnam Veterans Memorial Statue," November 11, 1984, Woolley and Peters, American Presidency Project, www.presidency.ucsb.edu/ws/?pid=39414.

56. Cindy Loose, "Women's War Memorial Brings Joy, Pain," *Washington Post,* November 12, 1993.

57. Richard Harwood and Haynes Johnson, "Vietnam: War We Never Won or Understood," *Washington Post,* November 10, 1982.

58. Note shared with author.

59. William Broyles Jr., "Remembering a War We Want to Forget," *Newsweek,* November 22, 1982, 82–83.

60. Poem shared with author.

61. Wayne Slater, "Vietnam Vet Still Haunted by War Becomes 'First Casualty of the Wall,' " *Los Angeles Times,* November 23, 1984.

62. Daniel Pollock et al., "Estimating the Number of Suicides Among Vietnam Veterans," *American Journal of Psychiatry* 147 (June 1990): 6; the follow-up study is Tim Bullman and Hans Kang, "The Risk of Suicide Among Wounded Vietnam Veterans," *American Journal of Public Health* 86, no. 5 (May 1996). Subsequent studies

include Janet Kemp and Robert Bossarte, "Suicide Data Report, 2012," Department of Veterans Affairs, Mental Health Services, Suicide Prevention Program; Bryant Jordan, "Older Vets Committing Suicide at Alarming Rate," August 31, 2014, www.military.com/daily-news/2014/08/31/older-vets-committing-suicide-at-alarming-rate.

63. Richard C. Paddock, "Bob Kerrey's War Record Fuels Debate in Vietnam on His Role in New University," *New York Times,* June 2, 2016; Tranh Van Minh, "War Record of Vietnam University's US Chairman Angers Some," *Stars and Stripes* (Pacific edition), June 14, 2016; Viet Thanh Nguyen, "Bob Kerrey and the 'American Tragedy' of Vietnam," *New York Times,* June 20, 2016. There has been reconciliation and even collaboration between the United States and Vietnam, but many Vietnamese also remember the trauma of war. Viet Thanh Nguyen challenged the evolving American version of memory and mourning. He argues that the Vietnam Veterans Memorial Wall frames a memory that may be recuperative for Americans but is incomplete — "where they and their soldiers are the victims and not the three million Vietnamese, is nothing less than Orwellian," (*Nothing Ever Dies,* 66). It is an important reminder of the magnitude of the suffering of Vietnamese. Their account needs to join

the narrative and expand the embrace.

64. Mike Ives, "In Search of Their Fathers: Seeking Redemption in Vietnam," *New York Times,* December 24, 2015.

65. Ronald Reagan, "Memorial Day Ceremonies Honoring an Unknown Serviceman of the Vietnam Conflict," May 28, 1984, reaganlibrary.archives.gov/archives/speeches/1984/52884a.htm. "One of 58,012 Vietnam Dead Joins the Unknowns," *New York Times,* May 29, 1984.

66. Bill Thomas, "Last Soldier Buried in Tomb of the Unknowns Wasn't Unknown," *Washington Post Magazine,* November 8, 2012.

67. For Defense Department tallies of the missing, www.dpaa.mil/portals/85/Documents/VietnamAccounting/2015_stats/Stats20160106.pdf. Evelyn Grubb describes the creation of the POW/MIA flag in *You Are Not Forgotten,* 197–99. Evelyn Grubb was one of the organizers and leaders of the National League of Families of POW/MIA. She believed her husband, air force pilot Wilmer Newlin "Newk" Grubb, was captured in 1966 — and learned in 1973 that he had died in captivity shortly after his capture. The fullest scholarly account of the POW/MIA tragedy and political endurance is Allen, *Until the Last Man Comes Home.*

68. "Witness Testimony of Charles R. Marmar, at a Hearing of House Committee on Veterans' Affairs," May 5, 2010, transcript provided by Dr. Marmar. An important contemporary report on the study of the 1980s is Richard A. Kulka et al., "Trauma and the Vietnam War Generation: Report of Findings from the National Vietnam Veterans Readjustment Study." Dr. Marmar was a coauthor of this report.
69. Benedict Carey, "Combat Stress Among Veterans Is Found to Persist Since Vietnam," *New York Times,* August 7, 2014.
70. Summary in *VVA Veteran Online,* January/February 2015.
71. Alan L. Gustman, Thomas L. Steinmeier, and Nahid Tabatabai, "Declining Wealth and Work Among Male Veterans in the Health and Retirement Study," National Bureau of Economic Research Working Paper 21736, November 2015.
72. For a full discussion of the enduring political impact of Vietnam, see Kalb and Kalb, *Haunting Legacy.*
73. Marlantes, *What It Is Like to Go to War,* 193–94.
74. Cleland and Raines, *Heart of a Patriot,* 126.
75. Stephen Hayes, personal diary kept in Vietnam, shared with author.

SELECTED BIBLIOGRAPHY

Abercrombie, Clarence L. *The Military Chaplain.* Beverly Hills: Sage Publications, 1976.

Ackermann, Henry F. *He Was Always There: The U.S. Army Chaplain Ministry in the Vietnam Conflict.* Washington, DC: Office of the Chief of Chaplains, Department of the Army, 1989.

Allen, Michael J. *Until the Last Man Comes Home: POWs, MIAs, and the Unending Vietnam War.* Chapel Hill: University of North Carolina Press, 2009.

Allison, William T. *Military Justice in Vietnam: The Rule of Law in an American War.* Lawrence: University Press of Kansas, 2007.

————. *My Lai: An American Atrocity in the Vietnam War.* Baltimore: Johns Hopkins University Press, 2012.

Anderson, David L. *Trapped by Success: The Eisenhower Administration and Vietnam, 1953–1961.* New York: Columbia University Press, 1991.

Andradé, Dale. *America's Last Vietnam Battle:*

Halting Hanoi's 1972 Easter Offensive. Lawrence: University Press of Kansas, 2001.

Appy, Christian G. *American Reckoning: The Vietnam War and Our National Identity.* New York: Viking, 2015.

————. *Patriots: The Vietnam War Remembered from All Sides.* New York: Penguin Books, 2004.

————. *Working-Class War: American Combat Soldiers and Vietnam.* Chapel Hill: University of North Carolina Press, 1993.

Asselin, Pierre. *A Bitter Peace: Washington, Hanoi, and the Making of the Paris Agreement.* Chapel Hill: University of North Carolina Press, 2002.

————. *Hanoi's Road to the Vietnam War, 1954–1965.* Berkeley: University of California Press, 2013.

Atkinson, Rick. *Where Valor Rests: Arlington National Cemetery.* Washington, DC: National Geographic, 2007.

Baker, Mark. *Nam: The Vietnam War in the Words of the Men and Women Who Fought There.* New York: Quill, 1982.

Bankston, Carl L., and Stephen J. Caldas. *Public Education, America's Civil Religion: A Social History.* New York: Teachers College Press, 2009.

Baskir, Lawrence M., and William A. Strauss. *Chance and Circumstance: The Draft, the War, and the Vietnam Generation.* New York:

Knopf, 1978.

Beattie, Keith. *The Scar That Binds: American Culture and the Vietnam War.* New York: New York University Press, 1998.

Becerra, Rosina M., and Milton Greenblatt. *Hispanics Seek Health Care: A Study of 1,088 Veterans of Three War Eras.* Lanham, MD: University Press of America, 1983.

Beidler, Philip D. *Late Thoughts on an Old War: The Legacy of Vietnam.* Athens: University of Georgia Press, 2004.

Belknap, Michal R. *The Vietnam War on Trial: The My Lai Massacre and the Court-Martial of Lieutenant Calley.* Lawrence: University Press of Kansas, 2002.

Berens, Charlyne. *Chuck Hagel: Moving Forward.* Lincoln: University of Nebraska Press, 2006.

Berg, Norman E. *Regret to Inform You: Experiences of Families Who Lost a Family Member in Vietnam.* Central Point, OR: Hellgate Press, 1999.

Bergsma, II. L. *Chaplains with Marines in Vietnam, 1962–1971.* Washington, DC: History and Museums Division, Headquarters, U.S. Marine Corps, 1985.

Berinsky, Adam J. *In Time of War: Understanding American Public Opinion from World War II to Iraq.* Chicago: University of Chicago Press, 2009.

Berman, Larry. *Lyndon Johnson's War: The*

Road to Stalemate in Vietnam. New York: Norton, 1989.

————. *No Peace, No Honor: Nixon, Kissinger, and Betrayal in Vietnam.* New York: Free Press, 2001.

Beschloss, Michael R. *Reaching for Glory: Lyndon Johnson's Secret White House Tapes, 1964–1965.* New York: Simon & Schuster, 2001.

————. *Taking Charge: The Johnson White House Tapes, 1963–1964.* New York: Simon & Schuster, 1997.

Biggs, David A. *Quagmire: Nation-Building and Nature in the Mekong Delta.* Seattle: University of Washington Press, 2010.

Bigler, Philip. *Hostile Fire: The Life and Death of First Lieutenant Sharon Lane.* Arlington, VA: Vandamere Press, 1996.

Bleier, Rocky, and Terry O'Neil. *Fighting Back.* New York: Stein and Day, 1980.

Bloom, Alexander, ed. *Long Time Gone: Sixties America Then and Now.* New York: Oxford University Press, 2001.

Boccia, Frank. *The Crouching Beast: A United States Army Lieutenant's Account of the Battle for Hamburger Hill, May 1969.* Jefferson, NC: McFarland, 2013.

Bogaski, George. *American Protestants and the Debate over the Vietnam War: Evil Was Loose in the World.* Lanham, MD: Lexington Books, 2014.

Boyle, Richard. *The Flower of the Dragon: The Breakdown of the U.S. Army in Vietnam.* San Francisco: Ramparts Press, 1972.

Bradley, Doug. *DEROS Vietnam: Dispatches from the Air-Conditioned Jungle.* North Hills, CA: Warriors Publishing Group, 2012.

Bradley, Doug, and Craig Werner. *We Gotta Get Out of This Place: The Soundtrack of the Vietnam War.* Amherst: University of Massachusetts Press, 2015.

Bradley, Mark Philip. *Imagining Vietnam and America: The Making of Postcolonial Vietnam, 1919–1950.* Chapel Hill: University of North Carolina Press, 2000.

Bradley, Mark Philip, and Marilyn B. Young, eds. *Making Sense of the Vietnam Wars: Local, National, and Transnational Perspectives.* New York: Oxford University Press, 2008.

Braestrup, Peter. *Big Story: How the American Press and Television Reported and Interpreted the Crisis of Tet 1968 in Vietnam and Washington.* New Haven: Yale University Press, 1983.

Bray, Gary W. *After My Lai: My Year Commanding First Platoon, Charlie Company.* Norman: University of Oklahoma Press, 2010.

Brigham, Robert K. *ARVN: Life and Death in the South Vietnamese Army.* Lawrence: University Press of Kansas, 2006.

Brinkley, Joel. *Cambodia's Curse: The Modern*

History of a Troubled Land. New York: PublicAffairs, 2011.

Broyles, William, Jr. *Brothers in Arms: A Journey from War to Peace.* New York: Knopf, 1986.

Burkett, B. G., and Glenna Whitley. *Stolen Valor: How the Vietnam Generation Was Robbed of Its Heroes and Its History.* Dallas: Verity Press, 1998.

Burner, David. *John F. Kennedy and a New Generation.* Boston: Little, Brown, 1988.

Burr, William, and Jeffrey P. Kimball. *Nixon's Nuclear Specter: The Secret Alert of 1969, Madman Diplomacy, and the Vietnam War.* Lawrence: University Press of Kansas, 2015.

Buzzanco, Robert. *Masters of War: Military Dissent and Politics in the Vietnam Era.* New York: Cambridge University Press, 1996.

Byrd, Barthy. *Home Front: Women and Vietnam.* Berkeley, CA: Shameless Hussy Press, 1986.

Caputo, Philip. *A Rumor of War.* New York: Henry Holt, 1977.

Chambers, John W. *To Raise an Army: The Draft Comes to Modern America.* New York: Free Press, 1987.

Chapla, John D. *The Men of Alpha Company: Combat with the 173rd Airborne Brigade, Vietnam, 1969–1970.* Alexandria, VA: The author, 2012.

Charles River Editors. *The Vietnam Veterans Memorial: The History of Washington D.C.'s Vietnam War Monument.* Charleston, SC: CreateSpace, January 26, 2015.

Clarke, Bruce B. G. *Expendable Warriors: The Battle of Khe Sanh and the Vietnam War.* Westport, CT: Praeger Security International, 2007.

Clarke, Jeffrey J. *Advice and Support: The Final Years, 1965–1973.* Washington, DC: U.S. Army Center of Military History, 1988.

Cleland, Max, and Ben Raines. *Heart of a Patriot: How I Found the Courage to Survive Vietnam, Walter Reed and Karl Rove.* New York: Simon & Schuster, 2009.

Clodfelter, Mark. *The Limits of Air Power: The American Bombing of North Vietnam.* New York: Free Press, 1989.

Clodfelter, Micheal. *Vietnam in Military Statistics: A History of the Indochina Wars, 1772–1991.* Jefferson, NC: McFarland, 1995.

Colby, William E., and James McCargar. *Lost Victory: A Firsthand Account of America's Sixteen-Year Involvement in Vietnam.* Chicago: Contemporary Books, 1989.

Combs, John. *Mercy Warriors: Saving Lives Under Fire.* Trafford Publishing, 2012, www.trafford.com.

Cooney, John. *The American Pope: The Life and Times of Francis Cardinal Spellman.* New York: Times Books, 1984.

Cortright, David. *Soldiers in Revolt: The American Military Today.* New York: Anchor Press, 1975.

Cosmas, Graham A. *MACV: The Joint Command in the Years of Escalation, 1962–1967.* Washington, DC: U.S. Army Center of Military History, 2006.

———. *MACV: The Joint Command in the Years of Withdrawal, 1968–1973.* Washington, DC: U.S. Army Center of Military History, 2007.

Cowie, Peter. *The "Apocalypse Now" Book.* Cambridge, MA: Da Capo Press, 2001.

Daddis, Gregory A. *No Sure Victory: Measuring U.S. Army Effectiveness and Progress in the Vietnam War.* New York: Oxford University Press, 2011.

———. *Westmoreland's War: Reassessing American Strategy in Vietnam.* New York: Oxford University Press, 2014.

Dallek, Robert. *Camelot's Court: Inside the Kennedy White House.* New York: Harper, 2013.

———. *Flawed Giant: Lyndon Johnson and His Times, 1961–1973.* New York: Oxford University Press, 1998.

———. *Lyndon B. Johnson: Portrait of a President.* New York: Oxford University Press, 2004.

———. *Nixon and Kissinger: Partners in Power.* New York: Harper, 2007.

————. *An Unfinished Life: John F. Kennedy, 1917–1963.* New York: Little, Brown, 2003.

Dancis, Bruce. *Resister: A Story of Protest and Prison During the Vietnam War.* Ithaca: Cornell University Press, 2014.

Đặng, Thùy Trâm. *Last Night I Dreamed of Peace: The Diary of Dang Thuy Tram.* New York: Harmony Books, 2007.

Davis, James W., and Kenneth M. Dolbeare. *Little Groups of Neighbors: The Selective Service System.* Chicago: Markham Publishing, 1968.

DeBenedetti, Charles, and Charles Chatfield. *An American Ordeal: The Antiwar Movement of the Vietnam Era.* Syracuse: Syracuse University Press, 1990.

Deiter, Gerry, Joan Athey, and Paul McGrath. *Give Peace a Chance: John & Yoko's Bed-in for Peace.* Mississauga, Ontario: Wiley, 2009.

Department of Defense. "U.S. Casualties in Southeast Asia, Statistics as of April 30, 1985." Washington, DC: Washington Headquarters Services, Directorate for Information, Operations and Reports, 1985.

Dicken, Chris. *The Foreign Burial of American War Dead: A History.* Jefferson, NC: McFarland, 2011.

Dienstfrey, Stephen J., and Robert H. Feitz. *Chart Book on Black and Hispanic Veterans:*

Data from the 1980 Census of Population and Housing. Washington, DC: Office of Information Management and Statistics, Statistical Policy and Research Service, Research Division (711), 1985.

Dooley, Thomas A. *Deliver Us from Evil: The Story of Viet Nam's Flight to Freedom.* New York: Farrar, Straus and Cudahy, 1956.

Doubek, Robert W. *Creating the Vietnam Veterans Memorial: The Inside Story.* Jefferson, NC: McFarland, 2015.

Downs, Frederick. *The Killing Zone: My Life in the Vietnam War.* New York: Norton, 2007.

Duncan, Jason K. *John F. Kennedy: The Spirit of Cold War Liberalism.* New York: Routledge, 2014.

Duncan, Stephen M. *Citizen Warriors: America's National Guard and Reserve Forces & the Politics of National Security.* Novato, CA: Presidio Press, 1997.

Ebert, James R. *A Life in a Year: The American Infantryman in Vietnam, 1965–1972.* Novato, CA: Presidio Press, 1993.

Ebert, John David. *Apocalypse Now, Scene-by-Scene.* Eugene, OR: Post Egoism Media, 2015.

Edelman, Bernard, ed. *Dear America: Letters Home from Vietnam.* New York: Norton, 1985.

Ehrhart, W. D. *Vietnam-Perkasie: A Combat*

Marine Memoir. Jefferson, NC: McFarland, 1983.

Ellsberg, Daniel. *Secrets: A Memoir of Vietnam and the Pentagon Papers.* New York: Viking, 2002.

Fall, Bernard B. *Street Without Joy: Indochina at War, 1946–54.* Harrisburg, PA: Stackpole, 1961.

Figley, Charles R., ed. *Stress Disorders Among Vietnam Veterans: Theory, Research and Treatment.* New York: Brunner/Mazel, 1978.

Figley, Charles R., and Seymour Leventman, eds. *Strangers at Home: Vietnam Veterans Since the War.* New York: Praeger, 1980.

Fisher, James T. *Dr. America: The Lives of Thomas A. Dooley, 1927–1961.* Amherst: University of Massachusetts Press, 1997.

FitzGerald, Frances. *Fire in the Lake: The Vietnamese and the Americans in Vietnam.* Boston: Little, Brown, 1972.

Flynn, George Q. *The Draft, 1940–1973.* Lawrence: University Press of Kansas, 1993.

———. *Lewis B. Hershey, Mr. Selective Service.* Chapel Hill: University of North Carolina Press, 1985.

Freedman, Dan, and Jacqueline Rhoads, eds. *Nurses in Vietnam: The Forgotten Veterans.* Austin: Texas Monthly Press, 1987.

Freedman, Lawrence. *Kennedy's Wars: Berlin,*

Cuba, Laos, and Vietnam. New York: Oxford University, 2000.

Fry, Joseph A. *The American South and the Vietnam War: Belligerence, Protest, and Agony in Dixie.* Lexington: University Press of Kentucky, 2015.

The Gallup Poll: Public Opinion, 1935–1997. Wilmington, DE: Scholarly Resources, 2000.

Garcia, Manny. *An Accidental Soldier: Memoirs of a Mestizo in Vietnam.* Albuquerque: University of New Mexico Press, 2003.

Gardner, Lloyd C., and Ted Gittinger. *The Search for Peace in Vietnam, 1964–1968.* College Station: Texas A&M University Press, 2004.

Gargan, Edward A. *The River's Tale: A Year on the Mekong.* New York: Knopf, 2002.

Gelb, Leslie H., and Richard K. Betts. *The Irony of Vietnam: The System Worked.* Washington, DC: Brookings Institution, 1979.

Gentile, Colonel Gian. *Wrong Turn: America's Deadly Embrace of Counterinsurgency.* New York: New Press, 2013.

Gibbons, William Conrad. *The U.S. Government and the Vietnam War: Executive and Legislative Roles and Relationships, Part II: 1961–1964.* Princeton: Princeton University Press, 1986.

Giglio, James N. *The Presidency of John F. Kennedy.* Lawrence: University Press of

Kansas, 2006.

Gillon, Steve. *Boomer Nation: The Largest and Richest Generation Ever, and How It Changed America.* New York: Free Press, 2004.

Gitlin, Todd. *The Whole World Is Watching: Mass Media in the Making and Unmaking of the New Left.* Berkeley: University of California Press, 1980.

Goff, Stanley, Robert Sanders, and Clark Smith. *Brothers: Black Soldiers in the Nam.* Novato, CA: Presidio Press, 1982.

Goldstein, Gordon M. *Lessons in Disaster: McGeorge Bundy and the Path to War in Vietnam.* New York: Times Books/Henry Holt, 2008.

Gottlieb, Sherry Gershon. *Hell No, We Won't Go! Resisting the Draft During the Vietnam War.* New York: Viking, 1991.

Graham, Herman. *The Brothers' Vietnam War: Black Power, Manhood, and the Military Experience.* Gainesville: University Press of Florida, 2003.

Graves, Ralph. *The Life I Led.* New York: Tiasquam Press, 2010.

Greene, Bob. *Homecoming: When the Soldiers Returned from Vietnam.* New York: Putnam, 1989.

Greene, Graham. *The Quiet American.* London: William Heinemann, 1955. Greiner, Bernd. *War Without Fronts: The USA in Viet-*

nam. New Haven: Yale University Press, 2009.

Grubb, Evelyn F., and Carol Jose. *You Are Not Forgotten: A Family's Quest for Truth and the Founding of the National League of Families.* St. Petersburg, FL: Vandamere Press, 2008.

Hackworth, David H., and Eilhys England. *Steel My Soldiers' Hearts: The Hopeless to Hardcore Transformation of 4th Battalion, 39th Infantry, United States Army, Vietnam.* New York: Rugged Land, 2002.

Hagan, John. *Northern Passage: American Vietnam War Resisters in Canada.* Cambridge, MA: Harvard University Press, 2001.

Hagopian, Patrick. *The Vietnam War in American Memory: Veterans, Memorials, and the Politics of Healing.* Amherst: University of Massachusetts Press, 2009.

Halberstam, David. *The Best and the Brightest.* New York: Random House, 1972.

————. *The Making of a Quagmire.* New York: Random House, 1964.

————. *The Powers That Be.* New York: Knopf, 1979.

Haldeman, H. R. *The Ends of Power.* New York: Times Books, 1978.

Hall, Mitchell K. *Crossroads: American Popular Culture and the Vietnam Generation.* Lanham, MD: Rowman & Littlefield, 2005.

————. *Vietnam War Era: People and Perspectives.* Santa Barbara, CA: ABCCLIO, 2009.

Hall, Simon. *Rethinking the American Anti-War Movement.* New York: Routledge, 2012.

Hammond, William M. *Public Affairs: The Military and the Media, 1962–1968.* Washington, DC: U.S. Army Center of Military History, 1988.

————. *Public Affairs: The Military and the Media, 1968–1973.* Washington, DC: U.S. Army Center of Military History, 1996.

————. *Reporting Vietnam: Media and Military at War.* Lawrence: University Press of Kansas, 1998.

Harris, Louis and Associates. *Myths and Realities: A Study of Attitudes Toward Vietnam Era Veterans on Their Readjustment to Civilian Life.* Washington, DC: Veterans Administration, 1980.

————. *A Study of the Problems Facing Vietnam Era Veterans on Their Readjustment to Civilian Life.* Washington, DC: Government Printing Office, 1972.

Hartman, Andrew. *Education and the Cold War: The Battle for the American School.* New York: Palgrave Macmillan, 2008.

Hauser, William L. *America's Army in Crisis: A Study in Civil-Military Relations.* Baltimore: Johns Hopkins University Press, 1973.

Heineman, Kenneth J. *Campus Wars: The Peace Movement at American State Universi-*

ties in the Vietnam Era. New York: New York University Press, 1993.

Heinemann, Larry. Close Quarters. New York: Farrar, Straus and Giroux, 1977.

Hellmann, John. American Myth and the Legacy of Vietnam. New York: Columbia University Press, 1986.

Helmer, John. Bringing the War Home: The American Soldier in Vietnam and After. New York: Free Press, 1974.

Helton, Bradley D. "Revolving Door War: Former Commanders Reflect on the Impact of the Twelve-Month Tour upon Their Companies in Vietnam." Master's thesis, North Carolina State University, 2004.

Herring, George C. America's Longest War: The United States and Vietnam, 1950–1975. 4th ed. New York: McGraw-Hill, 2002.

———. LBJ and Vietnam: A Different Kind of War. Austin: University of Texas Press, 1994.

Herrington, Stuart A. Stalking the Vietcong: Inside Operation Phoenix: A Personal Account. Novato, CA: Presidio Press, 1982.

Hersh, Seymour M. My Lai 4: A Report on the Massacre and Its Aftermath. New York: Random House, 1970.

Hess, Gary R. Vietnam: Explaining America's Lost War. Malden, MA: Blackwell, 2009.

Hixson, Walter L. Historical Memory and Representations of the Vietnam War. New

York: Garland Publishing, 2000.

Holm, Tom. *Strong Hearts, Wounded Souls: Native American Veterans of the Vietnam War.* Austin: University of Texas Press, 1996.

Holt, Marilyn Irvin. *Cold War Kids: Politics and Childhood in Postwar America, 1945–1960.* Lawrence: University Press of Kansas, 2014.

Huebner, Andrew J. *The Warrior Image: Soldiers in American Culture from the Second World War to the Vietnam Era.* Chapel Hill: University of North Carolina Press, 2008.

Hughes, Ken. *Chasing Shadows: The Nixon Tapes, the Chennault Affair, and the Origins of Watergate.* Charlottesville: University of Virginia Press, 2014.

———. *Fatal Politics: The Nixon Tapes, the Vietnam War, and the Casualties of Reelection.* Charlottesville: University of Virginia Press, 2015.

Hunt, David. *Lyndon Johnson's War: America's Cold War Crusade in Vietnam, 1945–1968.* New York: Hill and Wang, 1996.

———. *Vietnam's Southern Revolution: From Peasant Insurrection to Total War.* Amherst: University of Massachusetts Press, 2009.

Inboden, William. *Religion and American Foreign Policy, 1945–1960: The Soul of Containment.* New York: Cambridge University Press, 2008.

Jacobs, Robert A. *The Dragon's Tail: Americans*

Face the Atomic Age. Amherst: University of Massachusetts Press, 2010.

Jacobs, Seth. *America's Miracle Man in Vietnam: Ngo Dinh Diem, Religion, Race, and U.S. Intervention in Southeast Asia, 1950–1957.* Durham, NC: Duke University Press, 2004.

Johns, Andrew L. *Vietnam's Second Front: Domestic Politics, the Republican Party, and the War.* Lexington: University Press of Kentucky, 2010.

Johnson, James D. *Combat Chaplain: A Thirty-Year Vietnam Battle.* Denton: University of North Texas Press, 2001.

Jones, Frank L. *Blowtorch: Robert Komer, Vietnam, and American Cold War Strategy.* Annapolis, MD: Naval Institute Press, 2013.

Jones, Gregg. *Last Stand at Khe Sanh: The US Marines' Finest Hour in Vietnam.* Boston: Da Capo Press, 2014.

Jones, Howard. *Death of a Generation: How the Assassinations of Diem and JFK Prolonged the Vietnam War.* New York: Oxford University Press, 2003.

Jordan, James F. *Over and Out.* Charleston, SC: CreateSpace, 2013.

Just, Ward. *To What End: Report from Vietnam.* New York: PublicAffairs, 2000.

Kahin, George M. T. *Intervention: How America Became Involved in Vietnam.* New York: Knopf, 1986.

Kaiser, David E. *American Tragedy: Kennedy, Johnson, and the Origins of the Vietnam War.* Cambridge, MA: Harvard University Press, 2000.

Kalb, Marvin L., and Deborah Kalb. *Haunting Legacy: Vietnam and the American Presidency from Ford to Obama.* Washington, D.C.: Brookings Institution Press, 2011.

Karnow, Stanley. *Vietnam: A History.* New York: Penguin, 1997.

Kearns, Doris. *Lyndon Johnson and the American Dream.* New York: Harper, 1976.

Keegan, John. *The Face of Battle.* New York: Viking, 1976.

Kerrey, Robert. *When I Was a Young Man: A Memoir.* New York: Harcourt, 2002.

Khong, Yuen F. *Analogies at War: Korea, Munich, Dien Bien Phu, and the Vietnam Decisions of 1965.* Princeton, NJ: Princeton University Press, 1992.

Kimball, Jeffrey P. *Nixon's Vietnam War.* Lawrence: University Press of Kansas, 1998.

———. *The Vietnam War Files: Uncovering the Secret History of Nixon-Era Strategy.* Lawrence: University Press of Kansas, 2004.

Kirk, Donald. *Tell It to the Dead: Stories of a War.* Armonk, NY: M. E. Sharpe, 1996.

Kirkpatrick, Rob. *1969: The Year Everything*

Changed. New York: Skyhorse Publishing, 2009.

Kissinger, Henry. *Ending the Vietnam War: A History of America's Involvement in and Extrication from the Vietnam War.* New York: Simon & Schuster, 2003.

Kissinger, Henry, and Clare B. Luce. *White House Years.* Boston: Little, Brown, 1979.

Klassen, Albert D. *Military Service in American Life Since World War II: An Overview.* Chicago: National Opinion Research Center, 1966.

Kovic, Ron. *Born on the Fourth of July.* New York: McGraw-Hill, 1976.

Kramer, Michael J. *The Republic of Rock: Music and Citizenship in the Sixties Counterculture.* New York: Oxford University Press, 2013.

Krulak, Victor H. *First to Fight: An Inside View of the U.S. Marine Corps.* Annapolis, MD: Naval Institute Press, 1984.

Kulik, Gary. *"War Stories": False Atrocity Tales, Swift Boaters, and Winter Soldiers — What Really Happened in Vietnam.* Washington, DC: Potomac Books, 2009.

Kulka, Richard A., William E. Schlenger, John A. Fairbank, Richard L. Hough, B. Kathleen Jordan, Charles R. Marmar, and Daniel S. Weiss. *Trauma and the Vietnam War Generation: Report of Findings from the National Vietnam Veterans Readjustment*

Study. New York: Brunner/Mazel, 1990.

Kurlansky, Mark. *1968: The Year That Rocked the World.* New York: Ballantine Books, 2004.

Kurson, Robert. *Shadow Divers: The True Adventure of Two Americans Who Risked Everything to Solve One of the Last Mysteries of World War II.* New York: Random House, 2004.

Kuzmarov, Jeremy. *The Myth of the Addicted Army: Vietnam and the Modern War on Drugs.* Amherst: University of Massachusetts Press, 2009.

LaFeber, Walter. *The Deadly Bet: LBJ, Vietnam, and the 1968 Election.* Lanham, MD: Rowman & Littlefield, 2005.

Lair, Meredith H. *Armed with Abundance: Consumerism & Soldiering in the Vietnam War.* Chapel Hill: University of North Carolina Press, 2011.

Lâm Quang Thi. *Hell in An Loc: The 1972 Easter Invasion and the Battle That Saved South Viet Nam.* Denton: University of North Texas Press, 2009.

Landers, James. *The Weekly War: Newsmagazines and Vietnam.* Columbia: University of Missouri Press, 2004.

Lang, Daniel. *Casualties of War.* New York: McGraw-Hill, 1969.

Lang, Michael, and Holly George-Warren. *The Road to Woodstock: From the Man*

Behind the Legendary Festival. New York: Ecco, 2009.

Laurence, John. *The Cat from Hué: A Vietnam War Story.* New York: PublicAffairs, 2002.

Laurent, Pauline. *Grief Denied: A Vietnam Widow's Story.* Santa Rosa, CA: Catalyst For Change, 1999.

Lee, Eddy J. "Getting the Command and Control Right: A Vietnam Case Study." Master's thesis, Army Command and General Staff College, Fort Leavenworth, Kansas School of Advanced Military Studies, 2013.

Lembcke, Jerry. *Hanoi Jane: War, Sex, and Fantasies of Betrayal.* Amherst: University of Massachusetts Press, 2010.

———. *The Spitting Image: Myth, Memory, and the Legacy of Vietnam.* New York: New York University Press, 1998.

Lepre, George. *Fragging: Why U.S. Soldiers Assaulted Their Officers in Vietnam.* Lubbock: Texas Tech University Press, 2011.

Lewis, Penny. *Hardhats, Hippies, and Hawks: The Vietnam Antiwar Movement as Myth and Memory.* Ithaca: ILR Press, 2013.

Lifton, Robert Jay. *Home from the War: Vietnam Veterans: Neither Victims nor Executioners.* New York: Simon & Schuster, 1973.

Linn, Brian M. A. *The Echo of Battle: The Army's Way of War.* Cambridge, MA: Harvard University Press, 2007.

Logevall, Fredrik. *Choosing War: The Lost Chance for Peace and the Escalation of War in Vietnam.* Berkeley: University of California Press, 1999.

———. *Embers of War: The Fall of an Empire and the Making of America's Vietnam.* New York: Random House, 2012.

———. *The Origins of the Vietnam War.* New York: Routledge, 2001.

Logevall, Fredrik, and Andrew Preston. *Nixon in the World: American Foreign Relations, 1969–1977.* New York: Oxford University Press, 2008.

Logsdon, John M. *John F. Kennedy and the Race to the Moon.* New York: Palgrave Macmillan, 2010.

Longley, Kyle. *Grunts: The American Combat Soldier in Vietnam.* Armonk, NY: M. E. Sharpe, 2008.

———. *The Morenci Marines: A Tale of Small Town America and the Vietnam War.* Lawrence: University Press of Kansas, 2013.

MacGarrigle, George L. *Combat Operations: Taking the Offensive, October 1966 to October 1967.* Washington, DC: U.S. Army Center of Military History, 1998.

MacPherson, Myra. *Long Time Passing: Vietnam and the Haunted Generation.* Garden City, NY: Doubleday, 1984.

Maraniss, David. *They Marched into Sunlight: War and Peace, Vietnam and America, Octo-*

ber 1967. New York: Simon & Schuster, 2003.

Mark, Eduard M. *Aerial Interdiction: Air Power and the Land Battle in Three American Wars.* Washington, DC: Center for Air Force History, 1994.

Marlantes, Karl. *Matterhorn: A Novel of the Vietnam War.* New York: Atlantic Monthly Press, 2010.

————. *What It Is Like to Go to War.* New York: Atlantic Monthly Press, 2011.

Marr, David G. *Vietnam 1945: The Quest for Power.* Berkeley: University of California Press, 1995.

Marshall, Kathryn. *In the Combat Zone: An Oral History of American Women in Vietnam, 1966–1975.* Boston: Little, Brown, 1987.

Martini, Edwin A. *Agent Orange: History, Science, and the Politics of Uncertainty.* Amherst: University of Massachusetts Press, 2012.

May, Elaine T. *Homeward Bound: American Families in the Cold War Era.* New York: Basic Books, 1988.

McEnaney, Laura. *Civil Defense Begins at Home: Militarization Meets Everyday Life in the Fifties.* Princeton, NJ: Princeton University Press, 2000.

McKenna, Thomas P. *Kontum: The Battle to Save South Vietnam.* Lexington: University Press of Kentucky, 2011.

McLean, Jack. *Loon: A Marine Story.* New York: Ballantine Books, 2009.

McNamara, Robert S., James G. Blight, and Robert K. Brigham. *Argument Without End: In Search of Answers to the Vietnam Tragedy.* New York: Public-Affairs, 1999.

McNamara, Robert S., and Brian VanDeMark. *In Retrospect: The Tragedy and Lessons of Vietnam.* New York: Times Books, 1995.

Miller, Edward G. *Misalliance: Ngo Dinh Diem, the United States, and the Fate of South Vietnam.* Cambridge, MA: Harvard University Press, 2013.

Milliken, James W. *Enter and Die!* Bloomington, IN: Xlibris, 2009.

Moïse, Edwin E. *Tonkin Gulf and the Escalation of the Vietnam War.* Chapel Hill: University of North Carolina Press, 1996.

Momyer, William W. *Airpower in Three Wars: WWII, Korea, Vietnam.* Maxwell Air Force Base, AL: Air University, 2003.

Moore, Harold G., and Joseph L. Galloway. *We Were Soldiers Once . . . And Young: Ia Drang — the Battle That Changed the War in Vietnam.* New York: Random House, 1992.

Morgan, Joseph G. *The Vietnam Lobby: The American Friends of Vietnam, 1955–1975.* Chapel Hill: University of North Carolina Press, 1997.

Moser, Richard R. *The New Winter Soldiers:*

GI and Veteran Dissent During the Vietnam Era. New Brunswick, NJ: Rutgers University Press, 1996.

Moskos, Charles C. *The American Enlisted Man: The Rank and File in Today's Military.* New York: Russell Sage Foundation, 1970.

Moyar, Mark. *Phoenix and the Birds of Prey: Counterinsurgency and Counterterrorism in Vietnam.* Lincoln: University of Nebraska Press, 2007.

———. *Triumph Forsaken: The Vietnam War, 1954–1965.* New York: Cambridge University Press, 2006.

Mrozek, Donald J. *Air Power and the Ground War in Vietnam.* Washington, DC: Pergamon-Brassey's International Defense Publishers, 1988.

Mueller, John E. *War, Presidents, and Public Opinion.* New York: Wiley, 1973.

Mullen, Robert W. *Blacks and Vietnam.* Washington, DC: University Press of America, 1981.

Murphy, Edward F. *Dak To: America's Sky Soldiers in South Vietnam's Central Highlands.* New York: Ballantine Books, 2007.

———. *The Hill Fights: The First Battle of Khe Sanh.* New York: Presidio Books, 2003.

Nagl, John A. *Learning to Eat Soup with a Knife: Counterinsurgency Lessons from Malaya and Vietnam.* Chicago: University of Chicago Press, 2005.

Napoli, Philip F. *Bringing It All Back Home: An Oral History of New York City's Vietnam Veterans.* New York: Hill and Wang, 2013.

National Advisory Commission on Selective Service. *In Pursuit of Equity: Who Serves When Not All Serve?* Washington, DC: Government Printing Office, 1967.

Neel, Spurgeon H. *Medical Support of the U.S. Army in Vietnam, 1965–1970.* Washington, DC: Department of the Army, 1973.

Neiberg, Michael S. *Making Citizen-Soldiers: ROTC and the Ideology of American Military Service.* Cambridge, MA: Harvard University Press, 2000.

Nelson, Deborah. *The War Behind Me: Vietnam Veterans Confront the Truth About U.S. War Crimes.* New York: Basic Books, 2008.

Nesser, John A. *The Ghosts of Thua Thien: An American Soldier's Memoir of Vietnam.* Jefferson, NC: McFarland, 2008.

Nguyen, Lien-Hang T. *Hanoi's War: An International History of the War for Peace in Vietnam.* Chapel Hill: University of North Carolina Press, 2012.

Nguyen, Viet Thanh. *Nothing Ever Dies: Vietnam and the Memory of War.* Cambridge, MA: Harvard University Press, 2016.

———. *The Sympathizer.* New York: Grove Press, 2015.

Nicosia, Gerald. *Home to War: A History of the Vietnam Veterans' Movement.* New York:

Crown Publishers, 2001.

Ninh, Båo. *The Sorrow of War: A Novel of North Vietnam.* New York: Pantheon, 1995.

Nixon, Richard M. *No More Vietnams.* New York: Arbor House, 1985.

————. *RN: The Memoirs of Richard Nixon.* New York: Grosset & Dunlap, 1978.

Nolan, Keith W. *Death Valley: The Summer Offensive, I Corps, August 1969.* Novato, CA: Presidio Press, 1987.

————. *Ripcord: Screaming Eagles Under Siege, Vietnam 1970.* Novato, CA: Presidio Press, 2000.

————. *Sappers in the Wire: The Life and Death of Firebase Mary Ann.* College Station: Texas A&M University Press, 1995.

Oberdorfer, Don. *Tet!* Garden City, NY: Doubleday, 1971.

O'Brien, Tim. *Going After Cacciato.* New York: Broadway Books, 1978.

————. *If I Die in a Combat Zone: Box Me Up and Ship Me Home.* New York: Dell Publishing, 1987.

————. *The Things They Carried: A Work of Fiction.* New York: Broadway Books, 1990.

Oliver, Kendrick. *The My Lai Massacre in American History and Memory.* New York: Manchester University Press, 2006.

Olson, James S. *The Vietnam War: Handbook of the Literature and Research.* Westport,

CT: Greenwood Press, 1993.

Olson, James S., and Randy W. Roberts. *Where the Domino Fell: America and Vietnam 1945–2010.* Malden, MA: Wiley Blackwell, 2014.

Pach, Chester J., and Elmo Richardson. *The Presidency of Dwight D. Eisenhower.* Lawrence: University Press of Kansas, 1991.

Palmer, Bruce. *The 25-Year War: America's Military Role in Vietnam.* Lexington: University Press of Kentucky, 1984.

Palmer, Laura. *Shrapnel in the Heart: Letters and Remembrances from the Vietnam Veterans Memorial.* New York: Vintage Books, 1988.

Pape, Robert Anthony. *Bombing to Win: Air Power and Coercion in War.* Ithaca, NY: Cornell University Press, 1996.

Parrish, John A. *Autopsy of War: A Personal History.* New York: St. Martin's Press, 2012.

Patterson, James T. *The Eve of Destruction: How 1965 Transformed America.* New York: Basic Books, 2012.

Peacock, Margaret E. *Innocent Weapons: The Soviet and American Politics of Childhood in the Cold War.* Chapel Hill: University of North Carolina Press, 2014.

Peake, Louis A. *The United States in the Vietnam War, 1954–1975: A Selected Annotated Bibliography.* New York: Garland Publishing, 1986.

Perone, James. *Songs of the Vietnam Conflict.* Westport, CT: Greenwood Press, 2001.

Peterson, Robert. *Rites of Passage: Odyssey of a Grunt.* Middleton, WI: Badger Books, 1997.

Petraeus, David Howell. "The American Military and the Lessons of Vietnam: A Study of Military Influence and the Use of Force in the Post-Vietnam Era." Ph.D. diss., Princeton University, 1987.

Phillips, Rufus. *Why Vietnam Matters: An Eyewitness Account of Lessons Not Learned.* Annapolis, MD: Naval Institute Press, 2008.

Piehler, G. K. *Remembering War the American Way.* Washington, DC: Smithsonian Institution, 2004.

Podlaski, John. *Cherries: A Vietnam War Novel.* Charleston, SC: CreateSpace, April 20, 2010.

Powell, Colin L., and Joseph E. Persico. *My American Journey.* New York: Random House, 1995.

Prados, John. *Vietnam: The History of an Unwinnable War, 1945–1975.* Lawrence: University Press of Kansas, 2009.

Preston, Andrew. *Sword of the Spirit, Shield of Faith: Religion in American War and Diplomacy.* New York: Knopf, 2012.

Pribbenow, Merle L., trans. *Victory in Vietnam: The Official History of the People's Army of Vietnam, 1954–1975.* Lawrence: University Press of Kansas, 2002.

Puller, Lewis B., Jr. *Fortunate Son: The Autobiography of Lewis B. Puller, Jr.* New York: Grove Weidenfeld, 1991.

Race, Jeffrey. *War Comes to Long An: Revolutionary Conflict in a Vietnamese Province.* Berkeley: University of California Press, 2010.

Randolph, Stephen P. *Powerful and Brutal Weapons: Nixon, Kissinger, and the Easter Offensive.* Cambridge, MA: Harvard University Press, 2007.

Record, Jeffrey. *The Wrong War: Why We Lost in Vietnam.* Annapolis, MD: Naval Institute Press, 1998.

The Report of the President's Commission on an All-Volunteer Armed Force. Washington, DC: Government Printing Office, 1970.

Reeves, Richard. *President Kennedy: Profile of Power.* New York: Simon & Schuster, 1993.

Remnick, David. *King of the World: Muhammad Ali and the Rise of an American Hero.* New York: Random House, 1998.

Rice, Gerard T. *The Bold Experiment: JFK's Peace Corps.* Notre Dame, IN: University of Notre Dame Press, 1985.

Robbins, James S. *This Time We Win: Revisiting the Tet Offensive.* New York: Encounter Books, 2010.

Roberts, Randy, and James S. Olson. *A Line

in the Sand: The Alamo in Blood and Memory. New York: Free Press, 2001.

Rochester, Stuart I., and Frederick T. Kiley. *Honor Bound: The History of American Prisoners of War in Southeast Asia, 1961–1973.* Washington, DC: Historical Office, Office of the Secretary of Defense, 1998.

Romine, Randall M. *A Vietnam War Chronology According to Military Assistance Command Vietnam (MACV).* Lexington: BookSurge, 2003.

Rothberg, Donald M. "Assuming Nothing: How Mortuary Practices Changed During the Vietnam War." *Vietnam Veterans of America,* August/September 2001, 2–3, www.vva.org/archive/TheVeteran/2001_09/mortuary.htm.

Ryan, Allan A. *Yamashita's Ghost: War Crimes, MacArthur's Justice, and Command Accountability.* Lawrence: University Press of Kansas, 2012.

Ryan, Maureen. *The Other Side of Grief: The Home Front and the Aftermath in American Narratives of the Vietnam War.* Amherst: University of Massachusetts Press, 2008.

Sabato, Larry. *The Kennedy Half-Century: The Presidency, Assassination, and Lasting Legacy of John F. Kennedy.* New York: Bloomsbury, 2013.

Sallah, Michael, and Mitch Weiss. *Tiger Force: A True Story of Men and War.* New York:

Little, Brown, 2007.

Sander, Robert D. *Invasion of Laos, 1971: Lam Son 719*. Norman: University of Oklahoma Press, 2014.

Scheibach, Michael, ed. *"In Case Atom Bombs Fall": An Anthology of Governmental Explanations, Instructions and Warnings from the 1940s to the 1960s*. Jefferson, NC: McFarland, 2009.

Schell, Jonathan. *The Real War: The Classic Reporting on the Vietnam War*. New York: Pantheon Books, 1987.

————. *The Village of Ben Suc*. New York: Knopf, 1967.

Schmitz, David F. *Richard Nixon and the Vietnam War: The End of the American Century*. Lanham, MD: Rowman & Littlefield, 2014.

————. *The Tet Offensive: Politics, War, and Public Opinion*. Lanham, MD: Rowman & Littlefield, 2005.

Scholastic Magazine editors, adapted by Matthew Mestrovic, Ph.D. *What You Should Know About COMMUNISM and Why*. New York: Scholastic Book Services, from the series of fifteen articles published under the same title in *Junior Scholastic,* November 1961–April 1962.

Schrader, Paul. *Taxi Driver*. New York: Faber and Faber, 1990.

Schultz, John. *No One Was Killed: The Democratic National Convention, August 1968*.

Chicago: University of Chicago Press, 1969.

Schwarz, Benjamin C. *Casualties, Public Opinion & U.S. Military Intervention: Implications for U.S. Regional Deterrence Strategies.* Santa Monica, CA: RAND, 1994.

Scott, Wilbur J. *Vietnam Veterans Since the War: The Politics of PTSD, Agent Orange, and the National Memorial.* Norman: University of Oklahoma Press, 2004.

Scruggs, Jan C., and Joel L. Swerdlow. *To Heal a Nation: The Vietnam Veterans Memorial.* New York: Harper, 1985.

Seebeth, Linda. *An Introduction to War: The Journey of a Medic's Heart.* BookSurge, 2008.

Shafer, D. Michael. *The Legacy: The Vietnam War in the American Imagination.* Boston: Beacon Press, 1990.

Shaw, John M. *The Cambodian Campaign: The 1970 Offensive and America's Vietnam War.* Lawrence: University Press of Kansas, 2005.

Shawcross, William. *Sideshow: Kissinger, Nixon and the Destruction of Cambodia.* New York: Simon & Schuster, 1979.

Shay, Jonathan. *Achilles in Vietnam: Combat Trauma and the Undoing of Character.* New York: Atheneum, 1994.

———. *Odysseus in America: Combat Trauma and the Trials of Homecoming.* New York: Scribner, 2002.

Sheehan, Neil. *A Bright Shining Lie: John Paul Vann and America in Vietnam.* New York: Random House, 1988.

Sheehan, Neil, Hedrick Smith, E. W. Kenworthy, and Fox Butterfield. *The Pentagon Papers.* New York: Bantam Books, 1971.

Sherbo, Paul. *Unsinkable Sailors: The Fall and Rise of the Last Crew of USS "Frank E. Evans."* Niceville, FL: Patriot Media, 2007.

Sherman, Ben. *Medic: The Story of a Conscientious Objector in the Vietnam War.* New York: Ballantine Books, 2002.

Shkurti, William J. *Soldiering on in a Dying War: The True Story of the Firebase Pace Incidents and the Vietnam Drawdown.* Lawrence: University Press of Kansas, 2011.

Shore, Moyers S. *The Battle for Khe Sanh.* Washington, DC: Historical Branch, G-3 Division, Headquarters, U.S. Marine Corps, 1969.

Sigler, David B. *Vietnam Battle Chronology: U.S. Army and Marine Corps Combat Operations, 1965–1973.* Jefferson, NC: McFarland, 1992.

Sills, Peter. *Toxic War: The Story of Agent Orange.* Nashville: Vanderbilt University Press, 2014.

Sledge, Michael. *Soldier Dead: How We Recover, Identify, Bury, and Honor Our Military Fallen.* New York: Columbia University Press, 2005.

Sloyan, Patrick J. *The Politics of Deception: JFK's Secret Decisions on Vietnam, Civil Rights, and Cuba.* New York: St. Martin's Press, 2015.

Sorley, Lewis. *A Better War: The Unexamined Victories and Final Tragedy of America's Last Years in Vietnam.* New York: Harcourt Brace, 1999.

————. *Thunderbolt: General Creighton Abrams and the Army of His Times.* New York: Simon & Schuster, 1992.

————. *Vietnam Chronicles: The Abrams Tapes, 1968–1972.* Lubbock: Texas Tech University Press, 2004.

————. *Westmoreland: The General Who Lost Vietnam.* Boston: Houghton Mifflin Harcourt, 2011.

Southard, John. *Defend and Befriend: The U.S. Marine Corps and Combined Action Platoons in Vietnam.* Lexington: University Press of Kentucky, 2014.

Spector, Ronald H. *After Tet: The Bloodiest Year in Vietnam.* New York: Free Press, 1993.

Spiller, Harry. *Death Angel: A Vietnam Memoir of a Bearer of Death Messages to Families.* Jefferson, NC: McFarland, 1992.

Stanton, Shelby L. *Vietnam Order of Battle.* Washington, DC: U.S. News Books, 1981.

————. *The Rise and Fall of an American Army: U.S. Ground Forces in Vietnam, 1965–*

1973. Novato, CA: Presidio Press, 1985.

Steinman, Ron. *Inside Television's First War: A Saigon Journal.* Columbia: University of Missouri Press, 2002.

Stevens, Jason W. *God-Fearing and Free: A Spiritual History of America's Cold War.* Cambridge, MA: Harvard University Press, 2010.

Stone, Gary. *Elites for Peace: The Senate and the Vietnam War, 1964–1968.* Knoxville: University of Tennessee Press, 2007.

Stone, Robert. *Dog Soldiers.* Boston: Houghton Mifflin, 1973.

Stur, Heather Marie. *Beyond Combat: Women and Gender in the Vietnam War Era.* New York: Cambridge University Press, 2011.

Suid, Lawrence H. *Guts & Glory: The Making of the American Military Image in Film.* Lexington: University Press of Kentucky, 2002.

Summers, Harry G. *On Strategy: A Critical Analysis of the Vietnam War.* Novato, CA: Presidio Press, 1982.

Taylor, Mark. *The Vietnam War in History, Literature, and Film.* Tuscaloosa: University of Alabama Press, 2003.

Taylor, Telford. *Nuremberg and Vietnam: An American Tragedy.* Chicago: Quadrangle Books, 1970.

Terry, Wallace. *Bloods: An Oral History of the Vietnam War by Black Veterans.* New York: Random House, 1984.

Thayer, Thomas C. *War Without Fronts: The American Experience in Vietnam.* Boulder, CO: Westview Press, 1985.

Thomas, Evan. *Being Nixon: A Man Divided.* New York: Random House, 2015.

Tomes, Robert R. *Apocalypse Then: American Intellectuals and the Vietnam War, 1954–1975.* New York: New York University Press, 1998.

Townley, Alvin. *Defiant: The POWs Who Endured Vietnam's Most Infamous Prison, the Women Who Fought for Them, and the One Who Never Returned.* New York: St. Martin's Press, 2014.

Tregaskis, Richard. *Southeast Asia: Building the Bases: The History of Construction in Southeast Asia.* Washington, DC: Government Printing Office, 1975.

Trullinger, James W. *Village at War: An Account of Revolution in Vietnam.* New York: Longman, 1980.

Turse, Nick. *Kill Anything That Moves: The Real American War in Vietnam.* New York: Metropolitan Books/Henry Holt, 2013.

US Veterans Administration, Department of Medicine and Surgery. *The Vietnam Veteran in Contemporary Society: Collected Materials Pertaining to the Young Veterans.* Washington, DC: Government Printing Office, 1972.

Useem, Michael. *Conscription, Protest, and*

Social Conflict: The Life and Death of a Draft Resistance Movement. New York: John Wiley, 1973.

Valentine, Douglas. *The Phoenix Program.* New York: Morrow, 1990.

Van Creveld, Martin. *The Age of Airpower.* New York: PublicAffairs, 2011.

Van Devanter, Lynda, and Christopher Morgan. *Home Before Morning: The Story of an Army Nurse in Vietnam.* New York: Beaufort Books, 1983.

Vu Hong Lien, and Peter D. Sharrock. *Descending Dragon, Rising Tiger: A History of Vietnam.* London: Reaktion Books, 2014.

Walker, Keith. *A Piece of My Heart: The Stories of 26 American Women Who Served in Vietnam.* Novato, CA: Presidio Press, 1985.

Watkins, J. R. *Vietnam: No Regrets: One Soldier's "Tour of Duty."* San Diego: Aventine Press, 2005.

Webb, James. *Fields of Fire.* New York: Bantam Books, 1978.

———. *I Heard My Country Calling: A Memoir.* New York: Simon & Schuster, 2014.

Webb, Willard J. *History of the Joint Chiefs of Staff: The Joint Chiefs of Staff and the War in Vietnam, 1969–1970.* Washington, DC: Office of Joint History, Office of the Chairman of the Joint Chiefs of Staff, 2002.

Weiner, Tim. *One Man against the World: The*

Tragedy of Richard Nixon. New York: Henry Holt, 2015.

Weiner, Tom. *Called to Serve: Stories of Men and Women Confronted by the Vietnam War Draft.* Amherst, MA: Levellers Press, 2011.

Wells, Jack. *Class of '67: The Story of the 6th Marine Officer Basic Class of 1967.* Charleston, SC: CreateSpace, 2010.

Wells, Tom. *The War Within: America's Battle Over Vietnam.* Berkeley: University of California Press, 1994.

West, Francis J. [Bing]. *The Village.* New York: Harper, 1972.

Westheider, James E. *The African American Experience in Vietnam: Brothers in Arms.* Lanham, MD: Rowman & Littlefield, 2008.

————. *Fighting on Two Fronts: African Americans and the Vietnam War.* New York: New York University Press, 1997.

Westmoreland, William C. *A Soldier Reports.* Garden City, NY: Doubleday, 1976.

White, Bobby, ed. *Post 8195: Black Soldiers Tell Their Vietnam Stories.* Silver Spring, MD: Beckham Publications, 2013.

Whitfield, Stephen J. *The Culture of the Cold War.* Baltimore: Johns Hopkins University Press, 1991.

Whitt, Jacqueline E. *Bringing God to Men: American Military Chaplains and the Vietnam War.* Chapel Hill: University of North Carolina Press, 2014.

Wiest, Andrew A. *The Boys of '67: Charlie Company's War in Vietnam.* New York: Osprey Publishing, 2012.

————. *Vietnam: A View from the Front Lines.* New York: Osprey Publishing, 2013.

————. *Vietnam's Forgotten Army: Heroism and Betrayal in the ARVN.* New York: New York University Press, 2008.

Wiest, Andrew A., Mary Barbier, and Glenn Robins. *America and the Vietnam War: Reexamining the Culture and History of a Generation.* New York: Routledge, 2010.

Wiest, Andrew A., and Michael Doidge. *Triumph Revisited: Historians Battle for the Vietnam War.* New York: Routledge, 2010.

Wiknik, Arthur. *Nam-sense: Surviving Vietnam with the 101st Airborne Division.* Havertown, PA: Casemate, 2005.

Wilkins, Warren. *Grab Their Belts to Fight Them: The Viet Cong's Big-Unit War Against the U.S., 1965–1966.* Annapolis, MD: Naval Institute Press, 2011.

Willbanks, James H. *Abandoning Vietnam: How America Left and South Vietnam Lost Its War.* Lawrence: University Press of Kansas, 2004.

————. *The Battle of An Loc.* Bloomington: Indiana University Press, 2005.

————. *A Raid Too Far.* College Station: Texas A&M University Press, 2014.

————. *The Tet Offensive: A Concise History.*

New York: Columbia University Press, 2007.

Wilson, Jim. *The Sons of Bardstown: 25 Years of Vietnam in an American Town.* New York: Crown, 1994.

Wirtz, James J. *The Tet Offensive: Intelligence Failure in War.* Ithaca: Cornell University Press, 1991.

Wolff, Tobias. *In Pharaoh's Army: Memories of the Lost War.* New York: Knopf, 1994.

Woods, Randall B. *Shadow Warrior: William Egan Colby and the CIA.* New York: Basic Books, 2013.

Woolley, John, and Gerhard Peters. The American Presidency Project, University of California at Santa Barbara, www.presidency.ucsb.edu.

Wright, James. *Those Who Have Borne the Battle: A History of America's Wars and Those Who Fought Them.* New York: PublicAffairs, 2012.

Wyatt, Clarence R. *Paper Soldiers: The American Press and the Vietnam War.* Chicago: University of Chicago Press, 1995.

Ybarra, Lea. *Vietnam Veteranos: Chicanos Recall the War.* Austin: University of Texas Press, 2004.

Young, Marilyn B. *The Vietnam Wars, 1945–1990.* New York: Harper, 1991. Zaffiri, Samuel. *Hamburger Hill, May 11–20, 1969.* Novato, CA: Presidio Press, 1988.

Zaroulis, N. L., and Gerald Sullivan. *Who Spoke Up? American Protest Against the War in Vietnam, 1963–1975*. Garden City, NY: Doubleday, 1984.

Zelizer, Julian E. *The Fierce Urgency of Now: Lyndon Johnson, Congress, and the Battle for the Great Society*. New York: Penguin, 2015.

ABOUT THE AUTHOR

James Wright is President Emeritus and Eleazar Wheelock Professor of History Emeritus at Dartmouth College and the author or editor of several books, including *Those Who Have Borne the Battle.* His efforts on behalf of veterans and education have been featured in the *New York Times, Boston Globe,* NPR, and more. He serves on the Boards of the Semper Fi Fund, the Iraq and Afghanistan Veterans of America, and the Campaign Leadership Committee for the Vietnam Veterans Memorial Fund Education Center. He lives in Hanover, NH.